RIGHTS IN DIVIDED SOCIETIES

This collection examines the role and value of domestic rights instruments in divided and post-conflict societies, approaching the subject from a comparative and theoretical perspective.

Societies emerging from violent conflict often opt for a bill of rights as part of a wider package of constitutional reform. Where conflict is fuelled by long-standing ethno-national divisions, these divisions are often addressed through group-differentiated rights. Recent constitutional settlements have highlighted the difficulties in drafting a bill of rights in divided/post-conflict societies, where the aim of promoting unity is frequently in tension with the need to accommodate difference. Similar controversies continue to play out in Bosnia-Herzegovina and Northern Ireland. In such cases, a bill of rights might be a rallying point around which both minorities and the majority can articulate a common vision for a shared society. Conversely, a bill of rights might provide merely another venue in which to play out familiar conflicts, further dividing an already divided society.

The central questions that animate the collection are: (1) Can constitutional rights provide a basis for unity and a common 'human rights culture' in divided societies? If so, how? (2) To what extent should divided societies opt for a universalistic package of rights protections, or should the rights be tailored to the specific circumstances of a divided society, providing for special group-sensitive protections for minorities? (3) How does the judiciary figure in the management or resolution of ethno-national conflict? (4) What are the general theoretical and philosophical issues at stake in a rights-based approach to the management or resolution of ethno-national conflict?

Volume 17: Human Rights Law in Perspective

Human Rights Law in Perspective

General Editor: Colin Harvey
Professor of Human Rights Law
School of Law
Queen's University Belfast

The language of human rights figures prominently in legal and political debates at the national, regional and international levels. In the UK the Human Rights Act 1998 has generated considerable interest in the law of human rights. It will continue to provoke much debate in the legal community and the search for original insights and new materials will intensify.

The aim of this series is to provide a forum for scholarly reflection on all aspects of the law of human rights. The series will encourage work which engages with the theoretical, comparative and international dimensions of human rights law. The primary aim is to publish over time books which offer an insight into human rights law in its contextual setting. The objective is to promote an understanding of the nature and impact of human rights law. The series is inclusive, in the sense that all perspectives in legal scholarship are welcome. It will incorporate the work of new and established scholars.

Human Rights Law in Perspective is not confined to consideration of the UK. It will strive to reflect comparative, regional and international perspectives. Work which focuses on human rights law in other states will therefore be included in this series. The intention is to offer an inclusive intellectual home for significant scholarly contributions to human rights law.

Recent titles in this series

The Role of National Human Rights Institutions at the International and Regional Levels
Rachel Murray

Terrorism and the Limitation of Rights
Stefan Sottiaux

The Tension Between Group Rights and Human Rights: A Multidisciplinary Approach
Edited by Koen De Feyter and George Pavlakos

Transitional Justice from Below: Grassroots Activism and the Struggle for Change
Edited by Kieran McEvoy and Lorna McGregor

Making Rights Real: The Human Rights Act in its First Decade
Ian Leigh and Roger Masterman

Children's Socio-Economic Rights, Democracy and the Courts
Aoife Nolan

Rights in Divided Societies

Edited by
Colin Harvey
and
Alex Schwartz

•HART•
PUBLISHING
OXFORD AND PORTLAND OREGON
2012

Published in the United Kingdom by Hart Publishing Ltd
16C Worcester Place, Oxford, OX1 2JW
Telephone: +44 (0)1865 517530
Fax: +44 (0)1865 510710
E-mail: mail@hartpub.co.uk
Website: http://www.hartpub.co.uk

Published in North America (US and Canada) by
Hart Publishing
c/o International Specialized Book Services
920 NE 58th Avenue, Suite 300
Portland, OR 97213-3786
USA
Tel: +1 503 287 3093 or toll-free: (1) 800 944 6190
Fax: +1 503 280 8832
E-mail: orders@isbs.com
Website: http://www.isbs.com

British Library Cataloguing in Publication Data
Data Available

ISBN: 978-1-84946-100-9

Typeset by Hope Services, Abingdon
Printed and bound in Great Britain by
Lightning Source UK Ltd

Contents

Author Biographies

Leonardo Álvarez-Álvarez is Associate Professor of Constitutional Law at the University of Oviedo and Professor-Tutor at the Centro de Estudios Políticos y Constitucionales [Centre for Political and Constitutional Studies/Research] (Madrid). Currently, he is a Fellow of the Max Planck Society (Germany) and is involved in the development of the research project entitled 'Legal Dilemmas in the Field of Education in the Context of a Multicultural Europe', at the Max Planck Institut für ausländisches öffentliches Recht und Völkerrecht (Heidelberg). He is the author of two books, *La lealtad constitucional en la Constitución Española de 1978* and *Sentencias básicas del Tribunal Constitucional alemán en las encrucijadas del cambio del milenio*, Centro de Estudios Políticos y Constitucionales (2008).

Amaya Alvez received her LLB from the University of Concepción, Chile. She was called to the Bar by the Supreme Court of Chile in 1998. She holds a DEA from the Faculty of Law at the University of Liège, Belgium and a LLM from the University of Toronto, Canada. She successfully defended her PhD dissertation entitled, *Chilean Judges Under Democratic Rule: Proportionality and Constitutional Rights* at Osgoode Hall Law School in 2011, and returned to Chile to work as an Associate Professor of Law at the University of Concepción, after a five-year leave of absence.

Sujit Choudhry joined New York University, School of Law in September 2011. He holds law degrees from Oxford, Toronto and Harvard, was a Rhodes Scholar, served as law clerk to Chief Justice Antonio Lamer of the Supreme Court of Canada, and was a Graduate Fellow at the Harvard University Center for Ethics and the Professions. Professor Choudhry has written widely on comparative constitutional law and comparative constitutional development, with a particular focus on Canada, South Africa, India and the United States. His work also addresses basic methodological questions in comparative constitutional law. Recently, he has written on constitutional design as a tool to manage the transition from violent conflict to peaceful democratic politics, especially in ethnically divided societies. He has published over 60 articles, chapters and reports. His edited collections include *Constitutional Design for Divided Societies: Integration or Accommodation* (2008) and *The Migration of Constitutional Ideas* (2006). He sits on the Board of Editors of the *International Journal of Constitutional Law*, is a member of the Editorial Board of the *Constitutional Court Review* (South Africa) and is on the Board of Advisers for the Cambridge Studies in Constitutional Law. In 2010, he was one of four Canadians to receive the Trudeau Fellowship.

David Feldman, QC, DCL, FBA, is Rouse Ball Professor of English Law, University of Cambridge, a Fellow of Downing College, Cambridge and an Academic Associate at 39 Essex Street, London. From 2002 until 2010 he was a Judge of the Constitutional Court of Bosnia and Herzegovina (Vice-President 2006–09). He was Legal Adviser to the Parliamentary Joint Select Committee on Human Rights 2000–04, and has advised several other parliamentary committees. He held posts at the Universities of Bristol (1976–92) and Birmingham (1992–2000) and the Australian National University (1989), and has been a visiting scholar at the University of Melbourne and the University of Nottingham. He has published extensively, particularly in the fields of police powers, administrative law, constitutional law and theory, comparative public law, civil liberties, human rights, the relationship between national and international law, and judicial remedies.

Yash Ghai studied law at Oxford and Harvard and was called to the English Bar by the Middle Temple. He has taught at the University of East Africa, Uppsala University, the University of Warwick and the University of Hong Kong (where he was the first Sir YK Pao Professor of Public Law until the end of 2006). He has been a visiting professor at Yale Law School, Toronto University, Melbourne University, London University, the National University of Singapore, University of Wisconsin and Harvard Law School. His research interests include constitutionalism and human rights, ethnic conflicts, sociology of law, and federalism and autonomy. He has published extensively and his books include: *Public Law and Political Change in Kenya* (1970, with Patrick McAuslan), *Law in the Political Economy of Public Enterprise* (1977), *The Political Economy of Law: Third World Perspectives* (1987, edited jointly with Robin Luckham and Francis Snyder), *Law, Politics and Government in Pacific Island States* (1988), *Heads of States in the Pacific: A Legal and Constitutional Analysis* (1990, with Jill Cottrell), *Hong Kong's New Constitutional Order: The Resumption of Chinese Sovereignty and the Basic Law* (1997, 1999, 2nd edn) and *The Millennium Declaration, Rights and Constitutions* (2011, with Jill Cottrell).

Colin Harvey is Professor of Human Rights Law, School of Law, Queen's University Belfast. His research interests include human rights and constitutionalism. He served as a Northern Ireland Human Rights Commissioner from 2005–11. He has held visiting positions at: University of Michigan, Fordham University, and the London School of Economics and Political Science.

Samuel Issacharoff is the Reiss Professor of Constitutional Law at New York University School of Law. His research addresses the law of the political process and constitutional law, as well as issues in civil procedure (especially complex litigation and class actions). He is a co-author of the seminal *Law of Democracy* casebook and recently served as the Reporter for the Project on Aggregate Litigation of the American Law Institute. Professor Issacharoff is a Fellow of the American Academy of Arts and Sciences.

Mara Malagodi was awarded her PhD from SOAS, University of London, in December 2009 with the thesis *Constitutional Nationalism and Legal Exclusion in Nepal* (1990–2007). She has a longstanding interest in Nepali law and politics, with a comparative South Asian perspective. She holds a BA (Hons) in Nepali and Politics, an MA in South Asian Area Studies from SOAS, and a Laurea Degree in International Relations and Diplomacy from the University of Trieste. She is the Deputy Chair of the SOAS Centre of South Asian Studies, the Treasurer of the Britain-Nepal Academic Council, and a member of the UK Constitutional Law Group, the Association for the Study of Ethnicity and Nationalism, and the Law and Society Association.

Ruth Rubio-Marín holds a Chair in Constitutional and Public Comparative Law at the European University Institute in Florence, Italy. Formerly, she was Professor of Constitutional Law at the University of Seville, Spain, and a member of the Faculty of The Hauser Global Law School Program at New York University. She has taught at several other academic institutions including Columbia Law School and Princeton University, where she was selected as a Fellow for the Program in Law and Public Affairs at Princeton University in 2000–01. Her interests include migration, minority rights, citizenship, gender justice and transitional justice, areas which she addresses mostly from a constitutional, human rights and political theory angles. She is the author and editor of several books including *Immigration as a Democratic Challenge* (2000) and *The Gender of Reparations: Subverting Sexual Hierarchies while Redressing Human Rights Violations* (2009).

Alex Schwartz is a Banting Fellow with the Department of Political Studies, Queen's University (Canada). He was previously a postdoctoral fellow with the Canada Research Chair in Quebec and Canadian Studies at Université du Québec à Montréal. His current research concerns the tensions between state constitutionalism and sub-state constitutionalism in circumstances of national pluralism.

Richard Stacey holds degrees in political theory and law. He served as a law clerk at the Constitutional Court of South Africa before joining the Department of Public Law at the University of Cape Town Law School. He is currently a PhD Candidate at the Institute for Law and Society at New York University.

Stephen Tierney is Professor of Constitutional Theory, School of Law, University of Edinburgh, Director of the Edinburgh Centre for Constitutional Law and was a British Academy Senior Research Fellow 2008–09. He has published seven books including *Constitutional Law and National Pluralism* (2004). Another monograph, *Constitutional Referendums: The Theory and Practice of Republican Deliberation*, will be published in 2012.

Daniel Weinstock holds the Canada Research Chair in Ethics and Political Philosophy in the Department of Philosophy of the University of Montreal. He has written extensively on a wide range of issues in moral, political and legal philosophy. His most recent publications include 'How Political Philosophers Should Think About Health' in the *Journal of Medicine and Philosophy*, and 'Self-Determination for (Some) Cities' in A Gosseries and Y Vanderborght (eds), *Thinking About Justice. Essays for Philippe Van Parijs,* and 'On Voting Ethics for Dual Nationals' in K Breen and S O'Neill (eds), *After the Nation?*

1

Introduction

COLIN HARVEY AND ALEX SCHWARTZ

ONE OF THE defining features of contemporary constitutionalism is that it subjects public power to the discipline of rights. The catalogue of rights can be more or less expansive; rights are not always entrenched or superior to ordinary legislation; and the degree to which rights are enforceable by judicial review also varies considerably. But despite great variety in constitutional substance, a certain image of the polity typically informs contemporary constitutionalism: a consolidated political community of free and equal citizens constituted as such by a system of rights.

Whatever the utility of this model for many established liberal democracies, its implications are more complicated for polities that are fragmented by cleavages of group membership or identification. We will refer to these places here as 'divided societies'; for the most part, we use the term with respect to those polities where ethnic, ethno-national, or national affiliation are politically salient and contested. As we see it, divided societies complicate rights-based constitutionalism for at least two broad reasons.

The first reason concerns the individualistic meaning often ascribed to rights based constitutionalism. The standard model understands the individual as the foundation of constitutional value; the ultimate purpose of constitutional rights is to protect the individual against the abuse of public power. According to Ronald Dworkin's famous metaphor, rights are 'trumps' that individuals hold against the community: 'Individuals have rights when . . . a collective goal is not a sufficient justification for denying them what they wish, as individuals, to have or to do, or not a sufficient justification for imposing some loss or injury upon them'.[1] The individual is also at the heart of Robert Alexy's account in which rights are understood as principles requiring that certain interests or values be

[1] R Dworkin, *Taking Rights Seriously* (Cambridge, Harvard University Press, 1978) xi. See also R Dworkin, 'Rights as Trumps' in J Waldron (ed), *Theories of Rights* (Oxford, Oxford University Press, 1984). We agree with Jeremy Waldron's reading of Dworkin – Dworkin's idea of 'trumps' refers to the way rights impose limits on the public reasons that the state can appeal to in its dealings with the individual. See J Waldron, 'Pildes on Dworkin's Theory of Rights' (2000) 29 *Journal of Legal Studies* 301.

optimised to the greatest extent possible.[2] Any interference with the rights of the individual must therefore be justified as being suitable, necessary and proportionate to the realisation of some competing value or interest of comparable importance.[3]

It is not obvious, however, that individualistic rights can effectively address the problems of group-based domination or exclusion that often arise in divided societies. To be sure, the usual catalogue of individual rights provides some protection for minorities against certain kinds of abuses – after all, regardless of group affiliation, everyone is also an individual. However, the worry in divided societies is not only that majority factions will violate the individual rights of minorities (although this is a danger), but also that certain group-specific interests (eg, culture, language, national identity) will be disregarded or marginalised. The problem then is that, from the perspective of the standard model of rights-based constitutionalism, group-based concerns may not even register as matters of principle. If so, the interests of minorities (qua group) will be treated as matters of policy to be determined by majority-rule. For this reason, the circumstances of divided societies test the limits of rights-based constitutionalism to thwart the 'tyranny' of perpetual majorities. [4]

The second complication concerns the communitarian meaning of rights-based constitutionalism. Rights are not only matters of significance for the individual; rights often also express or define the nature of a political community – this is what Sujit Choudhry calls the 'constitutive' function of rights.[5] The Preamble to the Constitution of the United States, for example, invokes 'We the People . . .', imbedding the image of a collective 'macro-subject' at the very foundation of the system of rights.[6] To this day, constitutional rights help to define the image of the 'Popular Sovereign' that animates the American political imagination.[7] Similarly, Dworkin encourages us to personify the political community and imagine a collective agent whose moral character (or 'integrity') is defined by fidelity to certain rights.[8] Perhaps the purest expression of the communitarian meaning of rights is the idea of 'constitutional patriotism', the

[2] R Alexy, 'Constitutional Rights, Balancing, and Rationality' (2003) 16 *Ratio Juris* 131, 135. See also, R Alexy, *A Theory of Constitutional Rights* (Oxford, Oxford University Press, 2002) 47; and Amaya Alvez-Marin's contribution to the present volume.

[3] Alexy, 'Constitutional Rights, Balancing, and Rationality' (n 2) 135–36.

[4] *cf* J Waldron, 'The Core of the Case against Judicial Review' (2006) 115 *Yale Law Journal* 1345, 1398.

[5] S Choudhry, 'Bills of Rights as Instruments of Nation-Building in Multinational States: the Canadian Charter and Quebec Nationalism' in J Kelly and C Manfredi (eds), *Contested Constitutionalism: Reflections on the Charter of Rights and Freedoms* (Vancouver, University of British Columbia Press, 2009). See also the contributions of Mara Malagodi and Daniel Weinstock to the present volume.

[6] US Constitution, Preamble.

[7] See generally P Kahn, *The Reign of Law: Marbury v. Madison and the Construction of America* (New Haven CT, Yale University Press, 1997). See also P Kahn, *Political Theology: Four New Chapters on the Concept of Sovereignty* (New York, Columbia University Press, 2011) 8–17.

[8] R Dworkin, *Law's Empire* (Cambridge, Harvard University Press, 1986) 167–75, 184–86.

notion that the system of rights (along with democratic procedures) can be the basis for a 'post-national' collective identity.[9]

In divided societies, however, the communitarian meaning of rights-based constitutionalism is more problematic. On the one hand, a common framework of rights might be unifying, a medium for a divided society to articulate a vision for a shared future. On the other hand, a common framework of rights may be in conflict with the recognition of difference. Indeed, the framework of rights may be a source of division in its own right, a relic of a contested constitutional history or the perceived property of one political tradition to the exclusion of others. In the case of national or ethno-national conflicts, for example, the constitutive role of rights may be seen as a kind of domination.[10]

In their different ways, all of the contributions to this collection grapple with the issue of how the circumstances of divided societies complicate or challenge the usual meanings of rights-based constitutionalism. To this end, the various chapters we have brought together touch on a broad but interrelated range of questions: Can individual rights be adapted to accommodate the problems of divided societies or does a common framework of rights impose a false unity and stifle the accommodation of difference? How do the circumstances of divided societies influence the conditions for judicial empowerment and the design and composition of the judiciary? Can group-specific rights ameliorate divisions by helping to constitute a more inclusive model of political community or does the explicit recognition of group difference undermine the viability of constitutional democracy? Can different approaches to rights and pluralism coexist within the same state? What effect might prevailing theories or methodologies of rights-adjudication have on the accommodation or management of divisions?

The first section of contributions to this volume considers the perennial question of the relationship between rights and democracy, albeit from the perspective of divided societies. The section opens on a cautionary note with a contribution from Stephen Tierney. According to Tierney, the apparently tension-free relationship between liberalism and national and cultural pluralism in much contemporary political theory is often contradicted in constitutional practice; while political theory has developed a school of liberal philosophy that is sensitive to the group-specific concerns of culture and nationalism, an unreformed and universalistic brand of liberalism continues to govern in the practical domain of rights. Tierney highlights what he argues are enduring individualistic, homogenising, and ultimately undemocratic tendencies in the practice of liberal constitutionalism He contends that, at least in the context of nationally divided societies, these tendencies may be exploited by dominant groups to the detriment of minorities. And – pace the contributions from Samuel Issacharoff and Yash Ghai – Tierney's contribution suggests that an emphasis on the structural role of

[9] See J Habermas, 'The European Nation-State' in C Cronin and P De Greiff (eds), *The Inclusion of the Other: Studies in Political Theory* (Cambridge MA, MIT Press, 2000); and JW Müller, *Constitutional Patriotism* (Princeton, Princeton University Press, 2007).

[10] See the contributions of Stephen Tierney and Daniel Weinstock to this volume.

rights may overlook the fundamental importance of collective self-government in the accommodation of national pluralism.

Samuel Issacharoff's contribution goes on to make the case for the structural role of rights and judicial review in limiting the excesses of majoritarian power. He argues that the experience of 'third wave' democracies suggests a viable alternative to formal ethnic power-sharing in divided societies. In such cases, as Issacharoff explains, constitutional courts can play a central role in checking the excesses of majoritarian power, not only through the enforcement of individual rights, but also by safeguarding the structural conditions for competitive democracy; courts can oversee impeachment proceedings, protect the party system, scrutinise election laws and lustration laws, and sometimes even prescribe the structure of government itself.

Yash Ghai continues the theme with further comparative discussion of the 'structural aspects' of rights in divided societies. He argues that the accommodation of ethnic divisions does not necessarily entail a rejection of the universality of human rights in favour of relativism; the 'framework' of rights can be adapted to meet the special needs of ethnically divided societies. To support his argument, Ghai traces the contribution of rights to the practical management of diversity in Canada, Fiji, India and South Africa. Although Ghai stresses the progressive potential of rights in divided societies, he also draws attention to the power struggles that inevitably influence bills of rights in processes of constitutional change.

The next section of the collection considers the role and power of the judiciary. Sujit Choudhry and Richard Stacey focus on the generally neglected theme of the design of apex courts in divided societies. As they explain, there is a tension between the standard constitutional norm of judicial independence and the goal of reforming institutions to make them more representative of relevant ethnic or ethno-national groups. On the one hand, judicial independence requires that judges be insulated from the political factions of their society. On the other hand, the assumption behind ethnic representation in the judiciary is that judges will be especially responsive to the interests of their own group. The danger with the latter approach is that the judiciary will become so politicised that rights adjudication is just one more venue for ethnic conflict to play itself out. In light of this concern, Choudhry and Stacey evaluate how ethnic representation on apex courts has been pursued in different ways in the cases of Bosnia-Herzegovina and Canada. With respect to both these cases, they observe that apex courts have been able, on occasion, to transcend ethnic difference and speak in a single voice. Nevertheless, Choudhry and Stacey suggest that the twin aims of independence and representation in divided societies might be better achieved by facially neutral judicial appointment rules. They look to the example of the Germen Federal Constitutional Court to explain how this might work.

Alex Schwartz and Colin Harvey address the problem of judicial empowerment in divided societies, with a particular focus on the still unfinished bill of rights process in Northern Ireland. The chapter considers the explanatory power of theories of judicial empowerment for the context of divided societies. While the leading theories converge on the view that the support of political elites is a necessary condition for any significant transfer of power to the judiciary, they disagree about what factors might motivate elites to support such a transfer. Drawing on the example of the Northern Ireland bill of rights process, Schwartz and Harvey argue that the circumstances of divided societies significantly complicate the problem of winning elite support for judicial empowerment. In a deeply divided society, a would-be bill of rights must secure sufficient support from (at least) two distinct sets of political elites whose attitudes and interests, being shaped by very different experiences, will often pull them in opposing directions. Schwartz and Harvey observe that the same pressures that produce consociational settlements in divided societies may also produce judicial empowerment. Beyond consociational settlements, however, the alignment of background ideational conditions and political triggers needed for judicial empowerment in divided societies is the political equivalent of a lunar eclipse.

The next section of the collection includes two focused case studies: the post-conflict Constitution of Bosnia-Herzegovina and the ongoing process of post-conflict constitutional change in Nepal. David Feldman's contribution provides a critical overview of the place of rights in the Constitution of Bosnia-Herzegovina. As he explains, the Constitution is an eclectic mix of international human rights standards and more contextually sensitive norms assembled in an unsystematic way to meet the exigencies of a divided post-conflict society. Thus, one finds standard individual rights alongside group-specific rights of 'peoples' and 'entities' but no clear relation or hierarchy among them. Moreover, as Feldman points out, there is no codified list of basic rights (as one would find in a formal bill of rights), nor does the Constitution identify specific limiting factors or exhaustively determine remedies for violations. Feldman argues that the lack of a systematic enumeration and classification of rights is partly responsible for some of the major difficulties that have arisen in implementing the Constitution of Bosnia-Herzegovina. In particular, Feldman underlines the tensions between the Constitution's collective guarantees and individual rights and the way in which the former have often hindered the progress of effective and democratic government.

Mara Malagodi's contribution looks at the 'constitutive' role of rights in constitutional reform in Nepal. She charts the changing definition of the Nepali nation, from the 1990 Constitution through to present-day post-conflict negotiations. Malagodi argues that the 1990 Constitution's mix of 'constitutional nationalism' and individual rights was responsible for certain patterns of legal exclusion in Nepal. As she explains, recent constitution-making endeavours have tried to expand the 'traditional' conception of the Nepali nation, in part by making provision for group-based rights and self-government to empower marginalised groups at the local level. However, Malagodi argues that the emancipatory potential of fundamental individual rights has been unduly discounted by an association with the old constitutional order. She cautions against the over-reliance on legally defined ethnic categories and group-differentiated rights in ways that would undermine democratic stability and equality.

The final section of the collection expands the discussion to consider questions of pluralism beyond ethnic, ethno-national or national divisions. The intention here is to illuminate how legal approaches to different kinds of pluralism interact or have implications for divided societies. Daniel Weinstock opens the section with an examination of the intersection of national pluralism and religious pluralism in Canada. His main concern is the Charter of Rights and Freedoms as the focal point for pan-Canadian unity on the one hand and the accommodation of religious diversity on the other. As Weinstock argues, the Charter continues to be, despite its integrative ambitions, a potential basis for 'a major unity crisis'. The competing national traditions of Canada and Quebec diverge in their approach to the accommodation of religious and cultural diversity. Echoing the concerns raised by Tierney in his contribution, Weinstock argues that the Charter's pan-Canadian approach to religious and cultural pluralism exacerbates tensions with Quebec and may yet resuscitate the now relatively dormant constitutional conflict in Canada.

Ruth Rubio-Marín and Leonardo Álvarez-Álvarez move the discussion beyond nationalist divisions to consider the accommodation of religious pluralism in the multicultural European setting. They show how the theory of rights that underlies the legal approach to pluralism can make a real difference. Specifically, they argue that the theory of rights that informs the prevailing legal approach to religious diversity in the classroom is flawed, reflecting a classic liberal model that is ill-equipped to deal with diverse and divided societies. They argue that rights in the classroom should be informed first and foremost by a democratic theory of education that aims to prepare students to actively participate in the public life of a pluralistic society. The implications of Rubio-Marín and Álvarez-Álvarez's contribution for divided societies are important: the theoretical basis for classic liberal rights can be reinterpreted and given new life in light of the imperatives of peaceful coexistence and cooperation.

The collection concludes with a contribution from Amaya Alvez-Marin. Alvez-Marin expands the discussion further still to consider the relationship between constitutional rights, the problem of deep ideological divisions and the effect of adjudicative methodology. Her specific topic is rights-based constitutionalism in Chile, a society she describes as being governed by a 'forced consensus' that is, in fact, very divided over the interpretation and application of constitutional rights. Alvez-Marin explores the potential for the methodology of proportionality in the adjudication of rights to facilitate a deeper and more democratic engagement between the legislature and the judiciary. The implication of Alvez-Marin's contribution for divided societies more generally is that judicial methodology may be just as important in managing divisions as the content of the catalogue of rights.

It is our hope that this collection of work will stimulate future comparative research and debate on the complex role of rights in divided societies. We hope in particular that the preponderance of legal scholars here will help to stimulate the growth of comparative *legal* scholarship on divided societies. Comparative scholarship in constitutional law has only recently been made aware of its own methodological frailties relative to other social sciences,[11] and comparative legal scholarship on constitutionalism in divided societies is still in its infancy.[12] For the most part, this collection brackets methodological concerns. Our hope is to provide a kind of map of the various points where an increasingly global discourse of rights intersects with the special problems of power and pluralism that arise in divided societies. Subsequent research will prove which normative theories and comparative methodologies are best equipped to traverse this challenging topography.

[11] See R Hirschl, 'On the Blurred Methodological Matrix of Comparative Constitutional Law' in S Choudhry (ed), *The Migration of Constitutional Ideas* (Cambridge, Cambridge University Press, 2006).

[12] See S Choudhry, 'Bridging Comparative Politics and Comparative Constitutional Law: Constitutional Design for Divided Societies,' in S Choudhry (ed), *Constitutional Design for Divided Societies: Integration or Accommodation?* (Oxford, Oxford University Press, 2008).

Part I

Divided Democracy

2

Rights versus Democracy? The Bill of Rights in Plurinational States

STEPHEN TIERNEY

I. INTRODUCTION

PLURINATIONALISM – THE EXISTENCE of more than one national identity within a particular state – has only recently been taken seriously by constitutional scholars, having been the subject of considerable interest for sociologists, political scientists and political theorists for more than two decades. This period has also seen: the growth of a global human rights culture manifested in new international instruments entrenching new rights; the ratification of these and of pre-existing instruments by more and more states; and the deeper and wider domestic entrenchment of rights standards within domestic constitutions. In this chapter I will consider the tension between, on the one hand, the new nationalism which asserts both the moral worth of discrete national societies and the duty of any democratic society to accommodate pluralism and, on the other, a parallel trend of rights cosmopolitanism that seems to demand the homogenisation of liberal values within and across states, increasingly it seems at the expense of difference.

A well-established trope left by the bitter ethnic hatreds of the twentieth century posits nationalism and liberalism as inherently incompatible.[1] It is therefore remarkable that a new turn in liberal political theory of the past 20 years has gained considerable ground in overturning decades of received wisdom among liberals. The primary point of focus for 'liberal nationalist' theory has been sub-state nationalism, but its implications for liberalism encompass the phenomenon of nationalism more broadly. This in turn has led to a reappraisal of the normative issues surrounding state as well as sub state nationalism and

[1] FA Hayek, *The Constitution of Liberty* (London, Routledge & Kegan Paul, 1960) 14–15; H Arendt, *On Revolution* (London, Penguin, 1963) 163; D Miller, *On Nationality* (Oxford, Oxford University Press, 1995).

the development of elaborate arguments from a liberal perspective to the effect that nationalism should be politically and constitutionally accommodated.[2] In fact, this new turn has asserted that such accommodation is *required*[3] if plurinational states are to remain true to liberal ideals of justice embedded in principles of freedom and equality.

In this chapter I will begin in Section II by exploring 'Liberalism II' as it has become known. Advocates for the constitutional accommodation of national identity present their arguments through the lens of key liberal principles such as freedom and equality, but in doing so they also emphasise some specific values which are not always stressed in classical liberalism: collective self-determination and the recognition of cultural difference among them. In doing so they assert with multiculturalists more generally the reality of cultural diversity and the importance of its political and constitutional management within a liberal system. Such has been the success of this alternative conception of liberalism, that it may well be that – at the theoretical level – liberal nationalists have won the argument that a coherent liberal system must be one that does justice to cultural and national difference. However, at the same time as arguments for the compatibility of liberalism and nationalism have been refined, we have also seen a parallel expansion in the scope and field of application of human rights law and policy. One of the great stories of the post-war period is the rise of human rights as an international legal phenomenon, bringing with it more and more legally binding, and increasingly judicially enforceable, norms. The overwhelming dynamic of this rights revolution has focused upon the civil and political rights of the individual.

In Section III, I will ask whether there is in fact a tension – at least in practice – between theoretical liberalism's embracing of the new nationalism and the parallel consolidation in practice of a universalist approach to liberal rights, and whether more needs to be done to analyse the coincidence and possible clash between these two developments. So successful has liberal nationalist theory been in defending the compatibility of nationalism and liberal rights, that it is easy to assume that the elasticity of liberalism can happily accommodate both the diversity demands of the new nationalism, which in practice is grounded in group-based interests, and the ever more pervasive spread of a human rights culture that is by disposition individualist, universalist, cosmopolitan and homogenising in outlook.

I will address two issues: supremacy and pluralism. The first brings us to a possible tension between democracy and rights. Although liberal nationalism has tended to address the normative issues surrounding national identity through the liberal *idée fixe* of individual rights, in doing so it perhaps over-

[2] R McKim and J McMahon, *The Morality of Nationalism* (Oxford, Oxford University Press, 1997); M Moore, *The Ethics of Nationalism* (Oxford, Oxford University Press, 2001).

[3] W Kymlicka, *Multicultural Citizenship: A Liberal Theory of Minority Rights* (Oxford, Oxford University Press, 1995); F Requejo (ed), *Democracy and National Pluralism* (London, Routledge, 2001).

looks the fact that the main political dynamic in the resilience of state nationalism and the revitalisation of its sub-state variant is the assertion of the autonomy of discrete communities and their entitlement to make their own policies and laws. In other words, popular democracy is made the ultimate political value. The second issue is pluralism. As I have noted, with its emphasis on diversity and difference this is a key elaboration for liberal nationalists upon the traditional liberal values of freedom and equality. Pluralism, however, in certain manifestations can seem more of a contradiction to, or at least qualification of, rather than elaboration upon, the liberal commitment to equality. We see how this tension can play out in arguments advanced by many liberal legalists for the universal application of international human rights standards. What is becoming clear is that international human rights instruments and the dominant mode of interpretation brought to them reflects the universalising and undifferentiated characterisation of rights in the Liberalism I tradition which flourishes within legal liberalism at a time when in political theory its essentialising and homogenising propensities have been significantly undermined.

This tension is particularly significant as a backdrop to any study of diversity and human rights in divided societies. Liberal nationalism, which has hitherto identified no great tensions between aspirations for autonomy and the prioritisation of individual rights, is open to criticism for a narrowness of focus that tends to concentrate upon already liberal societies. The extension of theories of national pluralism to non-western societies[4] and indeed to divided societies where groups are territorially intermingled,[5] whether liberal or otherwise, has only recently begun, and neither is an easy task. It is also the case that in a number of these societies international influence has encouraged the transplantation of traditional liberal rights instruments into municipal constitutions.[6] The potential for more deep-seated inconsistencies to emerge between, respectively, the pluralistic *theory* of the new liberalism and the homogenising *practice* of liberal legalism through different understandings of the demands of liberal justice is very real.

II. PLURALISM: REDEFINING THE LIMITS OF LIBERALISM

Recent developments in social science suggest that the continuing, and indeed revitalised, salience of sub-state national identity should not be characterised as a struggle between liberal democratic, 'civic nationalist' host states on the one

[4] B Berman, D Eyoh and W Kymlicka (eds), *Ethnicity and Democracy in Africa* (Ohio, Ohio University Press, 2004); W Kymlicka and Baogang He (eds), *Multiculturalism in Asia* (Oxford, Oxford University Press, 2005).

[5] W Kymlicka and M Opalski (eds), *Can Liberal Pluralism be Exported? Western Political Theory and Ethnic Relations in Eastern Europe* (Oxford, Oxford University Press, 2002); A Schwartz, *National Pluralism and the Constitution of Northern Ireland*, PhD Thesis, Queen's University of Belfast.

[6] eg, the Constitutions of Bosnia-Herzegovina, East Timor and Montenegro.

hand, and communitarian, 'ethnic nationalist' sub-state national societies on the other. As nationalism re-emerged in the western democracies such as Canada, Spain, Belgium and the UK from the 1960s onwards, and since 1989 in eastern and central Europe, one liberal response was to paint this new nationalism as illiberal, ethnically essentialist and reactionary.[7] But the work of sociologists[8] and political scientists[9] has served to refute these stereotypes. Analysts of nationalist movements in western Europe and Canada, and the resistance they have faced from state forces opposed to enhanced constitutional accommodation of their demands, have noted that both sides to these disputes frame their political and constitutional arguments within traditional liberal democratic rhetoric.[10]

Liberal nationalist theory has built upon this work, reappraising the relationship between liberalism and nationalism and the normative implications of this relationship. Since the empirical evidence showed that the political aspirations and the justice claims of sub-state nationalists were most commonly being formulated using liberal democratic discourse, this in turn led liberal theorists to reassess how liberalism could be re-deployed to meet these new demands for political recognition. Fundamental questions were consequently posed of the generally accepted foundational principles of liberal justice, or more precisely, their mode of operation. Indeed theorists of the new wave asked how far these needed to be reformulated to meet the demands of sub-state nationalists. Thus, the debate was not one between liberalism on the one hand and communitarianism or some other non-liberal theory on the other. Rather, the main issue was how liberalism could shake off some of its underpinning assumptions about the nature of nationalism and its relationship to the state. As Will Kymlicka put it a decade ago, it was within liberalism itself that the real action took place.[11]

It rapidly became apparent that, somewhat remarkably, many of the classical accounts of liberalism had simply taken nationalism and national identity for granted. Theorists discussed social contracts, veils of ignorance etc. against the background assumption that the locus within which justice theories would play out was a national space with a sufficiently homogenised unitary national identity to obviate the need for further analysis of the sociological specificity of this locus. Margaret Canovan has noted the paradox in Rawls' work:

[7] M Ignatieff, *The Warrior's Honour: Ethnic War and the Modern Conscience* (New York, Metropolitan Books, 1998).

[8] D McCrone, *The Sociology of Nationalism. Tomorrow's Ancestors* (London, Routledge, 1998).

[9] A-G Gagnon and J Tully (eds), *Multinational Democracies* (Cambridge, Cambridge University Press, 2001); M Keating, *Nations Against the State – The New Politics of Nationalism in Quebec, Catalonia and Scotland*, 2nd edn (London, Palgrave, 2001) 63.

[10] M Keating, *Plurinational Democracy: stateless nations in a post-sovereignty era* (Oxford, Oxford University Press, 2001).

[11] See Kymlicka, *Multicultural Citizenship* (n 3) 73; and W Kymlicka, *Politics in the Vernacular* (Oxford, Oxford University Press, 2001) 63.

> Although the explicit purpose of John Rawls' 'Original Position' and 'Veil of Ignorance' was to enable him to arrive at principles of justice undistorted by 'the accidents of nature and social circumstance' (such as birth into a privileged caste or race), Rawls took for granted that these principles applied only inside 'a self-contained national community' recruited primarily by birth, an assumption shared unreflectively by almost all those who debated the theory over twenty years.[12]

In a related way Requejo argues that in some of the major works of liberal theory, national pluralism 'is a question that is not so much badly resolved as completely unaddressed by the premises, concepts and normative questions of these theories'.[13]

The development of a new model of liberalism stemming in large part from Charles Taylor's seminal analysis[14] has questioned among other things how the liberal principle of equality plays out in practice, and in particular, the way in which it elides with the notion of neutrality. There is an assumption within classical liberalism that matters of religion, culture and identity belong to the private realm as matters of individual choice and that the liberal democratic state can act as an honest broker in the management of diversity, itself remaining neutral in cultural or societal terms. Liberalism II as it has become known has debunked this myth. The USA is often held up as an example of a civic nationalist state that acts in a culturally disinterested way. But Kymlicka points out that although diversity does indeed flourish within America, this diversity 'is balanced and constrained by linguistic and institutional cohesion; cohesion that has not emerged of its own, but rather is the result of deliberate state policies'.[15] In other words cultural neutrality, even in a liberal democratic state with a proclaimed commitment to multiculturalism, is an impossibility: 'both ethnic and civic nations have a cultural component'.[16] Requejo echoes this: 'practically speaking, all liberal democracies have acted as nationalising agencies for specific cultural particularisms'.[17] Accordingly, many of the normative prescriptions emerging from traditional liberal accounts have been built upon epistemological imprecision. Notions of justice centred upon equality and fairness have been formulated by a theory that has made assumptions about the liberal state that are empirically false.

[12] M Canovan, 'Sleeping Dogs, Prowling Cats and Soaring Doves: Three Paradoxes in the Political Theory of Nationhood' (2001) 49 *Political Studies* 203, 204. See also J Rawls, *A Theory of Justice* (Oxford, Oxford University Press, 1972) 102 and 357; and J Rawls, *The Law of Peoples* (Cambridge MA, Cambridge University Press, 1999). Similarly, Canovan has questioned the assumptions of demotic singularity behind Habermas' work. See Canovan, 'Sleeping Dogs, Prowling Cats and Soaring Doves' 205–06.

[13] F Requejo, 'Introduction' in F Requejo (ed), *Democracy and National Pluralism* (London, Routledge, 2001) 4.

[14] C Taylor, 'The Politics of Recognition' in A Gutmann (ed), *Multiculturalism and the Politics of Recognition* (Princeton, Princeton University Press, 1992).

[15] W Kymlicka, *Politics in the Vernacular* (n 11) 25.

[16] W Kymlicka, 'Misunderstanding nationalism' in R Beiner (ed), *Theorizing Nationalism* (Albany, State University of New York Press, 1999) 133.

[17] F Requejo, 'Introduction' in F Requejo (ed), *Democracy and National Pluralism* (London, Routledge, 2001) 4; and see also F Requejo, 'Democratic Legitimacy and National Pluralism' in F Requejo (ed), *Democracy and National Pluralism* 167–69.

Another deficiency of liberalism has been the reduction of national and cultural attachments to individualism. Liberal nationalists such as Kymlicka have argued that in a plurinational society the full realisation of liberal values can only be achieved with an a priori recognition of the sociological reality of this national pluralism; sub-state national societal cultures provide the necessary 'context of choice' for freedom.[18] It is a social fact that individual citizens within both sub-state and state nations relate respectively to the state and to the international community through the strong and often primary attachments – in terms of identity and loyalty – which they feel towards their own national society, since it was within the specificity of that culture that many of these values and aspirations were acquired. In this way the liberal commitment to individual self-determination can only be properly realised when the collective self-determination of the person's primary demos is also properly respected and allowed the autonomy and self-government which is needed to achieve communal goals.

Here the liberal nationalist seeks to turn the tables on traditional liberalism with its pejorative stereotypes of nationalism as restrictive of freedom. Instead national identity is presented as an important base from which the individual develops a sense of self. In the post-Enlightenment period it has also proven itself to be a vehicle for vernacular, popular models of democratic representation and accountability. Requejo expresses this viewpoint in relation to plurinational societies: 'A normative and institutional refinement of liberal democracies in plurinational societies means seeing national pluralism as a value worth protecting and not just as an inconvenient fact that must be borne as stoically as possible'.[19] By extension we might make the same point about national identity more generally within a globalising world.

As a consequence, individual citizens can find themselves disadvantaged directly or indirectly by the marginalisation of the sub-state society to which they belong if the state constitution does not take full account of their societal particularity. An undifferentiated approach to liberal rights can entirely overlook the need to accommodate the *context of the individual* as well as the individual himself, since rights are invariably applied without conditioning the position of the individual through the prism of his societal attachments; the result can be homogenisation masquerading as universalism. For sub-state nationalists, the primary 'right' that is sought is self-government. In short, it is this insight – that the republican commitment to the self-government of the nation is the essential precondition for the achievement of the rights of the individual – that is arguably the most important conclusion of the liberal nationalist project, but this autonomy, as we will see, is open to curtailment by the homogenising dynamics of international liberal rights in the practice of liberal legalism.

[18] Kymlicka, *Multicultural Citizenship* (n 3) ch 5.
[19] Requejo, 'Democratic Legitimacy' (n 17) 166.

The normative challenge posed by the second type of liberalism as developed by Taylor, Kymlicka and others therefore is immanent, from a self-assured liberal position, but one which calls for a revision of how liberalism operates in practice in its prioritisation of radical individualism over the group attachments people have, and in the elevation of entrenched individual rights over democratic decision-making. For the liberal nationalist it seems that rights claims must be situated within particular social settings – contextualising the application of individual rights against the backdrop of the historical particularity of each society – rather than approached with simplistic notions of their universal application in undifferentiated ways. This conclusion has been reached with an admirable degree of sophistication among the scholars of the Liberalism II tradition, but as we will see there is no guarantee that this interpretation of liberalism is being adopted or this subtlety fully understood in the application of the new rights culture, particularly by legal practitioners and judges.

III. LIBERAL RIGHTS: THE NEW ORTHODOXY

Perhaps the most powerful story in post-war international law is the rise of the human rights agenda. The early and seemingly idealistic commitment to human rights in the Universal Declaration of Human Rights and in Article 1 of the UN Charter was followed by legally binding Covenants which, initially at least, acted more as sources of rhetoric in the hands of Cold Warriors than meaningful or enforceable legal instruments. But in recent times we have seen how the standard-setting of the legally binding International Covenant on Civil and Political Rights (ICCPR) has worked its influence in a myriad of ways. More states than ever are now party to it.[20] Efforts are being made gradually to strengthen agencies established to ensure state compliance,[21] and respect for them, at least insofar as this is evidenced by the number of states becoming party to the Optional Protocol that recognises the jurisdiction of the Human Rights Committee, has increased.[22] New institutions have been established, most notably the UN Office of the High Commissioner for Human Rights in 1993, and we have seen a growth in the number of Special Rapporteurs engaged in improving human rights compliance in a number of specialist areas.

The post-war period has also seen a proliferation of human rights instruments in two ways – specialisation and regionalisation. The former involves global Conventions on specific issues. The early Convention on the Prevention and Punishment of the Crime of Genocide and the heavily influential Convention Relating to the Status of Refugees and Protocol Relating to the Status of

[20] As at 19 November 2010 the ICCPR had 166 parties.

[21] The United Nations Human Rights Council replaced the United Nations Commission on Human Rights: (A/RES/60/251) on 15 March 2006.

[22] As at 19 November 2010 the First Optional Protocol had 113 parties. http://treaties.un.org/Pages/ViewDetails.aspx?src=TREATY&mtdsg_no=IV-5&chapter=4&lang=en .

Refugees have been added to over time by the very (and surprisingly) strongly worded Convention Against Torture (CAT). More recently these have been joined by the Convention on the Elimination of All Forms of Racial Discrimination (ICERD); the Convention on the Elimination of All Forms of Discrimination Against Women (CEDAW); the Convention on the Rights of the Child (CRC) and the Convention on the Rights of Persons with Disabilities (CRPD).

The other influential development has taken place at the continental level. Conventions such as the African Charter on Human and Peoples' Rights, the American Convention on Human Rights and the European Convention on Human Rights (ECHR) offer general treatments of rights; the last of these now has a massive and expanding jurisprudence.[23] And we also see regional treaties on specific human rights issues emerge.[24] The European treaties have been concluded under the auspices of the Council of Europe but it is important not to overlook also the Charter of Fundamental Rights of the European Union (the European Charter) which acquired legal effect with the entry into force of the Treaty of Lisbon on 1 December 2009 and which provides that the European Union must act and legislate consistently with the Charter and that Member States must also do so in the implementation of EU law.[25]

It is notable that the dominant force in the rights revolution has been civil and political rights framed in individual terms. Economic and social rights are protected in the International Covenant on Economic, Social and Cultural Rights, but the obligations here are far less directive than in the ICCPR. They are also not always mirrored in regional treaties, and are rarely the subject of specialist instruments. Among civil and political rights instruments, although there are allusions to minority rights[26] these have had little impact on the ground with limited and inconsistent application by the Human Rights Committee (HRC).[27] Article 27 of the ICCPR is itself framed seemingly as an individual right.[28]

[23] Deciding some 1500 cases a year, with a backlog of over 100000 cases. 'European court of human rights: Courting disaster', *The Guardian*, 11 April 2009.

[24] The African Charter on the Rights and Welfare of the Child; the Inter-American Convention to Prevent and Punish Torture; the Inter-American Convention on Forced Disappearance of Persons; the Inter-American Convention on the Prevention, Punishment, and Eradication of Violence against Women; the Inter-American Convention on the Elimination of All Forms of Discrimination against Persons with Disabilities; European Convention for the Prevention of Torture and Inhuman or Degrading Treatment or Punishment; European Social Charter, and Revised Social Charter; European Charter for Regional or Minority Languages; and the Framework Convention for the Protection of National Minorities.

[25] This initiative might well have substantially greater implications for national prerogatives in the long run than just about any other international human rights instrument given that the EU legal order acts more like a federal regime than an international one, that the court system polices consistent state application of EU law very vigorously, and that it is supported in this task by municipal courts bound by the supremacy of EU law in its agreed fields of application.

[26] International Covenant on Civil and Political Rights, art 27.

[27] K Henrard, *Devising an Adequate System of Minority Protection* (Netherlands, Kluwer, 2000) 172–84.

[28] The rights apply to 'persons belonging' to minorities rather than minorities as groups.

Other instruments such as those in Europe are either not in force or offer very limited guarantees that are in any way legally enforceable.[29]

The rights revolution has a number of features beyond merely the spread of international instruments which we will return to below. Its real force has, however, been felt at the municipal level where many states have adopted human rights protections into domestic law. This has often been done constitutionally either through the direct transposition of international treaties in their entirety,[30] a number of specific human rights protections within the constitution which in effect constitute a bill of rights,[31] or through a dedicated bill of rights as a separate instrument.[32] These rights are invariably legally enforceable, and as constitutional rights can be a basis for declarations of illegality against public bodies and even the overturning of incompatible legislation. A plethora of other rights-oriented legislation has accompanied these constitutional provisions, often mirroring international developments in areas of discrimination etc.

One consequence of this has been a growing homogenisation of liberal standards throughout the world in the area of rights protection. It is no surprise that the spread of international human rights law has been accompanied by the active enforcement of rights by the courts.[33] And increasingly we are seeing the cross-fertilisation of these norms as courts in one jurisdiction look to those in others for guidance on human rights matters.[34]

IV. AN EMERGING TENSION BETWEEN THE NEW NATIONALISM AND THE NEW ORTHODOXY?

Although a plausible case has been made by Kymlicka and others to the effect that nationalism is compatible with liberalism, in practice the rights revolution has tended to mirror the values of traditional liberalism in its inclination towards homogenisation in the application of individual rights. I will explore this in Section IV.B below when addressing examples of how both international and domestic human rights law approach the issue of pluralism. Before doing so, and in light of Liberalism II's role in consolidating the republican commitment to the self-government of the nation as the essential precondition for the achievement of

[29] G Gilbert, 'Minority Rights Under the Council of Europe' in P Cumper and S Wheatley (eds), *Minority Rights in the 'New' Europe* (Netherlands, Kluwer, 1999) 53–70.

[30] The Constitution of Bosnia and Herzegovina, art 2.7 and Annex 1. See D Feldman's contribution to this collection.

[31] The US example is widely followed.

[32] The Canadian Charter of Rights and Freedoms 1982 is such a document which has constitutional status. The UK Human Rights Act 1998 transposes many of the catalogued rights of the ECHR into UK law but these are not formally entrenched as fundamental law (ss 3 and 4).

[33] As noted, this is most striking in Europe where two dedicated court systems oversee the implementation of the ECHR and the Charter of Fundamental Rights of the European Union respectively. This complements the obligations on Member States to ensure the compatibility of their domestic law with the ECHR and EU law.

[34] S Choudhry (ed), *The Migration of Constitutional Ideas* (Cambridge, Cambridge University Press, 2006).

the rights of the individual, I need clarify how the rights revolution of traditional liberalism has come into tension with republican democracy.

A. Republicanism v Entrenchment

Since the principal dynamic of the new nationalism is the assertion of the autonomy of discrete communities and their entitlement to self-government,[35] we can see these claims fitting within a broader re-emergence of popular republicanism. But this re-emergence has brought with it a challenge to the assumption that the supremacy of entrenched constitutionalism is preferable to the open dynamics of the political. Sub-state nationalists can in many cases be located within this trend, making claims that seem to prioritise the open political processes of republican democracy and positing the principle of democracy as a purported trump card in the face of claims by the state that the constitution forbids certain forms of constitutional change or certain avenues by which constitutional change might be effected. We saw this dynamic in the dispute about the legality of the Quebec referendum on sovereignty in 1995. A number of constitutional arguments were made by the Canadian federal government to the effect that the referendum being used by Quebec was unconstitutional and, in any event, that it could not of itself bring about constitutional change. The Quebec government responded that this was an issue of democratic will of the discrete people of Quebec and could not be resisted by constitutionalism, certainly not a constitutionalism imposed upon Quebec and serving the dominant community of the state.[36] It is interesting that the legal case in which this culminated was raised as an individual rights claim.[37] Nonetheless, the Supreme Court of Canada (in considering the secession question following a subsequent intervention by the federal government of Canada) took the principle of democracy very seriously as one that needed to be weighed against constitutionalism in determining the weight to be given to an expression of will by the people of a province in a referendum.[38]

So while it is too simplistic to elide sub-state nationalism with anti-entrenchment popular republicanism, it is often the principle of democracy, expressed in terms of autonomy, self-government, self-determination or independence, that is the primary goal of sub-state nationalists. It is also often the case that this principle, when applied as a means of advancing the discrete democratic aspirations of a community, will come up against the entrenched

[35] As Canovan argues: the 'democratic' strand as opposed to the 'liberal' strand of democracy 'is concerned with the sovereign will of the people': M Canovan, 'Populism for political theorists?' (2004) 9 *Journal of Political Ideologies* 241, 244.

[36] See the comments of Quebec Prime Minster Jacques Parizeau quoted in RA Young, *The Struggle for Quebec: From Referendum to Referendum?* (Montreal/Kingston, McGill-Queen's University Press, 1999) 106.

[37] *Bertrand v Quebec (Procreur General)* (1995), 127 DLR (4th) 408 (Que. SC).

[38] *Reference re Secession of Quebec* [1998] 2 SCR 217, paras 88 and 92.

constitution of the state.[39] And of course entrenched constitutions today are the main mechanisms with which liberals seek to protect individual rights from the vagaries of legislative prerogative. It is perhaps no surprise that nationalists, even liberal nationalists, have therefore come to see such a strategy of embedded, and homogenising, liberal rights – deployed through the ideology of traditional liberalism – as a potential Trojan horse with which the state can restrict recognition of difference and the freedom of sub-state nations to set their own societal priorities. Indeed the bill of rights has itself become a battleground for the playing out of different national prerogatives within the state.[40]

There seem to be two issues – anti-conservatism and collectivism – that offer common cause for republicans and sub-state nationalists in questioning the role of constitutional entrenchment. Sub-state nationalism's reaction to entrenchment as a vehicle to super-impose uniformity in the name of liberal rights seems to fit within the tendency of the broader republican movement to question the conservative tendency of constitutionalism, and in particular the way in which this conservatism is deployed to elevate liberal rights to a position of ascendancy within a constitutional structure at the expense of popular democracy. In other words, popular republicanism poses a strident challenge both to the function of constitutionalism as a vehicle for instantiating the entrenchment of law over political decision-making, and in more radical critiques, to the ideological structure – founded upon methodological individualism – which constitutionalism is seen to underpin within liberal democracies. This branch of democratic theory, which has enjoyed a recent renaissance,[41] is a broad church,[42] but a number of its advocates share a commitment to a politically engaged demos in partial realisation of the ideal of 'government by the people'.[43]

[39] S Tierney, 'Crystallising dominance: majority nationalism, constitutionalism and the courts' in A-G Gagnon, A Lecours and G Nootens (eds), *Dominant Nationalisms* (Montreal, University of Montreal Press, 2008) 87–110.

[40] A-G Gagnon and R Iacovino, 'Challenging the Constraints of State Nationalism in Canada' in A-G Gagnon, A Lecours, and G Nootens (eds), *Dominant Nationalisms* (n 39) 111–30. See also S Choudhry, 'Bills of Rights as Instruments of Nation-Building in Multinational States: The Canadian Charter and Quebec Nationalism' in JB Kelly and CP Manfredi (eds), *Contested Constitutionalism: Reflections on the Canadian Charter of Rights and Freedoms* (UBC Press 2010); and AC Cairns, *Charter versus Federalism: The Dilemmas of Constitutional Reform* (Montreal and Kingston, McGill-Queen's University Press, 1992).

[41] P Pettit, *Republicanism: A Theory of Freedom and Government* (Oxford, Oxford University Press, 1999); J Maynor, *Republicanism in the Modern World* (Cambridge, Polity, 2003); D Weinstock and C Nadeau (eds), *Republicanism: History, Theory and Practice* (London, Frank Cass, 2004); R Bellamy, *Political Constitutionalism: A Republican Defence of the Constitutionality of Democracy* (Cambridge, Cambridge University Press, 2007).

[42] Among those who might be thought of as republicans who are more interested in the negative (modern) freedom of liberalism than the positive (ancient) freedom of republicanism, we might list Pettit and Bellamy (n 41) and indeed John Rawls. See A de Francisco, 'A Republican Interpretation of the Late Rawls' (2006) 14 *Journal of Political Philosophy* 270. For the characterisation of modern and ancient freedoms see of course Benjamin Constant, 'The Liberty of the Ancients Compared with that of the Moderns' in B Fontana (ed), *The Political Writings of Benjamin Constant* (Cambridge, Cambridge University Press, 1988).

[43] Within the strain of republican thought that emphasises the imperative of an active citizenry are B Ackerman and JS Fishkin, *Deliberation Day* (New Haven, Yale University Press, 2004).

Of course one argument for entrenched constitutional supremacy which binds the people into the future is that this leads to stable government. But the populist strain of republicanism calls into question the inherent value of stability, at least insofar as it is used to justify an overwhelming constraint on the people's will. A common question which goes back to the revolutionary period of the late eighteenth century asks, whence comes the authority for such a foundational document to bind a republican people into the future? And one objection is that this ties popular will to tradition whereby entrenched constitutionalism becomes akin to 'rule from the cold graves of dead men of constitutions past',[44] and hence illegitimate. Jefferson argued against entrenchment, stating that one generation was to another what one independent nation is to another; nations cannot make laws for each other, neither should one generation have such a power.[45]

Another argument against the conservatism of constitutionalism, this time from a more 'critical' republican tradition, contends that constitutionalism can act as a hegemonic force, not only constraining the republican, political potential of the people, but in doing so serving to uphold powerful vested interests. This reacts to the liberal argument that the inclusion of individual rights within the constitution offers the substantive benefit of protecting minority and individual interests from the will of the majority. For the radical republican, entrenchment can in fact serve to protect the pre-existing prerogatives of the powerful while claiming to act in a neutral way.[46]

These arguments – that the people should not be constrained by decisions of a mythical people in the past and that such constraints are often in fact reactionary devices – support the conviction that popular sovereignty ought to be kept alive: the people should be able directly to challenge those vested interests that can otherwise deploy constitutionalism to protect privilege. There is also in the republican tradition an argument that the ideology of individualism misses the communal value that the individual finds in society, and is in fact an inade-

[44] AR Amar, 'Popular Sovereignty and Constitutional Amendment' in S Levinson (ed), *Responding to Imperfection: The Theory and Practice of Constitutional Amendment* (Princeton, Princeton University Press, 1995) 89, 115.

[45] T Jefferson, letter to John Cartwright, 1824. See also J Locke, *Two Treatises of Government* (Cambridge, Cambridge University Press, 1963) ch 8, s 116.

[46] Wood famously characterised the American Revolution in this way. See GS Wood, *The Creation of the American Republic, 1776-1787* (Chapel Hill, NC, The University of North Carolina Press, 1969). Or as Dryzek explains, liberal constitutionalism can be seen as the 'aggregation of predetermined interests under the auspices of a neutral set of rules: that is, a constitution': JS Dryzek, *Deliberative Democracy and Beyond: Liberals, Critics and Contestations* (Oxford, Oxford University Press, 2000) 9. A classic critique of how democracy can be undermined by hegemonic juridification is J Tully, *Strange Multiplicity: Constitutionalism in an Age of Diversity* (Cambridge, Cambridge University Press, 1995). See also E Christodoulidis, 'Against Substitution: the Constitutional thinking of Dissensus' in M Loughlin and N Walker (eds), *The Paradox of Constitutionalism: Constituent Power and Constitutional Form* (Oxford, Oxford University Press, 2007) 189–208; and AC Hutchinson and J Colon-Rios, 'What's Democracy Got To Do With It? A Critique of Liberal Constitutionalism' (Comparative Research in Law and Political Economy Network Papers, Osgoode Hall Law School, Canada, Vol 03, No 05, 2007).

quate device with which to build the bonds of rights and responsibilities to which liberalism aspires. This contends that the reification of rights within a democratic project carries with it the deeply contestable political assumption that the purpose of a polity is more to protect individuals from the state than to build a people jointly committed to a communal enterprise. Within the populist republican tradition such a vision not only under-estimates the importance of communal attachments to individuals but also misses the utilitarian necessity of the demos as a vital point of shared identification which consolidates the collective identity of a free people around the notion of the polity, with resulting benefits for the shared responsibilities of citizenship that attend such a project.[47] David Miller, for example, has argued that the idea of the nation is essential in building the civic resources necessary to establish a sense of mutual obligation within a particular, territorially bounded commonwealth.[48] And as a matter of reason there is also a strong argument that a sense of 'we the people' as a collective is *logically a priori* to any workable notion of either democracy or constitutional form.[49] Therefore, although it is important to achieve 'inclusiveness without exclusion',[50] the notion of a united people taking collective decisions is the basis of any democratic system.

Hutchinson and Colon Rios, in a strident defence of popular republicanism, take issue not only with the methodology of liberal constitutionalism but also with liberal rights in substantive terms as constraints on democracy:

> Under liberal constitutionalism, democracy is exhausted by a constitution that establishes representative government, protects liberal rights, and enables all citizens to 'participate' in government by the election of officials. This is an impoverished and disabling idea of democracy and one which has little place for the emancipatory potential of popular participation and democratic openness.[51]

Moreover, this model of constitutionalism leaves too much of the task of important political decision-making to the courts: 'Making courts into a primary venue for democratic engagement perpetuates the idea that social justice comes from a judicial act of noblesse oblige rather than a popular product forged in the furnace of political debate'.[52]

[47] SD Gerber, 'The Republican Revival in American Constitutional Theory' (1994) 47 *Political Research Quarterly* 985.

[48] D Miller, *On Nationality* (1995). See also B O'Leary, 'An iron law of nationalism and federation? A (neo-Diceyan) theory of the necessity of a federal *Staatsvolk*, and of consociational rescue' (2001) 7 *Nations and Nationalism* 273, 284–85.

[49] H Lindahl, 'Democracy, Political Reflexivity and Bounded Dialogues: Reconsidering the Monism-Pluralism Debate' in E Christodoulidis and S Tierney (eds), *Public Law and Politics: The Scope and Limits of Constitutionalism* (Aldershot, Ashgate, 2008) 110. This position is one of some pedigree. Mill took the view that a successful democracy depends on citizens sharing a sense of common national identity: JS Mill, *Considerations on Representative Government* (London, Parker and Bourn, 1861) ch 16.

[50] H Lindahl, 'Democracy, Political Reflexivity and Bounded Dialogues' (n 49).

[51] Hutchinson and Colon-Rios, 'What's Democracy Got To Do With It?' (n 46) 26.

[52] ibid 35.

My purpose here is not to assert that liberalism is necessarily aligned with reactionary vested interests, that it is an inflexible tool, or to suggest that liberals cannot and do not build highly viable polities with overwhelming popular support across cultural groups. Indeed, the work of Kymlicka and others has arguably shown liberalism's potential for flexibility in the context of multiculturalism. My purpose rather is to point out that a model of constitutionalism that entrenches a system of classical liberalism is only one ideologically fashioned possibility for democratic society among many, even if it tries to disguise itself as the logical end-point of human political development, and hence as an ideology that can and indeed should be replicated universally.[53] Such a view can serve to restrict the aspirations of national democracies to pursue distinctive policy agendas among and within states. Within a plurinational state this tension can be apparent even when values are in fact shared to a high degree among nations.[54] Because even with no substantial value-based differential, respective societal aspirations, priorities and policies may be highly incommensurable, and where these differences fall foul of juridified liberalism's thirst for homogeneity, judicial attempts to enforce sameness can undercut autonomy. This is particularly tendentious for divided societies, where it might be argued that the avenues for political decision-making should remain as open as possible, and in particular should not be shut down by pre-set 'rights' which may be no more than the legal codification of the values of a dominant group.

It is overstated to present the liberal-republican debate today in an excessively binary way: republican politics will secure what national peoples want, liberal rights will deny this opportunity; republican politics will not accept any legal codification of rights, liberalism is only concerned with rights to the exclusion of other political values. But it does seem that if a divided society is to move towards some form of entrenched constitution, there are risks if this brings with it a foreclosure of the political marketplace of values; setting out only one acceptable value catalogue and handing responsibility to judges – whose own legitimacy and neutrality may well be questioned – to police this disposition. Such an approach promises to beg rather than offer a solution to multinational co-existence. In the next section we will see how the move towards the homogenisation of Liberalism I as a global movement may confirm some of the fears of republicans as to the incompatibility of liberal constitutionalism and national pluralism.

[53] F Fukuyama, *The End of History and the Last Man* (New York, Free Press, 1992); T Franck, *The Empowered Self: Law and Society in the Age of Individualism* (Oxford, Oxford University Press, 2000).

[54] The ever closer alignment of values among nations within states at the same time as nationalist sentiment within these nations grows has been called 'de Tocqueville's paradox' by Stephane Dion. See S Dion, 'Le nationalisme dans la convergence culturelle: le Québec contemporain et le paradoxe de Tocqueville' in R Hudon and R Pelletier (eds), *L'engagement intellectuel: Mélange en l'honneur de Léon Dion* (Québec, Presses de l'Université Laval, 1991).

B. Diversity v Homogenisation

One of the central normative arguments of the Liberalism II tradition is that pluralism is a value. The notion of a discrete people, developing over time through its own culture and traditions, is central to contemporary arguments that national groups should have the opportunity to govern themselves and set their own societal priorities. As we have seen, Kymlicka has argued this from a liberal perspective, suggesting that 'societal cultures' offer their members a 'context of choice' within which to make important individual decisions against the backdrop of the culture and society through which they generate many of their values.[55]

There is a substantial body of literature that addresses how this liberal argument for pluralism might be squared with liberal rights. However, although as a matter of principle liberalism may be capable of, and arguably should, accommodate pluralism (including the opportunity for different societies to set their own priorities), the rights revolution (especially in the way it is being adapted by legislatures and courts) certainly qualifies the extent to which societies have the opportunity to set and maintain their own standards, values and priorities. International human rights standards, dominated as they are by Liberalism I, lean by their application towards universalisation, and in a number of features both procedural and substantive, they seem to encourage states to adopt these standards in a homogeneous way.

The rights revolution has a number of features beyond merely the spread of international instruments discussed above. One is reporting mechanisms in treaties. A number of human rights treaties contain reporting mechanisms, requiring states to inform the relevant treaty body periodically of what it has done to comply with its international obligations. These are the focus of increasing attention by human rights scholars and activists.[56] Another is courts and tribunals established by the treaties. A number of treaties have adjudicatory mechanisms. The most developed of these is the ECtHR. I have noted that its caseload has been expanding exponentially in recent years. It is also interesting for the way in which, in a number of cases, it has seemed to extend its own jurisdiction.[57] The ECtHR has developed an approach that gives leeway to the cultural or other specificities of states through the 'margin of appreciation' doctrine, but this is limited to certain provisions, and can be curtailed closely as

[55] See also Charles Taylor's argument that many of the individual's 'beliefs about value' are formed within a national society: C Taylor, 'The Politics of Recognition' (n 14).

[56] P Alston and J Crawford (eds), *The Future of UN Human Rights Treaty Monitoring* (Cambridge, Cambridge University Press, 2000).

[57] S Miller, 'Revisiting Extraterritorial Jurisdiction: A Territorial Justification for Extraterritorial Jurisdiction under the European Convention' (2009) 20 *European Journal of International Law* 1223. We also see the ECJ taking a more assertive approach in the area of fundamental rights, using them to question the normative reach of a UN SC resolution – Joined Cases-C 402/05 and C-415/05P *Kadi and another v European Union Council* [2008] All ER (D) 34 (Sep).

we will see in the *Lautsi* case below. We also see the force of the rights revolution within domestic courts particularly in light of the incorporation of international instruments into domestic law and the migration of principles of human rights jurisprudence across jurisdictions.

Let us take two examples of the implications of these developments, the first from international law, and the second from the domestic law of a territorially disaggregated state. Both of these issues highlight the way in which the rights explosion serves to elevate judges to a position as vital political actors.[58] The former in particular will show how decisions can be reached that go against the grain of the prevailing national culture and the overwhelming body of opinion within the state, arguably without sufficient reflection in the reasoned opinion of the judges as to the significance of such an intervention for national autonomy. The latter concerns the scope for policy differences to survive in devolving plurinational states and the power of the universalising dynamic of liberal rights within the central state to take back with one hand what autonomy legislation has given with the other.[59]

In the case of *Lautsi v Italy*[60] a Chamber of the ECtHR found that the display of crucifixes on the walls in Italian schools violated the ECHR by restricting the right of parents to educate their children in conformity with their convictions, and the right of children to believe or not to believe. The Court concluded, unanimously, that there had been a violation of Article 2 of Protocol No 1 (the right to education) taken jointly with Article 9 of the Convention (freedom of thought, conscience and religion).[61] Regardless of one's views of the substantive issue at stake, the decision of the Chamber is open to criticism first for the lack of reasoning offered to support its decision; secondly, for the ideological character of the decision; and thirdly, for the assumption that an international court is better able to make these kinds of judgments than the elected bodies of the state concerned, relegating in importance the doctrine of margin of appreciation which has hitherto been widely used in Article 9 cases.

On the first point, *Lautsi* emerges at a time of intense debate in Europe on the place of religion in the public sphere and how multiculturalism is complicating this picture. This is a very complex issue, engaging fierce and emotive disagreement on a wide range of issues. Yet the Chamber dealt with this entire issue in a fairly peremptory way, described by Joseph Weiler as 'impatient and apodictic'.[62] Secondly, in such a brief treatment it might be argued that the Court does not articulate how ideologically contested the issues are and consequently does not fully engage with the complex range of possibilities open when balancing the

[58] R Hirschl, *Towards Juristocracy: The Origins and Consequences of the New Constitutionalism* (Cambridge MA, Harvard University Press, 2004).

[59] S Tierney, 'Giving with one hand: Scottish devolution within a unitary state' (2007) *International Journal of Constitutional Law* 1.

[60] *Lautsi v Italy*, no 30814/06, § 55, 3 November 2009; Grand Chamber, 18 March 2011.

[61] The decision was overturned by the Grand Chamber in its decision of 2011.

[62] JHH Weiler, 'Lautsi: Crucifix in the Classroom Redux' (2010) 21 *European Journal of International Law* 1.

application of liberal values against important aspects of the national and cultural identity of the state. Instead it falls back upon the principle of 'neutrality'. The Court stated that on matters of Church and State: '[t]he duty of neutrality and impartiality of the state is incompatible with any judgment on its part of the legitimacy of religious beliefs or ways of expressing them'.[63] I have alluded to how Liberalism II exposes cultural neutrality as a simplistic notion which in the rarefied sense implied by the Court is not feasible in any society.[64] To assert a neutral position is often to attempt to disguise the prioritisation of a particular set of values surreptitiously elevating these as somehow value-neutral and above the level of political disagreement. We need to ask, what is the neutral position to which the Court aspires? It seems that this is secularism. But as Weiler points out, secularism is simply one of a number of value systems that must compete with religion in the public sphere.[65] He describes the Court's view that the duty of neutrality is incompatible with any judgment on the legitimacy of belief as 'breathtaking' and asks:

> May Irish schools no longer teach the Irish Constitution to schoolchildren because the Constitution endorses expressis verbis in its Preamble the Holy Trinity? Must Denmark, like Sweden, abandon Lutheranism as the official Danish Church or hide this fact from its children? . . . Can one have an established church, or an endorsed church, or a supported church, or a privileged church (one of the many modalities of the non-laique group of states who are, pace the Chamber, still part of Europe), as one does in so many European states, which does not, at a minimum, impinge on the issue of legitimacy of religious beliefs as the Court seems to say no state may?[66]

Again one may disagree about the merits of official religion etc. within one's own state, or indeed for any state. But what seems to emerge in this case is a narrow vision of religious freedom, with the Chamber circumscribing extremely tightly what an acceptable manifestation of this freedom is in contemporary Europe. The sense of permissible religious expression which the Court advances seems to dictate that the proper place for religion is exclusively the private sphere. As such, it leaves little space for a publicly endorsed, communal expression of religious belief or culture. However, for many believers religious faith, like language, is often expressed by way of a collective act and the affirmation by the community of a commonly held faith. The approach of the Chamber also seems to relegate the significance of Christianity in Europe's cultural development, failing to see

[63] *Lautsi* para 47(e). More straightforwardly it also declares the state must 'uphold confessional neutrality in public education': see *Lautsi* para 56.

[64] As Ferran Requejo argues: 'There are fewer and fewer liberal theorists who still maintain that liberal-democratic institutions are neutral when dealing with cultural issues'. F Requejo, 'Introduction' in *Democracy and National Pluralism* 2. See also I Peleg, 'Ethno-national state definition and liberal democratic practices: Beyond "neutrality" in deeply divided societies' in A Lecours and L Moreno (eds), *Nationalism and Democracy: Dichotomies, Complementarities, Oppositions* (London, Routledge, 2010).

[65] See Weiler, 'Lautsi: Crucifix in the Classroom Redux' (n 62): 'the naked wall in the school . . . is no more neutral than having a crucifix on the wall'.

[66] ibid.

the close connection between religious symbolism and deep cultural attachments ('to say that the cross is predominantly religious does not mean that it is only that and that Italian history and identity started with, say the French Revolution').[67] Its judgment is also dubious from the perspective of pluralism. European states have developed widely varying constitutional traditions, some overtly and indeed militantly secular, others imbued with the (often banal) symbolism of Christianity. The Chamber's ruling seems to threaten the validity of all but the aggressively secular tradition and with it the space for difference in Europe.

The third point concerns the democratic legitimacy of Italy being bound by a decision of an international court on a matter with which so many voices within the Italian state so vehemently disagreed. It is certainly the case of course that Member States of the ECHR have ratified a convention recognising internationally agreed standards and have undertaken to be bound by the decisions of the Court. However, in issues of religious sensitivity the Court has previously shown itself prepared to defer to the specific sensibilities of a particular state which, as an international court, it has not the specialist knowledge or democratic legitimacy to second guess.[68] The Chamber in this case does not seem to have taken seriously any scope for margin of appreciation in this case which would have allocated to Italy the right to form a view on the proper display of a symbol that is so central to Italian national identity. A succession of Italian courts had declared the crucifix to be a symbol central to Italian history and culture. Indeed in its submission to the Court the Italian state defended the school crucifix not on the basis that it was an important *religious* symbol but primarily because it has *cultural* symbolism for Italians that transcends its outward religious significance. Weiler is once again scathing on the issue of democratic legitimacy:

> The European Court of Human Rights is not an Oracle. It is a dialogical partner with the Member States Parties to the Convention, and the legitimacy and persuasiveness of its decisions resides both in their quality and communicative power. The ECtHR is simultaneously reflective and constitutive of the European constitutional practices and norms. When there is a diverse constitutional practice among the Convention States – and there certainly is in this area – the Court needs to listen, not only preach, and to be seen to be listening.[69]

[67] ibid.

[68] eg *Otto-Preminger-Institut v Austria* [1994] ECHR 26.

[69] Weiler, 'Lautsi: Crucifix in the Classroom Redux' (n 62). It is notable that the Grand Chamber did listen to Professor Weiler's arguments when he represented Italy in its appeal. By 15 votes to 2 it overturned the Chamber ruling and found that the mere presence of the crucifix in state-school classrooms was not a violation. Certainly, this conferred on 'the country's majority religion preponderant visibility in the school environment'. However, this in itself was not evidence of indoctrination to constitute a breach of the requirements of art 2 of Protocol No 1. A crucifix on a wall is an 'essentially passive symbol' and 'cannot be deemed to have an influence on pupils comparable to that of didactic speech or participation in religious activities': para 71–72. Grand Chamber, 18 March 2011.

It seems that the original Chamber decision is infused with the ideology of traditional liberalism with fairly simplistic assumptions about neutrality and equality, making no reference to the nuanced accounts of these values which have been developed within liberal theory over the past 20 years. Hutchinson and Rios, in a critique of the universalistic assumptions in Ronald Dworkin's account of liberal principles, suggest this type of radical individualism seems to 'leave little space for religious or other group commitments'.[70] The point is not that established religion is a good or bad idea. But rather that European constitutionalism in all its diversity has developed a pluralistic approach to this question and has left the future of religious establishment open to democratic debate from state to state. The proselytising zeal of a stridently homogenising secularism is a valid contributor to the debate. But when this particular ideology is adopted unreflectively by a court that assumes the neutrality of this position, what is in fact simply one political argument is crystallised into a sacrosanct and incontestable 'right' that can be both declared and demarcated by judges, thereby foreclosing the deeply contextualised debate that is the mark of every democratic national society.

The quest for homogenisation in the juridification of human rights can also be found within states. An example of this can be taken from the UK where a number of legal systems exist side by side: England, Scotland and Northern Ireland. My focus will be upon Scotland where a devolved system was created through the Scotland Act 1998 which provides autonomy for Scotland in the form of a Scottish Parliament and Scottish Executive, but requires both to act compatibly with Convention rights (which apply directly throughout the UK by virtue of the Human Rights Act 1998). There is scope for tension to emerge between devolution for Scotland and this UK-wide 'bill of rights' since the UK's highest court seems inclined towards uniformity across the UK even despite the historical differences which have developed within the discrete legal systems of the state.

It is notable that with the coming of devolution there were no strong claims that a separate bill of rights different from the regime of the Human Rights Act (HRA) should be created for Scotland, in a way similar to Canada for example where Quebec has its own which pre-dates the Canadian Charter.[71] This was perhaps because the HRA and Scotland Act both gave effect to the ECHR which was a broadly agreed set of European standards. Nor in their general application so far have the rights contained in the Convention caused particular controversy as a mechanism of restraint operating on the devolved institutions from the perspective of sub-state autonomy.

However, one exception to this has arisen over a fairly esoteric point of criminal procedure. Until 2009 (when the new UK Supreme Court took over the jurisdiction of both) the Scottish legal system interacted with two tribunals in

[70] Hutchinson and Colon-Rios, 'What's Democracy Got To Do With It?' (n 46) 10.
[71] *Charter of Human Rights and Freedoms*, National Assembly of Quebec, 27 June 1975.

London. The Judicial Committee of the Privy Council (JCPC) settled devolution issues arising under the Scotland Act, while the Appellate Committee of the House of Lords (Appellate Committee) heard civil appeals from the Court of Session in Edinburgh (the House of Lords had no jurisdiction to hear appeals in criminal matters from Scotland.

Two cases, one emerging from Scotland and the other from England, suggest that some senior judges are prioritising the achievement of homogeneity across the UK over the prerogatives of the devolved institutions and the distinctive historical trajectory of Scots criminal law. The issue in the former case concerned the role of the Lord Advocate, Scotland's senior law officer. In Scotland, with its long history of the independent criminal prosecution service, the Crown (represented by the Lord Advocate) has a significantly stronger role in the criminal process than it does in England and so the office is expected to assume considerable responsibility for failings in that process.

The importance of this difference emerged in these two cases with respect to the question of delay in trial deemed excessive in terms of Article 6 of the ECHR, and, in particular, remedies for breach of this Convention right. In the Scots case *HMA v R*[72] the JCPC split 3–2 with the three Scottish judges on the Committee, Lords Hope, Rodger and Clyde, emphasising the strict position on delay which has traditionally been taken in Scots law. They argued that this required that where a trial had been delayed for an unreasonable time in certain circumstances one consequence could be that the accused had a positive right not to be tried. In other words, the right to be tried within a reasonable time could include a right not to be tried at all after an unreasonable time. The two dissenting judges (both non-Scots lawyers) worried about the scope of this decision, seeming to assume it would have to be followed in English law where there is no such tradition. Subsequently, in the English appeal case *Attorney General's Reference (No 2 of 2001)*[73] a nine-judge panel of the Appellate Committee split 7–2 (the two Scots judges Hope and Rodger dissenting) to the effect that delay was not in itself contrary to a right to fair trial.

What is interesting is not the different approaches taken to Scots and English law, but the reaction by certain judges to the very idea that such a difference in outcome could be tolerable. The majority in the Appellate Committee took the view that *HMA v R* was 'wrongly decided'. This is odd for two reasons. The first is that the Appellate Committee was bound by the decisions of the JCPC by virtue of the Scotland Act and so this is an unusual position to take in relation to what was in effect the decision of a superior tribunal. Secondly, it is curious that this view should be taken about a decision in a Scots law case by a court adjudicating on English law. As David Feldman notes: 'the English majority

[72] *HMA v R* 2003 SC(PC) 21.

[73] *Attorney General's Reference (No 2 of 2001)* [2003] UKHL 68.

went out of its way to express the view that their conclusion was irreconcilable' with the decision of the JCPC in *HMA v R*.[74]

One must ask, what was so problematic about two jurisdictions drawing different conclusions about the seriousness of delay before trial when the role of the Crown prosecutor is itself so specific in each system? Scots law and English law differ in many ways, a fact often acknowledged by the highest tribunals; indeed if they were not different in some respects then there would seem little point in the state continuing to support separate legal systems at all. It seems that the determining issue here is, however, human rights. And certainly there is an argument to be made that, since both the HRA and the Scotland Act give effect to the ECHR, there should be a presumption of similarity of treatment across the state. But the ECHR itself in its margin of appreciation doctrine, and in its minimal standards approach, fully acknowledges and respects that rights will be applied differently in different jurisdictions provided minimum standards are met.

There seems no strong reason why this should not also extend within states where there exist separate legal systems. In light of the different legal traditions, it seems inevitable that in some cases the same law, in this case Convention rights, will apply with different nuances across jurisdictions. As with the ECHR itself there is of course a minimum standard required by the Human Rights Act that public authorities act compatibly with Convention rights (a duty expressly imposed also by the Scotland Act on the devolved institutions), but there seems to be scope here for a different standard of protection in each jurisdiction provided the jurisdiction offering weaker protection – in this case England – meets the minimum requirements of Convention rights. Again Feldman observes:

> In view of the special structure of the devolution settlement, there is no good reason why Scotland and England should not have gone their own ways, as long as each of them gave at least as much protection to the right to a hearing within a reasonable time as is required by Article 6 of the ECHR.[75]

He concludes:

> This attempt by 'English' judges to impose a particular view of the practical impact of Article 6 of the ECHR on Scottish judges is more than an exercise in English legal imperialism. It reveals that the English judges have not developed a vision or conception of the United Kingdom's constitution that gives particular weight to the nature of the devolution settlement. A probably outdated unitary vision of the state was dominant . . . [A]s an exercise in the development of constitutional law it is disappointingly monoscopic: the House of Lords passed up an opportunity to recognise that in different parts of a devolved state a multiplicity of constitutional visions may be equally valid.[76]

[74] D Feldman, 'None, One or Several? Perspectives on the UK's Constitution(s)' (2005) 64 *Cambridge Law Journal* 329, 349–50.
[75] ibid 349.
[76] ibid 350.

V. CONCLUSION

One of the great advances of the late 20th century has been the legal consolidation of a global human rights movement that carries with it the laudable and important goal of promoting the interests of all human beings across national boundaries. And indeed the denial of fundamental principles of justice to individuals within national boundaries should not withstand the interrogation of fundamental rights values which have been universally endorsed since 1948. But at the same time we must nuance the conclusion that the proliferation of global – and globalising – human rights standards has been an unqualified good. At the same time an alternative model of liberalism within political theory has been successful in highlighting the value of the vernacular alongside that of the cosmopolitan, and in offering an alternative universalisable value – that of pluralism. The universal promise of this more nuanced model of liberalism is not homogenisation but the general application of the principle of difference; a recognition that throughout the world cultural and national diversity is to be valued not traduced, particularity celebrated rather than assimilated.

But it is the classical forbearer of this model of liberalism which has largely been subsumed within the global explosion of human rights, bringing with it the renewed dominance of a certain strain of liberal legalism and a set of assumptions about the human condition that are individualistic in nature, and a set of political goals that are universalising by instinct. This hegemony of classical liberalism can serve to overlook, or indeed deny, serious recognition to the cultural and national attachments which are central to many people's sense of self.

This tendency towards uniformity as an almost unquestioned good is an issue even in liberal societies where deep societal divisions are absent. But the real threat it poses is for divided societies where the homogenising dynamics of liberalism can be hijacked by a particular dominant group or society to disguise and indeed validate its own hegemony. In this context it is perhaps time that pluralists sought to rely less on the emancipatory power of rights and directed their attention more to autonomy as the primary goal for sub-state peoples, emphasising the good of political action generated in the vernacular from below rather than over the language of rights offered (imposed?) from above and outside. This is not to deny the value of universal human rights standards or the merit in any national society adopting a bill of rights, provided there is scope to tailor these to the specific aspirations and political values of a particular people. Rather, it is a caveat against the imposition of standards, particularly by external courts, that serve to undermine democratic pluralism in the name of the individualistic uniformity of classical and increasingly outmoded liberalism.

3

Managing Conflict Through Democracy

SAMUEL ISSACHAROFF*

I. INTRODUCTION

THOUGH FREQUENTLY HERALDED as a panacea for societal ills, the advent of democratic rule in historically fractured societies often risks amplifying – rather than ameliorating – pre-existing social, ethnic and religious tensions. Emerging democracies must manage these tensions lest electoral processes and the demands of governance be the trigger and the means for renewed conflict. In the period immediately after World War II, the preferred mechanism for attempting to dampen historic animosities was through a mechanism of formalised power-sharing that has come to be known in political science by the name consociationalism. In attempting to lessen the explosive potential of historical societal divisions, these new democracies apportioned governmental authority, with political roles delineated along historical fault lines.

This chapter is concerned with the contrasting approach taken by what has been termed the 'third wave' of democratisation. This period followed the collapse of the Soviet Union and has spread democracy more broadly around the globe than ever before. In common with the earlier period of post-war democratisation, the new round confronts the need to stabilise governance in historically divided societies. By contrast to the earlier period, however, the post-Soviet efforts take as their defining characteristic not the formalised power-sharing seen in prior eras, but a system of democratic competition for political office under a strong system of constitutional constraints on the exercise of political power. While the means of resolving social divisions have evolved, this move away from a system of prescriptive allocation of political power does not suggest that the fundamental problem this system sought to redress has gone away.

Both in and out of Europe, recent developments shed light on a broader range of nation-reinforcing tools beyond some kind of pro rata formal power-sharing.

* Some of the material in this chapter is based on a fuller treatment in 'Constitutional Courts and Democratic Hedging', published in 2011 by the *Georgetown Law Journal*, and in 'Constitutionalizing Democracy in Fractured Societies', published in 2004 by the *Texas Law Review*.

Alongside increased attention to constitutional restraints on the exercise of political power has come the dramatic expansion, and apparent acceptance, of judicial review of the structures of governance. The role of judicially enforced constitutionalism offers a different avenue of nation-building than that assumed in the consociational models. Rather than securing national unity through formal power-sharing along the major axes of social division, constitutionalism tends to impose limits on the range of decisions that democratically elected governments may take.

This chapter examines the institutional contours of fragile 'third wave' democracies and their structural limitations on the exercise of majoritarian power; it also explores the potential for robust constitutional protections to channel historic tensions into fruitful democratic engagement. The aim is not to devise a one-size-fits-all model of proper constitutionalism. I find this a dispiriting and more than mildly chauvinistic enterprise. Instead, I look at structured forms of power in divided societies in the terms by which the constitutional courts of those societies analyse the difficulties they present. In part, this is recognition of how much more sophisticated the world has become since the simple consociational models that were supposed to yield stability through formal power-sharing. In part as well, this is recognition of the stakes in truly fractured societies. The unfortunate lesson of history is that stable civilian governance is most likely to emerge from post-conflict societies when one ethnic group has accomplished clear dominance or destruction of the other.[1] Even with the introduction of more aggressive international peace-keeping, the key issue in nation-building remains the creation of an integrated political authority claiming legitimacy beyond an ethnic or racial base.

II. DEMOCRACY IN DIVIDED SOCIETIES

Democratic constitutionalism faces many challenges in trying to secure tolerant governance in societies without a sense of common destiny. Among the most basic of challenges faced by emergent democracies is how to protect the fundamental liberties as political power coalesces around majoritarian preferences; particularly how to protect the vulnerable, who belong to what United States law has characterised as discrete and insular minorities. Under United States law, such minorities are not simply those who receive fewer votes in any particular election. They are instead the historically identifiable groups, such as racial minorities, who are unlikely to prevail through the political process and who are likely to be at the mercy of those who will emerge as the electoral victors. These minorities may ultimately turn to legally defined domestic rights protections, or

[1] See R Licklider, 'The Consequences of Negotiated Settlements in Civil Wars, 1945–1993' (1995) 89 *American Political Science Review* 681, 686, finding that in so-called identity civil wars 'negotiated settlements are less likely to be stable than military victories' (emphasis omitted).

appeal to broader international human rights protections, but the primary concern is whether there are political structures within the newly developed democratic framework that might reduce their vulnerability.

It is precisely in terms of protecting these embattled minorities that democracy is most suspect. Voting alone cannot legitimise state coercion. The role of elections in democracy is to assign governmental power to voting majorities. There are many protective conditions presupposed in the modern conception of democracy, including liberty of expression and association, as well as the orderly functioning of the electoral system. Yet persistent minorities will always be at risk of majoritarian disregard, either in the form of disinterest in the welfare of minorities or the active suppression of minority interests and political organisations through the exercise of state authority.

The idea of using democracy as the chief organising principle in divided societies is itself rather novel and uncertain. John Stuart Mill, a central proponent of liberty as the desired end state of human affairs, viewed democratic governance in fractured societies as a non-starter. In his words:

> Free institutions are next to impossible in a country made up of different nationalities. Among a people without fellow-feeling, especially if they read and speak different languages, the united public opinion, necessary to the working of representative government, cannot exist.[2]

Underlying Mill's scepticism about democracy in divided societies is a set of concerns about the ability to attain a common conception of 'the good' to be maximised and a sense of shared enterprise in a national endeavour. Presumably, deeply divided societies will take the opportunity of the democratic franchise as a means to pursue their divergent interests rather than cohere around a national enterprise. On this view, the franchise is simply a rough calculus of who is ahead and who is behind, who will get the uniforms of the state and who will be made subservient. If democracies respond to the will of the majority, minorities can not expect to have their interests redressed unless they too become part of the majority. Ideally, democracy is the process of new governing majorities forming and reforming over time such that the losers of today can form a part of a prevailing coalition in the future. Yet deep (and violent) divisions reflecting historical hatreds rob democracies of any credible prospect that voting will yield anything but a headcount along those same historical divisions – at least initially.

Modern political theory challenges at least some of these assumptions. The larger the group, the more difficult for the common purpose to be obtained – at least so goes the core intuition of public choice theory. The combination of free-rider problems, transaction costs, and other obstacles to acquiring information about the political process, means that small, well-defined groups with high-intensity preferences will dominate the legislative scene. These groups may be

[2] JS Mill, *On Liberty, and, Considerations on Representative Government* (New York, MacMillan Co, 1947) 292.

able to secure rent-seeking legislation that, for example, may limit competitive entry into a regulated market or directly subsidise some group at the public's expense. On this view, democracy over-rewards smaller groups that are at once more cohesive and more likely unified by a narrow set of common objectives. The true insight of public choice theory concerns the advantage a well-organised, discrete and insular minority will hold when faced with opposition of less intensity by a diffuse and amorphous majority. So long as the majority retains its diffuse and amorphous character, a well-disciplined minority should hold a relative advantage in the political arena. Yet this provides little comfort, as majorities are not always so unorganised.

The practical considerations that provide protections to minorities under public choice theory do not necessarily hold where the divisions are at the heart of the society and capable of being reduced to a simple operative cue: us or them. Religious/racial/ethnic divides are often central features in the history of emerging democracies, and group identities – along with fears and prejudices – may become the perfect mechanism to overcome the collective action problem in moving broad masses to act in a disciplined fashion. Group identity is the perfect rallying cry: it is a simple identifier and it elicits intensely held beliefs and values. The struggle in post-war democracies has been to find a mechanism to cabin the triumphant majority faction so that the first election does not become the last. With the risk of oppression of minorities by historically defined majorities and the ease of organising this oppression under group identity, there must be structural mechanisms to limit majority excesses.

New democracies have generally rejected programs of power-sharing and other formalised allocations of political office to temper the power of the majority. Instead, the limits on the exercise of state authority depend heavily on strong constitutions enforced through constitutional courts. These courts did not form a significant part of post-war democratic design, but have emerged as critical actors in the most recent democratisations. Constitutions and constitutional courts mediate among factions and safeguard the interests of groups subject to abuse by majoritarian rule through prescribed rights instead of prescribed representation. These institutions also facilitate the initial stability necessary for a gradual shift to increased governance through political channels.

III. THE DISTINCT LOOK OF MODERN DEMOCRACIES

To appreciate the recent transition, a look back in history is perhaps in order. Following World War I, new nations were created around the world from the sudden collapse of empires. Borders were superimposed on regions with no effort to reconcile these new national divides with historic boundaries between different peoples and ethnic groups. Throughout the Middle East and Africa, nations that developed at this time did not correspond to any pre-existing sense of national identity and the resulting states were necessarily unstable and prone to communal violence. By contrast, the period following World War II was marked by deep concern for the ethnic composition of the post-war states, and Europe witnessed a period of massive forced population transfers in an effort to create relatively stable, homogeneous national boundaries.[3] The recognition of the importance of the communal make-up of states could be a precursor to either positive consociational attention to the allocation of power, or, more perniciously, to ethnic cleansing designed to concentrate political and economic authority in the hands of the dominant population.

The sudden emergence of new democratic authority over the past quarter century harkens back to the inter-war era problem of states with superimposed boundaries having to govern themselves despite longstanding, fundamental divisions within their new borders. As observed in the post-Soviet republics of eastern Europe or in divided societies such as post-apartheid South Africa, rekindling the flames of separatism and group identity in fragile post-conflict or post-authoritarian states can lead to the emergence of new factional strife, if not outright civil war. New states have largely responded to these issues through the development of surprisingly similar structural mechanisms.

One of the interesting developments in this third wave of democratisation is the actual form that democracy takes.[4] Despite the formal differences across the range of parliamentary versus presidential systems, there are striking parallels in many of the governmental structures selected by new democracies.[5] Almost all regimes import some notion of proportional representation in order to give broad representational opportunities to all social groups and to try to forestall parliamentary dominance by a single faction. All the new democracies provide checks against the power of the dominant legislative coalition, and no new democracy has adopted a Westminster-style system of complete parliamentary sovereignty, particularly as regards the interpretation of legal rules. All new democratic regimes have specified many of the conditions and limitations of democratic rule in strong constitutional texts. And nearly all the new democracies[6] have either created constitutional courts or endowed supreme courts with ample power of judicial review to enforce the democratic commands of the constitution.

As these countries embarked on their experiments with majoritarian rule, constitutional courts have been invariably assigned a central role in the creation and maintenance of a democratic order. Notably, these courts appear to have

[3] T Judt, *Postwar: A History of Europe Since 1945* (New York, Penguin Press, 2005) 27.

[4] See S Issacharoff, 'Constitutionalizing Democracy in Fractured Societies' (2004) 82 *Texas Law Review* 1861, 1872 (analysing post-apartheid South Africa as a 'particularly salient example of the turn to constitutionalism as an alternative to consociational power-sharing').

[5] JA Cheibub, J Gandhi and JR Vreeland, 'Democracy and Dictatorship Revisited' (2010) 143 *Public Choice* 67. This dataset reveals that in the immediate post-Soviet period from 1991–93, six new democracies adopted pure parliamentary systems, five adopted presidential systems and 12 adopted some form of mixed system.

[6] Estonia has a 'Constitutional Review Chamber,' one of several of the chambers of the highest National Court. In effect, it functions as a specialised court directed to constitutional review of legislative acts. Formally, however, it is part of the central court structure.

been a required element for the creation of these new democracies. These courts were invariably established with the primary purpose of ensuring the constitutional pedigree of the actions of the new political orders, a charge that left them unencumbered by the United States' fixation with the source of the authority for judicial review and the accompanying hand-wringing over countermajoritarianism. If we were to look at these courts as being part of a common enterprise in constitutional democracy – leaving aside the structural and political differences within the varying new democracies – the question could become one of defining the role that these courts are expected to play under the broad rubric of constitutional democracy. More specifically, the inquiry is two-fold: First, how should we understand the role of these courts? And, second, how do these courts discharge that role?

Most new democracies across the former Soviet bloc of eastern Europe accepted the constitutional court model with little debate over the existence and role of the courts. The uniform adoption is not entirely surprising when the aspirations of these countries are considered. Most of the world's new democracies emerged from the former Soviet Union and strive for (or have achieved) entry into the EU. The post-war model of constitutional court review, particularly as exemplified by Germany, was the assumed standard for emulation. The form of review in these constitutional courts followed as well from the European post-war courts. The constitutional courts' focus on ex post review of statutes for constitutional infirmity (termed 'abstract' review, or what would be on its face review in the US) was for the most part a product of simple adoption of western constitutional innovations, again most notably those of Germany. These constitutional courts stand apart from the national court system that is empowered to adjudicate ordinary disputes, even if a constitutional question is present. To the extent that any dispute may turn on the constitutionality of a legislative enactment, however, the specific case in the normal court structure in which the constitutional question is raised must be suspended and the question of the constitutionality of the statute under review must be referred to the specialised constitutional tribunals.

Despite their origin in European structures where the role of the court had long since been established, courts of these new democracies were consumed with trying to make sense of an unstable and often underspecified constitutional order. In almost every one of these new democracies, courts have had to review deeply contested claims of improper internal lock-holds on power. A ready example would be the Ukrainian Constitutional Court in 2004 derailing efforts to close off the electoral process in that country, ordering a revote, and then allowing for election of the opposition candidate, Viktor Yushchenko. While subsequent developments in Ukraine have shown the vulnerability of democratic gains,[7] the role of an independent tribunal in at least providing the space for democratic challenge was critical.

[7] SL Myers, 'Stalled by Conflict, Ukraine's Democracy Gasps for Air' *New York Times* (New York, 1 June 2007) A 4.

IV. DEFINING THE POLITICAL INSTITUTIONS OF DEMOCRACY

First and foremost among the obstacles new constitutional courts confront is the exercise of executive political power in ways that threaten the viability of subsequent challenges to that power. For countries emerging from authoritarian rule, domination by the executive is the historic norm. Especially in the countries of the former Soviet bloc, democracy emerged without an antecedent set of civil society institutions, particularly political parties with experience in rallying followers on the basis of political positions. Without well-established parties, parliamentary coalitions that would otherwise provide a check against the executive are likely to be fragile. Unlike the delicate coalitions, which are unable to act quickly owing to many competing interests and attendant deliberations, the executive is likely to be the most swiftly energised force of government. A central issue arising in country after country in new democracies is the extent of the power of the executive over the political process itself; although, perhaps surprisingly, the question is just as often one of protecting, as well as limiting, the power of the executive.

A striking departure from the United States' position that the court should not have a determinative role in assessing a 'political question' emerges immediately as these newly created constitutional courts confront questions about the structure of governance with little hesitation. For example, it is hard to imagine a more central political issue in the life of a country than the possible removal from office of the president by the legislature. In older constitutional arrangements, as in the United States, the judiciary is given no formal role in the decision-making process, save for the ceremonial role of presiding over the actual impeachment session. But in a number of more recent democracies, the constitution explicitly gives the constitutional court (or analogous body) the authority to render final judgment by way of appellate review of the legislature's decision to impeach. This is true in Hungary and the Czech Republic,[8] as well as in South Korea, where this power was dramatically used in 2004.[9] At issue in Korea was the increasing antagonism between President Roh Moo-hyun and the National Assembly, which finally voted to impeach Roh by a vote of 193–2, with Roh's supporters either abstaining or being barred from the vote. The Constitutional Court of Korea found that Roh had indeed violated the law in three of the ways alleged by the National Assembly,[10] but that when weighed

[8] Apparently, this is quite common in the post-Soviet states. T Ginsburg, 'Ancillary Powers of Constitutional Courts' in T Ginsburg and RA Kagan (eds), *Institutions and Public Law: Comparative Perspectives* (New York, Peter Lang Publishing, 2004) 225–44.

[9] Y Lee, 'Law, Politics, and Impeachment: The Impeachment of Roh Moo-hyun from a Comparative Constitutional Perspective' (2005) 53 *American Journal of Comparative Law* 403, 407.

[10] Roh transgressed the law in the following ways: (1) violating a statute that required the political neutrality of officials during elections (Roh publicly stated his preference for the newly formed Uri Party prior to the parliamentary election); (2) not demonstrating proper respect for the Constitution and constitutional bodies by challenging the National Election Commission's ruling

against the consequences of removing him from office, the impeachment should be dismissed and he should be reinstated as President. The costs of removal, as determined by the Court, included prematurely ending the term of a democratically elected official and the political chaos that would be caused by requiring the election of a new president. The Court held that

> [t]he acts of the President violating the laws were not grave in terms of the protection of the Constitution to the extent that it would require the protection of the Constitution and the restoration of the impaired constitutional order by a decision to remove the President from office.[11]

In other circumstances constitutional courts have had to deal with the similarly political mechanics of the election system. Perhaps following the lead of the German Constitutional Court in directing attention to electoral opportunity, this has been a fertile area of judicial engagement. The Hungarian Court was one of the first to begin work and has been handing down important decisions since the early 1990s.[12] The Court memorably struck down a proposed amendment to the electoral law which stated that elected representatives of the 'social security self-governments' could not be put forward as candidates at the parliamentary elections.[13] A dominant social and political issue for democracies emerging from extended periods of authoritarian rule – especially former-Soviet states, but also including post-Nazi Germany, post-apartheid South Africa, and even post-Saddam Iraq – is coming to terms with the monopoly of technical expertise by those compromised by association with the prior regime. Newly created constitutional courts are often tasked with policing the difficult line between accountability and revenge, as observed in Romania,[14] Ukraine,[15] Macedonia[16] and perhaps most notably, Poland.[17]

Courts have been confronted with the even more troubling prospect of legally sanctioned retribution. Lustration laws frequently take a form that sweeps in an

that he had violated political neutrality and illegally called a national referendum; and (3) illegally calling a national referendum to assess the nation's confidence in his leadership.

[11] Constitutional Court, 2004 Hun-Na 1, May 14, 2004, (16-1 KCCR, 609) (S. Kor.), available in English translation at english.ccourt.go.kr/.

[12] V Jackson, 'What's in a Name? Reflections on Timing, Naming, and Constitution-Making' (2008) 49 *William and Mary Law Review* 1249, 1266.

[13] Decision No 16/1994 of 25 March 1994, *East Europ Case Rep* 1 (1994): 245–46.

[14] W Sadurski, *Rights Before Courts: A Study of Constitutional Courts in Postcommunist States of Central and Eastern Europe* (Dordrecht, Springer, 2005) 156. Sadurski reviews the decision of the Constitutional Court upholding the time-limited exclusion of prefects and other police officials from presenting themselves as candidates in the first post-communist election.

[15] Decision Nos 03/3600-97, 03-3808-97, 1-12/98 of 26 January 1998, summarised in *Bull Constit Case Law* 1998 (1): 146–48 (Constitutional Court invalidation of categorical ban on persons from candidacy because of former role as judges, public prosecutors or state employees).

[16] Decision No 16/97 of 12 March 1997, available at www.cecl.gr/RigasNetwork/databank/Jurisprudence/FYROM/Jur_fyrom.htm (Constitutional Court invalidation of exclusion from election to local councils or mayoral office of members of armed forces, police and intelligence officers).

[17] Judgment No K. 2/07, May 11, 2007 (translated into English and excerpted by the Court) at 20 (striking down sweeping disqualification of former 'collaborators' as being of such scope as to render 'the principle of the sovereignty of the Polish people . . . illusory').

ethnic group compromised by association with the old regime, but now subject to recriminations by resurgent ethnic claims, as in Moldova[18] or the Baltics.[19] Particularly in the Baltics, the presence of a Russian population associated with Soviet occupation provided an almost irresistible target for xenophobic retribution, even though the Russian population by the end of the Soviet era had a generations-long presence in the region.

A particularly striking example of courts entertaining first-order questions about the very heart of democratic governance is found in Mongolia, where a newly created Constitutional Court waded into the very heart of the political thicket in the first election that successfully displaced the embedded Mongolian People's Revolutionary Party, the longstanding communist rulers. The Court in 1996 interpreted the new constitutional order, ruling that members of Parliament could not hold cabinet positions in the new coalition government.[20] The ruling confronted a series of efforts by the Mongolian Parliament (the State Great Hural) to appoint acting members of Parliament to the presidential cabinet. The Constitutional Court ruled that such a practice was unconstitutional, first when the matter was brought on petition of a private citizen in 1996, and again by striking down a law passed by Parliament in 1998.[21] The issue of parliamentary control of executive functions continued to dominate Mongolian legal disputes for five years, until the political parties were sufficiently united in demanding parliamentary authority and the Court ultimately backed down.[22]

While the Mongolian case illustrates the ultimate vulnerability of these new constitutional courts to persistent political pressure, it is nonetheless noteworthy that the terms of engagement were framed by a first-order dispute as to whether Mongolia was a presidential or parliamentary system. This question had not been specified in the multiparty and broadly participatory Mongolian constitutional design. The issue hinged on the interpretation of Article 29(1), which read that members of Parliament 'shall not hold any posts and employment other than those assigned by law'.[23] In order to strike down the proposed dual role of ministers, the Court had to first decide that Mongolia was constitutionally obligated to adhere to a presidential system, and then conclude that a

[18] See, eg, M Wines, 'History Course Ignites a Volatile Tug of War in Moldova' *New York Times* (New York, 25 February 2002) A 3; A France-Presse, 'Moldova: Setback for Russian Language' *New York Times* (New York, 22 February 2002) A 6.

[19] See, eg, I Skucas, 'Lithuania: A Problem of Disclosure' (2004) 12 *Demokratizatsiya* 411; F Arias-King, 'Estonia: The Little Country That Could' (2003) 11 *Demokratizatsiya* 619 (describing western groups' condemnation of Estonia's lustration laws as a type of apartheid); MS Ellis, 'Purging the Past: The Current State of Lustration Laws in the Former Communist Bloc' (1996) 59 *Law and Contemporary Problems* 181.

[20] The account that follows is based on T Ginsburg, *Judicial Review in New Democracies: Constitutional Courts in Asian Cases* (Cambridge, Cambridge University Press, 2003) 158–205.

[21] T Ginsburg and G Ganzorig, 'When Courts and Politics Collide: Mongolia's Constitutional Crisis' (2001) 14 *Columbia Journal of Asian Law* 309, 313.

[22] S Fenwick, 'The Rule of Law in Mongolia: Constitutional Court and Conspiratorial Parliament' (2001) 3 *Australian Journal of Asian Law* 219.

[23] Mongolian Constitution, art 29(1).

division of functions between members of Parliament and members of the executive was necessary to maintain both separation of powers and political competition between the branches.

Mongolia may well present an extreme version of a court having to resolve the basic structure of democracy, but it is far from the only such case. Courts are critical to establishing the boundaries of governmental power in unstable democracies.

In another extreme example, in Bangladesh a retired judge must head a caretaker government during the election period in order to forestall incumbent manipulation of state powers.[24] More typical is the experience of Albania, where the power of judicial review was established in a series of opinions addressing the terms under which an independent constitutional officer, the general prosecutor (the equivalent of the United States Attorney General), could be removed from office by the Assembly and the President.[25] The Court eventually decided that in dealing with an independent officer, the political branches were constrained both substantively (only certain offences suffice to remove such an officer) and procedurally (certain procedures required for the removal to be valid).[26] As in Mongolia, the Court ultimately lost out politically when the Assembly undertook to follow the prescribed procedures and remove the general prosecutor from office.[27] Nonetheless, as noted by the Albanian legal academic Agron Alibali, the 'case evidenced an important role which Constitutional Courts can play in post-Communist societies . . . as a true guarantor of the Constitution and the rights provided therein to their citizens'.[28]

In other situations, courts must confront minimum thresholds for parliamentary office under proportional representation elections. The issue of exclusion thresholds has a rich history, drawing, most notably, from Germany's Federal Constitutional Court (*Bundesverfassungsgericht*). The German Court has pursued a functional balance in this area, recognising that high thresholds can be a barrier to political choice, while also recognising that low thresholds risk impotent governance as representation is fractured among minor parties. The Court repeatedly upheld thresholds of five per cent by recognising that there was a compelling governmental interest in effective governing bodies and that this in turn required avoiding the splintering of parties 'which would make it more difficult or even impossible to form a majority'.[29] Most interestingly, the Court

[24] N Robinson, 'Expanding Judiciaries: India and the Rise of the Good Governance Court' (2009) 8 *Washington University Global Studies Law Review* 1, 66.

[25] Decision No 76 of the Albanian Constitutional Court, 20 April 2002 (translated into English by the Court) at 4–5, available at www.accpuf.org/images/pdf/cm/albanie/052-jc-autres_jurisp.pdf; Decision No 75 of the Albanian Constitutional Court, 19 April 2002 (translated into English by the Court) at 8, available at www.accpuf.org/images/pdf/cm/albanie/052-jc-autres_jurisp.pdf.

[26] Decision No 75, (n 25) 11.

[27] See A Alibali, 'Two Landmark Decisions of the Albanian Constitutional Court: The Individual, the Employee, and the State' (2004) 29 *Review of Central and Eastern European Law* 219, 244–45.

[28] ibid 245.

[29] DP Kommers, *The Constitutional Jurisprudence of the Republic of Germany*, 2nd edn (Durham, Duke University Press, 1997) 187.

struck down the same five per cent threshold after German reunification, on the ground that it could not guarantee a sufficient level of representation for the former East Germany, whose nascent political actors were unlikely to forge sufficiently strong national lists for the first post-unification elections.[30] The *Bundestag* then amended the election law in accordance with the Court's suggestions, and in the ensuing elections some groups from the former East Germany did manage to achieve representation.[31]

Following the German lead prior to reunification, the Constitutional Courts of the Czech Republic and Romania similarly upheld five per cent thresholds for election against constitutional challenges. In each case, the claim was that the threshold violated a constitutional commitment to proportional representation and to a minimum access to electoral office.[32] Further, courts confronted with such claims have in all cases weighed the claimed right of representation against the 'excessive splintering of the political process'[33] and the need for efficient political decision-making.[34] Without hesitation, these courts have assumed that the primary responsibility for protecting the integrity and accountability of the political process lies with a constitutional commitment to democracy, as shepherded by the Constitutional Court.

V. PROTECTING DEMOCRACY

The argument thus far posits that the newly minted constitutional courts emerge from an uncertain moment of regime change. The presence of a constitutional court may facilitate the transition to a democratic regime and allow for the creation of civilian rule. In turn, these courts may serve as a hedge against one-party consolidation of exclusive political and military power. On this account of their role in new democracies, these courts should be relatively unconstrained by a legitimacy concern over interceding in the political process. Their creation works as a barrier against the excessive centralisation of power in much the same way as federalism, proportional representation and many other features of recent constitutional regimes serve to thwart a descent back into autocratic rule. If we imagine early elections in unstable democracies as having the potential to become a winner-take-all tournament,[35] then we appreciate the concerns of the founders of these regimes and the stakes present in the early stages of democracy. To complete the picture, courts become key actors,

[30] ibid 188–89 (trans of the 1990 *National Unity Election* Case).
[31] ibid 191.
[32] W Sadurski, *Rights Before Courts: A Study of Constitutional Courts in Postcommunist States of Central and Eastern Europe* (Dordrecht, Springer, 2005) 154–55.
[33] Decision Pl US 25/96, translated in *E Europ Case Reporter* 5 (1998) 159–75.
[34] Decision 2/1992 of 30 June 1992, translated in *E Europ Case Reporter* 2 (1995) 229–36 (Romania).
[35] I take the imagery from JS Hellman, 'Winners Take All: The Politics of Partial Reform in Post Communist Transitions' (1998) 50 *World Politics* 203.

not as a semi-legislative body competing to initiate social policy,[36] but rather as a guarantor of the limits of politics and an assurance to the losing and vulnerable minorities that electoral loss is not to be synonymous with wholesale oppression. Thus, it is not surprising that a substantial portion of the caseload of the new constitutional courts, reaching to more than half the total cases heard in the first few years of constitutional governance in some countries, may be classified as involving challenges to the structure of the political system.[37]

A. The Basic Structures of Democracy

Assuming part of the justification for constitutional courts in new democracies is as a hedge against excessive concentration of power, the courts thus created would be expected to generate a jurisprudence based on the maintenance of competitive democracy. Put another way, the issue for these courts is whether they can produce, within the confines of their emerging constitutional culture, a domestic version of the Indian doctrine of a 'basic structure' with the aim of stabilising democracy.[38] This is a difficult claim to assess on a generalised basis given the diversity of specific case presentations and the difficulties (linguistic being the most obvious) of creating a comprehensive picture of constitutional courts in new democracies.

Nonetheless, what is distinct about a basic structures approach to constitutional adjudication is that it protects the core features of contested democratic governance, even if it is not apparent from the outset of a democracy which provisions may prove to be central. The basic structure doctrine seeks to remove critical features of a democracy from immediate majoritarian pressure. A similar manifestation of this idea appears in the unamendable provisions of the German or Israeli Constitutions, or in the prohibition in France and Italy against amendments that compromise the republican character of the state, or

[36] There are those who claim just the opposite and try to find justification for judicial review either as a democratic expression of the true will of the majority or as integral to the legislative bargain. See, eg, KL Scheppele, 'Democracy by Judiciary; Or, Why Courts Can Be More Democratic than Parliaments' in A Czarnota, M Krygier and W Sadurski (eds), *Rethinking the Rule of Law After Communism* (Budapest, Central European University Press, 2005) (arguing the former); A Stone-Sweet, *Governing With Judges* (Oxford, Oxford University Press, 2000) (arguing the latter). Alternatively, some argue directly that constitutional courts are legitimated through the quasi-parliamentary nature of their review: Sadurski, *Rights Before Courts* (n 14) 61 (arguing that court legitimacy comes from quasi-legislative function). Needless to say, I find these arguments unpersuasive as providing a core justification for creating constitutional courts. As a general rule, the claim to democratic authority of non-elected judicial bodies as against the politically accountable branches must be suspect.

[37] SI Smithey and J Ishiyama, 'Judicial Activism in Post-Communist Politics' (2002) *36 Law and Society Review* 719, 724.

[38] As colourfully expressed by Justice Khanna of the Indian Supreme Court, 'Provision regarding the amendment of the Constitution does not furnish a presence for subverting the constitution nor can [it] be construed to embody the death wish of the Constitution or provide sanction for what may be called its lawful harikari'. *Kesavananda Bharati v State of Kerala*, AIR 1973 SC 1461, P 1437 (Khanna J).

in more recent vintage in the 2007 Constitution of Thailand, where the Constitution simply forbids amendments that 'chang[e] the democratic regime of government with the King as Head of State or chang[e] the form of State'.[39]

The difference between the basic structures approach and that seen in older democracies, however, is the level of precision required for the unamendable provisions of a constitution. Rather than specify ex ante which provisions of the constitution form the core and which occupy the periphery of the commitment to democracy, the basic structures doctrine leaves that open for subsequent judicial exposition. The basic structures doctrine seems most suitable to the incomplete character of the negotiations that mark most of the recent transitions to democracy. It also seems best directed to the threat of one-party consolidation of power that threatens to undermine weak democracies from within the processes of democratic decision-making. With the aim of protecting democracies from collapsing into autocratic power, the oversight of constitutional courts provides a constitutional remedy for a latent democratic disability.

Paradoxically, the new constitutional courts are cautious about trumpeting their new role as institutional stabilisers of democracy. They tend to disclaim the exigencies of the extraordinary moment of regime transition, and resort frequently to the more familiar language of human rights or basic civil rights in justifying their significant assertion of constitutional authority.[40] From the vantage point of outside observers, however, these courts are nonetheless devoting significant institutional resources to issues that go to the heart of democratic governance, even if the courts themselves are not likely to provoke the political authorities by trumpeting this role.[41] Despite the unwillingness to broadcast a broader judicial role, the constitutional courts do repeatedly engage issues that force the development of a basic structures-style approach. This initiative naturally involves a measure of risk that a court will step farther than it is politically safe to go, but there is every reason to believe that it is precisely when the political branches are immature and the stabilisation of democracy is precarious that courts emerge as central actors in consolidating the constitutional order.[42] This is, after all, the role played by the US Supreme Court under Chief Justice Marshall in the early days of the American Republic, and it is the role played by

[39] Somdet Phra Paramintharamaha Bhumibol Adulyadej [Interim Constitution] B.E. 2549 (2006) ch 15 (Thail).

[40] The wariness over structural arguments about stabilising democracy and the reliance on claims of protecting civil liberties or individual rights is well noted by Professor Sadurski. W Sadurski, 'Judicial Review in Central and Eastern Europe: Rationales or Rationalizations?' (2009) Sydney Law School Research Paper No 09/38, 13, ssrn.com/abstract=1401242.

[41] See, eg, Aharon Barak, 'Foreword: A Judge on Judging: The Role of a Supreme Court in a Democracy' (2002) 116 *Harvard Law Review* 16, 160–63 (contrasting the different demands made upon constitutional law in mature as opposed to immature democracies).

[42] This point is forcefully made in the many writings of Professor Scheppele on the role of processes of state formation in nascent democracies. See, eg, KL Scheppele, 'Guardians of the Constitution: Constitutional Court Presidents and the Struggle for the Rule of Law in Post-Soviet Europe' (2006) 154 *University of Pennsylvania Law Review* 1757, 1757–61 (describing 'the separation of powers as a contact sport' in which the constitutional courts play a central role).

the European Court of Justice as the European Union struggled to create its competent political institutions.[43]

The role of these constitutional courts is perhaps most critical in the transition period, precisely because of the immaturity and likely weakness of not only political institutions, but also the ancillary civil society participants in democratic life – most notably, program-based political parties. The relative reticence of the courts to announce their role reintroduces in a curious way the debates in more mature democracies over the role of judicial review of democratic decision-making. Even accepting that constitutional courts are expected to have the power of review over legislation does not establish what should be the aim of that power of review. Not surprisingly, the easiest justification comes in terms of the post-World War II rights discourse of civil liberties and fundamental human rights.[44] Even though they are often cast as a matter of fundamental rights, many of these decisions are significant both in terms of securing the liberties associated with liberal democracy *and* because they thwart the exercise of majoritarian political power against disfavoured *political* minorities. The emerging jurisprudence must not only have an individual rights dimension but must also lead the constitutional courts into a more active role (certainly in the initial period) in debates over political structures. Ultimately, much of the legitimacy of these courts depends on their ability to fulfil their role in facilitating the constitutional enterprise.[45]

B. Making Democracy Work

Despite the reluctance of new constitutional courts to broadcast their expanded authority over the political process, there are certain repeated themes in the early jurisprudence of constitutional courts that force a confrontation with broader questions concerning the integrity of democratic governance. For present purposes, the issue of efforts to curb the political opposition provides an insight into how courts discharge this safeguarding function.

Moldova presents a useful example of a constitutional court forced to respond to an attempt to restore one-party control of a former communist regime. In December 2001, the Moldovan government, led by the former Communist Party, announced that it was planning to make Russian compulsory

[43] See, eg, HA Johnson, 'Judicial Institutions in the Emerging Federal System: The Marshall Court and the European Court of Justice' (2000) 33 *John Marshall Law Review* 1063 (comparing the similar roles both courts played in providing 'shape and substance' to the emerging democratic institutions to which they belonged).

[44] I am indebted to Dieter Grimm for reminding me that no matter what structural role is assigned to constitutional courts, the discourse of fundamental rights remains the *lingua franca* of judicial review.

[45] Stressing the direct tie between the role of these courts in easing the initial constitutional bargain and the role of judicial review after the democratic transition was helpfully suggested by Owen Fiss.

in all Moldovan schools, an issue that exacerbated the ethnic divisions of the country.[46] The move prompted protests, with the opposition Christian Democratic People's Party (CDPP) taking a major role, which in turn prompted the government to ban all party activities for one month.[47] The ban was upheld by the docile Moldovan Supreme Court of Justice (a holdover court, as opposed to the post-Soviet Constitutional Court), a decision that 'temporarily took the steam out of the protests',[48] but the Constitutional Court declared the move unconstitutional.[49] The US Department of State cited the decision as one example of 'the Constitutional Court show[ing] strong signs of independence during the year', 'balancing out several controversial initiatives of the Communist authorities'.[50]

Poland provides an even stronger example of the limitations imposed by constitutional courts on the use of exceptional powers by the executive after the immediate transition period had ended. The actions of the court are particularly illuminating because of its early activism and broad legitimacy.[51] The clearest case comes with a 2007 decision of the Constitutional Court striking down the central provisions of a new lustration law, an issue that has presented itself repeatedly in the transition from authoritarian regimes.

Lustration laws are a common problem in post-authoritarian societies. Often, as was the case in eastern Europe, the sudden collapse of the prior regime means that democratic forces are poorly prepared to function in the new electoral arena. The only organised political forces are the holdovers from the ancien regime, whose removal from the political arena is often central to the survival of a new democratic politics. The perceived need to remove the former communist officeholders from the new contests for political power represents an uneasy mix of the healthy impulse for democratic stability and the less admirable (if understandable) desire for revenge. Even in its most defensible guise as a forceful closing of the door on a past oppressive regime, lustration presents difficult legal and moral questions. Invariably, lustration imposes the legal order of the new regime on actions undertaken in a different legal setting under different forms of state coercion. Furthermore, lustration laws are invariably roughly hewn and sweep in entire categories of persons associated with the former regime, even though the prohibitions have a criminal law-like quality to them.

The group-culpability sweep and criminal-like quality of lustration laws have created implementation issues for the courts, forcing them to grapple with the

[46] See, eg, M Wines, 'History Course Ignites a Volatile Tug of War in Moldova' *New York Times* (New York, 25 February 2002) A 3; A France Presse, 'Moldova Setback for Russian Language' *New York Times* (New York, 22 February 2002) A 6.

[47] 'Constitution Watch', *E Eur Const Rev*, Winter 2002, 2, 32; *Christian Democratic People's Party v Moldova*, [2007] 45 EHRR 13, paras 8–19.

[48] Constitution Watch (n 47) 33.

[49] ibid.

[50] US Department of State, Country Reports on Human Rights Practices, 2002: Moldova (31 March 2003) www.state.gov/g/drl/rls/hrrpt/2002/18381.htm.

[51] L Solyom, 'The Role of Constitutional Courts in the Transition to Democracy' (2003) 18 *International Sociology* 133, 148–49.

lack of individual findings and procedural protections for banned individuals. Further, in some cases, such as Moldova and particularly the Baltics, lustration quickly implicated critical ethnic divides between the local population and Russian speakers or ethnic Russians. In the Baltics, the latter group was a generations-long presence as part of the Soviet effort to establish control of the region, which included imposing Russian as the official language and filling the ranks of the security state with ethnic Russians. In Estonia, for example, the ethnic Russians came to represent one-third of the entire civilian population by the end of the Soviet period.

Poland's history is both revealing and representative in this regard. Poland had passed a sweeping lustration law in 1997 designed to force Soviet-era collaborators to identify themselves and be subject to removal from or disqualification for public office. The lustration law set the prohibitions in motion by requiring 'persons performing certain public functions to file a declaration as to whether they had collaborated with the ancien regime'.[52] Although the Polish Constitutional Court upheld the law as non-penal and providing sufficient procedural guarantees, the European Court of Human Rights disagreed and in 2007 held the law in violation of Article 6 of the European Convention on Human Rights, which guarantees basic rights of open and fair criminal trials.[53] Even while the challenge to the first Polish law was pending, the nastier side of lustration took hold.

Under the increasingly authoritarian regime of the late President Lech Kaczynski and his identical twin brother, Prime Minister Jaroslaw Kaczynski, the Polish government adopted in late 2006 a new lustration law that broadened the sweep of targeted individuals through an 'exponentially expanded definition of "persons performing a public function"'.[54] The law would have imposed a 10-year ban on office holding for any individual who failed to submit a declaration explaining how his or her name came to be on any government 'lists' from the communist regime. Given the pressures and pervasiveness of totalitarianism, innumerable individuals would have been compromised by such a loose definition of collaboration.[55] Indeed, during the 2000 election, both famous Solidarity leader Lech Walesa and the winning candidate, Aleksandr Kwasniewski, were charged with having been collaborators because their names appeared on lists of persons who had spoken to communist security officers – an almost inescapable fate for anyone of any public stature under the prior regime.

Coming in the wake of the ECHR's decision on the earlier lustration law, the new law sparked a good deal of criticism about witch-hunting from EU officials and the foreign press, as well as charges that the new lustration law was nothing

[52] 'International Legal Developments in Review: 2007: Europe' (2008) 42 *International Lawyer* 975, 1005.

[53] *Matyjek v Poland*, App No 38184/03 (2007). The ECtHR held that the law was penal in nature and failed to provide for a fair trial.

[54] 'International Legal Developments in Review' (n 52) 1005.

[55] W Osiatynski, Op-Ed, 'Poland Makes Witch-Hunting Easier' *New York Times* (New York, 22 January 2007).

more than a 'generational bid for power' – an effort by the Kaczynski brothers to see their opponents 'purged from offices and replaced by their own loyalists'.[56] Opponents charged that the lustration law was 'only one act among many in a systematic effort by [Kaczynski's] party and its supporters to undermine the country's democratic institutions'.[57]

The Constitutional Court's response was to caution the government that lustration was not an opportunity to settle political scores, but to serve the broader ends of justice.[58] The Court took pains to limit the reach of the law to those who were proven to have cooperated specifically with the state security agency (not other civil agencies). More significant perhaps, the Court limited the ability of the law to reach political opponents of the Kaczynki government – most notably, journalists were completely exempted from the requirement to submit a declaration.[59] As a matter of compassion for life under authoritarian rule, the Court further exempted those who acted 'under compulsion in fear of loss of their life or health [or that of] closest persons'.[60]

Of greater significance here are the steps taken to protect against lustration being the opportunity for Poland to revert to one-party governance. The Court held that officeholders who had been 'elected in universal elections' prior to the entry in force of the new law were not obligated to submit declarations,[61] deeming the application of the declaration requirement to incumbent officeholders a 'legal trap' that is 'inadmissible in light of the principle of protection of trust in the State and its laws'.[62]

In the words of Poland's most significant democratic intellectual, Adam Michnik, 'The Constitutional Court stood up to its responsibilities and, after repeated government efforts to postpone the court's session and to impeach its judges, it reviewed the new law and found it unconstitutional'.[63]

VI. CONCLUSION

Undoubtedly the most powerful judicial engagement with the political process of the post-World War II period has been in the field of human rights. It is tempting, and I suggest somewhat misleading, to view the emergence of strong constitutional courts in the post-Soviet period as one more manifestation of the importance of judicially enforced universalist rights. Instead, this chapter posits

[56] ibid.

[57] A Michnik, 'The Polish Witch-Hunt' *New York Review of Books* (New York, 28 June 2007).

[58] Judgment No K. 2/07, 11 May 2007 (translated into English and excerpted by the Court) 6.

[59] ibid 4–5. The lustration of journalists was described by the Court as consistent with 'the former goals of the Communist state, particularly interested in the control – at every stage – of publications as well as persons involved in the production thereof', but 'unproductive in the new democratic order of the State'. ibid 21.

[60] ibid 18.

[61] ibid 5.

[62] ibid 19.

[63] Michnik, 'Polish Witch Hunt' (n 57).

that these new constitutional courts emerge from the need to constrain the exercise of political power, to borrow Bruce Ackerman's phrase. Although the courts appear to be rights-enforcing, the sweep of their concerns points to a structural role of core judicial review in limiting the excesses of majoritarian power. In historically riven societies, without experience of trust and compromise across the critical social divisions, such limits have come to define the latest wave of democratic experimentation.[64]

[64] See Issacharoff, 'Constitutionalizing Democracy' (n 4) 1891–92 (discussing, from a comparative perspective, the tensions in the American jurisprudence addressing the racial and electoral fractures in the United States).

4

Ethnicity and Competing Notions of Rights

YASH GHAI*

I. INTRODUCTION

HUMAN RIGHTS HAVE been put to many uses in the last few centuries: taming powerful and tyrannical monarchs in favour of the authority of barons and landowners; providing the framework for the market economy and the dominance of the bourgeoisie; humanising capitalism; ushering in democracy; and asserting the equality of women with men. In the late twentieth century human rights were invoked to moderate relations between different communities divided on the basis of race, ethnicity, religion and language. At each stage specific aspects of human rights prevailed over other aspects, defining the dominant ideology of the period. Yet, at each stage human rights have also provided the basis and form of challenge to the dominant ideology. Human rights now speak to many, often competing, concerns.

As the core content of human rights expands, the challenge is to find ways to reconcile these concerns within a coherent framework. A particular concern is the mediation between the human rights concern of individuals and of communities – not new in itself (the Marxist attack on the ideology of rights in the nineteenth century was based on the emphasis on the individual in abstraction

* This chapter draws on several of my previous papers: *Human Rights and Governance: The Asia Debate* (San Francisco, Asia Foundation, Occasional Paper No 4, 1994); 'Rights, Duties and Responsibilities' in Josiane Cauqwuelin, Paul Lim and Birgit-Mayer-Koning (eds), *Asian Values. Encounter with Diversity* (Richmond, Surrey, Curzon Press, 1998); 'Universalism and Relativism: Human Rights as a Framework for Negotiating Interethnic Claims' (2000) 21 *Cardozo Law Review* 1095–140; 'Globalization, Multiculturalism and Law' in B Santos Sousa (ed), *Globalisation and Social Emancipation* (Spanish edition published November 2002, English edition 2004); 'Constitutional Asymmetries: Communal Representation, Federalism, and Cultural Autonomy' in Andrew Reynolds (ed), *The Architecture of Democracy: Constitutional Design, Conflict Management, and Democracy* (Oxford, Oxford University Press, 2002); 'Understanding Human Rights in Asia' in Caterina Krause and Martin Scheinin (eds), *International Protection of Human Rights: A Textbook* (Turku, Institute for Human Rights, Abo Akademi University, 2008); 'Constitutionalism and the challenge of ethnic diversity' in James J Heckman, Robert L Nelson, and Lee Cabatingan (eds), *Global Perspectives on the Rule of Law* (London, Routledge, 2010).

from society) but new in the characteristics of the groups. Contemporary international developments, where many issues – including the extensive movement of people and capital across national boundaries – not only bring in closer proximity competing cultures and claims, but compel a resolution at the global level. The old debate about the cultural relativism of human rights takes on a new twist: relativism not of peoples and cultures across national boundaries, but of citizens within the same jurisdiction; not primarily disputations among anthropologists and other academics, but critical questions of the values and structures within the state regarding the diversity of the people – and sometimes of the very survival of the state.

The question then is how to reconcile cultural and religious differences in developing and implementing a common regime of human rights. I try to answer this question not by examining only doctrinal differences between cultural communities but by locating them in a broader framework that entails an examination of the goals and structures of the state and the aspirations of the people. In that sense the chapter is on 'structural' aspects of human rights, how conceptions of human rights shape the state and determine relations between the state and communities and to some extent between communities. Already this is a very different arrangement from those under the traditional constitutional orders which value human rights (seen as individual rights) and a direct relationship between the citizen and the state.

Increasingly human rights are seen as a resource for claims and arguments: inevitably in this context differences between rights are argued and played out also in terms of policies. The rise of the doctrine of human rights in the west was based on assumptions of universal values (influenced by Greek and Roman thought and Christianity). One set of western values revolved around the market and emphasised liberty; the other around community and equality. To some extent the two have been reconciled, especially in social democracy. Within these frameworks, cultural and ethnic homogeneity of the people has been assumed, taken for granted. The situation in the South, where the people of most states belong to communities distinguished by race, religion, language and history, has forced a debate on the role of human rights (and appropriateness of particular rights) in the context of ethnic and cultural diversity. Here the dominant ideology of individual identity, liberty and equality seems less important than recognition of the diversity and claims and entitlements of communities.

II. POST COLONIAL DIVERSITY

The historical roots of this diversity lie in colonialism. Colonial powers paid scant regard to pre-existing polities, to boundaries or the characteristics of the people, so that the colony would bring together two or more polities, and people belonging to different faiths or speaking different languages. The heterogeneity also resulted from the state-sponsored migrations within the empires, from one colony to another, to meet the colonialists' need for skills and labour; thus there was a significant movement from China to Africa, the Caribbean, and North Africa, to work in mines or the construction of railways; and of Indians to Fiji, Sri Lanka, South and East Africa, and to the Caribbean, for construction of railways, as workers in plantations and the colonial administration. In addition, citizens of the colonial power also migrated to the colonies, not only as administrators but also sometimes as settlers. The problems of this heterogeneity were compounded by of significant differences of wealth, economic opportunities and access to the state, corresponding closely to ethnic origins and regulated by notions of the order of racial superiority.

The combination of state coercion, the assertion of economic and political power by the privileged, the submission of the weak, the opportunism of some, and a distant sovereignty seemingly unattached to these hierarchies, served to maintain this colonial order. But the move to independence, triggered in large part by inequities of colonial rule, threatened and jolted this hierarchy. The prospect of the transfer of power from the colonial authority to the local population seemed to promise much to some, and fear of loss to others. How to balance the competing interests of communities became the major pre-occupation of those negotiating the terms of independence, reflected particularly in terms of the structure of the state and the entitlements of communities. This concern was based on the nature of the colonial state – authoritarian, coercive, exclusionary, unjust – and the impossibility of turning it into an instrument for the welfare of all the communities. It was noted that the break-up of empires in Europe led to the fragmentation of its territories into 'national groups' (the nation state). But this approach was not adopted in the decolonisation of Latin America in the nineteenth century and was precluded in the case of Asia and Africa, essentially by the United Nations in favour of colonial borders.[1]

The outstanding exception was British India which was split into two, with the establishment of Pakistan. The claims of a sizeable portion of the Muslim community were based on the European theory of the nation state. The leading ideologue of the secessionist movement, the poet Muhammed Iqbal, said that the proposition that religion is a private matter is 'not surprising on the lips of a European', because Christianity is a 'monastic order, renouncing the world of matter and fixing its gaze entirely on the world of spirit'. In his view, the experience of the Prophet as revealed in the Quran is of a wholly different nature, 'creative of a social order':

> The religious ideal of Islam is, therefore, organically related to the social order it has created. The rejection of one will eventually involve the rejection of the other. Therefore the construction of a polity on national lines, if it means the displacement of the Islamic principle of solidarity, is simply unthinkable to a Muslim.

[1] TM Frank, 'Postmodern Tribalism and the Right to Secession' in Catherine Brolman, Rene Lefeber and Marjoleine Zieck (eds), *Peoples and Minorities in International Law* (Dordrecht, Martinus Nijhoff, 1993).

The negotiations on the terms of independence followed two approaches, agreed perhaps on the objectives, but differing in method. One was based on the primacy of the status and rights of the individual as citizen regardless of ethnic ties. The other was the recognition of ethnic communities as corporate entities, entitled to rights of representation and participation in the national system but also to forms of self-government. The first approach is concerned, in terms of rights, with the direct relationship between the citizen and the state, the second also with the relationship between the state and communities, and sometimes between the communities themselves.[2] For these reasons, the constitutional moment (i.e., the time when constitutional arrangements for the country are being negotiated) is a good time to examine the role that human rights play in two critical areas – the definition or understanding of the 'people' (whether or not as a nation, united by strong ties of common vision and destiny, and bounds of solidarity) and the state (as an instrument of power, consensus building and welfare). The two are of course closely connected, but each has its distinct characteristics and consequences. The importance of nationhood is obvious, but those of the state perhaps less so, tied as it is to access to power and protection against oppression.

Briefly the argument is that the growth of state and its constitutional ordering in the West responded to changing social power and relations. First, the feudal lords weakened the monarchy in the name of liberty. Then the industrial revolution produced powerful social classes, balanced to some extent later by working classes, but never fully. The power of the bourgeoisie shaped the purposes and operation of the state, just as earlier social forces had done. But as society became developed and diversified, it was not necessary that this control over the state should be direct or exclusive. Economy rather than force became the source of effective power as society was transformed by market relations. The democratisation of the state ensured that, to a considerable extent, it served the interests of society as a whole – it did not dominate society. In Africa and, to a lesser extent in Asia, the growth of the colonial state was not gradual or organic in this sense. It was not rooted in local developments but imposed from outside, designed to promote colonial goals. It was exclusionary, built on racial and ethnic distinctions, the bureaucracy rooted in the imperative of the domination of the various societies that made up the colony. This system was buttressed by a battery of repressive laws and an oppressive legal system, reinforced by the control of the armed forces.

[2] These two approaches competed vigorously in the debates and proposals on decolonisation in India, with the Muslim League and Britain favouring the communal approach and the Congress Party (and presumably most Hindus) advocating the individual citizenship approach. A study of these proposals and counter-proposals provides a good guide to the possibilities of the communal approach – separate representation in the major institutions of the state, federalism, dual/multiple official languages, complex systems of voting and decision-making – the precursors of contemporary 'consociation'. Secession was seen as the way out of the communal to the individual, obviating the necessity of special arrangements. See Sir Maurice Gwyer and A Appadorai (eds), *Speeches and Documents on the Indian Constitution 1921–47*, vol II (Bombay, London, New York, Oxford University Press, 1957) for numerous proposals by the Muslim League and British government on the constitutional settlement of the problems of India's diversity (435–703).

The state in developing countries, whatever its vulnerability to global forces, is dominant locally and not sufficiently rooted in society. It is 'overdeveloped', that is, in relation to local social forces (and went beyond what was necessary as 'Marxian superstructure').[3] The post colonial state is both powerful and weak. It is weak internationally, dependent on handouts from western governments, with some of its essential tasks performed by international organisations or civil society groups. But it is strong internally, in the sense that it represents a greater concentration of financial and other resources, bureaucracy, networks of security forces, and above all, armed might, than other groups. It has become the principal source of accumulation (the Marxian version of primitive accumulation). It has great potential both to reward and punish. Understandably, minorities are fearful of exclusion and insist (under the threat of secession) on sufficient representation in and influence over the state to safeguard their interests – a consideration reinforced by the absence of a sense of national solidarity.

The post-colonial state was soon faced with serious challenges. The notion of equal undifferentiated rights did not quite fit a state where the salient identity was not national, but communal, religious or ethnic. A nation-state-based approach in effect privileges the culture or language of the majority and marginalises that of other communities, even where the state professes neutrality. The opposition is sometimes expressed in terms of identity, which has become a fashionable term. Minorities in so-called 'nation states' do not get proper recognition of their culture or history or other basis of identity, and this is demeaning to them. While this attack is based on the psychological harm a community suffers, the marginalisation of minorities takes other forms as well: exclusion from or under-representation in the institutions of the state, limited opportunities in the economy, social discrimination, lack of access to the legal system and the denial of justice in many sectors of life.

III. THE CLAIMS OF ETHNICITY

The political claims that ethnicity makes vary from a constitutional or legal recognition of aspects of culture (such as relations within the family or dispute settlement mechanisms), through special measures to improve social and economic conditions, to inclusion through representation, and state support for religion or culture. Sometimes (especially when the claims are denied) there is progression from modest to the more substantial demands, including a fundamental re-design of the state or even secession (arguing that only through this radical reform can legitimate demands be met). Increasingly these claims are justified by reference to international norms of human rights.

[3] The concept of the 'overdeveloped' state was advanced by Hamza Alavi in 'The State in Post-Colonial Societies' in *New Left Review* 74, July/August 1972. For a critique, see Colin Leys, 'The "Overdeveloped" Post-Colonial State: A Re-Evaluation' in *Review of African Political Economy* 5, Jan 1976.

The presence of diverse people does not necessarily lead to politicised ethnicity. A distinguished Indian political scientist, Rajni Kothari, has argued that the rise of ethnicity is due to the consequences of the centralisation and monopolisation of the state (comparing the modern state to pre-colonial polities in Asia which did not aim at centralisation of all authority, recognised diverse communities with their religion and customary practices, and whose borders were porous).[4] The growth of market relations and globalisation has led to the marginalisation, and subsequent disruption of cohesion, of communities, causing insecurities produced by economic changes over which they have no control. This also affects the nature of ethnic consciousness, turning it from a positive and inclusive form to negativity, exclusion and violence.

In the West, it is more fashionable to talk of the resurgence of ethnicity in terms of the imperatives of identity, based on Kant's emphasis on the autonomy of the individual (particularly the work of Charles Taylor[5] and Will Kymlicka[6]). The antecedents of this approach can be traced to the influential work of the anthropologist, Clifford Geertz, who argued that ethnicity flows from 'primordial' affiliations in the context of a state. Primordial links were based on what he called 'givens', the accidents of birth in a community, to which one may be connected by ties of religion, language, descent, history. In new states, these primordial attachments are particularly strong and are in frequent tension with the affiliation with and expectation from the state – and deeply destabilising.[7]

Charles Taylor defines identity as 'a person's understanding of who they are, of their fundamental characteristics as a human being'. Identity is achieved through a person's search for their authentic self. At another point, he says, 'There is a certain way of being that is *my* way. I am called upon to live my life in this way . . . If am not true [to myself], I miss the point of my life'.[8] According to Taylor, this consciousness of the uniqueness of one's identity is the result of the breakdown of social hierarchies, which had defined our roles and gave us the understanding of our place in society. But with democracy and the re-ordering of society, our identity comes from self-reflection and contemplation. Identity has become essential to the sense of our own dignity, as an attribute of our being human. Thus dignity is closely related to equality. And equality in turn depends on recognition by others, in the form of demands for the equal status of cultures and gender.

Although identity understood in this sense is an intensely personal affair, achieving a satisfactory understanding of oneself and one's potential, and of

[4] In an article now re-printed in Rajni Kothari, *Rethinking Development: In Search of Humane Alternatives* (Delhi, Ajanta Publications, 1988) as 'Ethnicity'.

[5] This chapter relies largely on his contribution, 'The Politics of Recognition' in the anthology edited by Amy Gutmann, *Multiculturalism* (Princeton, Princeton University, 1994).

[6] This chapter relies principally on his first, important book, *Liberalism, Community and Culture* (Oxford, Oxford University Press, 1989) and several subsequent articles.

[7] Clifford Geertz, 'The Integrative revolution' in C Geertz (ed), *Old Societies and New States* (New York, Free Press, 1963).

[8] Charles Taylor, 'Alternative Futures: Legitimacy, Identity, and Alienation in Late Twentieth-Century Canada' in Charles Taylor, *Reconciling the Solitudes: Essays on Canadian Federalism and Nationalism* (Kingston, McGill-Queen's Press, 1985) 30.

orienting oneself, depends on our contacts with others. Kymlicka says that our orientation, the way we negotiate values and make choices, comes from our membership of a cultural community. Thus in their different ways, Taylor and Kymlicka place the individual securely within a cultural context, and the wider interactions within a community. In an earlier period, Herder and other German philosophers[9] had claimed uniqueness for these communities, a unique, historically, even ethnically derived identity for each nation. Thus Kant's emphasis on individual autonomy was given firm roots in the community. The politics of recognition, in public and private spheres, has since become central to our quest for just political and social orders.

Although there is now wide acceptance of the recognition of identity, and its corollary of social and cultural diversity, there are acute controversies about the nature of identity and the forms of its recognition.[10] If in the West identity is a matter of psychic satisfaction, in Africa and Asia, identity politics are significant as a means to resources; although just as in the West material benefits are not irrelevant, in Asia and Africa pride in one's community is also an important factor. Identity is more a matter of political mobilisation than a precise delineation of a community's characteristics or beliefs. Ethnicity has become a way of dealing and bargaining with the state. Because electoral politics and government interventions respond to ethnic pressures, economic issues are transformed into issues of cultural survival. For example, in most cases, ethnic fighting is not about religion, but about jobs; religion is used as a pretext, emptying religion of its sacred and ritual aspects.

A community's entitlements may depend on how it views itself and is perceived by others. A self-conscious ethnic group can place itself in different categories, deriving from political science or legal discourse – it can be a cultural, religious or linguistic group, or it can be a minority, or a nation, or a 'people' or 'indigenous peoples'. Each of these categories is associated with a specific set of claims – participation, representation, recognition of language, religion, education, land and autonomy. How does one establish a claim to one or the other category? They are in part derived from international political or legal norms, and sometimes the characterisation or classification under national law (as in Spain). I now briefly examine the responses to the demands of ethnicity.

IV. INTERNATIONAL PROTECTIONS FOR GROUP RIGHTS

Although the mandate of the United Nations was a response to Nazi atrocities against Jews and other minority groups, the mandate was formulated in terms of individual rights; the refusal to recognise minority rights as such was

[9] FM Barnard, *Herder's social and political thought: From enlightenment to nationalism* (Oxford, Clarendon Press, 1967).

[10] See the critiques of Amartya Sen, *Identity and Violence: The Illusion of Destiny* (London, Allen Lane, 2006) and Anthony Appiah, 'Identity, Authenticity, Survival: Multicultural Societies and Social Reproduction' in Amy Gutmann (ed), *Multiculturalism* (Princeton, Princeton University Press, 1994).

motivated also by the Nazi use of German minorities to justify invading where these minorities resided. Nevertheless, two of the earliest human rights instruments were the Genocide Convention (1948) and the International Covenant Against Racial Discrimination (CERD) (1965). These were essentially protective of the rights of particular communities that were shared with all other individuals. There are trends now, however, towards a greater recognition of cultural and ethnic bases of autonomy.[11]

Article 27 of the International Covenant on Civil and Political Rights was drafted in narrow terms, based on the rights of individual members of the minority community rather than the community itself. And the state is prohibited from discrimination rather than obliged to take positive steps to promote minority rights. However, in recent years, despite the parsimonious language, the UN Human Rights Committee has interpreted the Article to develop minority collective rights including a measure of autonomy, and some positive obligations on the states.[12] The Committee has given a broad meaning to 'culture', noting that culture manifests itself in many forms, including a particular way of life associated with the use of land resources, especially in the case of indigenous peoples. The Committee regards the provision as directed at the survival and continued development of the cultural, religious and social identity of minorities. This broader approach is reflected in a UN Declaration on the Rights of Minorities adopted by the General Assembly in 1992. It places particular emphasis upon the right of minorities to participation, especially in decisions on the national and where appropriate, regional level.

Although this chapter does not deal primarily with indigenous people, it is worth noting that considerable progress has been made in safeguarding their rights. There has been a reversal from the earlier paternalistic and assimilationist approach (in the 1957 ILO Convention) to recognising the 'aspirations of these peoples to exercise control over their own institutions, ways of life and economic development and to maintain and develop their identities, languages and religions, within the framework of the States in which they live' (the 1991 ILO Convention). This new approach is reinforced in the UN Declaration on the Rights of Indigenous Peoples, adopted by the UN General Assembly in 2007.

The broadest source of minority entitlement now is self-determination, in itself a difficult and controversial concept, but one which is increasingly being analysed in terms of the internal, democratic organisation of a state rather than in terms of secession or independence. The greater involvement of the UN or consortia of states in the settlement of internal conflicts has helped to develop the concept of self-determination as implying autonomy in appropriate circum-

[11] For European developments see, eg, the *Lund Recommendations on the Effective Participation of National Minorities in Public Life* (OSCE 1998), also *Hague Recommendations regarding the Education Rights of National Minorities* (1996) and the *Oslo Recommendations regarding the Linguistic Rights of National Minorities* (1998).

[12] Accepting that in some situations, art 27 rights may be associated with a territory, as when cultural rights consist in a way of life which is closely associated with territory and use of its resources.

stances (such as in Bosnia, Eastern Europe and Kosovo), and other forms of self-government. The right of minorities to participate in public affairs and in state institutions as well as to enjoy their culture now ranks high in the lexicon of self-determination.

Ethnicity both invokes and undermines human rights. The fundamental dilemma of rights and diversity is well captured by Charles Taylor when he writes:

> Now underlying the demand [for recognition of diversity] is a principle of universal equality. The politics of difference is full of denunciations of discrimination and refusals of second class citizenship. This gives the principle of universal equality a point of entry within the politics of dignity. But once inside, as it were, its demands are hard to assimilate to that politics. For it asks we give acknowledgement and status to something that is not universally shared. Or, otherwise put, we give due acknowledgment only what is universally present – everyone has an identity – through recognizing what is peculiar to each. The universal demands powers and acknowledgement of specificity.[13]

Attacks on the bias of the regime of rights highlight what seem to be various contradictions between human rights and ethnicity. Human rights seek to be colour-blind, aloof from religious or other affiliations; ethnicity makes these affiliations basic to identity and human existence. Human rights empower the individual; ethnicity the group. Human rights are the framework for relations between citizens *inter se* and between citizens and the state; ethnicity compels attention to and regulation of inter-ethnic relations, and the relations of the group to the state. Human rights aim to be inclusive, ethnicity exclusive. Thus ethnicity has posed problems for human rights in a way that nationalism did not. Nationalism did not seek accommodation of rights within an existing state, but sought its own state; ethnicity seeks accommodation within an existing state. It internalises to the state problems that would otherwise dissipate on the formation of a new state; it brings problems of cultural relativism not as concerns between distant societies, but as basic to the very definition and existence of a state. Ethnicity seeks to re-configure the state as the principal framework for the formulation and enforcement of rights, with fundamental implications for how the scope and nature of rights are perceived (in the ways outlined above). If the quarter century after the end of World War II saw the rise of the ideology of individual-oriented human rights, the last quarter saw a major challenge, in the name of the community, to that approach. If in the first period, self-determination was the foundation of state sovereignty, in the second period it was mobilised to challenge that sovereignty.

Ethnicity has not yet vanquished earlier understandings of human rights (and indeed feeds on it) but it has posed greater challenge to it than autocrats ever did

[13] Charles Taylor, 'Alternative Futures: Legitimacy, Identity, and Alienation in Late Twentieth-Century Canada' in Charles Taylor, *Reconciling the Solitudes: Essays on Canadian Federalism and Nationalism* (Kingston, McGill-Queen's Press, 1985) 39.

– precisely because it presents the challenge in the language of human rights. And the way that the western community, under 'Bushite hegemony', chose to fight that challenge, has eroded the legitimacy of rights more than any terrorist movement could. So the challenge of ethnicity to human rights is not free from ambiguities. How that challenge is met will to a significant degree determine the resilience and development of human rights. Now we tend to see ethnicity as a negative force and attribute to its rise, intolerance, displacement of people, victimisation of children and women, suicide bombers and massacres. But ethnicity is also emancipatory; it is a basis for resistance to oppression; it is a primary source of identity, pride and solidarity. It is because of this Janus-faced quality that it is hard to formulate responses to it.

The international community has been forced to recognise and accommodate ethnicity; it has intervened in several intra-state conflicts with armed force and it has imposed political solutions on states. There has been considerable preoccupation with establishing norms and institutions for the regulation of inter-ethnic relations, particularly under the seductive influence of the Lijphartian theory of consociation, based on the primacy of the community over the individual. For multicultural states, human rights (as the negotiated understanding of the acceptable framework for co-existence and the respect for each culture) are more important than for mono-cultural or mono-ethnic societies, where other forms of solidarity and identity can be invoked, to minimise or cope with conflicts. The conflict between human rights and cultural relativism cannot be treated simply as a philosophical or political discourse, but as a conflict which must be resolved concretely if some degree of order, stability and mutual respect is to be achieved. In other words, precisely where the concept and conceptions of rights are most difficult, they are most needed.

V. HUMAN RIGHTS AS FRAMEWORK FOR CONSTITUTIONAL NEGOTIATIONS

By the 'framework of rights', I mean the standards and norms of human rights reflected in international instruments and the institutions for the interpretation and enforcement of rights. Policies must be justified by reference to a recognised right, the qualifications that may lawfully be imposed on the right, or a balance between rights. The procedures and guidelines for the balance and trade-offs must themselves be located within the regime of rights. The notion of framework also refers to the process of negotiations or adjudication, which must be conducted fairly, according to core values of rights. This implies the ultimate authority of the judiciary to settle competing claims by reference to human rights norms.

Since I examine the role of human rights in relation to nation building and the structuring of the state, I explore a number of 'constitutional moments'. In most cases the framework of human rights (including the newer norms and instruments) was prescribed in the terms of the drafting body as pre-determined principle. And since constitution-making is essentially a process of negotiations, these case studies provide instructive examples of the utility of the human rights framework for diversity.

A. India

India is one of the world's most complex countries, with all major religions; numerous linguistic groups; strong regional affiliations; complicated social structures and great social disparities. Successive Indian requests that Britain introduce a bill of rights during the colonial period were rebuffed by the British. In its view

> a declaration of rights is of so abstract a nature that it has no legal effect of any kind or its legal effect will be to impose an embarrassing restriction on the powers of the legislature and to create a grave risk that a large number of laws may be declared invalid by the Courts because inconsistent with one or other of the rights so declared.

Indian interest in rights was not due to some abstract reason, but due to discrimination against Indians. However, Indians had to confront various dilemmas before agreeing on the form of the bill of rights. A bill of rights had to accommodate (a) cultural diversity; (b) minorities; (c) poverty; (d) social and societal oppression; (e) hierarchical relationships; and (f) national unity and integration. Far from these factors being regarded as obstacles to rights, rights were deemed essential. It was only when the Indian Constituent Assembly was established that Indian leaders had an opportunity to implement their ideas. Indians justified rights on the principle that 'All powers of government, legislative, executive and judicial are derived from the people'. Indian leaders were very conscious of the poverty of the masses; they had to reconcile rights directed towards maintaining the status quo, particularly property rights, with those directed towards social change and social justice. Conscious of the oppression that inhered in social and economic structures (such as untouchability or caste), they were committed to empowering the disadvantaged groups. This suggested some restrictions on liberal rights of property or equality – and an activist state, engaged in the distribution of resources and the direction of the economy. The Constitution-makers wanted to bring about social reform, especially among the Hindus. This required prohibiting socio-religious practices deeply embedded in civil society, which could only be done by extending, at least partially, the regime of rights to private conduct.

They were committed to protecting minorities (though after the partition of Pakistan, they wanted to avoid forms of entrenchment which might promote fresh demands of separatism). They wanted to move away from what they regarded as the divisive way the British had ruled India, abandoning the conferment of corporate identities on religious or cultural groups, shifting, on this point, towards a more liberal framework. They were, more generally, conscious of the cultural diversity of India and the need to fit rights within this diversity. At the same time they were pre-occupied by the imperative of 'nation building', cultivation of a common identity and common loyalties, especially as they were drawing the Constitution at a time when the country was being torn asunder, with horrendous problems of security, lawlessness and communal carnage.

To an extent these opposing objectives were balanced by adopting the device of an enforceable Bill of Rights for, but not exclusively, civil and political rights, and a non-justiciable charter of Directive Principles for measures of social and economic equality. Where the necessary social and economic reforms could only be achieved by qualifying civil or political rights, such as those of equality and property, this was clearly stated in the Bill of Rights and authority or obligation for remedial action laid down.

i. Social Reform

The Indian Bill of Rights is strongly oriented towards universalism and social reform. Most rights are drawn from western precedents. Rights are used as a critique of culture, especially Hindu culture. 'Untouchability' is abolished and its practice made a criminal offence (Article 17). Traffic in human beings and *begar* (a form of servitude) and similar practices of forced labour are also abolished (Article 23). The provisions concerning freedom of conscience and religion was drawn carefully to ensure that practices like *purdah* or *sati* (widow burning) were not somehow entrenched (Article 25(2) says that the freedom of conscience shall not prevent the state from regulating or restricting any economic, financial, political or other secular activity associated with religious practice, or to provide for social welfare and reform or the throwing open of Hindu religious institutions of a public character to all classes and sections of Hindus). Reform of Hindu practices is also aimed at in the provisions which prohibit discrimination on access to the use of wells, tanks, bathing ghats, roads and places of public resort maintained wholly or partly out of public funds or dedicated to the use of the general public – with the abolition of discrimination against lower castes the primary objective. The imperative of social reform is evident also in Directive Principles, particularly in Article 38(1), which requires the state to 'strive to promote the welfare of the people by securing and protecting as effectively as it may a social order in which justice, social, economic and political, shall inform all the institutions of the national life'.

ii. Religious and Minority Rights

Many provisions balance 'universality' with 'particularity', cultural or religious autonomy with common citizenship. The Constitution seeks to hold an even hand between different religions (and establish a modernist approach to public life) by establishing a secular state. No person can be compelled to pay any taxes the proceeds of which are specifically appropriated for payment to promotion or maintenance of any particular religion or religious denomination (Article 26). No religious instruction may be provided in educational institutions maintained wholly out of state funds (Article 28(1)). No person attending an educational institution funded or recognised by the state can be required to take part in religious instruction or worship (Article 28(3)). On the other hand, Indian secularism is less thorough going than in the US. On the one hand the state is authorised to regulate, even ban, practices associated with religion. On the other hand, there is recognition of the profound influence of religion on the people, and general support of religious organisations (see Article 28(2); Article 30(2)).

Understandably many provisions deal with minority rights. Since religion was a major source of division and conflict, there are several provisions for the protection of religious belief and practices (Article 25). All religious groups are entitled to set up institutions to own property and to manage their religious affairs (Article 27). Minorities have the right to conserve their languages, script and culture (Article 29) and to establish their own educational facilities (Article 30). However, there are limits to the autonomy of minorities, particularly religious minorities (to some extent language groups are protected through language policy provisions, particularly federalism, although the linguistic basis of federalism came later, under great pressure from linguistic groups, reshaping the basis of federalism). One point of considerable contention at the time of the drafting of the Constitution was the right of cultural minorities to their own personal laws. The Constituent Assembly had before it a proposal to require the state to adopt a uniform civil code which would cover marriage and family laws. The justification was that such uniform laws were necessary for a modern state and for cementing national unity. This was met with considerable resistance from Muslim leaders, in and out of the Constituent Assembly. The compromise was to move the provision to the chapter on Directive Principles, so that it would not be legally binding but would constitute guidance to the state (Article 44 provides that the state 'shall endeavour to secure for the citizens a uniform civil code throughout the territory of India'). The personal laws of Hindu and associated communities have been codified (and modernised), but for the most part the *sharia* has continued to govern the personal laws of Muslims – not without contention, both among the Muslim communities themselves and as between rather aggressive Hinduism and traditional Muslim leaders. In the landmark case of *Shah Bano*[14] the Supreme Court grappled with the validity of *sharia* which placed Muslim women divorcees in a less advantaged position than other women. *Shah Bano* did not succeed in balancing competing interests and served merely to aggravate religious animosities. So far as tribal peoples are concerned, the authority to make laws on succession to chieftaincy, the inheritance

[14] *Mohd. Ahmed Khan v Shah Bano Begum* (AIR 1985 SC 945).

of property, marriage and divorce, and social customs is vested in their own district or regional councils (section 3, Sixth Schedule).

iii. Equality and Affirmative Action

A major theme of constitutional discourse is the balance between guarantees of formal equality and the provision of effective equality (see Article 14, 15 and 16 and most of the Directive Principles). Article 16 guarantees equality of opportunity in public employment, but it also authorises the state to make any provision for the reservation of appointments or posts in favour of any class of citizens which, in the opinion of the state, is not adequately represented in state services (Article 16(4)). It is also provided that the 'claims of the members of the Scheduled Castes and Scheduled Tribes shall be taken into consideration, consistently with the maintenance of efficiency of administration, in the making of appointments to services and posts' in the state (Article 335). These groups are also ensured special representation in the national and state legislatures in proportion to their population (Article 330). A more general commitment was placed, by a Directive Principle, on the state to promote 'with special care the educational and economic interests of the weaker sections of the people, and, in particular, of the Scheduled Castes and the Scheduled Tribes, and shall protect them from social injustice and all forms of exploitation' (Article 46).

iv. Conclusion

The variety of objectives which the Constituent Assembly attempted to secure through the Bill of Rights resulted in compromises and a complicated regime of rights. However, there was a wide measure of agreement on the general approach and substance, forged under the hegemony of the Indian National Congress party. With the decision of the departing colonial power to partition the subcontinent into India and a (Muslim) Pakistan, the case for cultural autonomy and group rights was considerably weakened. Group rights, in the form of 'reservations' for representation in the legislature or public service, were an important technique of control during colonial rule. The establishment of Pakistan on a 'religio-nationalist' basis eased the path towards a liberal and secular constitution in India. The Constitution reduced considerably the scope of reservations as compared with the immediately preceding period under British rule when most positions in administration and politics were allocated according to communal quotas.[15] Henceforth, reservations were intended to became a device for equity, not balance of power (although, prompted by electoral politics, this is not how things worked out).

[15] Andre Beteille, *Society and Politics in India: Essays in Comparative Perspective* (London, Athlone Press, 1991).

It became possible to focus also on other values, particularly social justice, economic and social rights and compensatory justice. At the heart of the regime lay the dialectics between Fundamental Rights, made supreme by the Constitution (Article 13), and Directive Principles of State Policy, which while not judicially enforceable, 'are nevertheless fundamental in the governance of the country' and impose a duty on the state 'to apply these principles in making laws' (Article 37). Directive Principles were employed to record aspirations of social justice and economic rights for example, free and compulsory primary education (Article 45), just and humane conditions of work (Article 42), living wages for workers (Article 43), while Fundamental Rights protected, for the most part, liberal individual rights. While the notion of group rights was not missing from Fundamental Rights, it was in Directive Principles that they were most prominent. Directive Principles reflected the concern with the community and the wider interests of society. They also provided the vehicle for the espousal of elements of Gandhian philosophy, particularly in the emphasis on *panchyats* (village-based government, Article 40), the protection of cows (and in this way acknowledging the importance of Hindu perception of the sacredness of cows, Article 48), and the prohibition of consumption of alcohol (Article 47, which found support in Hinduism and Islam).

That there might be conflicts between Fundamental Rights and Directive Principles, as representing somewhat different philosophies of rights, appears not to have been clearly perceived. Indians had seen liberal rights and social justice as a seamless web. The idea of separating off 'negative' and 'positive' rights in this way was raised at a late stage during the deliberations of the Constituent Assembly. The fears which some members then expressed were not connected so much to conflicts as to the inefficacy of Directive Principles, since they were not to be judicially enforceable. It was after the adoption of the Constitution, as the Congress government began to implement policies of social justice (particularly with restrictions on property rights) that the conflicts became patent, and were bitterly pursued. Affirmative action policies added further fuel to these conflicts. The courts, whence all these disputes made their way, vacillated between giving primacy to rights or Directive Principles when the validity of social legislation, purportedly in breach of rights of property or equality, was under review. At least two developments are worth mentioning. Eventually the courts accepted that they had to harmonise rights and Directive Principles. Chandrachud CJ said in the landmark decision of *Minerva Mills v Union of India*: 'To give absolute primacy to one over the other is to disturb the harmony of the Constitution. This harmony and balance between fundamental rights and directive principles is essential feature of the basic structure of the Constitution'.[16] For a while the provisions for affirmative action were seen as a qualification on the right to equality. Later the courts have begun to view them as the implementation of the guarantees for equality. But the issue remains unsolved.

[16] (1980) 3 SCC 625.

The major post-independence political and judicial battles have revolved around classical controversies in political theory: between rights of property and formal equality versus social and compensatory justice. One judge, in favour of effective equality, has said that, 'Advantages secured due to historical reasons cannot be considered a fundamental right guaranteed by the Constitution'.[17] Another Supreme Court judge, Beg J, has put the point slightly differently:

> [D]irective principles as laying down the path of the country's progress towards the allied objectives and aims stated in the Preamble, with fundamental rights as the limits of that path, like the banks of a flowing river, which could be mended or amended by displacements, replacements or curtailments or enlargements of any part according to the needs of those who had to use the path.[18]

B. Canada

Cairns says of Canadians, 'Those issues that have most deeply divided us, and have agitated our passions to the point of frenzy, have revolved around race, ethnicity, religion, and language, all of which have pervasive symbolic overtones'.[19] 'Rights' have not traditionally been employed to cope with these issues. When Canada was constituted as a state in 1867, the principal issue concerned the respective identities and privileges of the English and the French communities. It was resolved through the grant of significant autonomy (particularly in relation to civil law and education) to the francophone community residing in Quebec by federalisation. The solution lasted for a very considerable time, but it came under stress a few decades ago. Several factors seem to have contributed: an increasing role of the state which generated controversy on social policies; a rising francophone professional class in Quebec resentful of economic domination by English speakers; immigration of other national groups, which diluted the proportion of francophones and challenged the notion of the two 'founding peoples'; and the politicisation of the first nations advancing their economic and cultural claims. Canadians seemed threatened with fragmentation, but it was the stridency of francophone claims, backed with the threat of Quebec separatism, which prompted the search for new constitutional solutions, in which a bill of rights came to play an important role.[20] The Canadian Charter of Rights was adopted only in 1982, over a century after Canada was constituted as a federal state. The primary aim of the Charter does not seem to have been the strengthening of rights, for they were on the whole well protected under the law

[17] Hegde J in *Viswanath v State of Mysore* AIR (1964) Mys 132, 136.

[18] *Keshavananda Bharati v State of Kerala* (1973) 4 SCC 225.

[19] Alan C Cairns, *Charter versus Federalism: The Dilemmas of Constitutional Reform* (Kingston, McGill-Queen's Press, 1992) 59.

[20] ibid; and Peter Russell, *Constitutional Odyssey: Can Canadians Become a Sovereign People* (Toronto, University of Toronto Press, 1993).

and traditions of Canadian polity (criminal law has been a federal subject, thus ensuring uniformity and allowing courts to review the criminal process in provinces).

The push for the Charter came from the then Prime Minister, Pierre Trudeau, who was worried about a growing feeling of provincialism and wanted to offer Canadians an identity they could all embrace. That identity was to come from a Bill of Rights. As Cairns states,

> The Charter was always more than an instrument to protect the rights of Canadians against their governments. The larger political purpose, which explains its tenacious sponsorship by the federal government, was to strengthen national unity by providing constitutional support to a new definition of Canadians as a rights-bearing citizenry regardless of location.[21]

It was to infuse a new identity of 'Canada' as a bilingual and multicultural state; in other words it was intended to overcome narrow parochialism. The association of rights with the idea of the nation state has of course ancient pedigree.

Trudeau was also a strong supporter of bilingualism; and considered that the 'universalism' he was aiming for could not be achieved without securing the Francophone minority the right to their language outside Quebec. Bilingualism was such a vital plank in his new edifice that it was placed above the 'notwithstanding clause' (see below). The Charter would also redefine provincial powers, for henceforth the floor for provincial policy would not only be the federal division of functions but also national standards of rights, supervised by federal authorities throughout the state. The proposal for a Charter was part of a wider constitutional movement to endow Canada with a clearer focus for its identity. It involved the 'repatriation' of the Constitution from London, by which was meant that Canada would no longer need the permission of the UK Parliament to amend its Constitution. The new dimension of sovereignty, far from reinforcing Canadian statehood and nationalism, produced anxieties among various groups about their rights and interests. The Charter proposal was seen as excluding important options to these groups, as it would prevent the recognition of their particular claims or interests. Provinces were opposed to the universalising tendency of the Charter as this would weaken diversity, the rationale of federalism. Aboriginal people feared that universal norms would undermine their culture and autonomy, which could only flourish if their own, different norms and values were preserved. The francophones, although presumably not opposed in principle to a liberal regime of rights, saw in the Charter a threat to the pursuit of their language and other policies as manifestations of their distinct society. The new immigrants wanted the Charter to recognise the diversity of their own cultures, not only of the 'founding races'. There was also a feminist challenge to universality, as that would smother women's claims to protection against their vulnerability or historic injustice to them. English speaking

[21] Cairns (n 20) 49.

Canada was opposed to exceptions, to variations and to the differential availability of rights, as offensive to the universalism inherent in the idea of a rights-bearing citizenry. Thus paradoxically, proposals for the Charter reinforced the very identities that Trudeau, given his liberal predilections, was most anxious to transcend through a universal regime of rights. The drafting of the Charter was therefore in large measure taken up by negotiating competing claims.

While many feared that Canadians were now being defined by differences between them, others criticised the Charter for overriding diversity. Charles Taylor said that the emphasis on individual rights not only atomises society but, with its nationalising, levelling propensities, is destructive of the smaller communities on which Canada, he alleges, is based.[22] Tully argues that the recognition of the francophones and first nations as cultural minorities or communities diminishes them, derogating from their status as self-governing nations.[23] The validity of these opposing views can be assessed after an examination of the specific accommodations to the claims of different groups.

i. Aboriginal Rights

The movement for a national charter of rights was regarded by aboriginal nations as a threat to their special status. The effect of the Charter had already been foreshadowed by case law under the Bill of Rights, holding that a law which contained special provisions applying only to native Indians was void.[24] However, this doctrine was effectively overruled when the Supreme Court held that disenfranchising an Indian (first nation) woman who married a non-Indian was valid, but not disenfranchising an Indian man who married an outsider also was valid, notwithstanding the discrimination.[25] Aboriginal communities feared the negative impact of the Charter on recognition of their sovereignty and the preservation of their social and cultural traditions and practices, premised on group rights, and that their cultural traditions and practices, unlike those of the francophones, were seen as alien to Charter values.

Negotiations were difficult. One concession to first nations was section 25 which reads:

> The guarantee in this Charter of certain rights and freedoms shall not be construed so as to abrogate or derogate from any aboriginal treaty or other freedoms that pertain to the aboriginal peoples of Canada, including
>
> (a) any rights or freedoms that have been recognised by the Royal Proclamation of October 7, 1763; and

[22] Charles Taylor, 'Alternative Futures: Legitimacy, Identity, and Alienation in Late Twentieth-Century Canada' in Charles Taylor, *Reconciling the Solitudes: Essays on Canadian Federalism and Nationalism* (Kingston, McGill-Queen's Press, 1985).

[23] James Tully, Strange *Multiplicity: Constitutionalism in an Age of Diversity* (Cambridge, Cambridge University Press, 1996) 182–83.

[24] *R v Drybones* [1970] SCR 282.

[25] *AG of Canada v Lavell* [1974] SCR 1349.

(b) any rights or freedoms that now exist by way of land claims agreements or may be so acquired.

Douglas Sanders states that the section protects the rights of Indians from the egalitarian provisions of the Charter,[26] preserving aboriginal customs and practices from the right to gender equality.

Another provision for the benefit of first nations is section 35, outside the four corners of the Charter, and so not amenable to the notwithstanding clause. It affirmed the 'existing aboriginal and treaty rights of the aboriginal peoples of Canada' (of which section Dickson CJ said in *Sparrow* that it 'represents the culmination of a long and difficult struggle in both the political fora and the courts for the constitutional recognition of aboriginal rights'[27]). As in *Sparrow*, courts have used these provisions to strengthen indigenous rights. In *Guerin v R*, the Supreme Court held that the Musqueam Indian band had legal rights to their reserve lands.[28] The judgment was based on pre-contact control and possession of land by the Indians and owed nothing to British or Canadian actions. In *Nowegijicj v R*, Dickson CJ said, that

> treaties and statutes relating to Indians should be liberally construed and doubtful expressions resolved in favour of the Indians . . . Indian treaties must . . . be construed, not according to the technical meaning of their words, but . . . in the sense in which they would naturally be understood by the Indians.[29]

ii. Multiculturalism

Section 27 of the Charter declares:

> This Charter shall be interpreted in a manner consistent with the preservation and enhancement of the multicultural heritage of Canadians.

Courts have made serious attempts to grapple with it and no clear consensus has emerged. It is agreed that it covers questions of religion, since religion is so intricately connected with culture. The effect of section 27 was considered in *R v Big M Drug Mart Ltd*, and concerned the freedom of conscience in a multifaith society. Section 4 of the Lord's Day Act (1907), prohibiting any work or commercial activity on the Lord's Day was challenged.[30] Dickson held that the validity of legislation depends on both purpose and impact; either can make legislation invalid:

[26] Douglas Saunders, 'Pre-existing Rights: The Aboriginal Peoples of Canada' in Gerald-A Beaudoin and Errol Mendes (eds), *The Canadian Charter of Rights and Freedoms* (Canada, Carswell, 1996).

[27] [1990] 1 SCR 1075, 1105.

[28] [1984] 2 SCR 335.

[29] [1983] 1 SCR 29.

[30] 1985] 1 RCS 299.

> [T]he consideration of the object of legislation is vital if rights are to be fully protected . . . What may appear good and true to a majoritarian religious group, or to the state acting at their behest, may not, for religious reasons, be imposed upon citizens who take a contrary view. The Charter protects religious minorities from the threat of the 'tyranny of the majority'.[31]

However in *R v Edwards Books*, the Supreme Court held that section 2(a) (the derogation section) does not require the legislature to provide a Sabbatarian exemption in order to relieve those who worship on Saturday from the burden they may suffer because of the Act (Business Retail Holidays Act).[32] The Court held that if the legislative goal (of a common pause day for retailers) was to be achieved, it will be to the detriment of some and would be valid if it met the test of proportionality. Wilson J dissented, arguing:

> A limit on freedom of religion which recognises the freedom of some members of the group but not of other members of the same group cannot be reasonable and justified in a free and democratic society. The effect of the disparate treatment is that the religious freedom of some is respected by the legislation while the religious freedom of others continues to be violated. The Charter, when it protected group rights, protects the rights of all members of the group because to do otherwise would introduce an invidious distinction into the group and sever the religious and cultural tie that binds them together.[33]

Section 27 was taken in account in the Supreme Court reaching its conclusion that legislation criminalising hate propaganda was a justified qualification of the freedom of expression. Speaking for the majority in *R v Keegstra*, Dickson CJ quoted from another decision, 'Multiculturalism cannot be preserved let alone enhanced if free rein is given to the promotion of hatred against identifiable groups'.[34]

It could be argued that none of these decisions required section 27, as they could be based on the more general principle of equality. The inability of courts to give much substance to the section is perhaps symptomatic of the wider, political and sociological, vagueness of the concept of 'multiculturalism' in Canada (compared, for example, to the clearer, though still somewhat diffuse, notion of indigenous rights and their recognition in international instruments). It is uncertain whether 'multiculturalism' implies state neutrality between cultures or active state engagement with the propagation of different cultures. Trudeau suggested the former when he announced the policy to meet the claims of newer immigrants, saying that while Canada has two official languages, it had no official culture.[35] Forbes concludes that this compromise ('multicultural-

[31] ibid 331.
[32] [1986] 2 SCR 713.
[33] ibid 719.
[34] [1990] 3 SCR 697.
[35] Hugh Donald Forbes, 'Canada: From Bilingualism to Multiculturalism' in Larry Diamond and Marc Plattner, *Nationalism, Ethnic Conflict and Democracy* (Baltimore, John Hopkins University Press, 1994) 94.

ism within a bilingual framework') entailed a patchwork of new policies. Some were designed to encourage cultural retention by minority ethnic groups (i.e., to inhibit or oppose assimilation); others, which promoted contact and opposed discrimination, aimed to encourage social integration (despite its tendency to increase assimilation); and still others tried to hasten linguistic assimilation by subsidising the learning of the official languages by recent immigrants.

iii. Override Provision (the 'Notwithstanding' Clause)

Section 33 of the Charter, adopted as a concession to the provinces, enables Parliament as well as provincial legislatures to override most provisions of the Charter, for five years at a time, in relation to a law by an express declaration to that effect. It cannot override 'democracy rights' (particularly franchise and elections) and mobility, language and minority language rights – thus securing important minority rights from this form of legislative suspension. Quebec tried at an early stage to take advantage of this provision to insulate *all* its previous laws (through the use of a law invoking the section); although the Court of Appeal rejected this attempt for failure to specify which particular rights were to be suspended.[36] However, this view was overruled by the Supreme Court in a case reviewing legislation from Quebec which, using the 'notwithstanding' clause, required all outdoor signs to be in French, holding that provinces' power to override rights was absolute.[37] The earlier, adverse, decision had provoked much resentment in Quebec, while the latter resulted in equally strong resentment in other provinces. This would suggest the failure of this provision to mediate between competing claims; it was all or nothing, rather than a balancing.[38]

iv. Conclusion

Trudeau's aspirations for the Charter (universalism) are reflected in the general rules for qualifying rights. Rights may be subject to 'only such reasonable limits prescribed by law as can be demonstrably justified in a free and democratic rights'.[39] In so far as culture is relevant, it is 'political culture', though of course the initial choice of rights is to some extent determined by 'culture'. But the context for the Charter is also reflected in the rules of interpretation – human rights guarantees not to be construed to abrogate or derogate from aboriginal treaties or rights or freedoms (Article 25); the Charter shall be interpreted in a manner consistent with the preservation and enhancement of the multicultural heritage of Canada (Article 27, which may become more problematic than envisaged with the increase in Asian and African immigrants, as the original

[36] *Alliance des Professeurs de Montreal v A-G of Quebec* [1985] 21 DLR 4th 354.
[37] *Ford v A-G of Quebec* [1988] SCR 712.
[38] *cf* Peter Russell, 'Standing up for Notwithstanding' (1991) 24 *Albany Law Review* 293–309.
[39] Section 1.

understanding of multiculturalism developed in the context of newer European immigrants); and the rights and privileges of 'denominational, separate or dissentient schools' are not affected (Article 29).

In any event, Canada accepted a more complex regime of rights than perhaps even India. It has a greater orientation to group rights than India. It seeks to accommodate the francophones and the first nations through forms of collective rights. In another respect also the Charter recognises groups, not just individuals (the jurisprudence of the Supreme Court on section 15, the equality provision, recognises the importance of group disadvantage or disability). Derogation from equal rights is permitted in respect of

> any law, programme or activity that has as its object the amelioration of conditions of disadvantaged individuals or groups including those that are disadvantaged because of race, national or ethnic origin, colour, religion, sex, age or mental or physical disability.

Two Canadian scholars have argued that section 15(2) is intended to redress the imbalance against those groups which have been subject to persistent disadvantage, by pointing to the grounds on which discrimination has been based. They also state (like the current Indian Supreme Court position) that the right to equality and the provision for affirmative action should be seen as serving a common purpose rather than incorporating two inconsistent conceptions of equality.[40] The Canadian Supreme Court's view of the Charter is of rights as governed by

> respect for the inherent dignity of the human person, commitment to social justice and equality, accommodation of a wide variety of beliefs, respect for cultural and group identity, and faith in social and political institutions which enhance the participation of individuals and groups in society.[41]

All these concessions and compromises have not eased Canada's problems of identity and cultural differences. It was early realised that the repatriation process (and the Charter) were not the end of the problem; rather the beginning, and in one sense, even a cause of the difficulties. The political process, long drawn out as it has been, has so far failed to resolve outstanding issues. Issues which were up for negotiations were a clearer recognition of the distinctiveness of the francophones and the greater acknowledgment by the first nations of the imperative of gender equality. The task of reconciliation has been complicated by the multiplicity of claims that have been advanced (themselves promoted by the introduction of the notion of 'rights as framework'), cutting across class, ethnic and gender distinctions, pointing to limits of the flexibility of that framework. The variety of interests, values and groups which must be taken into account in interpreting the Constitution that was contained in the Canada

[40] William Black and Lynn Smith, 'The Equality Rights' in Gerald-A Beaudoin and Errol Mendes (eds), *The Canadian Charter of Rights and Freedoms* (1996) (n 27).

[41] *R v Oakes* [1986] 1 SCR 103, 136.

clause of the Charlottetown Accord provides a clear indication of the difficult burden placed on the Charter. However, the impasse of that effort means that, at least for the time being, the baton has to some extent been passed to the courts, which have begun to grapple with the challenges of multiculturalism, Quebec's distinct society, and aboriginal claims.

C. Fiji

The primary political issue in Fiji has been the reconciliation of the conflicting interests of its two major ethnic communities, the indigenous Fijians and the Indo-Fijians (whose respective shares of the total population have varied from 41 per cent to 44 per cent and 60 per cent to 38 per cent in the last three decades). The communities are divided by race, religion, language and historical traditions, divisions which were aggravated by British policy of separating off the races geographically, politically, educationally and even economically. Consequently, there was considerable tension between them, which surfaced most often on the political question of how to organise the state.

Indigenous Fijians have wanted the constitutional dispensation to be based upon ethnic communities as corporate entities (in terms of electorates, land rights, entitlements to posts in public services and cultural rights) while the Indo-Fijians preferred the concept of equal citizenship – both positions, motivated in substantial part by considerations of political advantage, deeply embedded in history. Until the mid-1990s, this difference was not meditated through the discourse of rights. The independence Constitution (1970) did contain a Bill of Rights, based on a 'debased' version of the European Convention of Human Rights that the UK purveyed in its colonies as they became independent. This model was accepted uncritically; few seemed to have realised the implications of a bill of rights (and which have not been explored either by politicians or judges). In any event, there were more qualifications and derogations than rights in this model. In particular there was a major exemption in the equal rights provision in favour of personal laws: these were not subject to the requirement of equality. Nor were the land provisions subject to it. Consequently, both an essential element of culture and the major economic asset were excluded from the regime of rights. Various other legislative and administrative provisions which would undoubtedly have clashed with the Bill of Rights were expressly entrenched in the Constitution, and thus exempt from judicial review. Human rights played little role in the political or legal life of Fiji; there was only one minor case concerning human rights, on the right of expression, in the first 17 years of its existence. Many adjustments in the relations between the two communities were made in this period. Controversies centred around theories of ethnicity (pluralism, consociationalism or integration) or class rather than theories of rights.

In 1987, a military coup overthrew the government, when, for the first time in Fiji's history, a substantial number of Indo-Fijian politicians found themselves in the cabinet, having won the elections through the medium of a multi-racial coalition. In 1990, the military promulgated a new constitution. Such public discussion as there was concerned the respective shares of the ethnic communities in Parliament and the public service, and methods for the protection of land, cultural and other rights of indigenous Fijians. The Bill of Rights survived, with further attenuations, while large parts of the Constitution were in direct violation of human rights norms. The Constitution effectively elevated Christianity (the faith of most indigenous Figians) to the status of state religion, with legislation that forbade any commercial or sporting activity on Sundays.

In early 1995 the political leaders of the two major ethnic communities were able, after protracted negotiations, under some international pressure, to agree on the terms of reference of a review of the 1990 Constitution. For the first time Indo-Fijians were able to make human rights the basic framework for the negotiation of communal differences. The first response of the indigenous Fijians was that the concept of human rights belonged to an alien political and cultural tradition. Later, under considerable pressure from the opposition and some foreign governments, they agreed to include some reference to human rights norms, but claimed that the communal entitlements should be resolved within the framework of indigenous rights. Eventually the terms of reference required the reviewing commission to have regard to recognised international principles and standards of individual and group rights. The commission was required to 'take into account that the Constitution shall guarantee full protection and promotion of the rights, interests and concerns of the indigenous Fijian and Rotuman people'.[42] This was the first constitutional settlement in Fiji that was based on rights. The emphasis on rights as framework was in one sense a repudiation of the 1990 Constitution which had degraded rights and had erected principles and structures totally at odds with any recognisable regime of rights. As the politically underprivileged community, Indo-Fijians wanted the framework of rights to be constitutive of the political settlement.[43] Indigenous Fijians preferred prior occupation of the land to be the decisive factor, giving them the right to determine the terms for the settlement of subsequent migrants.[44] Their resistance was overcome in part by international pressure and, more substantially, because they believed that there was no one conception of rights and so their own interests might also be pursued through rights-based claims.

Public debates were dominated by conflicting claims of individual or group rights. The case for the largest party of indigenous Fijians was based on the premise that sovereignty passed to them after independence, and that this sover-

[42] Fiji Constitutional Review Commission, *Towards a United Fiji* (Suva, 1996) 754–55.

[43] National Federation Party and Fiji Labour Party, *Towards Racial Harmony and National Unity: Submission to the Fiji Constitution Review Commission* (1995).

[44] Soqosoqo ni Kakavulewa ni Taukei, *Respect and Understanding: Fijian Sovereignty, The Recipe for Peace, Stability and Progress: Submission to the Fiji Constitution Review Commission* (1995).

eignty was reinforced by the then Draft UN Declaration on Indigenous Peoples (although it should be noted that indigenous Fijians had shown little interest in the international efforts to formulate rights of indigenous peoples and the government has not signed any conventions). The Indo-Fijians argued that all the rights under conventions on indigenous peoples were already available to indigenous Fijians, particularly as regards their lands and culture; that the Indo-Fijians were in no way questioning these rights; and that in any case indigenous rights had to be consistent with the general norms of human rights.

The resulting constitution (1997 but now abrogated)[45] emphasises human rights; it provides for much stronger protections, substantively as well as institutionally. In addition to the jurisdiction of the courts, a Human Rights Commission has been established, and the powers of the ombudsman enhanced. Provisions for affirmative action have been revamped, now extending to 'all groups or categories of persons who are disadvantaged', instead, as in the 1990 Constitution, confined to indigenous people (section 44(1)). The regime of rights is brought more centrally within the international norms, as in the rule that the courts must have regard, where relevant, to 'public international law applicable to the protection of the rights' set out in the Constitution (section 43(2)).

But in several important respects the Constitution itself is not consistent with international norms. Large elements of the structure of the state are still built around ethnic corporate entities, particularly representation in Parliament and the public service, and control of land. A key institution, the Great Council of Chiefs, which appoints the President and effectively has a veto over constitutional and, frequently, legislative changes, is an entirely indigenous Fijian body. Indigenous Fijians are over-represented in the legislature, particularly in the Senate where they dominate, in addition to having a veto over changes to the Constitution and a substantial body of other law. The Constitution continues the exemption from the requirement of equal treatment for laws on adoption, marriage, divorce, burial, devolution of property on death or 'other like matters as the personal law of any person or the members of any group' (section 38(7)(e)). However, now these laws have to be 'reasonable and justifiable in a free and democratic society'. Several laws privileging indigenous Fijians in various ways, including a substantial autonomy through their 'traditional' institutions, continue to be entrenched. Throughout there are genuflections to the 'paramountcy' of indigenous Fijians.

The Constitution provides therefore an uneasy mixture of newer international norms and a privileged position for indigenous Fijians. To some extent this compromise was built into the constitution review exercise. Constitutional reform could only be brought about by the consent of the indigenous Fijians, for not only were they firmly entrenched in the 1990 Constitution, but the armed forces were composed almost entirely of them. But the fundamental problem

[45] For a discussion of 1970, 1990 and 1997 Constitutions, see Yash Ghai and Jill Cottrell, 'A Tale of Three Constitutions: Ethnicity and Politics in Fiji' in Sujit Choudhry (ed), *Ethnicity and Constitutional Ordering* (Oxford, Oxford University Press, 2008) ch 9.

was the ideology of 'traditionalism' carefully cultivated over decades, first by the British colonial authorities and subsequently by the indigenous Fijian elite. Any threat to that 'tradition' has always been strongly resisted; the justification offered for the 1987 coup was that the electoral victory of the coalition dominated by Indo-Fijians posed a major threat to Fijian traditional rights and authorities. The ideology is an amalgam of indigenous institutions and Christianity; it consists of the Church, chiefs and land which hold the community ('vanua') together. Land itself has been under chiefly control (mediated to some extent through public institutions). The Church provides an important base for organisation as well as legitimacy. But the centrepiece is chieftaincy – which is hereditary. Unlike many other parts of the British empire, chiefs maintained their control over their community into and beyond independence, monopolising key political and administrative posts. By convention (when not by law), all major policies have to be approved by the Council of Chiefs, which gives the community a strong hold over the state political process. Such is the ideological (and material) force of the trinity of Church, chiefs and 'vanua' that few Indo-Fijians challenged any of its assumptions during the negotiations for the new Constitution.

The ideology has strong components of 'traditionalism', 'indigenousness' and 'culture', carefully nurtured and manipulated by the elite. This despite the fact that another major component, Christianity, has done more to change the customs and mores of the community than even the economy. In fact the ideology has been used to control the unfolding of the economy, keeping the indigenous people insulated for long periods from the market; although now, more than before, the political ideology of Fijian interests flourishes on the theme of economic development of Fijians. These provide the major contradictions of the ideology of traditionalism, which while not entirely protective or defensive, would undoubtedly have collapsed but for the presence of a sizeable Indo-Fijian community, providing the 'otherness' necessary for its sustenance. The emigration of another substantial body of Indo-Fijians since the latest coup (2006) has drastically reduced the number of Indo-Fijians, diminishing their political clout – and already bitter divisions have surfaced among the indigenous Fijians. The ideology of traditionalism has countered the ideology of rights and democracy in two ways: first by denying the relevance of the latter, relying on the hierarchy and differentiations explicit in 'traditional' systems; and latterly, by advancing the paradigm of indigenous collective rights in opposition to individual rights and equality (possible only through a gross misunderstanding or misrepresentation of indigenous rights instruments).

Of the four case studies, rights played the smallest role in Fiji; the very terms of reference for the negotiations on the Constitution contained ambiguities on the scheme of rights and the system of government (consociation or integration). An independent commission's recommendations strongly supported integration under a fairly comprehensive bill of rights. This was not acceptable to Fijian politicians, who insisted on their community's paramountcy. They insisted on many aspects of the old regime which were inconsistent with the primary principle of equality. Given the trappings of consociation, community representation, vetoes, proportionality and communal autonomy, it is easy to overlook the tendency towards the hegemony of a community a massive degradation of human rights.

Surprisingly, no-one seems to have objected to the provision on affirmative action which was no longer directed just at the indigenous Fijians but at the poor of all the communities – need rather than ethnicity was the criterion. But the equality and other provisions of rights are qualified by the privileges for the indigenous Fijians. The right to equality exempts Fijian land law and customs from its application. The system of Fijian administration continues and other privileges of traditional authorities are preserved.

It remains to be seen whether the newer prominence given to rights, even in their 'compromised' form, will moderate the ideology of 'traditionalism', or will be rendered nugatory by the politics of the latter – as in the past. Perhaps there are other provisions in the Constitution, including fair shares for all groups in political power, which might in due course modify 'traditionalism'. It may also be that the numerous provisions dealing with rights will promote a discourse of rights which in time may offer an alternative ideology to traditionalism. It is also unclear whether the judiciary, unlike in the past, will play any significant role in the interpretation and implementation of rights, and if so, whether it will be equally creative in adjusting them to the realities of multiculturalism (as the courts in other countries discussed in this chapter). For now, it should be acknowledged that the theme of rights and the dialectics of individual and group rights played an important role in mediating competing claims, whose justifications had to be made within the general framework of rights. This mediation facilitated a way out of the straitjacket of the constraints imposed by entrenched ethnic difference.

D. South Africa

In the early 1990s apartheid collapsed, under the weight of its own of iniquity, internal resistance and external pressure. With the demise of the apartheid regime South Africans embarked upon the task of fashioning a new constitutional order. It was clear that the debate on rights and the negotiations on the terms of rights for inclusion in the Constitution would be central issues. There had been no bill of rights until then; the apartheid regime was based on a massive repression of rights of the non-white people. The South African state was organised on a racial categorisation of the people, with unequal citizenship and unequal rights. The campaign against apartheid was based on rights and democracy, rather than opposition to whites as such. The African National Congress had declared its commitment to non-racialism and rights as early as the 1950s; its predecessor, the South African National Congress, had done so in the 1920s.[46] The supporters of apartheid, who had spurned rights for others, began to see the virtues of rights in a new dispensation where they would be a minority.

The general support for rights therefore ensured that they would find a place in the Constitution. But that did not settle the issue of what regime of rights; and here there were significant problems. Central and difficult issues of justice, social policies, organisation of public power, and freedom revolved around the nature and scope of rights. The form of the regime was influenced by several factors. There was the overriding question of social justice; redressing the oppression of the past. Could formal equality satisfy the aspirations of those who had suffered so much in their struggle against apartheid? If for a fairer distribution of resources, there had to be a massive re-allocation of resources, how could this be achieved in the face of constitutional protections of property rights? Could schemes for social justice exist without the device of classification of people, a device that had been the organising matrix of oppression under the previous regime? Could social justice be achieved without imposing obligations under the Bill of Rights on the private sector (a position not favoured by the libertarians)? Would activist state policies implicit in these approaches be consistent with the proper protection of citizens against arbitrariness of the government?

These dilemmas vexed two major groups who had been long-term supporters of human rights, which du Plessis has called 'libertarians' and 'liberationists'.[47] The libertarians, mostly white opponents of apartheid, drew their inspiration from classical liberal thought, based on the autonomy of the individual, the protection of property and opposition to an active role of the state. The former supporters of apartheid found natural allies with the libertarians (although on another aspect of the constitutional settlement, the territorial, they continued to support a group approach, which would have earned them significant autonomy). The 'liberationists', with a longer history of commitment to rights (especially those within the ANC), based their approach on social democracy or democratic socialism. They supported effective equality and consequently an activist state. Notwithstanding these differences, they were united by a 'profound loyalty to a distinct core of time-honoured liberal and democratic values'.[48] In none of these approaches was culture or religion an issue. The only group which had a distinct cultural approach were some African traditionalists, mostly chiefs, who wanted recognition of their own status and the preservation of traditional institutions and laws.[49] Their most vocal opponents were the

[46] The statement by the Native National Congress was amplified by the African Claims in the early 1940s, following on the Atlantic Charter adopted by Roosevelt, Churchill and Stalin in 1941 (I am grateful to Hugh Corder for this information).

[47] Lourens du Plessis, 'A Background to Drafting the Chapter on Fundamental Rights' in Bertus de Villiers (ed), *Birth of a Nation* (Cape Town, Juta, 1994) 91–92.

[48] ibid.

[49] TW Bennett, *Human Rights and African Customary Law: Under the South African Constitution* (Cape Town, Juta, 1995).

female members of their own communities. Corder and Du Plessis state the problem in the following way:

> The compatibility of customary law with the rights entrenched in Chapter 3 was hotly debated . . . This has a direct bearing on the position of women living under customary law. It furthermore raises the essentially moral and ideological questions of whether a legal system, taking its cue from a Bill of Rights, should put up with (traditionalist) 'cultural' violations of universal human rights standards. Is passing such a judgment not by its nature condescending? And what exactly is the scope of the individual's right to 'participate in the cultural life' of his or her choice? These questions recurred repeatedly during the debate. [50]

After long negotiations, it was agreed that 34 constitutional principles would form the basis of the final constitution, compliance with which the Constitutional Court had to certify. As far as rights were concerned, the most general principle was that, 'Everyone shall enjoy all universally accepted fundamental rights, freedoms and civil liberties' (II). Racial, gender and other forms of discriminations were to be prohibited and the state was to promote racial and gender equality and national unity (III). The right to equality was strongly endorsed, 'between men and women and people of all races' (I). Equality was seen positively as including 'laws, programmes or activities that have as their object the amelioration of the conditions of the disadvantaged, including those disadvantaged on the grounds of race, colour or gender' (V). Two principles recognised diversity. Principle XI stated, 'The diversity of language and culture shall be acknowledged and protected, and conditions for their promotion shall be encouraged'. Principle XIII recognised the institution, status and role of traditional leadership, according to indigenous law, and the application of indigenous law, subject to the Constitution. Diversity was also facilitated by the recognition of the 'collective rights of self-determination in forming, joining and maintaining organs of civil society, including linguistic, cultural and religious associations . . . on the basis of non-discrimination and free association' (XII) and in the provision for a system of provincial government (XVIII–XXII). These principles were translated first in the interim constitution (1994) and then entrenched in the final constitution (1996). This task was likewise accomplished only with a careful balancing of interests.

As with other constitutions discussed in this chapter, the orientation regarding rights can be gleaned from the rules about interpretation. Section 7 says that the Bill of Rights is 'a cornerstone of democracy' and 'enshrines the rights of all people in our country and affirms the democratic values of human dignity, equality and freedom'. The application of the duties under the Bill of Rights extends to private parties in suitable cases; the compromise on this point is captured in the words that a provision binds 'natural and juristic persons if, and to the extent that, it is applicable, taking into account the nature of the right and

[50] Hugh Corder and Lournes Du Plessis, *Understanding South Africa's Transitional Bill of Rights* (Cape Town, Juta, 1994) 56–57.

of any duty imposed by the right' (section 8). Section 39 enjoins courts in the interpretation of rights to 'promote the values that underlie an open and democratic society based on human dignity, equality and freedom' and these principles also provide the parameters for the limitation of rights (section 36). Section 39 also requires courts to consider international law and permits them to consider foreign law. The same article requires the courts to suffuse other laws they interpret with the 'spirit, purport, and objects' of the Bill of Rights. The broad mandate of rights and their international provenance are thus acknowledged.

i. Equality and Social Justice

I turn now to more specific rights. The right to equality, prohibiting discrimination on various grounds, also includes in its definition 'full and equal enjoyment of all rights and freedoms', and authorises 'legislative, and other measures designed to protect or advance persons, or categories of persons, disadvantaged by unfair discrimination'. Unfair discrimination by private persons is also prohibited (section 9). This approach to social justice is reinforced by social and economic rights – housing (section 26); health, food, water and social security (section 27); education (section 29) and employment-related rights (sections 22 and 23). The balancing of interests is perhaps nowhere more clearly provided than in relation to property. The relevant section (section 25) begins with the general principle: property can only be appropriated for a public purpose or in the public interest, and subject to compensation. The principle for compensation is not specified. Guidelines are given for 'the amount, timing, and manner of payment' of compensation: these must be just and equitable, 'reflecting an equitable balance between the public interest and the interests of those effected', having regard to a number of factors, including the current use of the property and the history of the acquisition and use of property. Public interest justifying acquisition of property includes 'the nation's commitment to land reform, and to reforms to bring about equitable access to all South Africa's natural resources'. The state has to take measures to 'foster conditions which enable citizens to gain access to land on an equitable basis'. Persons or groups whose land was taken away or title rendered insecure due to past racially discriminatory policies are entitled to compensation or redress.

ii. Cultural Rights

Finally I turn to provisions on culture. Everyone is assured the right to use the language and to participate in the cultural life of their choice, consistently with the Bill of Rights (section 30). Similar consistency is required for the right of persons belonging to a cultural, religious or linguistic community in conjunction with others to 'enjoy their culture, practise their religion and use their language and to form associations for this purpose' (section 31). The Constitution also provides for the creation of a Commission for the Promotion and Protection of the Rights of Cultural, Religious and Linguistic Communities, a gesture towards traditional leaders, and towards some of the more right-wing white sections of the population (section 185). The institution, status and role of traditional leadership, according to customary law, are recognised subject to the Constitution, and the application of customary law is permitted so long as it is consistent with the Constitution and relevant legislation (section 211). It is thus clear that the exercise of cultural rights is always subject to the general norms of the Constitution, including those of human rights. In so far as customary law is concerned, this represents a significant victory for African women, whose position under such law is generally inferior to that of men.

V. CONCLUSION

In all these countries, there were serious ethnic conflicts or competing claims. It might have been possible to deal with them through negotiations and compromises. However, at least in South Africa and Fiji, where the conflict was intense and a clear framework for the settlement of competing claims was hard to establish, the process would have been protracted, and even then, might not have succeeded. In all the cases, the relevance of human rights to the construction of the state was acknowledged. In South Africa and Fiji a prior agreement on this question was a prerequisite to the start of negotiations on other matters. It was in Fiji that there was perhaps the greatest initial resistance (by the indigenous Fijians) to accepting rights as the framework. The rights framework facilitated the application of norms that enjoyed international and some domestic legitimacy and was sufficiently malleable to provide broadly satisfactory outcomes.

The contents and orientation of rights were drawn from external sources: in India's case from foreign national precedents (the Universal Declaration of Human Rights had just been adopted), but in other instances from international instruments. A comparison of precedents used in India (1947) and Fiji (1995) provide insights that speak to the concerns of universality. At the time of the Indian independence, there was no internationally accepted body of norms or procedures. Nor was there a consensus that constitutions had to include a bill of rights. By the 1990s there was both a substantial body of internationally negotiated norms *and* a consensus that they had to be implemented in national constitutional systems. Likewise, between the Canadian Bill of Rights (1960) and the Charter (1982) a certain distance had been travelled in the use of international norms. In this way the international regime of human rights can help to build a presumption of 'universality' into the negotiating process.

'Culture' has nowhere been the salient element determining attitudes to rights. It has been important in Fiji, Canada and South Africa – but in different ways. Quebeckers do not object to the philosophical basis of rights (indeed they could hardly object to an instrument which draws its inspiration from the

French Revolution), but see their 'universalising' tendency as a threat to the survival of their culture (closely connected with language). In that sense, it can be seen as a defensive reaction. In Fiji, on the other hand, rights were presented as antithetical to underlying values of indigenous social and political organisation. 'Culture' was very broadly defined. It was used in an aggressive rather than a defensive way – as justifying claims to Fijian 'paramountcy', which implied a wide degree of political and economic supremacy which had little to do with culture. Using human rights as a framework helped to pare down but not eliminate this issue. Demands by South Africa's traditional leaders and the Inkatha Party were based on culture, and the ability of the latter to derail the transition to democracy gave its demands an importance that would otherwise have had little traction. It was perhaps in the stance of the Canadian aboriginals that 'culture' was most crucial. It was central to their demands of autonomy, the settlement of outstanding claims and the preservation of their internal social organisation. It was also the hardest case of the accommodation of cultural claims within the general framework of the Charter. The accommodation was secured through wide exclusions from the Charter rather than through forms of balancing, as in other instances discussed in this chapter.

With the exception of the Canadian first nations, the proponents of the cultural approach to rights were not necessarily concerned about the general welfare of their community's cultural traditions. They were more concerned about the power they obtain from espousing those traditions. It is widely recognised that Quebec's separatist politics were mobilised by young francophone professionals who found it difficult to compete with the more established English-speaking professionals. The manipulation of 'tradition' by the Inkatha Party is well documented. Fijian military and politicians who justified the *coup* were accused of similar manipulations by a variety of respectable commentators.

Difficult questions arise if the culture of a group can only be maintained at the expense of the rights of another community, or via the agency of the state. Cultural relativism in a homogenous community (where the issue is purely between local values and international standards) is less problematic than in a multicultural state, where it can be divisive, leading to the subordination of one community. Thus the debate about relativism in Tonga or Samoa (both homogenous Polynesian societies) is of a different dimension than in Fiji. The aboriginal claims in Canada are easier to negotiate because for the greater part, aboriginal peoples live in reservations where contact with other communities is minimal.

In my view, the more interesting issues arose when the question of the relationship of rights to culture was debated *within* the cultural community itself. In most of the cases women opposed the claims of the 'traditionalists', as with the first nations in Canada, the Muslims in India with regard to the application of the *sharia*, and the traditional leaders in South Africa. Hindus in India were divided over reforms of Hindu law, which followed from the mandate to codify and unify personal laws. More generally, significant numbers within the cultural community were anxious to build a more inclusive community instead of isolating their own community from the mainstream. Such divisions provided opportunities for using rights to interrogate culture, and gave interesting insights into the nature of rights. In no case are rights seen merely as protections against the state. They are instruments for the distribution of resources; a basis for identity; linked to hegemony; and to a social vision of society. Rights are not necessary deeply held values, but a mode of discourse, of advancing and justifying claims. Thus important sectors of the white community in South Africa opt for group rights when it comes to autonomy, but settle for individual rights when it comes to economic rights.

Groups present their claims in different paradigms of rights: individual versus group; equality versus preference; uniformity versus group identity. In Fiji, for example, the conflict between the two communities is played out in the competing currencies of human rights. These case studies also undermine the myth that those who push for universalism are westerners and those who oppose it are easterners.

Constitutional settlements in multi-ethnic societies require the balancing of interests. This balancing is particularly important if there are prior, existing disparities of economic, social or political resources, and particularly if these disparities are the result of state policies. Achieving this balancing has various implications for the regime of rights. Firstly, it involves the recognition of corporate identities as bearer of rights (which issue, however, remains deeply controversial, as does the scope of the recognition). It is in that sense that one can talk of collective rights. However, we also find individual rights which are connected to group membership. Most rights of affirmative action in India perhaps fall into this category.

Secondly, there cannot be, in relation to most rights, a notion of absolutism; there must be an acceptance of qualifications on rights.

Thirdly, this 'exercise of qualification' forces constitution-makers to understand and define the core of the rights concerned.

Fourthly, selecting the appropriate formulation and protection of social, economic and cultural rights, and thus emphasising the 'positive duties' of the state, is often fundamental to a settlement, both to acknowledge the importance of culture and the redress of ethnic inequalities. This is perhaps less so in Canada, where the Charter is more oriented towards civil and political rights, but there too problems associated with first nations are dealt with through redistribution. Thus for this (and other reasons of 'ethnic' management) there arises the necessity for an activist state.

Finally, since inter-ethnic relations are so crucial to an enduring settlement and past history may have been marked by discrimination or exploitation, a substantial part of the regime of rights has to be made binding on private parties.

The balancing of competing interests is also done by courts. They make use of limitation clauses; rules of interpretation which require emphasis on prescribed values; setting the scope for 'positive' rights (property or merit versus affirmative action and other forms of justice); juxtaposition of rights with directive principles (particularly in India); and overcoming these dichotomies by new conceptualisation, eg, 'equality' defined in substantive terms as in India and South Africa. A particular consequence of using the framework and language of rights and juridical techniques is the increase in the power and responsibility of the judiciary for the settlement of claims and disputes. It then falls ultimately to the courts to do the balancing of interests and rights that is an essential part of using the human rights framework. They may represent a different understanding of the permissible limits of the balance, and may come into conflict with determinations by the legislature or the executive. This was the Indian experience with the courts on the primacy of property rights over social rights. On the other hand, vesting the final authority in courts means that close attention is paid to the framework of rights, and that the balance between the core of the right and its modification is done in a reasoned and principled way. Usually the prestige of the courts helps also to bring the dispute to some resolution, although the Indian experience with *Shah Bano* suggests that judicial decisions can themselves be a source of conflict.

On the more general question of universalism and relativism, it is not easy to generalise. It cannot, for example, be said that bills of rights have a universalising and homogenising tendency; by recognising languages and religions, and by affirmative policies, they may in fact solidify separate identities. On the other hand, there may be some necessity for a measure of universalism of rights to transcend sectional claims for national cohesion. Simple polarities, universalism versus particularism, secular versus religious, tradition versus modernity, are not helpful; a large measure of ambiguity is necessary for the accommodations that must be made. Consequently most bills of rights are Janus faced (looking in the direction of both liberalism and collective identities). What is involved in these arrangements is not an outright rejection of either universalism or relativism; but an acknowledgment of the importance of each, and a search for a suitable balance, using for the most part the language and parameters of rights.

Part II

Judicial Independence and Empowerment

5

Independent or Dependent? Constitutional Courts in Divided Societies

SUJIT CHOUDHRY AND RICHARD STACEY

I. INTRODUCTION: JUDICIAL INDEPENDENCE IN DIVIDED SOCIETIES

WHY IS A bill of rights now regarded as an indispensable feature of a liberal democratic constitutional order, especially in an ethnically divided society emerging from protracted and often violent conflict? There are two answers to this question. On one view, the function is to arm ethnic minorities with the legal means to check the abuse of public power. In post-conflict settings, the breakdown of the previous constitutional order may have been accompanied by widespread violations of human rights, especially with respect to ethnic minorities. Indeed, the failure of the previous regime to protect human rights may have been a reason for ethnic minorities to impugn the legitimacy of, and to withdraw support from, the previous constitutional order. A post-conflict constitutional settlement includes a bill of rights, both to acknowledge the precise character of past wrongs and to serve as a credible commitment to ensure such abuses do not occur in the future. A bill of rights provides incentives to parties to put aside violence and to settle their political disagreements peacefully through the institutions of the new constitutional order operating according to the rule of law. Call this the *regulative* conception of a bill of rights. But, on another view, the function of a bill of rights is to constitute the very *demos* that it constrains. A bill of rights calls upon citizens to abstract away from group markers, like race, religion, ethnicity and language, which previously served as the grounds for political identity and political division. Instead, a bill of rights encodes a vision of political community built around citizens who are equal bearers of constitutional rights – a constitutional patriotism or civic nationalism – whose political membership is unmediated by group identity. Thus, a bill of rights is an instrument of nation-building that is meant to transform the very self-understanding of citizens. It dissolves and privatises the political salience of ethnic difference, and replaces it with a transcendent form of political identification. This is the *constitutive* function of bills of rights.

One of us has expressed scepticism on the capacity of bills of rights to do all the work that is expected of them in ethnically divided societies and we will not rehearse those arguments here.[1] On this occasion, we explore a related but neglected theme – the design of the apex court charged with the ultimate responsibility of interpreting a constitutional rights-protecting instrument. In divided societies – particularly in post-conflicting settings – there are two constitutional agendas regarding the design of the apex court charged with interpreting the bill of rights. On the one hand, alongside the creation of a bill of rights, there are demands for judicial independence for all courts, up to and including the apex court itself. While judicial independence is open to many interpretations, a core meaning is the idea that courts must enjoy independence from the other branches of government that wield political power. Owen Fiss has usefully termed this 'political insularity'.[2]

A central justification for judicial independence is that it flows from the very idea of a bill of rights. In ethnically divided societies, a bill of rights – to the extent that it is able to control the state – protects ethnic minorities from the tyranny of an ethnic majority. Independent courts that are free from the control of the ethnic majority are perceived as providing an important – perhaps indispensable – institutional mechanism for making a bill of rights a credible commitment to minorities. Indeed, if the breakdown of the previous constitutional order entailed not just the widespread abuse of human rights, but also the breakdown in the machinery of human rights enforcement, the demand for independent courts is that much stronger. The logic of a commitment to judicial independence manifests itself in a number of aspects of the design of the apex court – for example, in an appointments process that seeks to insulate the court from majoritarian capture. But in some divided societies there is an attempt to institutionalise ethnic divisions in the design of the apex court itself. In some post-conflict contexts there are measures to ensure that the major ethnic groups are institutionally empowered to choose a proportion of the justices, and consequently, that distinct ethnic communities are represented on apex judicial institutions.

Although they share the goal of protecting ethnic minorities, these two constitutional agendas are deeply in tension. The first seeks to render courts

[1] S Choudhry, 'Bills of Rights as Instruments of Nation-Building in Multinational States: the Canadian *Charter* and Quebec Nationalism' in J Kelly and C Manfredi (eds), *Contested Constitutionalism: Reflections on the Charter of Rights and Freedoms* (Vancouver, University of British Columbia Press, 2009) 233; S Choudhry, 'Not a New Constitutional Court: The Canadian *Charter*, the Supreme Court and Quebec Nationalism' in P Pasquino and F Billi (eds), *The Political Origins of Constitutional Courts: Italy, Germany, France, Poland, Canada, United Kingdom* (Rome, Adriano Olivetti Foundation, 2009) 39; and S Choudhry, 'After the Rights Revolution: Bills of Rights in the Post-Conflict State' (2010) 6 *Annual Review of Law and Social Science* 301.

[2] O Fiss, 'The Right Degree of Independence' in Irwin P Stotzky (ed), *Transition to Democracy in Latin America: The Role of the Judiciary* (Westview Press, Boulder, 1993) 55, 56.

independent of political actors. The second appears to seek precisely the opposite: to ensure that individual judges are in effect representatives of particular ethnic groups. For minority groups that demand the institutionalisation of ethnic difference in the design of the court, the expectation is that judges appointed by and/or drawn from the minority community would act to protect minority interests. But the corollary is that judges appointed by an ethnic majority would likewise act to further the majority's interests. Instead of a court appealing to impartial standards of justice that transcend group divides, the image that emerges is one of a court whose very design is part of the ethnic politics of the state. The implications for the interpretation of a bill of rights may be serious. Disagreements are unavoidable in the interpretation of bills of rights and frequently divide an apex court. But if those interpretive disagreements map onto ethnic divisions within the court, they pose the risk of drawing the bill of rights into ethnic politics, thereby undermining both the regulative and constitutive function of bills of rights.

In short, the constitutional politics of the design of apex courts in divided societies warrants careful examination, but this is a topic that has been neglected in the vast literature on constitutional design in divided societies. In this chapter, we explore the demands for ethnic representation on courts in divided societies. With respect to the cases we discuss in this chapter – Bosnia and Herzegovina and Canada (and some others we mention in less detail) – we describe and evaluate a number of mechanisms by which the imperative of representation might be pursued.

II. TWO KINDS OF JUDICIAL POLITICS

The politics of the design of apex courts in deeply divided societies is the product of the interaction of two kinds of judicial politics: the politics of judicial independence and the politics of constitutional interpretation.

Over the past decade, a large literature has addressed the emergence and persistence of judicial independence. As Matt Stephenson has usefully explained,[3] the claim that courts are independent and check government power appears to imply 'that the court is preventing the government from doing something that it would otherwise like to do', when even the most independent of courts are dependent on governments for financial support and the enforcement of their judgments. So the real question is '[w]hy . . . would the government accept the limits imposed by a truly independent court? Why would people with money and guns ever submit to people armed only with gavels?'[4] For constitutional scholars, the answer has resided in the various constitutional safeguards associated with judicial independence, which has traditionally encompassed security

[3] Matthew C Stephenson, '"When the Devil Turns . . .": The Political Foundations of Judicial Independence' (2003) 32 *Journal of Legal Studies* 59.

[4] ibid 60.

of tenure, financial security and administrative independence, and now may extend to the design of the judicial appointments process. Indeed, this legalist premise underlies the whole practice of constitutional design and expert advice in post-conflict constitutional processes, as well as the framing of the international declarations that inform these processes.

However, even the most rigid constitutional guarantees of judicial independence cannot stand in the way of a government determined to capture the courts. Indeed, these guarantees may themselves be endogenous, products of the same political factors that give rise to judicial independence. The answer to the puzzle of judicial independence is to be found, not in theories of judicial independence, but rather, in the notion of political competition. Where there are regular elections and party alternation, political parties that face the future risk of electoral loss will create independent courts to provide them with the institutional resources to check government power when they are in opposition. Parties are willing to fetter their decision-making while in office in exchange for the insurance provided by courts when they lose office. Conversely, if a party is politically dominant and does not fear electoral loss, it will likely prevent the rise of independent courts through its power of appointment.[5] Moreover, similar assessment of the prospects of future electoral success also frames constitutional choices regarding the appointment mechanism, jurisdiction and composition of the court.[6]

This line of analysis has not yet been extended to ethnically divided societies. This is surprising; it has long been recognised that in ethnically divided societies normal political competition is absent because of the character of political cleavages.[7] In societies that are not ethnically divided, political and ethnic cleavages are cross-cutting, which promotes political moderation and blunts partisan divisions. In addition, this account of political cleavages is closely tied to the case for a competitive model of democratic politics. It assumes that politics is characterised by shifting coalitions and majorities, that political parties will compete for median voters at the centre of the spectrum and, hence, that political competition creates pressures toward moderation. In addition, there is no permanent exclusion of any segment of society from political power, encouraging political losers to accept their loss in the hopes that they will win another day. Not one of these assumptions holds for ethnically divided societies. In such cases, cleavages are mutually reinforcing, not cross-cutting, with ethnic division mapping onto political division and political competition not producing moderation, but immoderation. The danger is of a majority dictatorship in democratic form that will not have the same incentives to check the abuse of public

[5] MJ Ramseyer, 'The Puzzling (In)Dependence of Courts: A Comparative Approach' (1994) 23 *Journal of Legal Studies* 721.

[6] T Ginsburg, *Judicial Review in New Democracies: Constitutional Courts in Asian Cases* (New York, Cambridge University Press, 2003).

[7] S Choudhry, 'Bridging Comparative Politics and Comparative Constitutional Law: Constitutional Design for Divided Societies' in S Choudhry (ed), *Constitutional Design for Divided Societies: Integration or Accommodation?* (Oxford, Oxford University Press, 2008).

power produced by political competition. Ethnic minorities, who are persistent losers with no prospect of wielding political power, would therefore have an incentive to exit politics and turn to violence.

The implications of the absence of normal political competition has been explored for a wide range of issues in constitutional design in divided societies such as electoral system design, the structure of and relationship between the executive and the legislature, federalism[8] and legal pluralism. By contrast, courts (and bills of rights) have attracted no sustained analysis, despite the necessary implication that constitutional arrangements would be enforced by judicial review. Indeed, Lijphart's *Democracy in Plural Societies*[9]and Horowitz's *Ethnic Groups in Conflict*[10] – the two classic texts in the field – barely mention courts.[11]

How would the absence of normal political competition in ethnically divided societies shape the constitutional politics of apex court design? Dominant ethnic majorities are merely a subset of the larger problem of political domination and the absence of political competition. Majority ethnic groups (who do not face the prospect of losing power) will attempt to capture courts and undermine judicial independence or prevent the establishment of independent courts in the first place. But there is another issue that has not been explored – how ethnic minorities, who will be perpetual political minorities, will address the issue of apex courts. The implicit assumption in the literature on judicial independence is that perpetual political minorities simply have no ability to set the constitutional agenda on this issue. But the fact that ethnic minorities can shape other dimensions of constitutional design in divided societies suggests that the structure of politics may likewise afford opportunities for them to do so with respect to courts.

There are two ideal-type scenarios here. First, in cases of divided societies emerging from prolonged, violent conflict, the design of the apex court charged with interpreting the post-conflict constitutional settlement could be an issue on the negotiation agenda. The leverage possessed by ethnic minorities would be the threat of a return to violence. Bosnia, Kosovo and Cyprus are examples of this scenario. The second scenario is that of a deeply divided but consolidated democracy in which there is no history of violent conflict or any realistic prospect of a descent into violence. Nonetheless, in at least one subset of these kinds of divided societies – plurinational places – national minorities have

[8] S Choudhry and N Hume 'Federalism, Secession & Devolution: From Classical to Post-Conflict Federalism' in T Ginsburg and R Dixon (eds), *Research Handbook on Comparative Constitutional Law* (Edward Elgar Publishing, forthcoming 2011).

[9] A Lijphart, *Democracy in Plural Societies: A Comparative Exploration* (New Haven, Yale University Press, 1977).

[10] D Horowitz, *Ethnic Groups in Conflict* (Berkeley, University of California Press, 1985).

[11] Where Lijphart does discuss judicial review in a chapter in *Patterns of Democracy: Government Forms and Performance in thirty-six Countries* (New Haven, Yale University Press, 1999), he does so in order to investigate the relationship between constitutional rigidity (ie, the ease of constitutional amendment) and the institutional nature of judicial review. He does not consider judicial review in the context of divided societies.

successfully mobilised through democratic politics to achieve the reconfiguration of these states from unitary mononational entities to plurinational states whose institutions reflect the existence of multiple nations and nationalisms. Although the focus of the literature on constitutional design in plurinational places has been federalism and executive power-sharing, the design of the apex court could be part of this constitutional agenda. Examples include Canada, Spain and Belgium.

What would the demand of minority ethnic groups be? One possible strategic objective would be to gain some control over the various features of the design of apex courts. An obvious mechanism for this end would be the *appointments* process, for example, through granting the authority to federal sub-units controlled by ethnic minorities to appoint a number of judges, through super-majority or concurrent majority requirements that empower minority legislators, or through minority control over nominations (eg, the exclusive power to generate shortlists). A closely related, but distinct issue would be the *composition* of the court. Certain seats could be designated for judges drawn from ethnic minorities, or all seats could be designated for members of different ethnic groups. Yet another aspect of design would be the judges' *legal expertise*. In bijural jurisdictions, such as Canada and the United Kingdom, a certain number of seats on the apex court may be set aside for judges trained in the component legal traditions where that tradition is tied to questions of minority ethnic identity. Finally, there are the *decision-rules* of the apex court. A court may constitute special panels of subsets of judges, to hear cases of special interest to ethnic minorities. These panels would contain a disproportionate number of judges appointed by minority ethnic communities, and/or ethnic minority judges. Alternatively, a court may require super-majority or concurrent majority to reach decisions, either on all issues or those of special concern to ethnic minorities.

Now this is not the only option on the table. The other would be for minorities to demand independent courts – for example, through the creation of a judicial services commission that buffers appointments from political influence. So what would determine an ethnic minority's constitutional priorities on the design of the apex court? Demography and relative political power may rule out the institutionalisation of ethnic identity in the apex court. But even in cases where ethnic minorities had sufficient political resources to choose either approach, the very nature of constitutional interpretation in divided societies may drive them toward the institutionalisation of ethnic difference. To understand why, we need to turn to the second kind of judicial politics, the politics of constitutional interpretation.

Recent comparative research on constitutional adjudication has confirmed what scholars of judicial politics have long presupposed – that formal sources of law rarely dictate definitive outcomes to questions of constitutional interpretation. However, it does not follow that constitutional reasoning is unconstrained. As Jeff Goldsworthy has recently argued, courts across jurisdictions rely on a shared set of interpretive methods in constitutional interpretation.[12] These include textual (including intra-textual methods), originalist (both original intent and original meaning), teleological or purposive, doctrinal or precedent-based, structuralist (drawing inferences from a single provision or sets of related provisions), prudential, and ethical or moral approaches to constructing constitutional provisions. Each national constitutional tradition differs in the relative emphasis and interrelationship they accord to those methods. The methodological matrix of a national constitutional tradition defines an argumentative space within which acceptable forms of constitutional argument occur.

Within a given constitutional tradition, a particular constitutional outcome may be demanded by the combination of local sources and by the methodological distinctiveness of that tradition. But in most cases, those contingent features of a constitutional tradition merely rule out, and do not require, specific constitutional decisions. Rather, they create an argumentative space within which a tradition is open to elaboration, reinterpretation, contestation and change. These spaces provide openings for competing ideologies to shape and direct constitutional interpretation. For example, clauses entrenching specific rights (eg, the right to equality) are framed abstractly, and incorporate principles of political morality by reference. They therefore invite courts to articulate an underlying theory of the right in question and to craft constitutional doctrine to implement that theory. Judges may rely on competing theories of the right in question to the extent permitted by a national constitutional tradition. Interpretive stances on the correct interpretation of particular provisions may cluster together and be united by a shared ideological commitment – for example, to an egalitarian or libertarian political morality – that organises, unites and justifies judgments in particular cases.

In divided societies, the design of the constitution may create an additional set of issues where judicial ideology can shape constitutional interpretation. This is because these constitutions may contain competing logics. On the one hand, these constitutions may institutionalise ethnic identity in the very design of federalism, the electoral system, the legislature, the political executive, etc. On the other hand, they almost invariably contain a bill of rights according to which individuals hold rights irrespective of their ethnic identity. Moreover, many of these rights are hostile to the institutionalisation of ethnic difference. Rights to equality and non-discrimination presumptively prohibit the distribution of rights and opportunities on the basis of ethnic identity – for example, through rules governing preferential treatment in public sector employment, the receipt of public services or in land ownership. A right to mobility renders constitutionally suspect a range of government policies designed to maintain the ethnic character of specific regions by discouraging migration by members of

[12] J Goldsworthy, 'Introduction' in J Goldsworthy (ed), *Interpreting Constitutions: A Comparative Study* (New York, Oxford University Press, 2007).

other ethnic groups. Moreover, the guarantee of rights on equal terms (eg, the right to vote and hold public office, the right to property) presumptively forbids the unequal enjoyment of the interests protected by those rights, including on the basis of ethnicity.

Now to be sure, almost every right in contemporary bills of rights is subject to reasonable limitations to be assessed on the basis of some test of proportionality. But as the well-known decision of the European Court of Human Rights in *Mathieu-Mohin and Clerfayt v Belgium*[13] illustrates, all this does is reframe the problem. The case turned on whether limitations on European Convention voting rights, imposed by Belgian statute, could be justified by the objectives of political accommodation and linguistic power-sharing, and whether those limits were proportional to the objectives they were intended to achieve. Article 3 of Protocol 1 of the European Convention on Human Rights obliges states parties to hold regular and fair elections that ensure the 'free expression of the opinion of the people in the choice of the legislature'. In considering the implications of this provision, the Court noted that it is not an absolute right and that 'there is room for implied limitations' in the wording of the Convention.[14] A majority of the Court concluded that 'any electoral system must be assessed in the light of the political evolution of the country concerned'.[15]As the aim of the Belgian electoral legislation was to 'defuse language disputes in the country', the majority held that the limitation of voting rights was 'not a disproportionate limitation such as would thwart "the free expression of the people".'[16]

The dissenting minority disagreed, arguing that the electoral system 'should be assessed on its own merits',[17] and that the particular national circumstances which motivate the design of an electoral system should never be allowed to justify violations of rights. The broader lesson of *Mathieu-Mohin* is that proportionality analysis, in principle, provides the state with the legal opening to invoke the constitutionalisation of ethnic difference as the constitutional underpinning for specific measures that limit individual rights. At the end of the day, it falls to judges of the apex court to sort out this clash between conflicting constitutional logics, and to determine which one has priority.

Here is the link between the two kinds of judicial politics. These disputes over how to resolve the conflict between competing constitutional agendas will often divide ethnic groups within a divided society who may have different interests on the issue in question. Moreover, those differences in interest may be nested in deeper disputes over the very character and identity of the state. So the reason that ethnic minorities might seek to institutionalise ethnic difference on a court

[13] *Mathieu-Mohin and Clerfayt v Belgium,* series A no 113 (1987).

[14] ibid para 52.

[15] ibid para 54.

[16] ibid para 57.

[17] ibid (joint dissenting judgment of Judges Cremona, Binschedler-Robert, Bernhardt, Spielmann and Valticos) at 18.

is not to transform judges into agents to serve the narrow political agendas of the ethnic minority politicians who appointed them, but to ensure those judges bring to bear on constitutional adjudication an interpretive agenda that is congenial to the protection of minority interests, at least in cases where the clash between bills of rights and the constitutionalisation of ethnic difference is at stake.

We explore these questions in the rest of the piece through three case studies, two representing both of the ideal-type scenarios we have described (Canada and Bosnia), and a third case (Germany) offering a different perspective on apex-court design.

III. THREE CASES

A. Post-transition Divided Societies: Bosnia and Herzegovina

The Republic of Bosnia and Herzegovina (hereafter Bosnia) emerged from the break-up of the Socialist Republic of Yugoslavia in the early 1990s. Three major ethnic groups – Muslim Bosniacs, Orthodox Christian Serbs and Roman Catholic Croats – inhabit the country. Between 1991 and 1995 the area was riven by civil war and ethnic cleansing of Bosniacs and Croats by Serbs in the entity now known as Republika Srpska and the reverse in the territory now known as the Federation of Bosnia and Herzegovina.[18] The constitutional reconstruction of the country has been driven by two competing agendas. In the wake of a war fought to secure ethno-national self-determination, the protection and preservation of ethno-national identity and autonomy are important foundations of the new political arrangement.[19] At the same time, this reconstruction attempts to protect individual rights of the kind enshrined in the European Convention on Human Rights.

The tension between these two agendas plays out in the very pages of the Bosnian Constitution, which commits the country both to collective rights and ethno-national autonomy within a federal state, as well as to individual civil and political rights. Article II(2) of the Constitution of Bosnia, for example, provides that the 'rights and freedoms set forth in the European Convention for

[18] NL Cigar, *Genocide in Bosnia: The Policy of 'Ethnic Cleaning'* (College Station, Texas A&M University Press, 1996); Laura Silber and Alan Little, *The Death of Yugoslavia* (London, Penguin, 1995); and David Feldman, 'Renaming Cities in Bosnia and Herzegovina' (2005) 3 *International Journal of Constitutional Law* 649, 650.

[19] See David Feldman's contribution to this collection. See also RC Slye, 'The Dayton Peace Agreement: Constitutionalism and Ethnicity' (1996) 21 *Yale Law Journal* 459, 460; RM Hayden, 'The Continuing Reinvention of the Square Wheel: The Proposed 2009 Amendments to the Bosnian Constitution' (2011) 58 *Problems of Post-Communism* 3, 4, 12; AM Mansfield, 'Ethnic but Equal: The Quest for a New Democratic Order in Bosnia and Herzegovina' (2003) 103 *Columbia Law Review* 2052, 2056; and EM Cousens, 'Making Peace in Bosnia Work' (1997) 30 *Cornell International Law Journal* 789.

the Protection of Human Rights and Fundamental Freedoms and its Protocols shall apply directly in Bosnia and Herzegovina [and] shall have priority over all other law'.[20] The Constitution includes a domestic bill of rights, with a list of individual rights enumerated in Articles II(3)(a) through to (m). At the same time, the political structure set up by the Constitution turns on ethnic and group identity and operationalises ethnic identity in the processes of government. While Bosnia's Constitutional Court has been influential in charting a course through these opposing currents, the limits of its ability to do so have become apparent, in part because ethnic difference has been constitutionalised in the appointments process to the court.

i. Bosnia's Consociational Peace Deal

The 1996 General Framework Agreement for Peace in Bosnia and Herzegovina, which ended conflict and restored political stability to the region, was negotiated and signed at Dayton, Ohio.[21] The Dayton Accords constitute Bosnia as a confederation of two autonomous 'constituent entities', the Federation of Bosnia and Herzegovina and the Republika Srpska. The Federation of Bosnia and Herzegovina itself distributes responsibilities between cantons and the Federation's central government,[22] making Bosnia a 'two-layer' federation. The Constitution establishes a three-member federal presidency representing each ethnic group and a bicameral legislature with representation guaranteed for each ethnic group.[23] The Constitution requires that of the 42 members elected to the House of Representatives, Bosnia's lower chamber, two-thirds are elected from the Federation of Bosnia and Herzegovina and one third from the Republika Srpska. The Election Act sets up a complicated system of mixed proportional representation and compensatory mandates based on cantonal divisions, designed to ensure more or less equal representation of Bosniacs and Croats in the House.[24] The 15 members of the upper chamber, the House of Peoples, include five representatives of each ethnic group delegated by the subnational legislative caucuses of the respective constituent peoples. The formal

[20] Annex I to the Constitution of Bosnia lists a number of additional international human rights agreements to be applied in Bosnia. They include the International Convention on the Elimination of all Forms of Racial Discrimination, the International Covenant on Civil and Political Rights and the International Covenant on Economic, Social and Cultural Rights. For a discussion of the status of international law in Bosnia, see Z Paji , 'A Critical Appraisal of Human Rights Provisions of the Dayton Constitution of Bosnia and Herzegovina' (1998) 20 *Human Rights Quarterly* 125.

[21] These documents are available through the website of the Office of the High Representative (OHR) at www.ohr.int/dpa/default.asp?content_id=380. The OHR is a position created under the Dayton Accords to oversee the implementation of the agreements. The OHR serves also as the European Special Representative to Bosnia and Herzegovina.

[22] Constitution of the Federation of Bosnia and Herzegovina, Official Gazette, 1/94, 13/97, 16/02, 22/02, 52/02, 60/02, 18/03, 63/03, available online from the OHR website at www.ohr.int/ohr-dept/legal/oth-legist/doc/fbih-constitution.doc, pt III and pt V.

[23] Articles V and IV of the Constitution of Bosnia and Herzegovina, 1995.

[24] Election Act, 2001, Official Gazette of Bosnia and Herzegovina, 23/01, 07/02, 09/02, 20/02.

distribution of power mirrors the political reality that has produced a tripartite partition along ethnic lines in every election since 1910.[25]

Against this ethno-political background, Bosnia's consociational power arrangements establish a system of checks and balances weighted according to ethnicity. All federal legislation must be approved by both chambers, and special majority voting procedures and quorum requirements ensure that decisions cannot be taken without the support of at least one-third of each of the representatives of each constituent people in the lower chamber, or without the participation of at least three out of five of the representatives of each constituent people in the upper chamber.[26] Further, the Constitution creates express veto points for members of the presidency and ethnic communities in the federal House of Representatives in respect of measures 'destructive of a vital interest of the Bosniac, Croat or Serb people'.[27]

The appointment procedure for the Bosnian Constitutional Court follows this consociational logic. Article VI (1) of the Constitution provides that four members of the Court will be appointed by the House of Representatives of the Federation of Bosnia and Herzegovina, and two members by the National Assembly of the Republika Srpska. The remaining three members are appointed by the European Court of Human Rights on the advice of the federal presidency and cannot be citizens of Bosnia or of any neighbouring state. The six judges selected by the constituent entities are not required to be of any particular ethnic background. In practice, however, these six positions on the Court have, since its inception, been filled by two Serbian judges, two Bosniac judges and two Croat judges.[28]

ii. Impact and Performance of the Court and its Judges

Two decisions of the Bosnian Constitutional Court, along with one that reached the European Court of Human Rights, stand out for exemplifying the implications of the Court's power for ethnic nationalism. In turn, these decisions help to explain the perceived importance of ethnic representation on the Court.

a) The *Constituent Peoples* Decision

The *Constituent Peoples* decision of 2000 declared provisions of both constituent entities' constitutions to be incompatible with the Constitution of Bosnia

[25] RM Hayden, 'Moral Vision and Impaired insight: The Imagining of Other Peoples' Communities in Bosnia' (2007) 48 *Current Anthropology* 105; and Hayden, 'The Continuing Reinvention' (n 19) 6. See also S Sebastian, 'Leaving Dayton Behind: Constitutional Reform in Bosnia and Herzegovina' Working Paper 46, November 2007 (*Fundacion para Relaciones Internacionales y el Dialogo Exterior*), 2–3 and N Caspersen, 'Good Fences make Good Neighbours? A Comparison of Conflict-Regulation Strategies in Postwar Bosnia' (2004) 41 *Journal of Peace Research* 569, 575–80.

[26] These requirements are set out in the Constitution at art IV(3)(c) and (d). See also Hayden, 'The Continuing Reinvention' (n 19) 7.

[27] Articles V(2)(d) and IV(3)(e).

[28] Feldman, 'Renaming Cities' (n 8) 655.

for identifying certain ethnic groups as the 'constituent people' of those particular entities.[29] The Constitution designates Bosniacs, Croats and Serbs as constituent peoples *throughout* the entire territory of Bosnia.[30] Thus, a majority of the Court held that Bosnia's territorial delimitation cannot be allowed to justify 'ethnic domination, national homogenisation, or a right to uphold the effects of ethnic cleansing'.[31]

The tension between the commitments to individual rights and the imperatives of an ethnic consociational peace deal are apparent in the judgments of the Court, which divided on ethnic lines. The majority of the Court – the international judges and the two Bosniac judges – held that provisions seeking to designate or emphasise each of the entities as 'the state of' one or other particular people indicate a 'purposeful discriminatory practice . . . with the effect of upholding the results of past ethnic cleansing'.[32] The discriminatory effect of these provisions in turn denuded rights of free movement and return to homes and residences from which people had fled or been removed during the war and periods of ethnic cleansing.[33] The Court then turned to the question of whether discrimination and violations of individual rights could be justified by the imperatives of ethnic power-sharing and consociationalism under the principle of proportionality.[34] On this question, the majority concluded that 'ethnic segregation can never be a "legitimate aim" with respect to the principles of "democratic societies" as required by the European Convention on Human Rights and the Constitution'.[35] Moreover, the majority went further and rejected the argument that individual rights undermine the peaceful co-existence of ethnic groups. On the contrary, they reasoned that individual rights are as important to peaceful co-existence between ethnic groups as the collective rights of the constituent entities themselves. Indeed, as the consociational institutions of government are meant to encourage the peaceful co-existence of ethnic groups, individual rights that promote ethnic intermingling must be protected.

[29] Constitutional Court of Bosnia, Request for Evaluation of Constitutionality of Certain Provisions of the Constitution of Republika Srpska and the Constitution of the Federation of BiH, 1 July 2000, Case No U 5/98, partial decision pt III of 1 July 2000, available online at www.ccbh.ba/eng/odluke/povuci_pdf.php?pid=22214. An excellent discussion of the tension in the judgment between ethnic power distribution and the imperatives of democratic government appears in S Issacharoff, 'Constitutionalizing Democracy in Fractured Societies' (2003–04) 82 *Texas Law Review* 1861.

[30] U 5/98 (above n 29) para52.

[31] ibid para 61.

[32] ibid para 95.

[33] ibid para 95. The rights in question are entrenched in art II(5) of the Constitution:

> Refugees and Displaced Persons
>
> All refugees and displaced persons have the right freely to return to their homes of origin. They have the right, in accordance with Annex 7 to the General Framework Agreement, to have restored to them property of which they were deprived in the course of hostilities since 1991 and to be compensated for any such property that cannot be restored to them. Any commitments or statements relating to such property made under duress are null and void.

[34] ibid para 79.

[35] ibid para 96. See also para 113.

The four judges in the minority, by contrast, privileged the logic of ethnic consociation over individual rights. A dissenting opinion by one of the Croat-appointed judges concluded that the various international agreements such as the International Convention on the Elimination on all forms of Discrimination and the European Framework Convention for the Protection of National Minorities, as well as the provisions of the Bosnian Constitution enshrining individual rights to movement and property, were 'totally beside the point' and of no application to the dispute.[36] A minority opinion by a Serb-appointed judge similarly argued that were constitutional equality rights to alter the ethnic power-sharing arrangements in the various constituent entities, the raison d'etre for the entities would cease to exist.[37] The other two dissenting opinions also saw the majority's conclusion as posing a threat to the ethnic character of the entities.[38]

b) The *Place Names* Case

In February 2004, the Constitutional Court declared unconstitutional parts of two statutes passed by the Republika Srpska, pursuant to which a number of cities and towns had been renamed to suggest their Serbian ethnic character.[39] The objection to these name changes parallels the concerns raised in the *Constituent Peoples* case: the emphasis on the Serbian character of places in the Republika Srpska privileged Serbian identity over Bosnian and Croat identity in the Republika Srpska, and violated rights to freedom from ethnic discrimination.[40] The Court also held that emphasising the Serbian character of places in the Republika Srpska discouraged members of the Bosniac and Croat communities from moving to or settling in the Republika Srpska or from returning to homes in the Republika Srpska from which they had fled during the war, and infringed rights of return and free travel within Bosnia.[41] In contrast to its earlier decision in the *Constituent Peoples* case, the Court was unanimous.

[36] Dissenting judgment of Judge Zvonko Miljko, Partial Decision in case U 5/98 (n 29) at 48–49.

[37] Dissenting judgment of Judge Snežana Savić, Partial Decision in case U 5/98 (n 29) at 63.

[38] See the Dissenting judgment of Judge Vitomir Popvić (Serb-appointed), Partial Decision in case U 5/98 (n 29) at 80–81 and Mirko Zovko (Croat-appointed), Partial Decision in case U 5/98 (n 29) at 93–94.

[39] Constitutional Court of Bosnia, Request of Sefjudin Tokić, 27 February 2004, Case No U 44/01 (available online at www.ccbh.ba/eng/odluke/povuci_pdf.php?pid=2277. The statutory provisions in question were arts 11 and 11(a) of the Law on Territorial Organisation and Local Self-Government, Official Gazette Republika Srpska, numbers 11/94, 6/95, 26/95, 15/96, 17/96, 19/96 and 6/97, and arts 1 and 2 of the Law on the City of Srpsko Sarajevo, Official Gazette Republika Srpska, numbers 25/93, 8/96, 27/96 and 33/97.

[40] ibid paras 51–55. See also Feldman, 'Renaming Cities' (n 18) 658. Rights to freedom from discrimination are conferred by art II(4) of the Constitution, read with the International Convention on the Elimination of all Forms of Racial Discrimination, art 26 of the United Nations International Convention on Civil and Political Rights and the Council of Europe Framework Convention for the Protection of National Minorities.

[41] See arts II(5) and II(3)(m) of the Constitution of Bosnia and art 2 of Protocol 4 to the European Convention on Human Rights.

The Court considered and rejected various justifications for the limitation of these rights. One possible justification was that name changes intended to emphasise the Serbian ethnic identity of towns within the Republika Srpska are consistent with the very designation of a Serbian constituent entity. The Court rejected this justification, saying that it would be illegitimate to emphasise the ethnic character of a town when that ethnic character was the result of ethnic cleansing and forced removal.[42] Another possible justification was that the name changes would distinguish towns in the Republika Srpska from towns in the Federation with similar names. To rename the towns to emphasise the Serbian nature of those towns, the Court reasoned, was disproportionate to that objective. The same purpose could be achieved, the Court went on, by choosing names less invasive of rights to movement and rights of return.[43]

The *Places Names* case very clearly pits the ability of constituent entities to emphasise their ethnic identity against individual rights to move around and settle anywhere in Bosnia. Both the *Constituent Peoples* and *Place Names* decisions demonstrate that ethnic nation-building will be subjected to the constraints of classic civil and political individual rights enshrined in familiar documents like the European Convention.

c) Limits to Individual Rights: the *Finci* and *Sejdić* case

There have been limits to the Court's ability to marry the two competing agendas of Bosnia's constitutional project. The *Finci and Sejdić* case is an example of where the Bosnian Constitutional Court, at least in the view of the European Court of Human Rights, did not do enough to ensure that individual rights were insulated against the demands of ethnic power-sharing government structures. Two Bosnian citizens, one being a member of the Jewish community and the other being a member of the Roma community, argued before the European Court that the provisions of the Constitution restricting membership of the presidency to Bosniacs, Serbs and Croats were inconsistent with the European Convention on Human Rights. The Bosnian Constitutional Court rejected three previous challenges to the consistency of these electoral provisions with the Convention. One of these judgments – which went only to the admissibility of the issue – was unanimous. The other two judgments were split, with an international judge from Germany and the Court's president in dissent on both occasions.[44] In late 2009, the European Court handed down judgment in *Finci and Sejdić* declaring the restriction incompatible with Convention rights to equality and anti-discrimination.[45] The difference in approach between the two

[42] *Place Names* Case (n 39) para 52.

[43] ibid para 63.

[44] Case No U-5/04 (unanimous), Case No U-13/05 (with Judge Constance Grewe and Vice President Seada Palavric in dissent) and Case No AP-2678/06 (with Judge Constance Grewe and Vice President Seada Palavric in dissent).

[45] *Finci and Sejdić v Bosnia and Herzegovina* (22 December 2009, applications nos 27996/06 and 34836/06).

courts highlights the tension that exists between commitments to individual rights and an explicitly ethnic distribution of political power. For the Bosnian Constitutional Court, individual rights against non-discrimination gave way to the demands of ethnic consociationalism because, in the Court's view, those infringements were justifiable in the broader context of Bosnian ethnic politics. In one decision, the Court relied on the European Court of Human Rights' decision in *Mathieu-Mohin*[46] to hold that the ethnic restrictions on membership of the presidency were both in service of the legitimate aim of 'peace and dialogue between opposing parties' and not disproportionate to the achievement of that aim.[47] The Bosnian Constitutional Court's decisions on this issue can be reconciled with its judgments in the *Constituent Peoples* and *Place Names* decisions – which established a strong norm of non-discrimination – on the basis that the elections cases concerned ethnic power-sharing and the distribution of public offices, which the *Constituent Peoples* and *Place Names* cases did not. Confronted with the tension between the rights against ethnic discrimination and consociationalism, the Constitutional Court has had no choice but to choose between these two constitutionally mandated imperatives. As David Feldman, sitting as a judge of the Bosnian Constitutional Court, explained:

> I accept that . . . different parts of the Constitution appear to have conflicting values and objectives, but constitutions are never entirely coherent. They are always shaped by, and are a compromise between, conflicting values and objectives. The task of the Constitutional Court under Article VI is to give effect to the Constitution, with all its inconsistencies, and make it as effective as possible in all the circumstances.[48]

The European Court of Human Rights, holding that racial discrimination is repugnant in all its forms and under any circumstances, was unable to uphold the presidency's ethnic exclusivity.[49] The European Court was itself divided on the issue, however, with one dissenting opinion criticising the majority for its insensitivity to the fragility and delicacy of the peaceful relations between dominant ethnic groups in Bosnia.[50]

iii. Applying the Bosnian Constitutional Court Model to Other Jurisdictions

In the *Constituent Peoples* case, a bare majority of five votes to four carried the decision, with the two Serbian and the two Croat judges in the minority and the

[46] *Mathieu-Mohin and Clerfayt v Belgium* (n 13).

[47] Case No AP-2678/06, majority judgment of Hatidža Hadžiosmanović, available online at www.ccbh.ba/eng/odluke/povuci_pdf.php?pid=67930, paras 20–23.

[48] Case No AP-2678/06, Feldman J's concurring opinion, para 4, available online at www.ccbh.ba/eng/odluke/povuci_pdf.php?pid=67930.

[49] See the case note by Marko Milanovic in (2010) 104 *American Journal of International Law* 636, 638.

[50] *Finci and Sejdić* (n 45), dissenting opinion of Justice Bonello (Malta). A separate, partly dissenting judgment of Justices Mijović (Bosnia) and Hajiyev (Azerbaijan) found no rights violations in the applicants' exclusion from the House of Peoples. See also S Bardutzky, 'The Strasbourg Court on the Dayton Constitution: Judgment in the case of *Finci and Sejdić v Bosnia and Herzegovina*, 22 December 2009' (2010) 6 *European Constitutional Law Review* 309, 326–27.

two Bosniac judges and the three international judges in the majority. David Feldman points out that during the first five years of the Court's operation – before he served on it – the judges of the Court tended to vote according to the interests of their ethnic affiliations, and many of the cases involved bare majorities of two ethnic judges and the three international judges.[51] The addition of three international judges was intended to neutralise the effects of ethnic polarisation on the Court. Since the Court is entrusted with adjudicating disputes between explicitly ethnic political organs, there is a strong justification for ensuring that the Court remains insulated from ethnic bias.[52] But since the three international judges and two judges from any one constituent people constitute a majority, the presence of international judges may have had the perverse effect of facilitating the Court's ethnic polarisation. More recently, however, the Court has shown a greater propensity for unanimity (eg, the *Place Names* case).[53] Moreover, this trend towards unanimity has been accompanied by a privileging of the integrative values of the Bill of Rights over the logic of consociational power-sharing.[54] It is not clear what shifted within the Court. One possibility is that the presence of the international judges on the Court had its intended effect and promoted the convergence of the domestic judges from a variety of ethnic backgrounds on a constitutional patriotism embodied in the rights-protecting provisions of the Bosnian Constitution. Furthermore, the Court has been a driver of moves towards greater integration in Bosnia and the decline of the consociational power-sharing arrangements often seen as indispensable to forging peace in a massively divided society.[55] It has been widely recognised that post-war Bosnia's consociational arrangements were unworkable and that the Bosnian state was dysfunctional.[56] A fascinating consequence of the *Constituent Peoples* judgment was the extent to which the Sarajevo Agreement on the implementation of the judgment, concluded in

[51] Feldman, 'Renaming Cities' (n 18) 660.

[52] Mansfield, 'Ethnic but Equal' (n 19) 2060

[53] Feldman, 'Renaming Cities' (n 18) 660. See also K Nobbs, 'International Benchmarks: A review of minority participation in the judiciary' in Marc Weller and Katherine Nobbs (eds), *Political Participation of Minorities: A Commentary on International Standards and Practice* (Oxford, Oxford University Press, 2010) 589, 605.

[54] Feldman, 'Renaming Cities' (n 18); H Stokke, 'Human Rights as a Mechanism for Integration in Bosnia-Herzegovina' (2006) 13 *International Journal on Minority and Group Rights* 263, 264; and Mansfield, 'Ethnic but Equal' (n19) 2089. In Germany, this shift in loyalty from nation to legal principles has been called 'constitutional patriotism': see D Kommers, 'The Federal Constitutional Court in the German Political System' (1994) 26 *Comparative Political Studies* 470, 488.

[55] D Wippman, 'Practical and Legal Constraints on Internal Power Sharing' in D Wippman (ed), *International Law and Ethnic Conflict* (Ithaca, Cornell University Press, 1998) and S Issacharoff, P Karlan and R Pildes, *The Law of Democracy: Legal Structure of the Political Process* (New York, Foundation Press, 2007).

[56] Hayden, 'The Continuing Reinvention' (n 19) 4; Mansfield, 'Ethnic but Equal' (n 19) 2055. In 1997, in the face of political stalemate to which Dayton's consociational arrangements frequently led, the parties to the Dayton Accords agreed at a meeting in Bonn, Germany, to imbue the Office of the High Representative with almost dictatorial powers to govern the country. These have become known as the Bonn Powers of the Office of the High representative.

March 2002,[57] limited the ability of the entities to pursue aggressive nation-building projects. The agreement requires that the upper chambers of each of the two constituent entities' legislatures be constituted on the basis of parity, so that each constituent people has the same number of delegates regardless of population distribution.[58] Further, in order to give effect to the Court's prohibition on ethnic domination in government structures,[59] the agreement insists on 'proportionate representation' in government based on the 1991 census, which reflects population distributions before ethnic cleansing and internal displacement occurred.[60]

The Sarajevo Agreement also makes significant changes to the procedures for the protection of vital ethnic interests. It defines vital interests,[61] avoiding the possibility of 'pretextual ethnic vetoes',[62] and, and more importantly, creates a route for the judicial review of declarations of vital interest.[63] The *Constituent Peoples* decision refined the model established by the Dayton Constitution into 'a restrained form of consociationalism' in which the vital interest veto is more a platform for governance than a trapdoor to deadlock, proportional representation is based on ethnically mixed pre-war demographics, and power-sharing is dependent on the 'facially neutral process of geographic concentration of the various ethnic groups'.[64] The shifting balance in Bosnia between consociationalism of the Lijphart-mould and a more integrative political arrangement favoured by Lijphart's interlocutor, Donald Horowitz, has been documented before now.[65] What is important for us here is how a court designed to mirror ethnic divisions in the country has contributed to this integrative process.

The Bosnian experience may be instructive for other divided societies facing questions of constitutional design, such as Kosovo and Cyprus. The Constitution

[57] Sarajevo Agreement available online from the OHR website at www.ohr.int/print/?content_id=7274.

[58] ibid pt I art3.

[59] Partial Decision (above n 29) Reasons, para 60.

[60] Sarajevo Agreement (n 57) pt IV. See also Stokke, 'Human Rights as a Mechanism for Integration in Bosnia-Herzegovina' (n 54) 277.

[61] Sarajevo Agreement, (n 57) pt I art 4. Vital interests are listed as the exercise of the rights of constituent peoples to be adequately represented in legislative, executive and judicial bodies; identity of one constituent people; constitutional amendments; organisation of public authorities; equal rights of constituent peoples in the process of decision-making; education, religion, language, promotion of culture, tradition and cultural heritage; territorial organisation; public information system; and any other interest as claimed by two-thirds of one of the caucuses of the Federation House of Peoples or the Republika Srpska Council of Peoples.

[62] Mansfield, 'Ethnic but Equal' (n 19) 2074.

[63] Sarajevo Agreement (n 57), pt I art 5. Other commentators have noted the softening effect the *Constituent Peoples* decision has had on the consociational nature of the Bosnian political settlement. See Richard H Pildes, 'Ethnic Identity and Democratic Institutions: A Dynamic Perspective' in Choudhry (ed), *Constitutional Design for Divided Societies* (n 7) 173, 197.

[64] Mansfield, 'Ethnic but Equal' (n 19) 2085.

[65] See generally, Nina Caspersen, 'Good Fences make Good Neighbours? A Comparison of Conflict-Regulation Strategies in Postwar Bosnia' (n 25). For a sample of Horowitz's work, see generally *Ethnic Groups in Conflict* (n 10); *A Democratic South Africa: Constitutional Engineering in a Divided Society* (Berkeley, University of California Press, 1991); and 'Democracy in Divided Societies' (1993) 4 *Journal of Democracy* 18.

of Kosovo provides for consociational power-sharing arrangements similar to Bosnia's. Seven of the nine seats on the Constitutional Court of Kosovo are designated for filling by a two-thirds majority of the unicameral legislature. The remaining two seats are designated for filling by a simple majority of the legislature with the consent of a majority of the legislative representatives of ethnic minorities, whose representation in the legislature is itself guaranteed.[66] The recently rejected Annan Plan for Cyprus included an apex court staffed by an equal number of Cypriot and Turkish judges alongside three international, non-Cypriot judges.[67] It seems from the Bosnian experience that an ethnically diverse and representative apex court is important to developing the legitimacy of the court, just as consociational mechanisms are necessary for political compromise. At least in Bosnia, however, the apex court has been able to overcome the ethnic divisions reproduced on the court and hand down ethnically non-partisan judgments that privilege the rights-protecting parts of the Bosnian Constitution. The international, neutral, presence on the Court may have ensured the independence and impartiality of the apex court and prevented its capture by sectional ethnic interests.

B. Divided Democracies: Canada

In 1980, and again in 1995, Quebeckers voted in referenda on whether the province of Quebec should remain part of Canada or secede to form a sovereign independent nation. French-speakers are a majority in Quebec, but a minority in Canada as a whole. Throughout Canada's history the French-speaking minority has tried to protect its distinct linguistic and cultural identity. Linguistic nationalism in Canada has been central to three sets of constitutional questions – about provincial autonomy, about Quebec's unique civil law tradition, and about the effect of the 1982 Canadian Charter of Rights and Freedoms[68] on Quebec's policies linguistic nation-building.

The Supreme Court of Canada has addressed these questions, and in doing so has confronted directly the question of how pan-Canadian individual rights enshrined in Canada's bill of rights, the Canadian Charter of Rights and Freedoms, limit or constrain Quebec's ability to forge a distinct cultural and political identity. Its record in this regard can be assessed through three sets of cases, all centred on language rights. On the matter of language in the private sector, the Court has at times been generous to Quebec. With respect to the language of education, the Court's judgments have been more restrictive of

[66] Constitution of the Republic of Kosovo, 2008, art 114(2) and (3). The representation of ethnic minorities is set out in art 64.

[67] See the draft Constitution for Cyprus, Annex I to the Annan Plan, available online from the UN website at www.hri.org/docs/annan/Annan_Plan_April2004.pdf, art 36.

[68] Canadian Charter of Rights and Freedoms, Part I of the Constitution Act, 1982, being sch B to the Canada Act 1982 (UK), 1982, c 11 (the Charter).

Quebec's autonomy. Regarding the language of government, the Court has been firm in upholding constitutionally mandated requirements of bilingualism.

i. Quebec Nationalism and the Design of the Court

Two significant changes to Canada's constitutional landscape brought together the issue of the institutional design of the apex court and the three constitutional questions of Quebec nationalism. The first was the abolition of appeals from Canada to imperial courts in 1949, and the second was the introduction of the Charter of Rights and Freedoms.

The starting point is the British North America Act,[69] which established the nation state of Canada as a confederation of several provinces and is still in force today. The Act was textually ambiguous on a number of important elements of federalism, including the respective scope of provincial and federal jurisdiction, the relationship between the federal and provincial governments and the relationship between the provincial executive and legislative power. Quebec and the federal government consequently developed very different conceptions of Confederation. It fell to the courts to resolve basic disagreements over the nature of Canada. At first, Canada's court of final appeal was the Judicial Committee of the Privy Council – the British appellate body for colonial courts – rather than the Supreme Court of Canada. The conception of Confederation set out by the Privy Council favoured strong provinces and a weak federal government, a conception in which the provinces had jurisdiction over major aspects of social and economic policy.[70] With the abolition of appeals to the Privy Council in 1949,[71] the Supreme Court became Canada's final court of appeal. Quebeckers were concerned that Quebec's autonomy would be eroded by a Supreme Court of Canada biased in favour of the federal government.[72]

As it became clear in the 1940s that the Privy Council would no longer be Canada's apex court, Quebec began to make proposals for a new apex court. An early proposal included a nine-member specialist Constitutional Court, consisting of five judges appointed by the federal government, and one judge

[69] Constitution Act, 1867 (UK), 30 & 31 Vict, c 3.

[70] See, eg, *Maritime Bank of Canada v Receiver-General of New Brunswick*, [1892] AC 437, *Hodge v The Queen*, [1883] 9 AC 117 (PC), *Ontario (AG) v Dominion (AG)*, [1896] AC 348 (PC), *Reference Re Board of Commerce Act, 1919 (Canada)*, [1922] 1 AC 191, 60 DLR 513, *Citizens Insurance Company v Parsons*, [1881] 7 AC 96 (PC), *Canada (AG) v Alberta (AG)* [1916] 1 AC 589 and *Toronto Electric Commissions v Snider*, [1925] AC 396, 2 DLR 5 (PC). Indeed, two prominent Quebec legal scholars and future Justices of the Supreme Court, Louis-Philippe Pigeon and Jean Beetz, praised the Privy Council for its protection of provincial autonomy. See Pigeon, 'The Meaning of Provincial Autonomy' (1951) 29 *Canadian Bar Review* 1126 and Beetz, 'Les attitudes changeantes du Quebec a l'endroit de la Constitution de 1867' in P Crepeau and CB Macpherson (eds), *The Future of Canadian Federalism* (Toronto, University of Toronto Press, 1965) 113.

[71] *Act to Amend the Supreme Court Act*, S.C. 1949 (2nd sess), c 37, s 3.

[72] See the 'Tremblay Report', Quebec's *Report of the Royal Commission of Inquiry on Constitutional Problems* (Royal Commission of Inquiry on Constitutional Problems Imprint, Quebec City 1956) Vol III, Book I at 287.

appointed by each by the executives of each region of Canada (Quebec, Ontario, Atlantic Canada and Western Canada).[73] Another proposal empowered provincial executives to appoint two-thirds of the Constitutional Court with one-third of the judges appointed by Quebec, and another one-third appointed by the other provinces.[74] The federal government was concerned that such a court would become a representative tribunal for the negotiation of regional interests rather than an independent judicial body.[75]

Quebec shifted its focus from the creation of a specialist constitutional court to the reform of the Supreme Court of Canada. The 1971 Victoria Charter proposed that appointments require the agreement of the federal and provincial executives,[76] and that every case involving Quebec's civil code be heard by a panel of five judges, including three from Quebec. Another variation reduced the federal executive role to nomination with legislative confirmation, and linked this to reforms to the composition of the federal upper chamber such that it would consist of members appointed by the federal House of Commons and provincial legislatures.[77] Proposals included in the Meech Lake Accord in 1987 (an abortive attempt to generate Quebec's support for the 1982 Constitution Act) were for federal appointment of a guaranteed number of judges from Quebec to the Court, from a list of candidates prepared by Quebec.[78] Appointments to the non-Quebec seats would be made from lists provided by the other provinces. A final set of proposals involved expanding the Court and increasing the number of sitting judges from Quebec, as well as ensuring that constitutional cases be heard by a smaller panel on which all the Quebec judges would sit.

Limited concessions were made to Quebec in 1985, in the aftermath of the breakdown of negotiations between the federal government and the provinces over the adoption of the Charter of Rights and Freedoms in 1980. The Supreme Court Act of 1985 formalises a convention that judges from Quebec serve on the Court, by setting the number of judges on the Court at nine and designating three of those seats for judges from Quebec.[79] However, Quebec has no say in who the three judges from Quebec will be; the judges are appointed by the federal government with no input from Quebec.[80] Canada's Constitution Act of 1982, which includes the Charter, entrenches Quebec's privileged position on the Court by requiring that changes to the 'composition of the Supreme Court'

[73] Tremblay Report' (n 72).
[74] *Quebec's Positions on Constitutional and Intergovernmental Issues from 1936 to March 2001* (Québec City, Secretariat of Canadian Intergovernmental Affairs, 2001) 38, 52.
[75] Otto E Lang, 'Constitutional Reform: The Supreme Court of Canada' in Anne F Bayefsky, *Canada's Constitution Act 1982 and Amendments: A Documentary History* (Toronto, McGraw-Hill Ryerson, 1989) 476.
[76] Victoria Charter 1971 c 38.
[77] Constitutional Amendment Bill, Bill C-60, 1978.
[78] Meech Lake Accord, Amendment to the Constitution 1987, c 11 s 5.
[79] Supreme Court Act, RSC c S-26, ss 4(1) and 6.
[80] Supreme Court Act, s4(2).

require unanimous federal and provincial consent.[81] The distribution of the remaining seats – three from Ontario, one from Atlantic Canada, one from British Columbia and one from the Prairie provinces– is a matter of sub-constitutional political convention rather than statute.[82]

The above reforms occurred against the background of the introduction of the Canadian Charter of Rights and Freedoms – itself the federal government's response to centrifugal pressures from Quebec.[83] Until the 1960s, Quebec's constitutional claims had been defensive, aimed at safeguarding its existing areas of jurisdiction. In the 1960s Quebec's goals shifted to ethno-linguistic nation-building and an expansion of its jurisdiction over social and economic policy.[84] The basic political objective of the Charter was to combat Quebec nationalism both by *regulating* ethno-linguistic nation-building in Quebec and by *constituting* a pan-Canadian political community throughout Canada.[85]

In regulative terms, the Charter imposes legal restraints on minority nation-building through rights to inter-provincial mobility[86] and to minority language education.[87] A flashpoint of controversy within Quebec has been the right of Canadian citizens who received their primary school instruction anywhere in Canada in English to have their children educated in English in Quebec (the so-called 'Canada Clause'). Quebec objected to the entrenchment of these rights because the province 'legitimately discriminates in its legislation to preserve and enhance its integrity as a culturally differend [sic] society'.[88] The Charter of Rights and Freedoms was drafted specifically to render objections like this unconstitutional.[89] The federal government, through the Charter, was able to protect minority language rights for Anglophones in Quebec at the same time as it protected language rights for francophones across Canada.[90]

In constitutive terms, the Charter of Rights and Freedoms was intended to function as the germ of a pan-Canadian constitutional patriotism. In a federal state such as Canada, since citizens share rights irrespective of language or province of residence, a bill of rights is meant to serve as a transcendent form of

[81] Constitution Act 1982, s 41(d).

[82] See P Hogg, *Constitutional Law of Canada* 5th edn (Scarborough, Thomson Carswell, 2007) ch 8.3.

[83] PH Russell, 'The Political Purposes of the Charter of Rights and Freedoms' (1983) 61 *Canadian Bar Review* 30. See also *Federalism for the Future,* released by the federal government in 1968 (Ottawa, Queen's Printer, 1968) 2.

[84] See generally K McRoberts, *Quebec: Social Change and Political Crisis* (Toronto, McLelland and Stewart, 1988).

[85] On the regulative and constitutive functions of bills of rights, see Choudhry, 'After the Rights Revolution: Bills of Rights in the Postconflict State' (2010) 6 *Annual Review of Law and Social Science* 301.

[86] Charter, s 6(2).

[87] ibid s 23.

[88] 'Letter from Premier Rene Levesque to Prime Minister Margaret Thatcher, December 19, 1981', reprinted in (1985) 30 *McGill Law Journal* 645, 710.

[89] The Supreme Court upheld the Charter against Quebec's language policy in one of its earliest Charter cases, *Quebec (AG) v Quebec Protestant School Boards* [1984] 2 SCR 66.

[90] See *Federalism for the Future* (n 83) 4.

political identification. In this light, the minority language education rights communicate a conception of linguistic identity that is subsumed by a Canadian constitutional identity.

ii. Assessing the Court

The Court has had a large role in defining the constitutional relationship of Quebec to Canada. In three sets of language rights cases the Court has addressed the tensions between the logics of plurinational accommodation and individual rights.

First, in a pre-Charter case dealing with the language of government, the Court struck down provisions of the 1977 Quebec Charter of the French Language[91] purporting to make French the exclusive language of Quebec's legislature and courts.[92] These provisions were held to be in direct contravention of section 133 of the British North America Act, which requires that all Acts of Parliament and the Quebec legislature be published in both English and French.[93]

Second, with respect to the language of commerce and the private sector, the Court's influence on Quebec's fortunes has been mixed. The Court struck down requirements in the Charter of the French Language that commercial signage be exclusively French, on the grounds that the law imposed unreasonable limitations on the Canadian Charter right to freedom of expression.[94] However, the Court accepted the legitimacy of Quebec's stated objective for the provision, to ensure that 'the "visage linguistique" of Quebec would reflect the predominance of the French language'.[95] The provision was struck down because it was disproportionate to that objective; a measure requiring that French be predominant would have sufficed. Moreover, in a companion case, the Court accepted that Quebec has the constitutional authority to regulate 'the language of commerce and business', and that doing so in a way that promotes the use of French in commerce and business falls within provincial jurisdiction.[96] The Charter of the French Language obliges employers to provide written communications to their staff in French, prohibits employers from making employment conditional on the knowledge of a language other than French unless necessary, and authorises the provincial government to require larger businesses (50 employees or more) to engage in a process of 'francisation', whereby the use of French is generalised throughout the firm. The Court's view is that these rules are matters of

[91] Charter of the French Language, RSQ c C-11 (2007).

[92] *AG Quebec v Blaikie* [1979] 2 SCR 1016.

[93] The portions of the Charter of the French Language that establish French as the exclusive language of work within the civil service, however, have never been constitutionally challenged and remain in force. These provisions have cemented the place of French as the dominant language of work in Quebec, by creating strong economic incentives for individuals who desire to secure public sector employment or contract with the state to master French.

[94] *Ford v Quebec (AG)* [1988] 2 SCR 712.

[95] ibid para 72.

[96] *Devine v Quebec (AG)* [1988] 2 SCR 790, paras 16–20.

intraprovincial commerce and thus are within provincial jurisdiction, even though they have an obvious impact on interprovincial and international trade, which are matters of federal competence. This approach reflects an interpretation of Canadian federalism that protects provincial autonomy – long a primary driver of Quebec's push for judicial reform. Moreover, these provisions have not been subject to Charter challenge.

Finally, on matters of French as the language of public education, the Court has upheld English minority language rights in the face of Quebec's attempt to promote French as the dominant language of education. The 'Canada Clause' grants citizens educated in English at primary level anywhere in Canada the right to have their children educated in English in Quebec.[97] In the *Quebec Protestant School Board* decision, the Court struck down the provision of the Charter of the French Language that completely denied this right and, in its proportionality analysis, held that Quebec's purpose was impermissible because it attempted to completely negate the effect of the Canada Clause (as opposed to merely limiting it).[98] The Charter also grants the right to children who have received schooling in English anywhere else in the country the right to continue schooling in English in Quebec, another right the Quebec Charter on the French Language attempted to limit.[99] The Court blocked this measure in *Solski*.[100] However, rather than holding that there had been a violation of the Charter and that the violation was not justified (as it had in *Quebec Protestant School Board*), the Court narrowly interpreted the provision to keep it on safe constitutional terrain. It therefore did not have to address the question of whether Quebec had acted for a constitutionally permissible purpose.

While the outcome for Quebec in these cases has been mixed, two points are noteworthy. First, in all five cases, the Court has been unanimous, handing down a judgment of 'The Court' as an institution rather than a judgment authored by an individual judge in which the rest of the Court has concurred. The Court's practice seems to indicate its awareness that, with respect to these divisive issues, it is important for it to present a collective front in order to emphasise the fact that what drives the judgments is not the identity of the judge authoring the opinion, but the Court's understanding of the constituent elements of the Canadian constitutional order and their interrelationship. It also reflects an agreement among judges from across Canada's linguistic divide. Joint authorships signals a stronger degree of agreement on the Court than a mere concurrence.

Second, the Court has applied the Charter to check Quebec's linguistic nation-building policies, but at the same time has left space for Quebec to pursue these policies. While the Court's decisions on minority language education rights and commercial advertising appear to limit Quebec's ability to recognise,

[97] Charter, s 23(1)(b).
[98] *Quebec Protestant School Boards* (n 89) at 87–88.
[99] ibid s 23(2).
[100] *Solski (Tutor of) v Quebec (AG)* 2005 SCC 14; [2005] 1 SCR 201.

protect and enhance the status of French in education and commerce, over time it has come to accept Quebec's objectives as constitutionally legitimate, either explicitly or implicitly. The early post-*Charter* decision, *Quebec Protestant School Board*, can be read either to impliedly suggest that the objective of preserving and enhancing the status of French as Quebec's common language was per se illegitimate, or that the means chosen were disproportionate. But in *Ford* the Court accepted the legitimacy of this objective and struck down the law for not using a less intrusive means. This raised the question of whether it would be legitimate to pursue this objective with respect to access to English language education. *Solski* stayed clear of this issue because it interpreted the challenged measure to comply with the minority language education rights in the Charter and so did not have to consider the question of proportionality. But the Court went out of its way to say that the measure as interpreted would still meet Quebec's objectives, impliedly accepting that such an objective is constitutionally legitimate.

What the Court has not done is to expressly root the legitimacy of this objective elsewhere in Canada's constitutional structure. The answer is federalism, which in large part was designed to accommodate Quebec's distinctive linguistic and cultural identity. Federalism has therefore conditioned the interpretation of the Charter, while at the same time, the Charter constrains the extent of provincial diversity under federalism.

iii. Applying the Model

The Canadian experience may offer some insight to divided democracies going through similar constitutional reforms, such as the United Kingdom and Spain. Two sets of changes have recently been made in the United Kingdom: first, greater power has been devolved to Scotland, Northern Ireland and Wales;[101] and second, in 2009 the Supreme Court of the United Kingdom replaced the Appellate Committee of the House of Lords as the apex court in the UK.[102] By statute, the composition of the Supreme Court must reflect 'knowledge of, and experience of practice in, the law of each part of the United Kingdom'.[103] The Supreme Court itself interprets this to impose a substantive requirement that judges from both Scotland and Northern Ireland serve on the Court.[104] In practice, this continues the informal convention of designating at least one seat each for Law Lords from Scotland and Northern Ireland.

[101] The Scotland Act 1998 c 46, the Government of Wales Act 1998 c 38, the Government of Wales Act 2006 c 32 and the Northern Ireland Act 1998 c 47.

[102] Constitutional Reform Act 2005 c 4.

[103] ibid s 27(8).

[104] 'Procedure for appointing a Justice of the Supreme Court of the United Kingdom', available on the Supreme Court of the United Kingdom website at www.supremecourt.gov.uk/docs/appointments-of-justices_V2.pdf. It should be noted that a single legal system governs both England and Wales. To the extent that they are sub-national units within a federated legal system, they form a single jurisdictional entity within that system.

A justification for diversity on the Court is expertise. It is possible that as the Home Unions grow into their devolved powers they will encounter the same sorts of tensions as arose between Quebec and the Canadian government.[105] As Stephen Tierney's contribution to this volume points out, the approach taken to the rights in the European Convention on Human Rights may acceptably differ between jurisdictions, as long as they meet minimal standards. There seems no reason why this margin of appreciation would not apply in the UK, where there are different legal systems within a single state. Yet the Appellate Committee of the House of Lords held, considering fair trial rights in the Convention and the Human Rights Act of 1998 which gives effect to the Convention, that provisions of Scots law different from English law were bad law.[106] The concern then is that this 'homogenisation' of law is a form of legal imperialism that undermines the multiplicity of otherwise valid constitutional visions in the different parts of a devolved state. The guaranteed representation of the Home Unions on the Supreme Court may prove important if and when these tensions continue to arise. However, while the two Scots judges dissented in this case, there is no guarantee that judges in this position will emphatically pursue ethnic or sub-national interests in their judicial roles.

In Spain, too, tensions between the federal government and the autonomous communities have led to at least one controversial and divisive Constitutional Court decision on the place of language in the autonomous communities. The Statute of Autonomy of Catalonia, which functions as a constitution for Catalonia, provides that Catalan and Spanish are official languages in Catalonia. Amendments to the Statute provided further that Catalan is the 'preferred' language of government,[107] but the Constitutional Court held that entrenching Catalan as a preferred language was unconstitutional because it undermined the status of Spanish in Catalonia.[108] Tensions like these have arisen at the same time that the autonomous communities have expanded their influence on the composition of the Constitutional Court. The 12 judges of the Court are appointed four-apiece by the upper and lower houses of the federal Parliament by a three-fifths majority, and two-apiece by the government and the independent General Council of the Judiciary.[109] Changes to the organic law of the

[105] Indeed, Stephen Tierney makes just this kind of argument in noting that while the Scottish devolution can be seen as an 'accommodationist' move, there are undeniable integrative tendencies involved which, as in Quebec's case, have the effect of restricting sub-national nation-building in Scotland and undermining efforts to reorient the United Kingdom in a plurinational direction. See S Tierney, 'Giving with one hand: Scottish devolution within a unitary state' (2007) 5 *International Journal of Constitutional Law* 730.

[106] *Attorney General's Reference (No 2 of 2001)* [2003] UKHL 68.

[107] Organic Law on the reform of the Statute of Autonomy of Catalonia, 6/2006, 19 July 2006, art 6(1) and (2).

[108] The Court did, on the other hand, uphold provisions establishing Catalan as the 'normal' language of education. See the *Decision on the constitutionality of amendments to the Statute of Autonomy for Catalonia*, Judgment 31/2010, 28 June 2010. See the report of the judgment, in English, commissioned by the government of Catalonia, available online at www10.gencat.cat/drep/binaris/Informe%20STC_eng_tcm112-133021.pdf.

[109] Spanish Constitution 1978, art 159(1).

judiciary now require that the Senate appoint its four judges from a list of nominees provided by the legislative assemblies of the autonomous communities.[110] The autonomous communities are thus assured of some procedural input into the composition of the Court. This could prove to be influential if clashes between the federal government and the communities continue to appear before the Constitutional Court.

C. Facially Neutral Institutional Rules: Germany

Our final case study is Germany. Germany is not a divided society in the way that Bosnia and Canada are. Germany's apex court in constitutional matters – the Federal Constitutional Court (FCC) – does, however, face a similar tension between the impetus for independence and the impetus for the representation of political interests on the FCC. In Germany's case, the political interests are ideological and organised around political parties rather than ethno-cultural or linguistic groups. The design of the FCC reflects these conflicting political interests, but it does not institutionalise them in the same way as in Bosnia and Canada. The political rules governing appointments, which require broad political consensus, are facially neutral and can adapt to changing patterns of political mobilisation. They do not freeze the current pattern of political identity into place. Moreover, the FCC has adjudicated constitutional disputes in which the competing legal positions track these ideological divisions.

i. The Politics of Judicial Appointments in Germany

The FCC is a product of the constitutional document drafted for the new West German state in the wake of the Second World War. Section IX of the German Basic Law establishes the Court, but leaves institutional details such as the Court's jurisdiction, the number of judges, their terms of service and their selection, to be determined by legislation. The Federal Constitutional Court Act (FCCA) was eventually passed in February 1951 and the first judges were appointed to the Court in September 1951 after months of deadlock and fierce competition between political parties.[111]

Of the three cases presented here, Germany is the most faithful to the 'insurance model' theories of judicial independence presented by Tom Ginsburg and others.[112] The political parties represented in the structures of government and

[110] Organic Law on the Constitutional Court, 2/1979, art 16 (as amended by Organic Law 6/2007, 24 May 2007).

[111] For a fuller account of the details and circumstances of the Court's establishment, see Georg Vanberg, *The Politics of Constitutional Review in Germany* (Cambridge, Cambridge University Press, 2005) 62–66.

[112] Ginsburg, *Judicial Review in New Democracies* (n 6); Stephenson, '"When the Devil Turns . . ."' (n 3); Ramseyer, 'The Puzzling (In)Dependence of Courts' (n 5); and J Ferejohn, 'Judicializing Politics, Politicizing Law' (2002) 65 *Law and Contemporary Problems* 41. See also the contribution of Alex Schwartz and Colin Harvey to this volume.

responsible for appointments to the FCC were concerned to prevent partisan domination of the FCC in order to ensure as much as possible the independence of the Court down the road. The outcome has been a highly politicised appointment process and an apex court apparently strongly committed to unanimity in its judgments.

a. Structure of the FCC and Appointment of Judges

The FCC has 16 judges. It is a 'twin court' composed of two senates with distinct and mutually exclusive jurisdiction. Eight judges sit in each senate and are appointed for a non-renewable term of 12 years.[113] The president of the FCC heads one senate and the vice-president heads the other. Although the federal president formally appoints the judges elected by the chambers, the power of appointment rests with the two chambers of the legislature, the *Bundestag* and the *Bundesrat*. Each chamber appoints a total of eight judges, four to each senate.[114] In the *Bundestag*, judges are chosen indirectly through a 12-member committee, the membership of which reflects party representation in the *Bundestag*. Election as a judge requires a supporting vote of eight of the 12 members of the electoral committee (reduced from nine in 1956).

In the *Bundesrat*, election of judges is by a two-thirds majority of the votes of the chamber. The *Länder* represented in the *Bundesrat* have on occasion formed an ad hoc commission to make recommendations to the full chamber on candidates for the FCC, but such a commission is not required by law and is not always constituted.[115]

In contrast to Bosnia and Canada, the rules for the appointment of judges are neutral with respect to political or social groups. The super-majority requirements for the election of judges in both the upper and lower chambers, however, have ensured that the main parties on the German electoral landscape, the alliance between the Christian Democratic Union (CDU) and the Christian Social Union (CSU), and the Social Democrats (SPD), each enjoy a practical veto over appointments.[116] The result has been the development of a sub-constitutional practice by which partisan political interests represented in the legislature play a decisive role in the election of judges, through three primary mechanisms.

[113] FCCA, arts 2 and 4. The number of judges in each senate has been gradually reduced by legislation from 12 to 10 in 1956, and finally to eight in 1962. Also, when the FCC was established in 1951, judges were appointed either for life, or for a renewable term of eight or four years. This arrangement was abolished in 1970 and the present system introduced. See GN Schram, 'The Recruitment of Judges for the West German Federal Courts' (1973) 21 *American Journal of Comparative Law* 691, 693; and Vanberg, *The Politics of Constitutional Review* (n 111) 85.

[114] This aspect of the appointment procedures is required by art 94(1) of the German Basic Law. The specific procedures for the appointment of judges are set out in arts 6–10 of the FCCA.

[115] Schram, 'The Recruitment of Judges' (n 113), 698; David S Clark, 'The Selection and Accountability of Judges in West Germany: Implementation of a *Rechtsstaat*' (1987–88) 61 *Southern California Law Review* 1796, 1828.

[116] Vanberg, *Politics of Constitutional Review* (n 111) 83.

First, when vacancies on the FCC have meant that both the *Bundestag* and the *Bundesrat* have had to elect judges, negotiations between representatives of the two houses have occurred, providing an opportunity for horse-trading between the parties represented in the legislature, with the interests of the *Länder* represented by negotiating teams from the *Bundesrat*. In 1971, for example, four new judges were to be appointed by the *Bundesrat* and two by the *Bundestag*. The negotiating teams were formed by the two major parties at the time, the CDU and the SPD, and the manifest purpose of the negotiation was the realignment of the membership of the Court to reflect party sympathies.[117]

Second, the *Länder* themselves occasionally seek representation on the FCC and bring pressure to bear accordingly. The election of a Hessian civil servant to the FCC in 1963 has been explained as a result of the influence of a Hesse minister on the ad hoc *Bundesrat* commission,[118] while Bavaria and 'the north-German element' were successful in having representative judges appointed in 1975.[119] Disputes and disagreements between *Länder* and between *Länder* and the federal government often take on a party political character,[120] with the result that *Land* pressure for one candidate or another is taken up by politically sympathetic parties.

Third, and most significantly, the dominant parties in the legislature have allocated seats on the FCC among them, and indeed are thought to own them.[121] The practice arose in order to avoid the partisan deadlock that delayed the appointment of judges in 1951. Now, half of the judges are appointed by the CDU/CSU, while the other half are appointed by the SPD. When either of the smaller parties, the Greens or Liberal Free Democrats (FDP), have been part of a governing coalition, they have usually been able to secure control over the appointment of one seat. When a judge retires, the party to which the seat belongs chooses the replacement with no opposition in the legislature – provided the candidates are moderate enough to be acceptable to the other party. The president of the FCC has always been appointed by the CDU/CSU, while the vice-president has always been appointed by the SPD. In Germany, seats on the apex court are 'double-designated', according to which chamber of the legislature fills them and again according to which party fills them. The result is an FCC fairly evenly representative of the large parties in Germany, with little drastic ideological shift over time.[122]

[117] Clark, 'Selection and Accountability of Judges' (n 115) 1828, fn 157; Schram, 'The Recruitment of Judges' (n 113) 696.

[118] Schram, 'The Recruitment of Judges' (n 113) 698.

[119] PM Blair, *Federalism and Judicial Review in West Germany* (Oxford, Oxford University Press, 1981) 21.

[120] See D Kommers, 'The Federal Constitutional Court in the German Political System' (1994) 26 *Comparative Political Studies* 470, 481–82, and G Vanberg, 'Establishing Judicial Independence in West Germany: The Impact of Opinion Leadership and the Separation of Powers' (2000) 32 *Comparative Politics* 333, 338–39.

[121] Vanberg, *Politics of Constitutional Review* (n 111) 83–85, Schram, 'The Recruitment of Judges' (n 113) 699.

[122] Vanberg, *Politics of Constitutional Review* (n 111) 85.

b. Assessing the FCC in the Context of Germany's Multiparty Democracy

In Canada and Bosnia ethnicity has emerged as a primary factor in the composition of the apex courts, which have had an important influence in adjudicating disputes arising out of ethnic federalism and ethnicity more broadly. In Germany, the primary factor in the composition of the FCC is party politics, and many of the most significant cases the German FCC has decided have dealt with disputes of party politics and matters arising out of Germany's constitutional commitment to multiparty democracy. Generally, tensions have arisen between the FCC and the government, such as during the early face-off between Konrad Adenauer's CDU government and an SPD-dominated second senate on Germany's accession to the European Defence Community treaties.[123] The kind of tension that we are more specifically interested in here, however, arises between Germany's commitment to a conception of democracy and rights to participate in the political process. Article 21(1) of the Basic Law, for example, provides that political parties 'may be freely established', but that their 'internal organisation must conform to democratic principles'. The right to participate in the democratic process through political parties is immediately limited by the constraints of democracy. The details of those constraints are themselves left to federal law (Article 21(3)).

Three sorts of cases in the FCC's 60-year history stand out as focal points of this tension between rights and democracy and for the direct effect they have had on the political vitality of political parties. The first set of cases involves the participation of political parties in the legislative system. The FCC has jurisdiction to decide on the constitutionality of political parties,[124] and has upheld petitions to ban the Neo-Nazi Socialist Reich Party and the Communist Party.[125] The FCC reasoned that 'in a free democratic state . . . freedom of political opinion and freedom of association are guaranteed to individual citizens as basic rights' and that, by implication, 'the establishment and activity of political parties must not be restrained'.[126] Nevertheless, since the framers of the Basic Law had felt it necessary to limit the absolute freedom conferred by basic political rights in order to safeguard democratic institutions from undemocratic activities, limiting political individual rights in the service of the democratic political system was, in the FCC's view, justifiable. The decisions were hugely influential in cementing the importance of party-based democracy in Germany, not only because their direct result was to exclude extremist parties from the party system altogether, but also in highlighting the power the FCC holds to protect the

[123] See Vanberg, 'Establishing Judicial Independence' (n 120), and Vanberg, *Politics of Constitutional Review* (n 111), 67–77.

[124] Article 13(2) of the FCCA, read with art 21(2) of the German Basic Law.

[125] The *Socialist Reich Party* case, 2 BVerfGE 1 (1952) and the *Communist Party* case, 5 BVerfGE 85 (1956).

[126] *Socialist Reich Party* case, ibid.

ideology of 'militant democracy'.[127] The FCC has extended its guardianship over the 'party state' in other ways too. It has developed a rich jurisprudence on the role of parties, relying on the statement in the Basic Law that 'political parties shall participate in the formation of the political will of the people'[128] to hold that when the state is engaged in the process of will formation, political parties are 'integral units of the constitutional state'.[129] In seeking to ensure the character of German democracy, the FCC has handed down decisions

> ordering higher salaries for legislative representatives; invalidating laws unduly restricting political parties from gaining access to the ballot; forbidding political parties from changing the order in which candidates appear on party list ballots; limiting the conditions under which a minor parliamentary party can be excluded from representation on a legislative committee; barring Parliament from excluding a representative from a legislative committee merely because he or she is not a member of a political party; and vindicating the rights of parliamentary minorities to establish investigative committees to hear evidence of illegal or improper conduct by a ruling governmental majority.[130]

An important decision on multiparty democracy involves the expansion of the system by abolishing electoral thresholds for representation in the legislature. German electoral law requires a party to win at least five per cent of the vote in order to take PR seats in the legislature.[131] The adoption of thresholds has been explained as an attempt to negate the instability that splinter parties bring to a PR system.[132] In the National Unity Elections case, however, the FCC held that the rule would not apply to the first post-unification elections in Germany in 1990.[133] This was to ensure that the parties of the former East German republic, now minority parties in the unified Germany, 'would have a fighting chance to enter the new, all German Parliament'.[134] In a subsequent decision related to the 1994 election, the FCC upheld the waiver of the five per cent rule for a minority party from the former East Germany, allowing it to takes seats in the legislature even though it won less than five per cent of the vote.[135] In these cases, the FCC

[127] Kommers, 'The Federal Constitutional Court' (n 120) 474. The phrase 'militant democracy' was introduced by the FCC in the *Communist Party* case (n 125) at 139. The FCC has rejected three other applications for declarations that a political party is unconstitutional. See D Kommers, *Constitutional Jurisprudence of the Federal Republic of Germany* 2nd edn (Durham, Duke University Press, 1997) 11–12.

[128] German Basic Law, art 21(1).

[129] *Schleswig-Holstein Election case*, BVerfGE 208 (1952) 225.

[130] D Kommers, 'The Federal Constitutional Court: Guardian of German Democracy' (2006) 603 *Annals of the American Academy of Political and Social Science* 111, 116 (emphasis and citations omitted).

[131] Federal Electoral Law, art 6(6).

[132] See K Bawn, 'The logic of Institutional Preferences: German Electoral Law as Social Choice Outcome' (1993) 37 *American Journal of Political Science* 965, 986. Despite objections, the FCC has upheld the principle of the 5% threshold (*Bavarian Party* case, 6 BVerfGE 84 (1957)).

[133] 82 BVerfGE 322 (1990).

[134] Kommers, 'The Federal Constitutional Court' (n 130) 117.

[135] *Basic Mandate Clause* case, 95 BVerfGE 408 (1997). See also Kommers, 'The Federal Constitutional Court' (n 130) 118.

upheld rights of political participation ahead of mechanisms intended to strengthen the party-political system against the threats that splinter parties might pose to a parliamentary system.

Second, the FCC has been called on to adjudicate directly in electoral disputes between the two very parties who select its judges. In what has been called Germany's *Bush v Gore*, the Hessian Election Review case,[136] the FCC was asked to decide whether the CDU's electoral victory in the largely SPD-dominated Hesse *Land*, on the back of illegal campaign financing, was void. While the FCC held that the CDU's actions did not violate the statutory standard of public morality by which the validity of the election was to be assessed,[137] the importance of the case lies not in its outcome but in the direct role that the party-political appointed FCC played in partisan electoral politics.

The third category of cases shows that partisan concerns arise in cases that are at least on the surface not about party politics, a demonstration of just how important partisan concerns are to constitutional adjudication in Germany. The FCC has jurisdiction in disputes involving public law between the federal government and *Länder*.[138] Relations between the federal government and the *Länder* in Germany, however, have often been shaped by partisan considerations. In the 1961 *Television* case, nullifying a decree establishing a national television service because it infringed *Land* competence in respect of cultural matters, the FCC rebuked the government, not only for the content of its action, but for having consulted only with *Länder* controlled by the CDU and not those controlled by the SPD. Thus, the government had unconstitutionally treated the *Länder* differently on the basis of party orientation.[139] Indeed, Chancellor's Adenauer's plan to create the national television service had been strongly opposed by states under SPD control.[140] In another case, five CDU-controlled *Länder* and a number of CDU members of the *Bundestag* challenged a liberal abortion law passed by an SPD-FDP coalition.[141] The rights conflict in this case was whether the Basic Law's protection of an 'inner core of personal freedom' had to submit to 'certain norms governing the whole of society' – in this case the norms contained in Article 6 of the Basic Law articulating the state's 'special protection' of marriage and the family.[142] The case was an abstract judicial review proceeding. Such cases frequently take on partisan overtones simply because the Basic Law contemplates abstract review only where a third of the members of the *Bundestag*, a state government, or the federal government

136 103 BVerfGE 111 (2001). Kommers, 'The Federal Constitutional Court' (n 130) 121.

137 Kommers, 'The Federal Constitutional Court' (n 130) 122. See also RA Miller, 'Lords of Democracy: The Judicialization of "Pure Politics" in the United States and Germany' (2004) 61 *Washington & Lee Law Review* 587, 627ff.

138 Article 13(8) FCCA and art 93(4) of the Basic Law.

139 12 BVerfGE 354 (1961).

140 Kommers, *Constitutional Jurisprudence* (n 127) 69–70.

141 *Abortion Reform Law* case, 39 BVerfGE 1 (1975). See also Kommers, 'The Federal Constitutional Court' (n 120) 474–75.

142 Kommers, *Constitutional Jurisprudence* (n 127) 346.

request it. Abstract review is usually initiated by opposition parties and the proceedings often result in a reiteration of party positions in court.[143] The FCC divided on the judgment, but not on the interpretation of the rights at issue. Rather, the court divided on the question of how the political system should approach the objective values at the heart of the Basic Law. The two dissenting judges argued that the implementation of the Basic Law's objective values is a task for the legislature, not the courts. A wide range of options for the translation of values into law and policy exists, and the decision on how to do so is one that 'rests with the legislature upon which the people directly confer legitimacy.' The majority, in engaging the legislature's decision, entered into the political fray while the minority chose to defer to the legislative majority; the minority aligned with SPD politics while the majority favoured the more conservative CDU opposition.

ii. Applying the Model

Canada is often looked to as a model of institutional design for divided societies.[144] Increasingly, Bosnia is coming to be seen in a similar light, at least in post-conflict states.[145] However, the German model, with its facially neutral rules, might offer a better solution for the design of apex courts in divided societies. In Peru, for example, a similar sub-constitutional power-sharing arrangement has arisen between the four dominant political parties against the background of facially neutral rules for the appointment of judges to the apex court. Judges are appointed by a super-majority in the legislature, but an agreement now exists in terms of which the seats on the court are designated for parties represented in the legislature.[146]

The benefit of facially neutral rules of this kind is that they accommodate shifting electoral dominance. The rules are flexible enough to allow for the kind of sub-constitutional arrangements that ensure all the major political parties are involved in the political process of selecting judges to the apex court. In Germany's case this has resulted in an effective and independent apex court. In addition, the FCC does not reveal the names of dissenting judges unless they write separate, dissenting opinions. Dissenting opinions have only been allowed

[143] Vanberg, *The Politics of Constitutional Review* (n 111) 89–90 and Alec Stone Sweet, *The Birth of Judicial Politics in France* (Oxford, Oxford University Press, 1992).

[144] Will Kymlicka, eg, describes Canada as a 'world leader . . . now seen as a model by many other countries' for the management of ethno-cultural relations (*Finding our Way: Rethinking Ethnocultural relations in Canada* (Oxford, Oxford University Press, 1995) 2–3. See also S Choudhry, 'Does the World need more Canada? The Politics of the Canadian model in constitutional politics and political theory' (2007) 5 *International Journal of Constitutional Law* 606, 607–08).

[145] Katherine Nobbs takes a largely positive view of the Bosnian Court's performance in bettering ethno-cultural relations in Bosnia. See Nobbs, 'A review of minority participation in the judiciary' (n 53).

[146] Eduardo Dargent, 'Determinants of Judicial Independence: Lessons from three "Cases" of Constitutional Courts in Peru (1982–2007)' (2009) 41 *Journal of Latin American Studies* 251.

since 1971, and since then have been prepared in only six per cent of decisions.[147] Analysis of the voting patterns of judges is difficult as a result, and investigating the link between a judge's performance and the partisan interests associated with the designation on his or her seat is all but impossible.

Why have the judges on the FCC generally chosen not to reveal their votes by writing dissenting opinions? Perhaps the judges on the FCC are concerned to prevent the party-political analyses of its members that are common in jurisdictions like the United States. While it is clear that political parties have a determinative say on the appointment of judges, the FCC has taken an approach that makes it very difficult to assess whether judges favour their appointing party, perhaps to preserve its own independence or at least the appearance of independence. While party politics enters the FCC both in the process by which it is staffed and in the cases that come before it, it cannot be said whether those politics influence the way the judges decide. Another possibility is that the judges' behaviour is itself explicable in terms of the insurance model of judicial politics. The idea here is that dissenting judges anticipate that they will be in the majority in future cases. In those future cases, the same judges will benefit from the institutional legitimacy the FCC derives from minimising the opportunities for political analysis of its judges' decisions.

The disadvantage of the Canadian or the Bosnian model is the very fact that ethnic concerns are explicitly and concretely integrated into the appointment and institutional foundations of the courts. Because the rules are not facially neutral there is no room for responsive adjustment should ethnic concerns fade over time or realign in any number of ways we cannot predict. The facially neutral rules in Germany and Peru have resulted in a situation where electoral outcomes have been central in shaping the process for the appointment of judges. These rules allow for a creative and flexible response to the contingent dominance of electoral processes. There is no reason that rules like these should not be able to accommodate or respond to ethnicity-based electoral or political outcomes in the same way.

The difference between the German approach to the representation of a diversity of interests on the apex court and the Bosnian and Canadian approaches is similar to the difference between liberal consociational and corporate consociational approaches to representation in the elected branches of government.[148] A liberal consociation allows groups to 'self-determine' their identity, and rewards whatever group identities emerge from the democratic process. These identities could be ethnic or religious or linguistic, but they could also be purely political or ideological or policy-centric. Corporate consociation,

[147] Vanberg, *The Politics of Constitutional Review* (n 111) 91. See also at 55, pointing out that the FCC is broadly representative of established political interests, 'including the interests of the states as corporate entities within the German system'.

[148] This point is taken from the discussion in J McGarry, B O'Leary and R Simeon, 'Integration or Accommodation? The Enduring Debate in Conflict Regulation' in Choudhry (ed), *Constitutional Design for Divided Societies* (n 7) 61–62.

in contrast, predetermines the identities that groups carry. Group identity is assigned according to ascriptive characteristics like ethnicity or mother tongue, and those identities in turn become politically salient as the mechanism or marker by which seats in parliament or portfolios in cabinet are allocated. The rules for consociation in liberal consociational systems are thus facially neutral just as are Germany's rules for the composition of the FCC. It seems, then, that differences in approach to broader questions of constitutional design reappear in these debates about apex courts. Thus, the politics of representation in these broader political areas may prove to be relevant to the investigation of the politics of representation in apex courts.

IV. CONCLUSION

In this chapter, we have argued that the politics of the design of apex courts in deeply divided societies is the product of the interaction of two kinds of judicial politics, the politics of judicial independence and the politics of constitutional interpretation. We suggested that in divided societies ethnic minorities that were likely to be perpetual political minorities have an interest in shaping the appointment procedures, composition, expertise and decision-rules of the apex court charged with ultimate responsibility for constitutional interpretation. We also suggested that in such societies the interrelationship between bills of rights that guarantee universal human rights for all citizens irrespective of ethnic identity, and elements of the constitutional order that institutionalise ethnic difference, would be at the heart of important constitutional cases and would yield interpretive disagreement. These constitutionally divisive issues would divide a divided court.

But what we have witnessed in the Bosnian and Canadian cases is how courts can arrive at a consensus and speak in a single voice on precisely these difficult questions. So the question for future research is how judges on a multi-member court reason across these divides. We cannot fully explore that issue here, but offer the following preliminary observations. In contemporary debates on representative democracy in diverse societies, one of the central questions has been whether legislatures should be designed to ensure the representation of historically excluded groups. Anne Phillips has argued in favour of these policies under the rubric of a politics of presence.[149] For Phillips, the value of guaranteeing representation of historically excluded groups is the increased likelihood that they will be particularly alert to the interests of their communities, of how they are affected by public policies, and will advance arguments and adduce evidence that would be neglected by members of the majority. But it does not follow that members of other groups are incapable of understanding these arguments, and hence, that absent vetoes or super-majority rules, members of excluded groups

[149] Anne Phillips, *The Politics of Presence* (New York, Oxford University Press, 1995).

are doomed to lose in politics. On the contrary, the claim is that in the process of legislative deliberation, these arguments may resonate with members of the majority, who will be persuaded by the strength of the reasons and evidence offered.

Phillips's institutional focus is the legislature. In a highly suggestive passage, she explores the extension of her argument to the judiciary:

> [C]ertain decisions are legitimated only by the representativeness of those who take them, while others stand independently of this. When this is so, the precise composition of the judiciary may not be such a salient concern. This conclusion, however, would follow only if we believed in impartiality as that 'view from nowhere', untouched by the experiences of where we have come. If, on the contrary, we see the pursuit of impartiality as depending on gathering the views from everywhere, then securing the diversity of the judiciary becomes as important as securing the diversity of the legislative assembly. In both cases, experience will affect our judgment, and a body that draws overwhelmingly on one set of experiences will be limited in its range of concerns. The difference is that, while members of the legislature can legitimately engage in special pleading . . . members of the judiciary cannot so legitimately regard themselves as 'representing' particular concerns. This is an important distinction . . . and it makes it harder to argue for strict guarantees along the lines of equal or proportionate presence. But the composition of the judiciary is an additional and significant concern, and particularly so where the judiciary adjudicates constitutional concerns.[150]

Phillips helps to frame the problem of adjudication on a divided court in a divided society. Judges are not simply delegates of the ethnic politicians who appointed them. But on constitutional questions that go to the very nature of citizenship and identity in a multi-ethnic state, judges from excluded groups bring to bear arguments and evidence that draw upon their experience in order to persuade their fellow judges from outside the community. The details of how that process takes place, and how the institutional factors that establish, empower, shape and constrain courts can promote this kind of deliberative engagement, we leave for another day.

[150] ibid 197, quoting IM Young, *Justice and the Politics of Difference* (Princeton, Princeton University Press, 1990) for the phrase 'view from nowhere'.

6

Judicial Empowerment in Divided Societies: The Northern Ireland Bill of Rights Process in Comparative Perspective

ALEX SCHWARTZ AND COLIN HARVEY

I. INTRODUCTION

THE BELFAST/GOOD FRIDAY Agreement (the Agreement) contemplates the possibility of a bill of rights for Northern Ireland. To that end, the Agreement provides for the establishment of a Northern Ireland Human Rights Commission who, inter alia, is tasked to 'consult and . . . advise on the scope' of a possible bill of rights for the jurisdiction (to be enacted by Westminster legislation).[1] After a decade of controversy and false

[1] Agreement reached in the multiparty negotiations 10 April 1998, 'Rights, Safeguards and Equality of Opportunity', para 4. The idea of a bill of rights for Northern Ireland actually predates the Agreement of 1998, but the Agreement provided relatively clear elite-level confirmation (and popular endorsement by referenda in both Ireland and Northern Ireland) to a longstanding idea whose time had finally arrived (or so it appeared). On the history of the bill of rights process (both before and after the Agreement), see generally C Harvey and A Schwartz, 'Designing a Bill of Rights for Northern Ireland' (2010) 60 *Northern Ireland Legal Quarterly* 181. By the time of the Agreement, rights and equality had moved from the 'margins to the mainstream', see P Mageean and M O'Brien, 'From the Margins to the Mainstream: Human Rights and the Good Friday Agreement' (1999) 22 *Fordham International Law Journal* 1499. References to human rights, and a bill of rights, are to be found throughout the long peace process. See C Harvey and S Livingstone, 'Human Rights and the Northern Ireland Peace Process' [1999] *European Human Rights Law Review* 162. As Stephen Livingstone noted, '[t]hroughout the past thirty years of conflict in Northern Ireland widespread agreement on the need for a Bill of Rights as one element of any constitutional settlement was one of the few beacons of political consensus': S Livingstone, 'The Need for a Bill of Rights in Northern Ireland' (2001) 52 *Northern Ireland Legal Quarterly* 269. See also A Smith, 'The Drafting Process of a Bill of Rights for Northern Ireland' [2004] *Public Law* 526; C Harvey and D Russell, 'A New Beginning for Human Rights Protection in Northern Ireland?' (2009) *European Human Rights Law Review* 767–86; and C Harvey, 'Implementing a Bill of Rights in Northern Ireland' (2001) 51 *Northern Ireland Legal Quarterly* 342.

starts, the Human Rights Commission delivered its 'final' advice in December 2008.[2] Successive UK governments have yet to implement that advice. Given the general scepticism expressed in the Northern Ireland Office's consultation document and outright opposition from the two major unionist parties, it seems unlikely that a bill of rights for Northern Ireland will materialise any time soon.[3]

There are several reasons why a bill of rights might be of value in Northern Ireland. At the very least, a bill of rights has the potential to compensate for deficiencies in existing human rights protections and to challenge inequities that have thus far been neglected by legislatures at Westminster and Stormont.[4] One might also legitimately suppose that a more just society will also be a less divided one.[5] In addition, a bill of rights has the potential to build on the Agreement's abstract commitments to 'parity of esteem' and 'mutual respect' between unionists and nationalists.[6] By consolidating these matters within a single rights instrument, the bill of rights could promote a more coherent and principled approach overall.[7] Finally, a bill of rights for Northern Ireland might even become a unifying device around which an otherwise divided society might articulate 'a collective commitment to a set of common values'.[8] To this end, a bill of rights ought – ideally – to be based on a broad political consensus spanning the ethno-national divide. But the pursuit of particular goals in the bill of rights inevitably jeopardises the basis for a cross-community consensus. People disagree about rights even in relatively homogenous societies.[9] So it is no surprise that the question of a bill of rights for Northern Ireland has been beset by

[2] Northern Ireland Human Rights Commission, *A Bill of Rights for Northern Ireland: Advice to the Secretary of State for Northern Ireland* (NIHRC 2008).

[3] See Northern Ireland Office, *A Bill of Rights for Northern Ireland: Next Steps* (NIO 2009); and Lady Daphne Trimble, 'Letter from Commissioner Daphne Trimble to the Secretary of State for Northern Ireland', at www.bbc.co.uk/blogs/ni/2008/12/daphne_trimble_explains_why_sh.html. It should be noted that one possibility is for a UK Bill of Rights to 'make special provision for Northern Ireland to reflect its need to tackle the particular circumstances there'. Dominic Grieve QC MP, 'Can the Bill of Rights do better than the Human Rights Act?' (30 November 2009), available online at www.dominicgrieve.org.uk/record.jsp?type=speech&ID=82.

[4] See A Kavanagh, 'The Role of a Bill of Rights in Reconstructing Northern Ireland' (2004) 26 *Human Rights Quarterly* 956–82; see also C Harvey, 'The Need for a Bill of Rights in Northern Ireland', at www.borini.info/uploads/documents/The%20need%20for%20a%20BoR%20in%20NI%20-%20Colin%20Harvey.doc; and S Livingstone, 'The Need for a Bill of Rights in Northern Ireland' (2001) *Northern Ireland Legal Quarterly 52, 269*.

[5] John Rawls, for one, thought that a polity whose people came to accept a theory of justice for the right reasons would also be politically stable: see generally J Rawls, *Political Liberalism* (Columbia University Press, 1993).

[6] See the Agreement, 'Constitutional Issues', para 1(v).

[7] On the role and value of 'integrity' for divided societies, see A Schwartz, 'Patriotism or Integrity?: Constitutional Community in Divided Societies' (2011) 31 *Oxford Journal of Legal Studies* 503.

[8] Harvey, 'The Need for a Bill of Rights in Northern Ireland' (n 1); see also Committee for the Administration of Justice, 'Comments on "Making a Bill of Rights"' (CAJ, 2001) para 1.4.

[9] See J Waldron, 'The Core of the Case Against Judicial Review' (2006)115 *Yale Law Journal* 1346, 1366–69 (discussing the problem of reasonable disagreement about rights).

deep disagreement.[10] Issues of particular contention have ranged from group identity rights (and the right not to identify with either of Northern Ireland's two main communities), to the rights of victims of the conflict, to the inclusion of socio-economic rights.[11]

This chapter considers the conditions for achieving a bill of rights in a deeply divided society like Northern Ireland. In pursuing this inquiry, we look at what leading theories of 'judicial empowerment' might have to contribute to the discussion.[12] As we will explain, the circumstances of divided societies, especially where these are accompanied by 'consociationalism', significantly complicate the problem of judicial empowerment. In so far as judicial review is a counter-majoritarian device, its emergence may coincide with and complement a larger scheme for accommodating group differences. But in a deeply divided society, a would-be bill of rights must also pass through a kind of double 'veto-gate'; the bill must secure sufficient support from (at least) two distinct sets of political elites whose attitudes and interests will have been shaped by very different experiences. Consequently, the alignment of background ideational conditions and elite support needed for judicial empowerment will tend to be particularly ephemeral.[13] We conclude the chapter on a more optimistic note with some 'Ackermanian' reflections on how popular mobilisation might ultimately overcome the problem of elite obstinacy.

II. POPULAR PARTICIPATION AND ELITE INITIATIVE

Despite the evident legal, political, social and other differences, the bill of rights debate in Northern Ireland has often been compared with bill of rights processes in Canada and South Africa.[14]As in Northern Ireland, the processes in

[10] The persistence of disagreement was evidenced by the dissent of the two Commissioners from the Human Rights Commission's final advice on the proposed bill of rights. See Trimble, 'Letter from Commissioner Daphne Trimble to the Secretary of State for Northern Ireland' (n 3).

[11] For an overview and critical analysis of the debate see R Whittaker, 'Debating Rights in the New Northern Ireland' (2010) 25 *Irish Political Studies* 23; see also Harvey and Schwartz, 'Designing a Bill of Rights for Northern Ireland' (n 1).

[12] Our use of the term 'judicial empowerment' follows Ran Hirschl's in his *Towards Juristocracy: The Origins and Consequences of the New Constitutionalism* (Cambridge MA, Harvard University Press, 2004). The term refers to a transfer of power to the judiciary from other branches of government. A common mechanism for judicial empowerment is, of course, a bill of rights.

[13] Our argument in this respect builds on David Erdos's 'post-materialist trigger theory' (or PTT) of bill of rights genesis. See D Erdos, *Delegating Rights Protection: The Rise of Bills of Rights in the Westminster World* (Oxford, Oxford University Press, 2010).

[14] See, eg, R Murray, 'The Importance of a Bill of Rights in Northern Ireland as a Process: Comparative Reflections from South Africa' (2002) 52 *Northern Ireland Legal Quarterly* 385; Whittaker, 'Debating Rights in the New Northern Ireland' (n 11) (comparing Northern Ireland with Canada), Committee on the Administration of Justice, *Human Rights and Peace-Building in Northern Ireland* (CAJ, 2006), chapters by B McLachlin, A Sachs, R Goldstone and B Porter; G Marcus, 'A Bill of Rights for Northern Ireland: Lessons from South Africa' in Amnesty International, *Northern Ireland: An Inclusive Bill of Rights for All* (AI, 2001). Northern Ireland is, of course, a sub-state polity endowed with devolved legislative powers and not a sovereign state in

Canada and South Africa occurred against the backdrop of politically salient group differences. It is the extent of public consultation and civil society participation in these three processes, however, that most invites comparison. Although there was a distinctive political context in each case – the transition to a post-apartheid South Africa, the 'patriation' of the Constitution of Canada and a peace process in Northern Ireland – each process sought widespread societal engagement in a constitutional conversation about rights.[15]

In the case of Northern Ireland, public consultation and the participation of civil society were central elements from the outset.[16] Shortly after beginning its work, the Northern Ireland Human Rights Commission (the Commission) launched a series of outreach efforts designed to raise awareness and elicit discussion about a possible bill of rights. These included human rights training and education, promotional publications and consultation with political parties, the voluntary sector and children and young people.[17] During the first two years of its work, the Commission received over 600 written submissions from political parties and civil society groups.[18] The establishment of a 'Bill of Rights Forum' in 2006 facilitated further public input; while half of the Forum's 28 members were drawn from Northern Ireland's main political parties – three each from the Democratic Unionist Party (DUP), Sinn Féin, Ulster Unionist Party (UUP) and the Social Democratic and Labour Party (SDLP), and two from the Alliance Party – the other half was made up of representatives from civil society/the voluntary sector (including representatives of the major Christian churches, the business sector, the human rights sector and various groups representing children, the disabled, the elderly, ethnic minorities, gays and lesbians, trade unions and women).[19] The Human Rights Consortium also assisted the

its own right. Thus, despite the considerable autonomy enjoyed by the Northern Ireland Assembly and the Executive, the power to effect constitutional change rests, at least in a technical sense, with outside elites. For the purposes of the discussion here, however, we will be, for the most part, treating Northern Ireland as though it were a self-contained polity on the assumption that the power to effect change enjoyed by elites at Westminster will be exercised in a way that is responsive to the preferences of governing elites in Northern Ireland. This has not always been a realistic assumption. Since the Agreement, however, Westminster has been increasingly deferential to the will of Northern Ireland's governing politicians.

[15] This focus on participation has also found its way into discussions of a UK/British bill of rights: see C Harvey, 'Taking the Next Step? Achieving another Bill of Rights' [2011] *European Human Rights Law Review* 24.

[16] See the comments of the departing Chair (Michael Lavery) of the Standing Advisory Commission on Human Rights in July 1998: 'Since its earliest days, SACHR has advocated the introduction of a Bill of Rights for Northern Ireland. The Multi-Party Agreement makes the process of consulting and advising on such a Bill the job of the new commission. SACHR has urged you to ensure that the process of drafting a Bill of Rights includes two key elements: firstly, that it involve wide-ranging consultation and education for the public and, secondly, that it draw upon individual international expertise of drafting Bills of Rights'. SACHR, *Report for 1997–1998* (1998) iii.

[17] See Northern Ireland Human Rights Commission, *Taking Forward a Bill of Rights for Northern Ireland* (NIHRC 2005) 8–11.

[18] See Northern Ireland Human Rights Commission, *Summary of submissions on a Bill of Rights* (NIHRC, 2003).

[19] See Bill of Rights Forum, *Final Report* (2008).

process of wide public consultation,[20] and the Northern Ireland Assembly has debated the bill of rights on a number of occasions.[21] More recently, the publication of the Northern Ireland Office's consultation document on the bill of rights has provided yet another opportunity for public input.[22] The responses to this exercise were published in late 2010, again demonstrating continued public engagement.[23]

The process leading up to the adoption of the Canadian Charter of Rights and Freedoms in 1982 also involved extensive public engagement.[24] In a series of televised hearings, a specially appointed parliamentary committee heard submissions from a broad spectrum of organisations representing the interests of linguistic minorities, aboriginal peoples, the 'multicultural community', labour unions, the poor, sexual minorities and women.[25] This phase of consultation had a tangible impact on the ultimate content of the Canadian Charter of Rights and Freedoms, prompting a stronger general equality provision, enhanced criminal procedure protections, an explicit guarantee of gender equality, and recognition of traditional aboriginal rights.[26]

The South African bill of rights process was even more broadly inclusive than the one in Canada. Indeed, the South African process is often regarded as the exemplar of how popular participation can engender constitutional legitimacy in a divided polity. The Constitutional Assembly (the body responsible for drafting the South African bill of rights) launched a massive multimedia campaign to raise awareness and elicit input from the public, including workshops in towns and villages, televised debates, a telephone hotline and an educational website.[27] In total, the Constitutional Assembly received a remarkable two million submissions from the public and consulted with nearly six hundred civil society organisations.[28]As Simone Chambers explains, these efforts to reach out and engage with the general population have a unifying effect:

[20] The Human Rights Consortium was established in 2000 to 'encourage widespread community participation in the Bill of Rights consultation'. The Consortium is made up of 120 non-governmental organisations, trade unions and community groups. See the Consortium's website: www3.billofrightsni.org/about_us/.

[21] See, eg, Northern Ireland Assembly, Official Report, 1 March, 2010; 3 November 2009 and 25 September 2001.

[22] Northern Ireland Office, *A Bill of Rights for Northern Ireland: Next Steps* (NIO, 2009).

[23] See www.nio.gov.uk/index/public-consultation/archive-consultation/content-responses-bill-of-rights.htm .

[24] For an overview of the process leading up to the patriation of the Canadian Constitution and the entrenchment of the Charter of Rights and Freedoms, see R Romanow, J Whyte and H Leeson, *Canada . . . Notwithstanding* (Toronto, Carswell/Methuen, 1984) ch 8; Peter Russell, *Constitutional Odyssey: can Canadians become a sovereign people?* 3rd edn (Toronto, University of Toronto Press, 2004) ch 8; and L Weinrib, 'Of diligence and dice: Reconstituting Canada's constitution' (1992) 42 *University of Toronto Law Journal* 207.

[25] See B Perry, 'The role of popular mobilizations in the struggle for the Canadian Charter of Rights and Freedoms' (1994) 22 *Crime, Law and Social Change* 183; and Erdos, *Delegating Rights Protection* (n 13) 77–82.

[26] See the discussion in Erdos, *Delegating Rights Protection* (n 13) 78.

[27] See S Chambers, 'Democracy, Popular Sovereignty, and Constitutional Legitimacy' (2004) 11 *Constellations* 153, 161–64.

[28] ibid 162.

> South Africans needed to create a 'people,' but faced a situation of pluralism and diversity, not to mention past injustice and deep scars. They approached this problem by getting citizens to identify with, and participate in, a process that gave them dignity and thereby created a sense of a 'people'. Rather than identification with one abstract statement, there is an identification with a process in which all are involved.[29]

Whatever the value and extent of popular participation in the bill of rights processes in Canada and South Africa, however, it should not be forgotten that those processes were primarily elite-driven affairs. In the Canadian case, the Federal Liberal Party (led by Prime Minister Pierre Trudeau) spearheaded and dominated the drive for a constitutionally entrenched bill of rights. In fact, beginning with his appointment as Federal Justice Minister in 1967, the 'Charter'-project was a kind of personal political mission for Trudeau.[30] The project was designed with explicitly 'integrative' purposes in mind: to undermine Quebec nationalism and foster a pan-Canadian identity based on individual rights and official bilingualism.[31] Later, as Prime Minister, Trudeau led the constitutional 'patriation' process that saw the plan for a constitutional bill of rights through to its ultimate fruition.[32] The notion of actually involving the 'People' of Canada in that process was only begrudgingly agreed to by the Trudeau government (after significant political pressure) and the public hearings that followed were carefully orchestrated so as to discredit the Charter's opponents.[33]

In the case of South Africa, the process had two distinct stages, each of which was dominated by political elites (albeit in different ways). The first stage involved a series of 'consensus-building' elite negotiations, primarily between the still-governing National Party and the recently legalised and the soon-to-be ascendant African National Congress (ANC).[34] The purpose there was to devise a provisional framework for the eventual transition to a permanent post-apartheid constitutional order. The resultant 'Interim Constitution' was, as Heinz Klug puts it, 'the epitome of an elite pact' – to assuage the anxieties of the National Party (and also the Inkatha Freedom Party), the Interim Constitution guaranteed a system of power-sharing subject to a 'sunset clause' after the first five years of the transition.[35] In return, the Interim Constitution

[29] ibid 164.

[30] Romanow, Whyte and Leeson, *Canada . . . Notwithstanding* (n 24) 227–29.

[31] See P Russell, 'The Political Purposes of the Canadian Charter of Rights and Freedoms' (1983) 61 *Canadian Bar Review* 30; see also S Choudhry 'Bills of Rights as Instruments of Nation-Building in Multinational States: The Canadian Charter and Quebec Nationalism' in JB Kelly and CP Manfredi (eds), *Contested Constitutionalism: Reflections on the Canadian Charter of Rights and Freedoms* (Vancouver, University of British Columbia Press, 2010).

[32] See Romanow, Whyte and Leeson, *Canada . . . Notwithstanding* (n 24) 229–47.

[33] ibid 246–48.

[34] H Klug, *The South African Constitution: A Contextual Analysis* (Oxford, Hart Publishing, 2010) 46–50. For critical discussion of the first phase of the constitutional transition, see Hugh Corder 'Towards a South African Constitution' (1994) 57 *Modern Law Review* 491.

[35] H Klug, *Constituting Democracy: Law, Globalism, and South Africa's Political Reconstruction* (Cambridge, Cambridge University Press, 2000) 104; and 'Participating in the Design: Constitution-Making in South Africa' (1996) 3 *Review of Constitutional Studies* 18.

provided for the ANC's preferred option for the second stage of the process: a democratically elected 'Constitutional Assembly' (in which the ANC would easily command an overwhelming majority) with a mandate to draft the final constitution.[36] In keeping with the spirit of the initial 'elite pact', the Constitutional Assembly's final draft had to be certified by the South African Constitutional Court as being consistent with the general principles agreed to in the interim settlement.[37]

In contrast to the Canadian and South African examples, the process in Northern Ireland has been driven all along by an appointed committee of experts: the Northern Ireland Human Rights Commission.[38] Together with a consortium of human-rights friendly non-governmental organisations, the Commission advocates a strong and expansive bill of rights for the jurisdiction.[39] Meanwhile, support from political elites for a bill of rights in Northern Ireland has, on the whole, been more ambivalent. To be sure, all major political parties – unionists and nationalists alike – have professed their support for the abstract idea of *a* bill of rights.[40] However, unionist elites have generally insisted on a narrowly circumscribed rights instrument or, in the alternative, no bill of rights at all.[41] Meanwhile, nationalist elites (although much more supportive of

[36] See Klug, *The South African Constitution* (n 34) 46, 53.

[37] ibid 50.

[38] Section 68(3) of The Northern Ireland Act 1998 provides that appointments to the Commission are made by the Secretary of State for Northern Ireland who is required to ensure that 'as far as practicable . . . the Commissioners, as a group, are representative of the community in Northern Ireland'.

[39] See Northern Ireland Human Rights Commission, *A Bill of Rights for Northern Ireland: Advice to the Secretary of State for Northern Ireland*. The rationale for an inclusive process that also gains traction with elites was neatly captured by the-then UN High Commissioner for Human Rights, Mary Robinson, in an address to the Human Rights Consortium in Belfast on 18 May 2002: 'Real change will only happen if those in positions of power recognize their own responsibility in bringing change about – and, indeed, become genuine agents of change . . . In arguing for active party political involvement in the debate, you are arguing that those in positions of influence be part of the change process. In arguing for a cross-party, cross-community approach to the debate you are challenging your political representatives to reflect the diversity that is this society'. See also Mary Robinson, 'Equality and Human Rights: Their Role in Peace Building', Belfast, 2 December 1998: 'The process of engaging society in a broad and inclusive debate about the content of a written Bill of Rights will be a major building block in the creation of a culture of human rights, which is the only sure protection in the longer term'.

[40] See Committee for the Administration of Justice, *A Bill of Rights for Northern Ireland through the Years – The Views of the Political Parties* (CAJ, 2003). See also K Boyle and T Hadden, *Northern Ireland: The Choice* (London, Penguin Books, 1994) 180: 'The protection of individual and communal rights may be thought to be equally straightforward. All the parties in Northern Ireland are committed to the introduction of a Bill of Rights and the British government has indicated that it will not raise any objections to this despite its opposition to the introduction of any such Bill of Rights for the rest of the United Kingdom'. See also K Boyle and T Hadden, *Ireland: A Positive Proposal* (London, Penguin Books, 1985) 83.

[41] See the submissions of political parties to the Northern Ireland Human Rights Commission, available at www.nihrc.org/dms/data/NIHRC/attachments/dd/files/53/summarybor.pd. And note the comment of the Commission in 2005: 'The Ulster Unionist Party . . . and the Democratic Unionist Party . . . have not played a very active part in the Commission's consultation process . . .the DUP clearly retains deep reservations about the need for, and wisdom of, a comprehensive Bill of Rights that would make the position regarding human rights in Northern Ireland noticeably different from that in Great Britain'. Northern Ireland Human Rights Commission, *Taking Forward a Bill of Rights for Northern Ireland* (NIHRC 2005) 24.

the latest proposals) have never made the bill of rights a deal-breaking issue in their negotiations with political unionism.[42] Despite the apparent ambivalence of political elites (and especially mainstream unionists), recent opinion polls indicate a great deal of popular support for a bill of rights within both nationalist and unionist communities in Northern Ireland.[43] It would seem then that the primary obstacle to a bill of rights for Northern Ireland is not a lack of social demand, but what we might call (following David Erdos) 'elite-supply blockage'.[44] In other words, Northern Ireland would already have a bill of rights (in some form or another) if only its political elites *really* wanted one.

III. THEORISING ELITE SUPPORT FOR JUDICIAL EMPOWERMENT

Leading theories of judicial empowerment converge on the view that the support of political elites is a decisive factor in the realisation of a bill of rights.[45] No amount of public consultation, civil society engagement or expert advice will deliver a bill of rights unless it is also supported by those elites who are effectively 'veto players' with respect to constitutional change.[46] But it is not obvious why political elites would support a bill of rights; bills of rights tend to restrict the legislative and administrative freedom of political elites.[47] Why would elites ever choose to disempower themselves in this way?

According to one school of thought, elite support for bills of rights can be explained primarily by reference to rational-strategic considerations; certain

[42] In the last round of devolution negotiations, eg, the bill of rights question was a non-issue. The main concern of nationalist elites was to negotiate terms for the devolution of policing powers, an objective they achieved by consenting to unionist demands for reform of the Parades Commission. See *Agreement at Hillsborough Castle*, online at www.nio.gov.uk/agreement_at_hillsborough_castle_5_february_2010.pdf .

[43] See, eg, Opinion Poll (MRNI 2004), online at www.borini.info/opinion-polls.aspx.

[44] D Erdos, 'Elite supply "blockages" and the failure of national Bill of Rights initiatives in Australia: a comparative Westminster analysis' (2008) 46 *Commonwealth & Comparative Politics* 341.

[45] See T Ginsburg, *Judicial Review in New Democracies: Constitutional Courts in East Asia* (Cambridge University Press, 2003) 11; Hirschl, *Towards Juristocracy* (n 12); D Erdos, *Delegating Rights Protection* (n 13) 27; and L Hilbink, 'The Constituted Nature of Constituents' Interests: Historical and Ideational Factors in Judicial Empowerment' (2009) 62 *Political Research Quarterly* 781.

[46] On the role of 'veto players' in politics more generally, see generally G Tsebelis, *Veto Players: How Political Institutions Work* (Princeton NJ, Princeton University Press, 2002).

[47] Awareness of this in Northern Ireland was evident in an early response to the Commission from the Northern Ireland Office: 'Decisions on matters like these are for democratically elected politicians to take, not the courts. It seems to me that it would be wrong to seek to tie the hands of Government Ministers or Ministers in the Executive in this way through a Bill of Rights made at Westminster. Indeed, given the absence of locally elected governance in Northern Ireland over the past 30 years, it could be argued that the "particular circumstances" of Northern Ireland make it even more important for decisions to be taken by the Executive rather than the courts on foot of Westminster legislation'. (emphasis in original) Letter of 18 November 2001 from Des Browne, Parliamentary Under-Secretary of State for Northern Ireland to Brice Dickson, Chief Commissioner NIHRC.

conditions create strategic incentives for elites to cede some of their power, *via* a bill of rights, to the judiciary. In this vein, Tom Ginsburg argues for what he calls the 'insurance model' of judicial empowerment.[48] According to Ginsburg, judicial review provides elites with a kind of insurance against the possibility of future electoral loss: 'Under conditions of high uncertainty, it may be especially useful for politicians to adopt a system of judicial review to entrench the constitutional bargain and to ensure they can challenge government action after future electoral change'.[49] Thus, according to the insurance model, one can expect elite support for judicial empowerment to increase as perceived prospects for electoral success diminish; conversely, elite support for a bill of rights will decline where a single political party is dominant or where electoral success can be expected with greater confidence.

In a similar vein, Ran Hirschl argues that judicial empowerment is best explained in terms of the efforts of threatened elites to preserve their hegemony; elites will seek judicial empowerment in order to safeguard their cultural, economic and ideological dominance when that dominance is challenged within conventional majoritarian decision-making arenas.[50] Hirschl's account relies on the interplay of three groups of elites: political elites who seek to insulate their policy preferences, economic elites who see judicial review as as a means of promoting a 'neoliberal' free-market agenda, and judicial elites 'that seek to enhance their political influences and international reputation'.[51] In so far as it relies on ideational factors (especially neo-liberalism), Hirschl's explanation of judicial empowerment is 'thicker' and more contextually sensitive than Ginsburg's insurance model. Nevertheless, both theories can usefully be described as 'rational-strategic' theories because of the emphasis they place on the means-end calculations of political elites.[52]

Not everyone agrees, however, that judicial empowerment can be explained primarily by the rational-strategic motivations of elites.[53] Lisa Hilbink argues that the motivations of political elites cannot be understood in isolation from historical and ideational factors.[54] According to Hilbink, 'shared experiences, beliefs, identities, ideologies, and interpretations of events and sequences of events at home or abroad' significantly influence what political elites understand their interests to be and how they decide to pursue them.[55] Thus the motivations of political elites are not always so obviously self-serving; the

[48] Ginsburg, *Judicial Review in New Democracies* (n 45) 25.

[49] ibid 30.

[50] See Hirschl, *Towards Juristocracy* (n 12) 44.

[51] ibid 43.

[52] Our terminology here follows Woods and Hilbink. See PJ Woods and L Hilbink, 'Comparative Sources of Judicial Empowerment: Ideas and Interests' (2009) 62 *Political Research Quarterly* 745.

[53] For a helpful overview of the debate see ibid; and M McCann, 'Interests, Ideas, and Institutions in Comparative Analysis of Judicial Power' (2009) 62 *Political Research Quarterly* 834.

[54] L Hilbink, 'The Constituted Nature of Constituents' Interests: Historical and Ideational Factors in Judicial Empowerment' (2009) 62 *Political Research Quarterly* 781.

[55] ibid 782.

institutional preferences of elites can also reflect sincere beliefs about what is best for their societies:

> In delegating power to courts, they are not always or only seeking to enhance or extend their own wealth, power, or prestige, but are sometimes doing what seems proper in terms of their nation's history or what they think a theory or model of good government (e.g., democratic, liberal, or modern) requires.[56]

Another challenge to the rational-strategic paradigm comes from recent work by David Erdos. He argues that while rational-strategic motivations are important in many cases, they are neither necessary nor sufficient conditions for judicial empowerment.[57] According to Erdos, bill of rights genesis is also dependent upon and substantively influenced by 'long-range background pressures favouring a bill of rights', the most important of these being the growth of what he calls a 'postmaterialist rights constituency'.[58] Such a constituency is the product of wider ideational change in the advanced industrialised world leading to the emergence of a general postmaterialist value orientation associated with an increasing emphasis on 'a wider array of (non-economic) values and concerns' coupled with the 'declining salience of traditional ascriptive identities and communities'.[59] This 'postmaterialisation' of values stimulates the emergence of a coalition of civil liberty and social equality groups who will tend to champion a bill of rights as an instrument for furthering their postmaterial interests. But the emergence of a postmaterialist rights constituency is not, all by itself, sufficient to provoke judicial empowerment; some 'contingent and discrete political trigger' is also needed to motivate elites in the right way.[60] In some cases, as Erdos concedes, elite support for judicial empowerment may well be rooted in a 'strictly rational, prospective, power-focused calculation'.[61] Thus, Erdos argues that a 'threat to political stability' triggered elite support for the Canadian Charter; the rise of Quebecois nationalism

> directly threatened the prospective power and position of the federal elite. Given that the Charter was devised to counter this, it follows that, in addition to any ideological factor at play, this project was strongly linked to the future oriented rational self-interest of this group.[62]

In other cases, however, Erdos argues that judicial empowerment may be triggered instead by 'a reactive or "aversive" response rooted in past negative political experiences'.[63] In such cases, 'a long period in the political wilderness loosens commitments to the power-hoarding, executive-minded approach associated

[56] ibid 783.
[57] Erdos, *Delegating Rights Protection* (n 13).
[58] ibid 23.
[59] ibid 25.
[60] ibid 23.
[61] ibid 43.
[62] ibid 74.
[63] ibid 43.

with parties of government' and 'the experience of such opposition under a government perceived as heavy-handed and authoritarian leads to growing support for specific institutional restraints on political power'.[64] According to Erdos, it was this kind of retrospective aversive trigger that generated the Labour Party's enthusiasm for the UK Human Rights Act in the late 1990s.[65]

As we will explain later, we think that Erdos's theory is actually the most helpful of the leading theories for understanding the challenges of judicial empowerment in divided societies like Northern Ireland. In order to appreciate why this is so, however, it is first necessary to understand how the circumstances of divided societies, and especially consociationalism, complicate the problem of judicial empowerment.

IV. CONSOCIATIONALISM AND JUDICIAL EMPOWERMENT

By 'divided society' we mean a polity in which cleavages of group identity or membership (ie nationalism, ethnicity, religious affiliation, etc) are politically salient in the sense that they are the predominant (or very prominent) bases for political behaviour.[66] In such cases, elections tend to proceed 'like a census' and so simple majoritarian democracy will tend to construct perpetual minorities.[67] One of the institutional remedies for this kind of problem is what Arend Lijphart called 'consociational democracy'.[68] The chief feature that distinguishes consociational democracy from majoritarian democracy is that power is shared amongst representatives of all politically salient groups.[69] Lijphart and his followers have identified certain arrangements that are said to be characteristic of the consociational model of democracy: (1) a power-sharing executive inclusive of all major societal 'segments'; (2) territorial or cultural autonomy; (3) proportional representation in government and the civil service and the proportional allocation of public funds; and (4) minority/mutual veto power (at least on issues of vital concern to the major societal segments).[70]

[64] ibid 29.

[65] See ibid ch 7.

[66] On politics in divided societies, see generally D Horowitz, *Ethnic Groups in Conflict* (Berkeley and Los Angeles, University of California Press, 1985); and A Rabushka and KA Shepsle, *Politics in Plural Societies* (Columbus OH, Charles E Merrill, 1972).

[67] See M Moore, *The Ethics of Nationalism* (Oxford, Oxford University Press, 2001) 89.

[68] For seminal works on consociational democracy see A Lijphart, *The Politics of Accommodation: Pluralism and Democracy in the Netherlands* (Berkeley and Los Angeles, University of California Press, 1968); 'Consociational Democracy' (1969) 21 *World Politics* 207; and *Democracy in Plural Societies: A Comparative Exploration* (New Haven CT, Yale University Press, 1977). For influential applications of consociational theory to the Northern Ireland conflict, see J McGarry and B O'Leary, *The Northern Ireland Conflict: Consociational Engagements* (Oxford, Oxford University Press, 2004). For an overview of contemporary debates on consociational democracy and Northern Ireland, see generally R Taylor (ed), *Consociational Theory* (London, Routledge, 2008).

[69] See generally Lijphart, *Democracy in Plural Societies (n 68).*

[70] ibid 25.

There are some important connections between consociational democracy and judicial review. First of all, to the extent that they both limit the power of majority communities to impose their will upon minorities, they are both counter-majoritarian institutions. For this reason, Lijphart considers both judicial review and consociationalism to be characteristic expressions of the more general style of government he calls 'consensus democracy'.[71] But the connection between the two institutions goes further. Where consociationalism is formally prescribed in some kind of constitutional (or quasi-constitutional) document, judicial review provides a way of checking that public power is in fact exercised in accordance with the consociational scheme.[72] And this same logic can be extended to justify the expansion of judicial power beyond the formal dimensions of consociationalism to include rights-based review as well: in a divided society, rights-based judicial review provides further reassurance to minorities that their interests will not be disregarded by majorities. Thus, the same kind of pragmatic reasons that prompt elites to converge on a consociational settlement may also prompt them to support judicial empowerment; judicial empowerment helps to construct a stable and functional system of government in the otherwise destabilising circumstances of divided societies.[73] Call this the 'accommodation theory' of judicial empowerment.[74]

It is important to notice that the accommodation theory does not propose that there is anything like a necessary connection between consociationalism and judicial empowerment; it posits only that the two institutions share a certain functional affinity. But if this is so, then we would seem to be no closer to understanding why the bill of rights process in Northern Ireland has been so fraught with difficulty. According to the accommodation theory of judicial empowerment, a bill of rights would buttress Northern Ireland's consociational scheme with one extra level of counter-majoritiarian protection. So why haven't the same conditions that induced Northern Ireland's consociational settlement also induced a bill of rights?

Rational-strategic theories of judicial empowerment suggest one possible answer to this puzzle: from a rational-strategic perspective, consociationalism ought to *discourage* the genesis of rights-based judicial review. Two of the four elements of consociationalism – inclusive power-sharing and minority/mutual

[71] A Lijphart, *Patterns of Democracy: Government Forms and Performance in Thirty-Six Countries* (New Haven, CT: Yale University Press, 1999) 3–4.

[72] See ibid 228–30, discussing the logical connection between judicial review and constitutional rigidity.

[73] See M Adams and Gvan der Schyff, 'Political Theory Put to the Test: Comparative Law and the Origins of Judicial Constitutional Review' (2010) 10 *Global Jurist* 1, 32–33.

[74] Erdos and Hirschl refer to this kind of account as, respectively, 'institutionalist' and 'functionalist'. See Erdos, *Delegating Rights Protection* (n 13) 35; and Hirschl, *Towards Juristocracy* (n 12) 35. Those labels are accurate, but we have used the term 'accommodation' here to highlight the specific affinity between judicial review and consociationalism. For another good example of an accommodationist/institutionalist/functionalist theory of judicial review, see B Weingast, 'The Political Foundations of Democracy and the Rule of Law' (1997) 91 *American Political Science Review* 245.

veto power – either weaken or totally negate rational-strategic incentives for elites to support judicial empowerment. First, inclusive power-sharing guarantees that all parties with a significant degree of electoral support can confidently expect to share in some degree of executive power. Thus, the anxiety of changing electoral fates is considerably defused and so the insurance function of judicial review is superseded. Second, veto power provides insecure political elites with a simple and very effective mechanism for protecting their interests against legislative incursions; they can block whatever prospective laws or decisions they do not like. In comparison with the indirect and unpredictable mechanism of judicial review, hegemonic elites would surely prefer to rely only on veto power as an *alternative* to taking their chances with judicial empowerment.

The above hypothesis concurs to some extent with the substance of Northern Ireland's settlement. In Northern Ireland, both executive power-sharing and mutual veto power are present in relatively strong forms. Executive power-sharing in Northern Ireland is premised on a relatively low threshold for representation in the Assembly (14.3 per cent) in each of the territory's six-member constituencies. The Northern Ireland Executive is then constituted according to an algorithm, the d'Hondt formula, whereby ministerial posts are allocated in a way that is roughly proportionate to the number of seats a party wins in the Assembly.[75] The minority/mutual veto power relies on a system of community designation, whereby members of the Assembly are required to self-designate as 'unionist', 'nationalist', or 'other'.[76] Thereafter, certain 'key' decisions, such as standing orders and budget allocations, are made on the basis of 'cross-community consent', requiring either at least a majority of designated unionists and nationalists, as well as a majority in the Assembly, or, in the alternative, a weighted majority of 60 per cent of members present and voting, including at least 40 per cent each of designated unionists and nationalists present and voting.[77] The cross-community consent rules may also apply to any decision where a 'Petition of Concern' is brought by at least 30 members of the Assembly.[78]

So, if rational-strategic theories of judicial empowerment are right, then the lack of a bill of rights in Northern Ireland might be attributed (at least in part) to the consociational nature of the constitutional settlement. In other words, neither unionist nor nationalist political elites have reason to support a bill of rights so long as they can expect to enjoy the benefits of power-sharing and mutual vetoes.[79] And so, counter to what the accommodation theory of judicial

[75] Northern Ireland Act 1998, s 18(5).

[76] Northern Ireland Act 1998, s 4(5); see also The Agreement, 'Strand One', para 6.

[77] See Northern Ireland Act 1998, ss 4(2A), 4(3), 4(5), 17, 28A(4(a)), 30, 39, 41 and 63(3).

[78] ibid s 42.

[79] Note the speech by Mark Durkan, then leader of the Social Democratic and Labour Party (SDLP), at the British Irish Association Conference in New College, Oxford (5 September 2008), where in discussions of moving beyond communal designation he appeared to suggest that a bill of rights might provide the needed assurances: 'There are those who dismiss the need for such a bill or for it to be robust and extend to some social and economic issues. Maybe they and the rest of us need to start thinking about how a sound Bill of Rights in Northern Ireland might offer more productive and articulate protection for all our rights in a new democratic society than vote-locks and

empowerment would have us believe, the functional affinity shared by constitutionalism and judicial review would be a reason *not* to find the latter in conjunction with the former (or, at the very least, we would expect to see less judicial review where there is greater consociationalism).

But judicial review has in fact often followed or been accompanied by varying degrees of consociationalism (eg, Belgium and Bosnia-Herzegovina).[80] The example of Belgium is especially instructive. Since the 1970s, Belgium has enjoyed a system of government that is strongly consociational with respect to its two ethno-linguistic communities, combining executive power-sharing at the federal-level and later also within the Brussels-Capital Region governments, a de facto mutual veto power at the federal executive level, formal mutual vetoes over federal legislation with specifically regional implications, and an 'alarm bell' procedure whereby any legislation may require the approval of the federal or Brussels-Capital Region executives.[81] As we saw earlier, power-sharing and veto power mechanisms undercut rational-strategic incentives to support judicial empowerment. Nonetheless, the judicial power in Belgium has also expanded considerably since the 1970s.[82] First, a special court – the Court of Arbitration – was established in the early 1980s to adjudicate disputes concerning the competencies of Belgium's federal, regional and community legislatures.[83] At that time, the power of judicial review was seen as just a necessary outgrowth of Belgium's federalisation.[84] The Court of Arbitration's jurisdiction was later expanded in 1988, however, to allow review for compliance with education rights and principles of equality and non-discrimination.[85] This second spate of judicial empowerment was brought on by the devolution of education

tit-for-tat vetoes in perpetuity. "One man-one vote" was the start of a journey – made longer and harder than it needed to be. "One side-one vote" should not be the final destination of that journey'. The speech generated considerable discussion in Northern Ireland.

[80] We rely here on Rupert Taylor's list of consociational systems. R Taylor, 'Introduction' in R Taylor (ed), *Consociational Theory* (London, Routledge, 2009) 5. For judicial review, we rely on Arend Lijphart's index for measuring the strength of judicial review. See Lijphart, *Patterns of Democracy* (n 71) 226; David Erdos's index for what he calls 'bill of rights institutionalization'. See Erdos, *Delegating Rights Protection* (n 13) 16–17; and the index for measuring 'constitutional review' developed by Rafeal La Porta et al. See R La Porta, F Lopez-de-Silanes, C Pop-Eleches and A Shleifer, 'Judicial Checks and Balances' (2004) 112 *Journal of Political Economy* 445, app B.

[81] See K Deschouwer, 'And the Peace Goes On? Consociational Democracy and Belgian Politics in the Twenty-First Century' (2006) 29 *West European Politics* 895. For an historical overview of Belgium's path from a simple consociational democracy to a federal consociational democracy, see K Deschouwer, 'From consociation to federation: how the Belgian parties won' in KR Luther and K Deschouwer (eds), *Party Elites in Divided Societies* (London, Routledge, 1999).

[82] Belgium's score on Erdos's index for 'bill of rights institutionalization' is relatively high at 3.58. That score is higher than the overall average score of 2.82 and higher even than the United States's score of 3.25. See Erdos, *Delegating Rights Protection* (n 13) 16–17, Table 2.1.

[83] See M Adams and Gvan der Schyff 'Political Theory Put to the Test: Comparative Law and the Origins of Judicial Constitutional Review' (2010) 10 *Global Jurist* 1, 11–12; see also P Peeters, 'Expanding Constitutional Review by the Belgian "Court of Arbitration"' (2005) 11 *European Public Law* 475, 476–77.

[84] Adams and van der Schyff, 'Political Theory Put to the Test' (n 83) 11–12.

[85] Adams and van der Schyff, 'Political Theory Put to the Test' (n 83) 13; see also Peeters, 'Expanding Constitutional Review' (n 83) 480–83.

powers from the federal government to Belgium's linguistic Communities; the liberal minority within the jurisdiction of Flemish Community and the Roman Catholic minority within the jurisdiction of the Walloon Community, both being anxious that their respective interests would not be properly respected by the Communities, insisted on justiciable rights-based protections.[86]

To be sure, a single case cannot decisively vindicate any particular theory of judicial empowerment.[87] That being said, 'process tracing' within a single case can be used to generate a plausible causal narrative for the observation in question.[88] In the Belgian process we have just outlined,[89] the expansion of judicial power (beyond the initial systemic need to manage conflicts over legislative competence) was apparently driven by some combination of intra-group solidarity and inter-group suspicion: elites in Group A care about the fate of other A's but they do not trust elites in Group B to do the same (and vice versa). Some A's are subject to Group B's jurisdiction (and vice versa). By accepting judicial supervision over their own powers, Group A's elites gain confidence that their counterparts in Group B will be subject to the same constraints (and vice versa). Significantly, this account situates elite support for judicial empowerment within a larger scheme of group accommodation. In other words, judicial empowerment in the Belgian scenario is part of the politics of accommodation. And this is just what the accommodation theory of judicial empowerment maintains.[90]

So we would appear to have come full circle. On the one hand, there is a functional affinity between consociationalism and judicial review. On the other hand, recognising this affinity only makes the problem of 'elite-supply blockage' in Northern Ireland all the more puzzling. As we have seen, one explanation for this puzzle – building on rational-strategic theories – is that the usual incentives to support judicial empowerment are neutralised by the consociational nature of the settlement. But, as we have also seen, this explanation does not account for those consociational settings (like Belgium) where judicial review is part of a broader logic of inter-group accommodation. Given this apparent stalemate, we have good reason to extend our inquiry beyond *both* rational-strategic and accommodation theories to incorporate historical-ideational variables as well. As we will explain, the way in which the circumstances of divided societies

86 Adams and van der Schyff, 'Political Theory Put to the Test' (n 83) 13–14.

87 See Gary King, Robert Keohane and Sidney Verba, *Designing Social Inquiry: Scientific Inference in Qualitative Research* (Princeton, Princeton University Press, 1994) 209–13.

88 See Alexander L George and Andrew Bennett, *Case Studies and Theory Development in the Social Sciences* (Cambridge MA, MIT Press, 2005) ch 10. See also James Mahoney, 'After KKV: The New Methodology of Qualitative Research' (2010) 62 *World Politics* 120.

89 For a more detailed 'process tracing', see Adams and van der Schyff, 'Political Theory Put to the Test' (n 83).

90 Indeed, Maurice Adams and Gerhard van der Schyff offer precisely this kind of account of the Belgian scenario as a challenge to Hirschl's rational-strategic theory. See ibid. It should be noted, however, that the Belgian scenario presumes a specific kind of setting: a federal or quasi-federal polity in which groups are imperfectly concentrated within different territorial units of government and so have reason to want additional protections beyond consociational guarantees at the centre.

generate diverging patterns of ideas and interests among political elites helps to explain why, *despite* the consociational settlement, it has been so difficult to realise a bill of rights in Northern Ireland.

V. IDEAS AND INTERESTS IN DIVIDED SOCIETIES

In moving on to consider historical-ideational factors, we ought to be wary of falling prey to a lazy kind of cultural essentialism. It has become a sort of cliché to contrast an Irish nationalist political culture that stresses human rights and equality with a British unionist political culture that emphasises responsibility and loyalty to the state.[91] To be sure, nationalist politicians have tended to support a stronger and more comprehensive bill of rights while unionist politicians have tended to favour a more limited model. Nevertheless, positing a rigid dichotomy between unionist and nationalist political cultures is misleading for several reasons. As Robin Whittaker observes, the Progressive Unionist Party has been strongly supportive of the more expansive proposals for a bill of rights for Northern Ireland; unionist political parties in Northern Ireland have expressed support for human rights (if not versions of a bill of rights);[92] many of the civil society activists who have supported the expansive model come from Protestant/unionist backgrounds; and opinion polls further serve to undermine the cultural stereotype of the rights-averse unionist.[93] So the unionist perspective on rights and equality is not as monolithic as it is often portrayed.[94]

If there are general patterns in the attitudes of political elites with respect to the bill of rights, these have less to do with hard-wired cultural propensities and more to do with divergent circumstances and experiences. Historically, nationalist and unionist elites in Northern Ireland have been situated differently vis-a-vis state power. From the perspective of historically marginalised nationalist elites, the language of equality and rights is empowering for obvious reasons. But from the perspective of historically dominant unionist elites, the discourse of human rights is seen by many as antagonistic to the interests of the state and, by extension, to unionism itself. This contrast is a well-rehearsed conversation piece in Northern Ireland.[95] An important point that Hirschl's work highlights, however, it is that changing circumstances can provoke miraculous conversions to the cause of rights-based judicial review even among the most unlikely apos-

[91] For discussion and criticism of these stereotypes, see Whittaker, 'Debating Rights in the New Northern Ireland' (n 11).

[92] See Committee for the Administration of Justice, *A Bill of Rights for Northern Ireland through the Years – The Views of the Political Parties* (CAJ, 2003).

[93] See Opinion Poll (MRNI 2004), available online at www.borini.info/opinion-polls.aspx.

[94] Indeed, 'unionist' critiques of the bill of rights proposals often look more like familiar neo-conservative scepticism about rights in general and some rights in particular. The crude monolithic view also discourages more focused probing of the rhetorical flourishes of the nationalist political parties.

[95] See Whittaker, 'Debating Rights in the New Northern Ireland' (n 11).

tles – the white elite in South Africa, for example, became enthusiastic proponents of rights-based judicial review once they realised that they were destined to be a vulnerable minority in a post-apartheid democracy.[96]

The foregoing suggests a more general lesson about judicial empowerment in divided societies (a lesson that seems to have escaped Hirschl): where judicial empowerment is the result of some kind of bargain between antagonistic groups, the ideas and interests of at least two sets of political elites must be accounted for. By virtue of the divided nature of such polities, however, the relevant political elites will tend to have very different ideas and interests because each set of elites will have very different experiences. This is not to say that these attitudes cannot adapt to changing circumstances. The point, rather, is that experience provides the prism through which new events are interpreted. It is here that the merits of Erdos's post-materialist trigger theory really start to show.

Unlike more 'pure' rational-strategic theories, where elite support (or the lack thereof) is always understood in terms of the same motivations (ie political insurance or hegemonic preservation), PTT allows us to conceptualise a dynamic field of multiple and shifting motivations. PTT can do this (at least more effectively than rival theories) because it acknowledges that elite support for judicial empowerment can be triggered in more than one way. In other words, PTT countenances the idea that elites may be motivated to support judicial empowerment for very different reasons.[97] Thus, with the aid of PTT, we can formulate the following provisional hypothesis: elites in divided societies may, despite their disparate experiences, converge on some form of judicial empowerment *if* their respective political triggers happen to synchronise.

VI. A BILL OF RIGHTS FOR NORTHERN IRELAND?

We are now in a position to collect the various strands of the argument thus far and attempt an explanation for the lack of a bill of rights in Northern Ireland. First of all, PTT tells us that Northern Ireland is ideationally ripe for a bill of rights. The jurisdiction has long been home to a very large constituency of groups advocating for civil liberty and social equality. Indeed, the sheer number and variety of 'culturally left' non-governmental organisations in the jurisdiction is extraordinary.[98] These groups played an important role in the human rights and equality agenda leading up to the Agreement, and (as was noted

[96] See Hirschl, *Towards Juristocracy* (n 12) 92–93.

[97] See Erdos, *Delegating Rights Protection* (n 13) 27–30.

[98] The Northern Ireland Human Rights Consortium, eg, is made up of 120 non-governmental organisations, trade unions and community groups, all of whom are supportive of a maximal bill of rights. On the history of Northern Ireland's remarkably robust civil society/voluntary sector, see D Birrell and A Williamson, 'The Voluntary–Community Sector and Political Development in Northern Ireland, Since 1972' (2001) 12 *Voluntas: International Journal of Voluntary and Nonprofit Organizations* 205.

earlier) they have also been central to the campaign for a bill of rights. According to PTT, this terrain should be fertile ground for bill of rights genesis; all that would be needed is some political catalyst to open a window for judicial empowerment.

In fact, there *was* a spate of judicial empowerment following the Agreement of 1998. Several aspects of the Agreement (as implemented by the Northern Ireland Act 1998) *do* significantly empower the judiciary at the expense of local political elites. Pursuant to the Agreement, the Northern Ireland Assembly has no power to legislate in contravention of Convention rights, and ministers (or departments of the Northern Ireland government) have no power 'to make, confirm or approve any subordinate legislation, or to do any act' that is incompatible with Convention rights.[99] The Northern Ireland courts therefore possess a 'strike down' power in the area of human rights (although this power does not apply to primary legislation of the Westminster Parliament).[100]

The Agreement also includes a commitment to strengthen equality norms in Northern Ireland, specifically contemplating that a statutory duty would be imposed upon public authorities in Northern Ireland to promote equality of opportunity.[101] That commitment is implemented by section 75(1) of the Northern Ireland Act 1998, which requires that designated 'public authorities' shall, in carrying out their functions relating to Northern Ireland, 'have due regard to the need to promote equality of opportunity – between persons of different religious belief, political opinion, racial group, age, marital status or sexual orientation; between men and women generally; between persons with a disability and persons without; and between persons with dependents and persons without'. Also pursuant to established equality objectives, section 76 of the Northern Ireland Act makes it unlawful for a public authority 'to discriminate, or to aid or incite another person to discriminate, against a person or class of person on the ground of religious belief or political opinion'. Each of these provisions, albeit in very different ways, empowers the judiciary (and other institutions) to override the preferences of local political elites.[102]

[99] Northern Ireland Act 1998, ss 6(2)(c), s 24(1)(a).

[100] Interestingly, one of the concerns about a possible bill of rights for Northern Ireland was that aspects of it might stand in tension with the nature of the Agreement. Thus, Brendan O'Leary has expressed caution about potential anti-consociational consequences of a bill of rights: 'I do not think that any new Bill of Rights, however progressive, should permit the judicial striking down of any feature of the Agreement; any changes should occur within the established institutions and terms of the Agreement'. Brendan O'Leary, 'The Protection of Human Rights under the Belfast Agreement' in J McGarry and B O'Leary (eds), *The Northern Ireland Conflict: Consociational Engagements* (Oxford, Oxford University Press, 2004) 353.

[101] See the Agreement, 'Rights, Safeguards, and Equality of Opportunity: Human Rights', para 3.

[102] Section 75 remains distinctive given the role of the Equality Commission and the Secretary of State, and the clear judicial suggestion that enforcement is principally through the sch 9 route (while not ruling out judicial review). This may therefore be empowerment of a different sort. In *Re Neill's Application for Judicial Review [2006] NICA 5*, it was held that generally judicial review would not be available with respect to an alleged failure to comply with s 75. In coming to this conclusion, the Court of Appeal observed that the Northern Ireland Act 1998, under sch 9, creates a specific enforcement procedure with respect to s 75. Schedule 9 provides that the Equality Commission is to

If we can understand what made this earlier spate of judicial empowerment possible, then we may be able to account for the current impasse with respect to a bill of rights for Northern Ireland. The Agreement-era had a number of advantages (apart from the presence of a large post-materialist constituency noted earlier). First of all, the wider constitutional context in the United Kingdom in 1998, coupled with the historical residue of earlier quasi-constitutional mechanisms specific to Northern Ireland, made things easier than they might have otherwise been. At the time of the Agreement, the idea of giving domestic effect to the European Convention on Human Rights (ECHR) within the United Kingdom was already a key component of the Labour Party's agenda for constitutional reform, an idea realised in the Human Rights Act 1998.[103] Thus, although the Agreement gives the ECHR greater legal force within the jurisdiction of Northern Ireland, the fact that this coincided with a similar measure applying throughout the UK allowed the Northern Ireland instrument to 'piggyback', so to speak, on the essentially exogenous processes that led to the Human Rights Act in the rest of the UK. It also probably helped that the other elements of judicial empowerment – anti-discrimination and equality of opportunity – were not without precedent in Northern Ireland; between the suspension of Northern Ireland's government in 1972 and the Agreement in 1998, the British government introduced several pieces of anti-discrimination and equality legislation. First, the Constitution of Northern Ireland Act 1973 (an early effort at providing a constitutional settlement to the conflict) included an anti-discrimination provision making it unlawful for 'a public authority carrying out functions relating to Northern Ireland to discriminate, or to aid or incite another person to discriminate, against a person or class of persons on the ground of religious belief or political opinion'. As Christopher McCrudden observes, this anti-discrimination provision was 'reincorporated, substantially untouched, in the Northern Ireland Act of 1998',[104]

investigate complaints that a public authority has failed to comply with its equality scheme. The Commission has the power there to bring any such failure to the attention of the Northern Ireland Assembly. Thus, the Court found that, 'in the main at least', Parliament must have intended that the sch 9 procedure would be the principal mechanism for addressing any alleged breach of s 75. Nevertheless, the Court left open the possibility that judicial review might be available for 'substantive breaches' of s 75, an issue it said would have to be resolved 'on a case by case basis'. See also *JR1's Application* [2011] NIQB 5, at para 31 the Lord Chief Justice states, 'The court [*In Re Neill*] found at paragraph 28 of the judgment that the juxtaposition of Sections 75 and 76 with contrasting enforcing mechanisms for the respective obligations contained in those provisions strongly favoured the conclusion that Parliament intended that, in the main at least, the consequences of a failure to comply with Section 75 would be political, whereas the sanction of legal liability would be appropriate to breaches of the duty contained in Section 76. At paragraph 30 the court accepted that there may be occasions where a judicial review challenge to a public authority's failure to observe Section 75 would lie but declined to speculate on the circumstances where such a challenge might arise'.

[103] See Home Office, 'Rights Brought Home: The Human Rights Bill' (Cm 3782, 1997).

[104] C McCrudden, 'Mainstreaming Equality in the Governance of Northern Ireland' (1999) 22 *Fordham International Law Journal* 1696, 1705.

and continues to exist alongside robust fair employment legislation.[105] Second, the duty to promote equality of opportunity is only the latest in a series of similar measures. Most immediately, the Agreement's promise of a statutory equality duty followed dissatisfaction with an earlier non-statutory mechanism, the Policy Appraisal & Fair Treatment (PAFT) guidelines.[106] Thus, by the time of the Agreement the idea of a statutory duty to promote equality had won significant support locally and from the government of the United Kingdom and so easily found its way into the agenda for constitutional reform.[107] Of course, these earlier laws were not adopted by local elites; they were imposed from 'outside' by Westminster during the period of direct rule. But the fact that these kinds of laws were not new to Northern Ireland must have made them seem more 'natural' when local elites came to hammer out the details of Northern Ireland's new institutions.[108]

Coupled with the influence of a substantial rights and equality seeking constituency, the foregoing helps explain the 'demand-side' of the equation in Northern Ireland's previous spate of judicial empowerment. With respect to the 'supply-side', the reasons why elites actually supported judicial empowerment at the time of the Agreement can be attributed to two distinct but overlapping political triggers. For nationalist elites, the trigger was (to borrow Erdos's language) a clear case of an 'aversive reaction to prior negative political experiences'.[109] Moved as they were by the fresh memory of unionist political hegemony, discrimination in employment and housing, and conflict-related human rights abuses, nationalist political elites naturally championed a robust equality and human rights agenda in the multiparty talks leading up the Agreement.[110] It is against the historical backdrop of the nationalist experience that the Agreement promises 'a fresh start' premised on 'the protection and vindication of the human rights of all'.[111] Conversely, the motivation for unionist political elites was (again borrowing Erdos's terms) a prospectively oriented 'threat to political stability' trigger. In effect, the same pressures that prompted a consociational compromise also encouraged unionists to acquiesce to the mostly nationalist human rights and equality agenda. Traditionally, the unionist major-

[105] See C McCrudden, 'Affirmative Action and Fair Participation: Interpreting the Fair Employment Act 1989' (1992) 21 *Industrial Law Journal* 170; and McCrudden 'Mainstreaming Equality in the Governance of Northern Ireland' (n 104).

[106] For history and criticism of the PAFT guidelines, see McCrudden, 'Mainstreaming Equality in the Governance of Northern Ireland' (n 104) 1710–17.

[107] ibid 1723–34.

[108] As Horowitz explains, the substance of the Agreement is partly a function of the residue of earlier attempts at ameliorating or resolving the inter-communal conflict: D Horowitz, 'Explaining the Northern Ireland Agreement: The Sources of an Unlikely Constitutional Consensus' (2002) 32 *British Journal of Political Science* 193, 211–18.

[109] Erdos, *Delegating Rights Protection* (n 13) 5.

[110] See Mageean and O'Brien, 'From the Margins to the Mainstream: Human Rights the Good Friday Agreement' (n 1) 1503–10.

[111] The Agreement, 'Declaration of Support', para 2.

ity in Northern Ireland had no real incentive to compromise with the nationalist minority. As John McGarry points out,

> the default to compromise was the essentially unionist option of direct rule from Westminster. Unionists may have disagreed about whether direct rule was better than pre-1972 arrangements, when they governed Northern Ireland without interference from Westminster, but they agreed it was preferable to a deal with nationalists.[112]

By the late 1990s, however, a number of elements had converged to create a clear threat to the stability of the status quo. By then it was British policy (and had been since the Anglo-Irish Agreement of 1985) to allow the Irish government to play a greater role in the affairs of Northern Ireland; unionist elites would be denied an analogous policy-making role so long as they refused to negotiate for an internal settlement.[113] Nevertheless, unionist elites could effectively resist British-Irish pressure for compromise so long as the governing party in Westminster had to rely on unionist votes to hold on to power.[114] When the Labour Party won a majority government in 1997, however, unionist votes were no longer needed at Westminster.[115] Moreover, the unionist position was further weakened by the popular perception that within a generation or two unionists themselves might be a minority in Northern Ireland (at least in electoral terms if in terms of their actual numbers).[116] Given these circumstances, unionist intransigence had become more of a liability than an asset: refusing to compromise with nationalists might in fact strengthen Irish involvement in Northern Ireland in the short term while it would do nothing to protect unionist interests in the long term.[117] Thus, unionist elites – who would almost certainly have otherwise been averse to counter-majoritarian mechanisms – came to endorse a strongly counter-majoritarian settlement that, in addition to providing for consociational guarantees, also entailed a considerable degree of judicial empowerment.

Of course, the parties to the Agreement also imagined that the constitutional settlement would be complemented by an eventual bill of rights for Northern Ireland.[118] But that objective was deferred and the task of delivering it was delegated to the newly created Northern Ireland Human Rights Commission. This may have made some practical sense at the time (indeed, several matters, such as

[112] J McGarry, 'Political Settlements in Northern Ireland and South Africa' (1998) 46 *Political Studies* 853, 865.

[113] See *Agreement between the Government of Ireland and the Government of the United Kingdom, [Anglo-Irish Agreement] online at* http://cain.ulst.ac.uk/events/aia/aiadoc.htm. For critical discussion, see Brendan O'Leary, 'The Limits of Coercive Consociationalism in Northern Ireland' in John McGarry and Brendan O'Leary (eds), *The Northern Ireland Conflict: Consociational Engagements* (OUP, 2004).

[114] McGarry, 'Political Settlements in Northern Ireland and South Africa' (n 112) 868.

[115] See ibid; see also Horowitz, 'Explaining the Northern Ireland Agreement' (n 108) 206.

[116] McGarry, 'Political Settlements in Northern Ireland and South Africa' (n 112) 866; Horowitz, 'Explaining the Northern Ireland Agreement' (n 108) 201.

[117] See McGarry, 'Political Settlements in Northern Ireland and South Africa' (n 112) 868.

[118] This much is evident in the language of the Agreement, with references in 'Strand One' to the possible bill of rights.

policing reform and criminal justice were not comprehensively addressed in the Agreement). Having to agree on the substance of a bill of rights would have only complicated (and maybe even jeopardised) the already arduous task of brokering agreement on a constitutional settlement. However, by the time the Human Rights Commission produced its final advice in 2008 the window for judicial empowerment in Northern Ireland may have already closed. From the perspective of unionist political elites, there is no longer a clear 'threat to political stability trigger'; political violence in Northern Ireland has (almost) entirely abated, the question of Northern Ireland's status as part of the United Kingdom has been settled for the foreseeable future, and unionists will benefit from consociational protections regardless of their demographic and electoral future. Thus, whatever compromise inducing pressures may have acted on unionist political elites in the late-1990s, these pressures no longer apply. Meanwhile, nationalist political elites are increasingly accustomed to having a stake in executive and legislative power and so the aversive reaction to their long-time political marginalisation may already be starting to wane. How the dynamics of discussions around a UK bill of rights will impact on the Northern Ireland debate remains to be seen.[119]

The foregoing explanation is consistent with the group accommodation theory outlined earlier; the same compromise-inducing pressures that lead to consociational settlements can also induce elite support for judicial empowerment. However, our explanation here goes further and incorporates insights from PTT to explain why judicial empowerment occurs at some times and not at others. As we have seen, judicial empowerment in divided societies ultimately depends on the attitudes and interests of two differently situated sets of elites aligning on the question of judicial empowerment (encouraged by compromise-inducing pressures and a certain kind of ideational background); the convergence of these various elements is the political equivalent of a lunar eclipse. In the case of Northern Ireland, this explains both the initial spate of judicial empowerment following the Agreement as well as the subsequent trials of realising a bill of rights in the Agreement's aftermath.

VII. BEYOND THE IMPASSE?

Admittedly, the foregoing paints a rather pessimistic picture of the prospects for further judicial empowerment in Northern Ireland. Still, we do not think that proponents of a bill of rights for Northern Ireland have no grounds at all for hope. As we have explained, an elite consensus on judicial empowerment in divided societies is likely to be especially ephemeral. But elites are not aliens. To the extent that they share experiences with the publics they represent, elites

[119] See C Harvey, 'Taking the Next Step? Achieving another Bill of Rights' [2011] *European Human Rights Law Review* 24.

cannot help but be influenced by popular mobilisation.[120] On this point we think that proponents of the bill of rights may yet have some reason for optimism.

To be sure, Hirschl is certainly right to deride the naivety of what he calls the 'Ackermanian' narrative in which the spread of constitutionalism since World War II is simplistically attributed to the triumph of popular human rights movements:

> the vast majority of the constitutional revolutions of the past few decades do not fit this story. They were either negotiated among rival parties during times of political transition (even the constitutional revolution in South Africa – a poster child of democratic constitutionalism – has been the product of a long negotiation process steeped in power relations, political interests, and strategic calculations); were promoted by external actors (e.g., the new constitutions of Afghanistan 2004 or Iraq 2005); or were initiated by powerful political elites whose interests did not exactly reflect popular will at the time.[121]

Nevertheless, it is enlightening to return to what Bruce Ackerman himself actually says in defence of his theory of transformational 'constitutional moments'.[122] Ackerman acknowledges four ways of modelling change: (1) the unconscious direction of impersonal 'invisible hand'-like forces; (2) the self-conscious action of elites; (3) the gradual evolution of a community's 'folkways'; and (4) outright 'revolutionary transformation'.[123] The various theories of judicial empowerment we have considered here have made use of the first three of these models to different degrees. Erdos's PTT, for example, relies mostly on the first two: the 'invisible hand' of post-materialist ideational drift and rational-strategic triggers that motivate the self-conscious actions of elites. Ackerman's account does not discount the explanatory power of any of these models. His point, rather, is that an account of constitutional change that refers exclusively or primarily to the self-serving actions of political elites gives insufficient weight to the role of popular 'movements':

> In this cynical age, it is easy to tear down the aspirations of any civic movement for greater justice and a deeper legitimacy. The harder job is to understand the process through which a civic movement manages, despite the inevitable political compromises, to win a deep, and broadly based, sense of popular consent for its exercise in civic renewal.[124]

[120] On this point, we agree with Hilbink. See Hilbink, 'The Constituted Nature of Constituents' Interests' (n 54).

[121] R Hirschl, 'The Realist Turn in Comparative Constitutional Politics' (2009) 62 *Political Research Quarterly* 825, 826.

[122] Ackerman develops the theory of 'constitutional moments' in several places, but see especially B Ackerman, 'Constitutional politics/constitutional law' (1989) 99 *Yale Law Journal* 46; *We the People Vol. 1: Foundations* (Cambridge MA, Harvard University Press, 1991); and *The Future of Liberal Revolution* (New Haven CT, Yale University Press, 1992).

[123] B Ackerman 'Revolution on a human scale' (1999) 108 *Yale Law Journal* 2279.

[124] B Ackerman 'Constitutional Economics/Constitutional Politics' (1999) 10 *Constitutional Political Economy* 415–24, 419.

Ackerman contends that popular movements have actually played a vital and transformative role throughout the constitutional history of the United States. He relies on three major examples to support his case – the Founding, the post-Civil War Reconstruction and the New Deal of the 1930s. In all these cases Ackerman discerns a definite pattern: a transformational movement gathers strength in the 'political wilderness', the movement's agenda is pushed to the forefront of public debate by some major institution, and a phase of focused constitutional reappraisal follows.[125] The proponents of constitutional change succeed if their program is ultimately ratified and consolidated by popular approbation.

Ackerman calls this kind of activity 'higher-lawmaking'.[126] 'Higher-lawmaking' is revolutionary in the sense that it entails 'a self-conscious effort to mobilise the relevant community to reject currently dominant beliefs and practices in one or another area of social life'. [127] Change here is first and foremost a function of 'mass movements mobilizing on behalf of grand ideals'.[128] Elites still matter in this equation, but only to the extent that they can 'earn the authority to speak in the name of their mobilized fellow citizens'.[129] If Ackerman is right about the United States, then proponents of the bill of rights in Northern Ireland may also have some cause for hope. A groundswell of grassroots mobilisation in Northern Ireland may yet initiate a process of higher-law making that eventually culminates in a bill of rights.

Unfortunately, Ackerman's major examples – the Founding, the Reconstruction and the New Deal – are not terribly helpful for our present purposes. Popular mobilisation in each of those cases was spearheaded by political parties – our aim right now is to think around obstinate political elites. Furthermore, Ackerman's first and third examples do not speak directly to judicial empowerment. With the respect to the Founding, the power of judicial review would not be established until the Supreme Court's decision of *Marbury v Madison* in 1803.[130] With respect to the New Deal, the 'constitutional moment' in question empowered the President and Congress *against* the judiciary.[131] Meanwhile, the example of the Reconstruction Amendments is probably too idiosyncratic to be of much comparative value – constitutional change in the immediate aftermath of the Civil War was underwritten by the threat of renewed military conflict.

That being said, we do think some productive use might be made of Ackerman's other examples, especially the African-American civil rights move-

[125] B Ackerman, 'The Holmes Lectures: The Living Constitution' (2007) 120 *Harvard Law Review* 1727.

[126] See B Ackerman, *We the People* (n 122) ch 1.

[127] Ackerman, 'Revolution on a human scale' (n 123) 2283.

[128] ibid 2279.

[129] ibid.

[130] *Marbury v Madison*, 5 U.S. 137 (1803).

[131] See Ackerman, *We The People* (n 122).

ment (or what Ackerman sometimes calls 'the Civil Rights Revolution').[132] Unlike the 'big three' constitutional moments (in which party politicians directed popular movements), the Civil Rights Revolution was spearheaded all along by popular (as opposed to party) activism. As Ackerman explains, the Civil Rights Revolution is notable for lacking a dedicated 'movement-party':

> We most definitely observe a movement, led by Martin Luther King, Jr., and ultimately supported by millions of followers, both black and white, throughout the nation. But we definitely don't see a party that served as the political vehicle for this movement'.[133]

Nevertheless, the civil rights movement was eventually able to realise landmark legislation – the Civil Rights Act 1964 and the Voting Rights Act 1965.[134]

So the Civil Rights Revolution provides us with at least one example of the kind of grassroots success that a popular bill of rights movement in Northern Ireland might hope for: a mass movement operating independently of the party system that nevertheless manages to achieve a degree of judicial empowerment. There are, of course, many important differences between the Civil Rights Revolution and the movement for a bill of rights for Northern Ireland, the least of which being that the former sought to remedy specific and very grave injustices while the latter seeks to improve on an extant human rights regime. But in addition to whatever other contextual differences there may be, we would sound one final cautionary note about the prospects for 'Ackermanian' constitutional moments in divided societies like Northern Ireland. People in such places do not see themselves as a single 'People' in the way that Ackerman's theory presupposes. As divided as the United States was by the civil rights movement, Martin Luther King could nevertheless appeal to the moral sentiment of his fellow *Americans:*

> When the architects of our republic wrote the magnificent words of the Constitution and the Declaration of Independence, they were signing a promissory note to which every American was to fall heir. This note was a promise that all men, yes, black men as well as white men, would be guaranteed the unalienable rights of life, liberty, and the pursuit of happiness . . . We refuse to believe that there are insufficient funds in the great vaults of opportunity of this nation.[135]

However, as Stephen Tierney argues, in circumstances of national pluralism a constitutional settlement must speak on behalf of multiple *demoi*; it is not 'We the People' but 'We the Peoples' who can legitimately claim the constituent

[132] Bruce Ackerman, 'The Living Constitution' (n 125) 1757–92.

[133] ibid 1786.

[134] The second of these continues to be a significant source of judicial empowerment (although the Act also empowers the federal government to scrutinise changes to state voting regimes by way of a procedure known as 'preclearance'). See S Issacharoff, 'Is Section 5 of the Voting Rights Act a Victim of Its Own Success?' (2004) 105 *Columbia Law Review* 1710.

[135] Quoted in DD Hansen, *The Dream: Martin Luther King, Jr., and the speech that inspired a nation* (New York, Ecco, 2003) 104.

power in a plurinational context.[136] The bill of rights movement in Northern Ireland has had some real success in winning popular support from both of the two main communities (even if not from their political representatives). But Northern Ireland remains a deeply divided place. It may be some time before the 'Peoples' of Northern Ireland can come together to speak with a single sovereign voice.

VIII. CONCLUSION

To conclude, we can suggest a few lessons that might be elicited from the foregoing discussion for other divided societies that might be contemplating a bill of rights. First, elite 'ownership' and endorsement of a bill of rights is just as important as popular participation. A broadly inclusive and participatory bill of rights-making process (like the processes in Canada, Northern Ireland and South Africa) is certainly a good thing; at the very least, popular participation probably enhances the legitimacy of the final product.[137] But elite support will ultimately be necessary in any case. Consequently, proponents of bills of rights cannot afford to ignore the problem of elite support in arguing for their cause. Second, proponents of bills of rights need to be aware of just how tenuous and contextually contingent elite support for judicial empowerment actually is. As we have seen here, this difficulty is compounded in consociational settings by the need to secure support from two distinct blocs of elites. So timing really is crucial; proponents of judicial empowerment must seize the day when the conditions are ripe for a bill of rights. A final and related point concerns the structure of the process itself. Open-ended processes (like the one in Northern Ireland) are much less likely to 'deliver the goods' than processes where there is a clear time frame for completion (like the process in South Africa). Providing for a maximally inclusive public process may well help to legitimate the final product (and even generate admirably robust proposals), but it also risks delaying the product beyond the time frame in which elite support for a bill of rights is plausible. The dilemma for participants in these debates then is whether compromises are made in order to achieve a bill of rights during the tenuous alignment of elite triggers, or whether a stand is made for stronger or more expansive proposals whose time may come at some later 'Ackermanian' constitutional moment. There is no trite or easy answer to this dilemma.

[136] See S Tierney, 'We the Peoples: Balancing Constituent Power and Constitutionalism in Plurinational States' in N Walker and M Loughlin (eds), *The Paradox of Constitutionalism* (Oxford, Oxford University Press, 2007).

[137] See Chambers, 'Democracy, Popular Sovereignty, and Constitutional Legitimacy' (n 27).

Part III

Post-Conflict Constitutions

7

The Nature and Effects of Constitutional Rights in Post-conflict Bosnia and Herzegovina

DAVID FELDMAN

I. INTRODUCTION: DESIGNING A CONSTITUTION FOR A DIVIDED SOCIETY

THE CHARACTER OF a society's divisions and the nature of the problems which they cause naturally influence the structure of any constitution which is adopted to mitigate their impact. Divisions may have become more or less entrenched over longer or shorter periods. They may relate to different factors, including status, wealth, race, religion, birth and occupation. Grievances often relate to several factors, because birth, race, religion, occupation, wealth and status may be interconnected in different patterns. Existing social and political arrangements tend to embody the very divisions which are causing problems. When seeking ways of helping conflicting groups to live and work together peacefully, if not contentedly, societies frequently use a new statement of rights, and guarantees that the rights will be respected, as instruments for building confidence.

These statements and guarantees take different forms. Rights may be individual or collective; political, civil, social, economic or cultural. They may be enforceable by individuals or on behalf of collectives, and through political, social or judicial channels. These lists are not exhaustive, and characteristics may be combined in a multitude of ways, as the chapters in this volume show. Guarantees of rights may be a way of recognising but mitigating divisions and their effects. Alternatively, they may be a way of overcoming them, encouraging social cooperation and perhaps even integration. It takes generations rather than years, however, to overcome deep, social divisions and to build trust. It may therefore initially be necessary to respect and accommodate divisions within the design of the state to make it possible for hostile groups to live and work together, while building social and economic foundations for fuller cooperation in the longer term.

It is difficult, however, to design a state's constitution and statement of rights in such a way as to allow both short-term and long-term goals to be pursued effectively at the same time. The two aims may pull in different directions, and create obstacles to achieving either of them. This chapter considers the post-war 1995 Constitution of Bosnia and Herzegovina (BiH) as an illustration of the tensions that are characteristic of post-conflict constitutions in divided societies.[1] Combined with direct, international involvement in constitution-making, the Constitution generates certain oddities in the treatment of rights, to the point where it is questionable whether or not BiH can even be said to have a 'bill of rights' at all.

II. YUGOSLAVIA: A HOUSE DIVIDED

Divisions are deeply rooted in the Balkans, based on longstanding nationalist pride and aspirations. After the Battle of Kosovo in 1389, the kingdom of Serbia and most Slavic peoples in the region, including Bosnia, became subject to Ottoman rule. Serbia was ruled directly by the Ottomans until 1829, when it became a semi-autonomous principality. It became a fully independent kingdom again in 1878. At the Congress of Berlin in the same year, Austria became responsible for administering Bosnia, which, with a substantial population of Muslim Slavs as well as Christians, remained part of the Ottoman Empire until it was annexed by Austria in 1909 during the revolution by the Young Turks against Sultan Abdul-Hamid II. The Young Turks behaved even more repressively than their predecessors towards subject peoples. In 1912, this caused a major nationalistic uprising: 'Nothing but experience of Young Turkish rule could have caused Greeks, Serbs, Montenegrins, and Bulgars to unite into the common front of the Balkan League'.[2] Ultimately, it led to an expansion of Serbia, which worried Austria enough for the Treaty of Versailles in 1918 to create a Kingdom of Yugoslavia, merging the State of the Slovenes, Croats and Serbs with the Kingdom of Serbia (which included the Kingdom of Montenegro following annexation earlier in the year). Agitation by both nationalists and communists was successfully repressed until World War II, when Axis forces, supported by nationalist Croats, invaded and broke up the kingdom. They established an independent Croat state with a fascist government who oversaw the killing, expulsion, or conversion to Catholicism of nearly one million non-Croats (mainly Serbs but also Jews). Axis forces occupied the rest of the kingdom.

[1] R Holbrooke, *To End a War* (New York, Random House, 1998) 297, recording how the parties' obsession with territorial issues – who would get what from the partition of the country – 'revealed how little each side trusted the political aspects of the Dayton agreement to which they had both agreed . . . The argument over the land was, in effect, a continuation of the war in Dayton, while the political discussions were a tentative effort to build a political framework for a joint future. We were all too aware of the internal contradiction, but there was nothing that could be done about it'.

[2] D Thomson, *Europe since Napoleon* revised edn (Harmondsworth, Penguin Books, 1966) 473.

Communist Partisans, led by Josip Broz Tito, fought the Axis forces (supported initially by royalist Chetniks, who later, however, collaborated with the Axis powers) and drove them from Yugoslavia. In 1945, Tito was elected Prime Minister of the new Federal People's Republic of Yugoslavia, which succeeded the Kingdom of Yugoslavia. It consisted of six republics, the Socialist Republics (SRs) of BiH, Croatia, Macedonia, Montenegro, Serbia and Slovenia, each with a good deal of governmental autonomy. Within SR Serbia were two Socialist Autonomous Provinces, Kosovo (with a majority of ethnic Albanians) in the south, and Vojvodina (with a mixed population) in the north. These had significant governmental independence of SR Serbia.

The arrangement gave Albanians, Croats, Macedonians, Montenegrins, Serbs and Slovenians considerable autonomy in areas where they formed a majority of the population. But in each SR there were minority populations of other national groups. The Socialist Federal Republic of Yugoslavia (SFRY), as the state became in 1963, was thus highly diverse and decentralised. Nevertheless, Serbs formed the largest group in the population as a whole, and saw Yugoslavia as their historic homeland. Controlling competing nationalisms and maintaining the integrity of the state depended heavily on the personal authority of Marshal Tito, who had been named Life President in 1963. When he died in 1980, nationalist tensions resurfaced, and the collapse of the Communist bloc in 1989 heightened pressure for independence in the SRs.

The violence which erupted in SFRY in 1991 and 1992 was thus largely nationalistic. As SRs broke away, Serbs sought to maintain the state and protect Serb minorities. In Croatia, they tried to establish an autonomous area (Republic of Serb Krajina). When Croatia's government reasserted its authority, the Yugoslav People's Army (JNA) intervened. When the government of SR BiH moved towards declaring independence in 1991, Bosnian Serbs established a separate Serb republic (Republika Srpska, or RS) within SR BiH, loyal to the SFRY. Following a referendum (largely boycotted by Serbs), the government of SR BiH declared the Republic of BiH (RBiH) to be an independent, sovereign state. On 6 April 1992, the USA and a number of European states recognised the new state.

This triggered generalised warfare. In RBiH, Serb militias (secretly supported by the JNA from what had become the Federal Republic of Yugoslavia), and a Croat army supported by Croatia, attacked the fledgling RBiH, and made considerable territorial gains, until Serb attacks on Croat populations pushed Croats into a shotgun marriage with the Muslim-led government of the RBiH to form a somewhat uncomfortable coalition, the Federation of Bosnia and Herzegovina (FBiH), on territory they still controlled. Together they pushed Serb forces back to roughly the territory which the RS had controlled before the outbreak of hostilities, and NATO bombing and international sanctions brought the Serbs to the negotiating table.

III. THE DAYTON AGREEMENT AND ITS CONSTITUTION

The broad shape of the settlement had already been worked out by outsiders while the conflict raged. Previous peace plans had been developed without success, first by British Foreign Secretary, Lord Carrington, then by UN and EU representatives, Cyrus Vance and David Owen. When President Bill Clinton committed the US to trying to resolve the conflict, Richard Holbrooke, a US diplomat, commenced shuttle diplomacy which eventually brought the parties to reluctant agreement.[3]

The General Framework Agreement for Peace, negotiated at Dayton, Ohio in November 1995 and signed in Paris on 14 December, was only questionably workable, and left a legacy of dissatisfaction on all sides. Despite guaranteeing the continued existence of BiH (as it was now called) within its pre-war borders, the agreement accepted the partition of the state into two Entities, RS and FBiH, as a *fait accompli*. Bosniacs considered that this legitimised the effects of aggression and ethnic cleansing. Croats wanted an Entity of their own. Serbs regretted the independence of BiH and the break-up of SFRY.

Annex 4 to the Dayton Agreement contained the new Constitution of BiH. Despite being moulded round the military and political realities of BiH, the Constitution was (and to a great extent still is) regarded in the country as an alien imposition. It was drafted under great pressure by an international group of lawyers who had little knowledge or experience of the legal and constitutional systems of SFRY and its SRs. They assembled rights based on a mixture of free-market economics and social, economic and political group rights, implemented through a consociational, power-sharing democracy, and backed by constitutional judicial review on a German model. The language of the Constitution, as part of the Dayton Agreement, is English (except for the only amendment to have been enacted so far). There is no officially approved version of the Constitution in any of the local languages; indeed, it has never been approved by any constitutive or legislative body within the state.

At Dayton, it was accepted that two kinds of collectivities required special protection. The two Entities, FBiH and RS, would each have a significant degree of self-government, and the structure of the state would be based on power-sharing between them. They retained all functions not expressly conferred on the state, while being subject to the authority of state institutions acting within their powers.[4] Serbs and Croats expected the state to be relatively weak and the Entities strong and largely autonomous. For Bosniacs, the Americans, NATO and the UN, however, the overarching state of BiH was intended to be the mechanism by which divisions between Bosniacs, Serbs and Croats were to be progressively overcome. They hoped to build a strong state to which the Entities would be increasingly subordinated. This is a continuing cause of tension.

[3] For a first-hand account, see Holbrooke, *To End a War* (n 1).
[4] Constitution of BiH, arts I.3 and III.3/(a), (b).

A further governmental unit came into existence later. The RS consists of two large areas with the narrow Posavina corridor, in which lies the city of Brčko, between them. The Dayton negotiations failed to resolve the strategically vital issue of control over the corridor. It was referred to an arbitral tribunal, which decided that it should be a special administrative area, Brčko District, under international oversight. In 2009, an amendment to the Constitution recognised that Brčko District, which

> exists under the sovereignty of Bosnia and Herzegovina and is subject to the responsibilities of the institutions of Bosnia and Herzegovina as those responsibilities derive from this Constitution, whose territory is jointly owned by ([or] a condominium of) the Entities, is a unit of local self-government with its own institutions, laws and regulations, and with powers and status definitively prescribed by the Awards of the Arbitral Tribunal for the Dispute over the Inter-Entity Boundary in the Brčko Area. The relationship between the Brčko District of Bosnia and Herzegovina and the Entities may be further regulated by law adopted by the Parliamentary Assembly.[5]

However, Brčko enjoys none of the constitutional privileges of the Entities.

The other type of collective which has special constitutional privileges is the 'constituent people'. The Preamble to the Constitution declares (untruthfully) that the Constitution was determined by 'Bosniacs, Croats, and Serbs, as constituent peoples (along with Others), and citizens of Bosnia and Herzegovina', and that they were '*Dedicated* to peace, justice, tolerance, and reconciliation'.[6] The three constituent peoples were, of course, those which had recently subjected each other to irredentist, political and ethnic violence of an extreme kind. 'Others' were all who could not or would not be identified with one of the constituent peoples. They had often suffered as much as the constituent peoples. Nevertheless, the framers of the Dayton Agreement and of the Constitution were particularly concerned about relations between the constituent peoples, as only they had the capacity for renewing large-scale ethnic cleansing and military aggression.

Line 3 of the Preamble asserts 'that democratic governmental institutions and fair procedures best produce peaceful relations within a pluralist society', and Article I.2 requires BiH to be 'a democratic state, which shall operate under the rule of law and with free and democratic elections'. Doubting the depth of each other's dedication to peace, justice, tolerance and reconciliation, they wanted guarantees that a numerically dominant people in an area would not be able to use majoritarian democracy or control over institutions of public administration to override the interests of other peoples.

In these circumstances, rights have several important roles in the state. They offer guarantees of protection for individuals against renewed atrocities and discrimination, and for minorities against being politically overwhelmed. In these ways they help to provide a sense of security and an environment in which

[5] Constitution of BiH, art VI.4 as inserted.

[6] Constitution of BiH, Preamble, lines 10 and 2 respectively.

former enemies can trust each other enough to cooperate and make concessions in order to rebuild society and economy. The Constitution sets a demanding, perhaps unrealistically high, standard. The Preamble to the Constitution recites that the Constitution is '*Based* on respect for human dignity, liberty, and equality', and

> *Inspired* by the Universal Declaration on Human Rights, the International Covenants on Civil and Political Rights and on Economic, Social and Cultural Rights, and the Declaration on the Rights of Persons Belonging to National or Ethnic, Religious and Linguistic Minorities, as well as other human rights instruments.[7]

Article II.1 requires the state and both Entities to 'ensure the highest level of internationally recognized human rights and fundamental freedoms'. Rights and freedoms referred to in Article II of the Constitution are doubly entrenched by Article X.2: 'No amendment to this Constitution may eliminate or diminish' any of them 'or alter the present paragraph'.

IV. VARIETIES OF RIGHTS IN THE CONSTITUTION

The Constitution contains a somewhat uncomfortable assortment of rights based on different and potentially conflicting values and socio-economic and political aspirations. Classic civil and political rights, enforceable at the instance of individuals, abound. The Preamble (which is treated as having normative force)[8] announces that the framers of the Constitution desired 'to promote the general welfare and economic growth through the protection of private property and the promotion of a market economy'.[9] In one of its most significant decisions, the Constitutional Court held that this, together with freedom of movement of goods under Article I.4 and the right to property under Article II.3/k) and ECHR Protocol 1, Article 1, made it unconstitutional for the RS's Constitution to authorise or require state or social ownership of certain assets unless it could be justified as serving a legitimate aim, such as protecting items of special cultural or environmental importance. This gave constitutional status to a policy of privatisation.[10] Yet such rights sit alongside special rights and privileges attaching to collectivities, including the Entities and the constituent peoples, guaranteeing collective equality and, in some instances, collective superiority over less privileged groups. The sources of these rights are equally varied.

[7] Constitution of BiH, Preamble, lines 1 and 8.

[8] This is because the Constitution is part of a treaty, and has to be interpreted in accordance with the Vienna Convention on the Law of Treaties, art 31. See Case No U-5/98-III, *Request of Mr Alija Izetbegović*, Decision of 1 July 2000, paras 19, 23–26. On the potential normativity of preambles generally, see L Orgad, 'The preamble in constitutional interpretation' (2010) 8 *International Journal of Constitutional Law* 714.

[9] Constitution of BiH, Preamble, line 4.

[10] Case No U-5/98-II, Decision of 18 February 2000, CC of BiH, esp at paras 11, 14–24. All the decisions of the Constitutional Court mentioned in this chapter are available in English at www.ustavnisud.ba/eng/.

A. Rights Conferred Entirely by the Constitution

The Constitution itself expressly confers a number of rights. Of particular importance, though not easily or quickly given effect, are freedom of movement for persons, goods and services throughout the country (Article I.4) and a right for refugees and displaced persons to return freely to their homes of origin, to have restored to them property of which they were deprived in the course of the hostilities from 1991 to 1995, and to be compensated for any such property which cannot be restored (Article II.5). As a necessary condition for implementing this right, Article II.5 also provides, 'Any commitments or statements relating to such property made under duress are null and void'. The Constitutional Court used the right to property and the right to respect for one's home, together with the priority given by Annex 7 of the Dayton Agreement to allowing refugees and displaced persons to return to their homes of origin, to hold that transfers induced without duress would also be constitutionally unenforceable if one of the parties was vulnerable by reason of ethnicity at a time of ethnic cleansing.[11]

B. Rights Derived from International Human Rights Law

Many rights and freedoms derived from international human rights instruments have effect by virtue of the Constitution. Those in the European Convention for the Protection of Human Rights and Fundamental Freedoms (ECHR) and its Protocols 'shall apply directly in Bosnia and Herzegovina' and 'have priority over all other law'.[12] The reference to 'other law' suggests that domestically the ECHR has the status of law, and is thus subject to the Constitution rather than part of or superior to it. In December 1995, BiH was not yet a member of the Council of Europe and so could not become a party to the ECHR. Authority for implementing the ECHR domestically had to be provided by a norm of the municipal constitution or law, so Article II.3 provides that all persons are to enjoy those rights and freedoms, and offers (rather confusingly) a list of some but not all of them. Responsibility for giving effect to rights under the ECHR is shared by courts and all agencies of both state and Entities.[13]

Article II.7 is unusual in requiring the state to become a party to another 15 international human rights instruments, listed in Annex I to the Constitution: Convention on the Prevention and Punishment of the Crime of Genocide 1948; Geneva Conventions I–IV on the Protection of the Victims of War 1949, and their 1977 Protocols; Convention relating to the Status of Refugees 1951, and its

[11] Case No U-15/99, *Appeal of SZ*, Decision of 15 December 2000, CC of BiH.
[12] Constitution of BiH, art II.2.
[13] ibid art II.6.

1966 Protocol; Convention on the Nationality of Married Women 1957; Convention on the Reduction of Statelessness 1961; International Convention on the Elimination of All Forms of Racial Discrimination 1965; International Covenant on Civil and Political Rights and its 1966 and 1989 Optional Protocols; International Covenant on Economic, Social and Cultural Rights 1966; Convention on the Elimination of All Forms of Discrimination against Women 1979; Convention against Torture and Other Cruel, Inhuman or Degrading Treatment or Punishment 1984; European Convention against Torture and Other Cruel, Inhuman or Degrading Treatment or Punishment 1987; Convention on the Rights of the Child 1989; International Convention on the Protection of the Rights of All Migrant Workers and Members of their Families 1990; European Charter for Regional or Minority Languages 1992; and Framework Convention for the Protection of National Minorities 1994.

The selection of these instruments was clearly influenced by the ethnic and nationalist problems which had precipitated and, to a large extent, survived the war. It is significant, however, that the Constitution does not say what status they have in municipal law. Article II.4 provides that the rights or freedoms in Article II or in the instruments listed above

> shall be secured to all persons in Bosnia and Herzegovina without discrimination on any ground such as sex, race, color, language, religion, political or other opinion, national or social origin, association with a national minority, property, birth or other status.

This gives rise to two interlinked questions. First, are these rights justiciable, and, if they are, can courts review laws and administrative acts for compatibility with them? Secondly, does Article II.4 and 7 imply that BiH is generally a dualist state, on the principle *expressio unius, exclusio alterius*? These are questions to which the Constitutional Court has given inconsistent answers or no answer at all, depending on circumstances.

The Constitution makes it clear that Entities have positive obligations to uphold rights under Annex I treaties. Article III.2/b) requires each Entity to 'provide all necessary assistance to the government of Bosnia and Herzegovina in order to enable it to honor the international obligations of Bosnia and Herzegovina'. In addition, Article III.2/c) obliges each Entity to

> provide a safe and secure environment for all persons in their respective jurisdictions, by maintaining civilian law enforcement agencies operating in accordance with internationally recognized standards and with respect for the internationally recognized human rights and fundamental freedoms referred to in Article II above, and by taking such other measures as appropriate.

This does not expressly make the obligations judicially enforceable at Entity level. They arise from the state's Constitution, not the Entities', so only the Constitutional Court of BiH can finally decide whether Entities have complied with them.

The Constitution does not unequivocally impose obligations on the state and its institutions to comply with rights under Annex I treaties. Article II.4 could be read as requiring them to be secured either generally (and particularly without discrimination), or only against discrimination in relation to their enjoyment. If the former, it would allow state courts to enforce rights under Annex I treaties directly. If the latter, it would give rise to an inexplicable oddity: why should rights under non-discrimination treaties be enforceable only where the right not to be subjected to discrimination has been applied in a discriminatory way?

The Constitutional Court has also flirted with an argument that the Constitution is monist, so treaty obligations automatically form part of BiH's legal order. The final sentence of Article III.3(b) reads: 'The general principles of international law shall be an integral part of the law of Bosnia and Herzegovina and the Entities'. If, as is probable, those include obligations arising from *jus cogens*, treaty obligations which overlap *jus cogens* would be enforceable in domestic law. But the case law of the Constitutional Court potentially takes incorporation a stage further. The Court has held that *pacta sunt servanda* is a general principle of international law. It therefore forms part of the law in BiH, and imposes a constitutional obligation on state and Entity bodies to comply with obligations under treaties to which the state is a party. In consequence, the obligations of BiH under the Central European Free Trade Agreement (CEFTA), to which BiH is a party, form part of the law of BiH. What is more, it has supra-legal status, because of the constitutional status of the principle *pacta sunt servanda*. The Court held, therefore, that a law which restricted imports in a manner inconsistent with the CEFTA was invalid because it prevented the state from honouring its treaty obligations.[14]

Three judges dissented. President Simović considered that general principles of international law are part of the constitutional fabric, but

> the constitutional law position of this principle does not automatically lead to a conclusion that the entire international treaty law, which has to be entered into in accordance with the international law principle pacta sunt servanda, represents a constitutional law standard which, as such, the Constitutional Court of BiH is obliged to protect. Thus, neither the violation of an individual concrete international law agreement such as the Central European Free Trade Agreement (CEFTA) in this concrete case, regardless of the fact how apparent it may be, leads to an automatic violation of the principle of pacta sunt servanda. If interpreted in this manner, the entire international treaty law obtains a constitutional law level, which has not been the intention of the author of the Constitution.[15]

[14] Case No U-5/09, *Request of Mr Ilija Filipović*, Decision of 25 September 2009.
[15] ibid Separate Dissenting Opinion of President Miodrag Simović, para 5.

Judges Feldman and Pantiru noted in their joint dissenting opinion that this would be inconsistent with the express provisions of Article II of the Constitution providing for a limited number of human rights treaties to have effect directly within the legal system; *expressio unius, exclusio alterius*. Indeed, in their dissent they went further than the President, denying that general principles of international law had constitutional status. In their view, they had the status of law, not of the Constitution, so no Law could be invalid by reason only of inconsistency with a principle, and less still for inconsistency with a specific treaty provision. In the absence of a clear, express constitutional provision, they were unwilling to imply such a wide expansion of the constitutional limits on the Parliamentary Assembly's legislative competence under Article IV of the Constitution. With the President's concurrence, they also pointed out that the majority's reasoning led to uncertainty, and gave discretionary power to judges at the expense of the democratically accountable Parliamentary Assembly.[16]

Subsequently, the Court was reluctant to give effect expressly to the full breadth of the majority's reasoning where human rights treaties were in issue. Instead, the judges preferred to apply human rights treaties directly, without explicitly endorsing or applying the reasoning in Case No U-5/09. For example, in a later case the Court by a majority applied provisions of the International Covenant on Civil and Political Rights (ICCPR) relating to electoral rights directly, and accordingly quashed certain provisions of the Election Law of BiH relating to council elections in Mostar on the ground that they did not comply with the requirements of the ICCPR. They did not, however, say whether they were applying the ICCPR because it had quasi-constitutional status in domestic law on account of the constitutional status of the principle *pacta sunt servanda* or because of an interpretation of Article II.4.[17] Their silence on this point was deliberate; it avoided overt disagreement.

Uncertainty about the status of obligations under Annex I treaties results directly from the somewhat incoherent drafting of the Constitution. The Constitutional Court has perpetuated uncertainty by sometimes, but not always, applying Annex I treaties directly as a basis for reviewing the validity of laws, but without consistently endorsing any rationale for doing so (or, sometimes, for not doing so).

C. Political Privileges

The last class of rights in the Constitution consists of privileges for certain collectivities, which leave others in a relatively unfavourable position. They result from the need, recognised by the Dayton Agreement, to protect the previously warring parties against the possibility (or even likelihood) that an ordinary,

[16] ibid Separate Dissenting Opinion of Judge David Feldman and Judge Tudor Pantiru.
[17] Case No U-9/09, decision of 26 and 27 November 2010, CC of BiH.

majoritarian political system would allow the most populous group to impose its will on the rest, overriding the vital interests which those groups had fought a war to advance.

Article IX.3 of the Constitution requires officials in state institutions to be 'generally representative of the peoples of Bosnia and Herzegovina'. As this is not limited to constituent peoples, Others are also represented in, for example, the diplomatic service. This helps to combat direct discrimination, but can result in certain posts becoming effectively restricted to members of a particular people, or being required to rotate between peoples, regardless of the experience and qualifications of candidates for the position.

Politically, however, constitutional provisions discriminate against Others. The Constitution moderates majoritarian democracy with a form of power-sharing between the three constituent peoples and between the two Entities, based on the idea of collective political equality. This gives rise to a tension between structures for power-sharing, which seek to bolster confidence in conditions for peaceful co-existence, and the right of individuals to be free of discrimination. Most political parties at both state and Entity levels are identified with and draw their main support from a particular constituent people. Consociational democracy should ideally take the form of a dialogue between competing groups, but the process reinforces and institutionalises political, ethnic or religious differences, making integration less likely in the short to medium term. Furthermore, groups not privileged to share power are disadvantaged, and individual members of those groups suffer unfavourable treatment in the political process as compared with members of the privileged groups.

The Constitutional Court has held that constituent peoples must have equal rights to participate effectively in state authorities, but that their privileges over Others should be applicable only so long as they are required by the Constitution (including the Preamble) and do not undermine the efficiency of the state and its institutions.[18] Furthermore, the principle applies only to membership of bodies with power to make legally binding decisions affecting members of the public. This includes city councils, but not an administrative body such as the Steering Board responsible for public broadcasting.[19]

Where the principle of equal participation applies, people who want to participate in public life have to identify themselves as members of one or another ethnic group. Election results depend on guarantees of collective equality of peoples rather than the number of votes cast for each candidate.[20] In BiH, the impact is most obvious in relation to membership of the state's Parliamentary Assembly and Presidency. In the bicameral Parliamentary Assembly, Entities have

[18] Case No U-5/98-III, *Request of Alija Izetbegović*, Decision of 1 July 2000, esp paras 55, 68; Case No U-8/04, *Request of Mr Mustafa Pamuk*, Decision of 25 June 2004, paras 32, 33, 51.

[19] Case No U-4/05, *Request of Mr Nikola Špirić*, Decision of 22 April 2005; Case No U-10/05, *Request of Mr Velimir Jukić*, Decision of 22 July 2005, para 49; Case No U-5/06, *Request of Mr Ivo Miro Jovic*, Decision of 29 May 2009, para 49.

[20] Case No AP-35/03, *Appeal of Socijal demokratska partija Bosne i Hercegovine*, Decision of 28 January 2005.

guaranteed levels of representation in both the directly elected House of Representatives and the indirectly elected House of Peoples. Two-thirds are from the FBiH, and one-third from the RS.[21] The constituent peoples are guaranteed equal representation in the House of Peoples. Of the 15 indirectly elected Delegates, five must be designated as members of each of the three constituent peoples. Those designated as Bosniacs and Croats must come from the FBiH, and are chosen by the Bosniac and Croat caucuses respectively of the House of Peoples of the Federation's legislature. The Serbs must be from the RS, and are selected by the National Assembly of the RS. The position of the constituent peoples is further strengthened by constitutional rules of procedure. In the House of Representatives, a majority of all members constitutes a quorum. In the House of Peoples, nine Delegates form a quorum, but only if they include at least three designated Delegates from each constituent people.[22] This prevents the Parliamentary Assembly from operating without participation of representatives of all constituent peoples.

In the House of Peoples, a majority of Bosniac, Croat or Serb Delegates may declare a proposed decision of the Parliamentary Assembly (including decisions about legislation) to be destructive of a vital interest of that people. If a majority of Delegates of one of the other peoples objects to that declaration, the Chair of the House of Peoples must set up a commission to resolve the issue, consisting of one Delegate from each of the constituent peoples. If the commission fails to resolve it within five days, the matter is referred to the Constitutional Court, which must adopt an expedited procedure and review 'procedural regularity' of the declaration. If the Court decides that the declaration is procedurally regular, the proposed decision of the Parliamentary Assembly requires a majority of the Delegates from each of the three constituent peoples in order to pass.[23]

These provisions, well intentioned as they are, have caused practical, constitutional and human rights problems. At a practical level, the vital interest provisions gave each constituent people something approaching a veto on all legislation. Indeed, the power of the caucuses is colloquially called a 'vital national interest veto'. This has often made it impossible for the Parliamentary Assembly to function as an effective legislature. In 2006, a package of proposals for constitutional reform would have simplified matters by limiting the role of the House of Peoples in the legislative process, but the House would have retained its function in relation to vital interests. In the event, the proposals were rejected. Eventually, the Constitutional Court decided to break the deadlock by adopting an expansive interpretation of procedural regularity. It held that a declaration of vital interest was not procedurally regular unless the impugned law or other decision affected an interest which the Court itself

[21] Constitution of BiH, art IV.1, 2.
[22] Constitution of BiH, art IV.1, 2.
[23] Constitution of BiH, art IV.3/(e), (f).

regarded as a 'vital interest' of a constituent people, and was destructive of, rather than merely an interference with, that interest.[24]

Where the Court has been unable to break the deadlock, the High Representative has sometimes used his powers under Annex 10 to the Dayton Agreement to impose legislation which was being legitimately blocked by one or more of the constituent peoples. From a constitutional perspective, this is problematic. It deprives the elected representatives of constituent peoples in the House of Peoples of their constitutional right to control the passage of legislation to protect the vital interests of their people. On the other hand, when the Constitution guarantees the collective equality of the constituent peoples and their political leaders are determined not to compromise, something has to give if the state is to function. The Constitutional Court decided that it could not review a decision of the High Representative, although it could review a legal norm which he inserted into the state's legal order for compatibility with the substantive requirements of the Constitution.[25] This compromise effectively prevents constituent peoples from arguing that a law imposed by the High Representative to overcome a vital interest veto is unconstitutional because the law was not made in accordance with the procedure set out in Article IV of the Constitution.

The composition of the Presidency, based on a power-sharing arrangement between the three constituent peoples and the two Entities, has proved even more problematic. As noted above, Article V provides for a three-member Presidency: a Bosniac and a Croat from FBiH, and a Serb from RS. They are required to adopt all Presidency decisions about foreign policy, appointment of international representatives and representation in and membership of international and European organisations and institutions by consensus if possible. If adopted by a majority, a member of the Presidency who considers that a majority decision is destructive of a vital interest of the Entity from which he or she comes may make a declaration to that effect within three days. A declaration by the member from the RS is referred to the National Assembly of the RS; one by a member from the Federation is referred to the caucus of delegates to the House of Peoples in the legislature of the FBiH representing the constituent people to which that member belongs. If that body votes by a two-thirds majority to confirm the declaration, the decision of the Presidency 'shall not take effect'.[26] The interests in question here are those of an Entity, rather than a constituent people. The distinction is not clear-cut, however. The Serb member of the Presidency usually sees the interests of the RS as being the same as those of the Serb people. In the Federation, it is natural for the Croat and Bosniac members of the Presidency to seek to identify the interests of their respective peoples

[24] See particularly Case No U-2/04, *Request of Mr Mustafa Pamuk*, Decision of 28 May 2004, Case No U-8/04 (n 18); Case No U-4/05 (n 19), Case No U-10/05 (n 19); Case No U-5/06 (n 19).

[25] Case No U-9/00, *Request of Eleven Members of the House of Representatives of the Parliamentary Assembly of BiH*, Decision of 3 November 2000, paras 6–7.

[26] Constitution of BiH, art V.2/(d).

with the interests of the Federation. It is hard to separate them in political rhetoric and also, sometimes, in litigation. It tends to undermine the effectiveness of Presidency decision-making on politically controversial matters.

Entities and constituent peoples are all privileged in the composition of the Constitutional Court of BiH. Four of the six national judges are selected by the House of Representatives of the legislature of the FBiH, and two by the National Assembly of the RS. As an additional constraint on Entity-based voting when deciding cases, three of the Court's nine judges are international judges, appointed by the President of the European Court of Human Rights after consulting the Presidency of BiH. They must not come from BiH or any neighbouring state.[27]

The privileges granted to constituent peoples disadvantage Others, who are ineligible to stand for election to the Presidency or to be selected as Delegates in the House of Peoples of the state's Parliamentary Assembly. Serbs living in the FBiH, and Bosniacs and Croats living in the RS are similarly ineligible. The same is probably true of anyone who resides in the Brčko District, which had no place in the Constitution until 2009.

There were constitutional challenges to the validity of provisions of Articles IV and V on account of inconsistency with the fundamental value of equality protected by Article II of the Constitution and by international law. The Court held by a majority that it lacked competence to rule on the constitutionality of a provision of the Constitution. It could not discharge its overarching duty under Article VI of the Constitution to 'uphold this Constitution' by holding part of it to be unconstitutional. As a result, the composition of the House of Peoples had to be seen as a necessary concession to secure the conditions for peaceful co-existence of the constituent peoples after the war. At least one of the judges thought that this continued to provide an objective and rational justification for the unfavourable treatment of Others.[28]

When the issue was considered by the European Court of Human Rights in the context of human rights law rather than constitutional law, that Court, unconstrained by the need to uphold the Constitution, rejected the state's argument that the special arrangement was still justified, and found a violation of Article 14 taken together with Protocol No 1, Article 3 of the ECHR in relation to the House of Peoples and a violation of Article 1 of Protocol No 12 in relation to elections to the Presidency.[29] Unfortunately, the Court's reasoning failed to address seriously the problems still afflicting BiH, the issue of justification, or the use of the margin of appreciation in transitional states. The effect of the decision was to require the state to amend its Constitution. This has so far proved impossible, despite deadlines set by the Committee of Ministers of the

[27] Constitution of BiH, art VI.1(a).

[28] Case No U-5/04, *Request of Mr Sulejman Tihić*, Decision of 31 March 2006. See also Case No U-13/05, *Request of Mr Sulejman Tihić*, Decision of 26 May 2006.

[29] *Sejdić and Finci v Bosnia and Herzegovina*, Apps Nos 72996/06 and 34836/06, Judgment of 22 December 2009, ECtHR [GC].

Council of Europe, as anyone familiar with the political problems in the country would have anticipated. The difficulty of securing consensus among peoples and parties is tellingly illustrated by the fact that, at the time of writing (August 2011), it has still not been possible to elect a Council of Ministers to govern after indecisive results of the October 2010 general election. The European Court of Human Rights had unrealistic expectations of BiH which have reduced the Court's authority among the country's political elite.

V. CONCLUSION: DOES BiH HAVE A BILL OF RIGHTS?

We have seen that the Constitution of BiH makes a very large assortment of rights part of the legal order in BiH, and requires all institutions to secure the highest level of internationally recognised human rights in the country. But the Constitution does not specify all the rights individually and it does not codify them in the form usually associated with a bill of rights. Nor does it explain clearly the status of each category of rights in the hierarchy of constitutional and legal norms. Rights derive from multiple sources, and indeed different legal orders. The relationship between municipal and international law is contested and uncertain. Of those rights which derive from international law, some are enumerated but not defined, and others are merely incorporated by reference. The Constitution does not set out either the limiting factors which might justify interfering with rights or the remedies which are to be available for violations. The rights are also of different kinds. Individual rights stand together with the rights of 'peoples' and Entities, linked to a model of political consociationalism necessitated by the divisions in society and the nature of the war which the Constitution was instrumental in ending. These kinds of rights can conflict, particularly in the field of discrimination.

Is there, then, a bill of rights? Most of the oddities are shared with one or more of the bills of rights adopted by other countries and recognised as such. For example, Ireland, India and South Africa have constitutional bills of rights which mix individual and group rights, civil, political, social and economic rights. Neither the US Bill of Rights nor the New Zealand Bill of Rights Act 1990 expressly authorises remedies for violating rights. The US Bill of Rights does not include a clear statement of factors justifying interfering with constitutional rights. The UK's Human Rights Act 1998 (which may or may not be properly regarded as a bill of rights) leaves the relationship between municipal and international law opaque. All these issues have had to be addressed by administrators, politicians and judges in many jurisdictions.

Yet the absence of a full enumeration of the rights themselves is a major stumbling block to regarding BiH as having a bill of rights.[30] It is normal for the

[30] The Council of Europe Commission for Democracy through Law (Venice Commission), in criticism of a proposed amendment to art II in 2006, has by implication recognised the shortcomings of the current treatment of rights: see CDL-AD(2006)019,Opinion 375/2006, *Opinion on the*

scope of rights to be uncertain: social and political understandings and practices change, and rights can be interpreted in unexpected ways. For example, the Indian Supreme Court has implied a social right to education from a guarantee of the right to life in Article 21 of the Indian Constitution.[31] But where rights appear without having been expressly enumerated, they are normally developed by interpretation of, or implication from, enumerated rights and other constitutional provisions. The major oddity of the way the Constitution of BiH deals with rights is that it does not attempt to enumerate them thoroughly.

Two factors help to explain this deficiency. First, in the fevered effort to put in place a constitutional settlement capable of inducing previously warring parties to shoulder their arms and try to work peacefully alongside (if not with) one another, rights and privileges were selected for their instrumental value to the peace negotiation, and there was not time to think through the implications fully. It has been left to institutions working in the country to try to make practical, domestic sense of a diplomatic and military settlement. Secondly, the so-called 'international community' played a major part in the making of the Constitution. Despite the protestations of the Preamble, the citizens of BiH were not in control of the process and have never had a say in its adoption. This is not peculiar to that troubled country. Much the same can be said of the constitutional settlements in Japan and Germany after World War II, Afghanistan after the Taleban, Iraq after the second Gulf War, and Kosovo after independence.[32] Nevertheless, in BiH's case the Constitution was drafted as a part of the deal to end a war. In the other cases, the war was over, so there was less urgency to put a new constitution in place (although Iraq's Constitution shows that time to reflect does not necessarily produce coherence). The fact that the international community was working under pressure of time helps to explain some of the problems to which the Constitution has given rise.

Does it matter whether rights mentioned in the Constitution form a bill of rights? Perhaps the content of the rights and their effectiveness is more important than any issue of form or terminology. But form is not unimportant. The lack of systematic enumeration of the rights, let alone elaboration and classification, is partly responsible for the difficulties which have arisen in giving effect to them. The status of rights under the ECHR and other human rights treaties, the relationship between collective guarantees and individual rights, and the way in which those guarantees have hamstrung the political system of the state for much of the last 16 years, can all be attributed in part to the creation, largely

Draft Amendments to the Constitution of Bosnia and Herzegovina, available at www.venice.coe.int/, paras 77–83, 95.

[31] See *Mohini Jain v State of Karnataka* [1992] 2 SCC 666, as restricted in *Unni Krishnan v State of AP* [1993] 1 SCC 645. See also D Feldman, 'Public interest litigation and constitutional theory in comparative perspective' (1992) 55 *Modern Law Review* 47, and 'The contribution of human rights to improving public health' (2006) 120 *Public Health* 61–69; M Khosla, 'Making social rights conditional: lessons from India' (2010) 8 *International Journal of Constitutional Law* 739.

[32] See, eg, C Hahm and S H Kim, 'To make "We the People": constitutional founding in postwar Japan and South Korea' (2010) 8 *International Journal of Constitutional Law* 800.

by outsiders, of an incompletely worked out catalogue. The lessons of BiH's experience with constitutional rights are simple: find out what is going on; make sure that expectations are realistic; think things through. A better formulated system of rights might not have made the country's government more effective or its social and economic progress more positive, but the way in which the Constitution was made has not made it easy for politicians, officials, and judges to make it effective.

8

Constitutional Change and the Quest for Legal Inclusion in Nepal

MARA MALAGODI

I. INTRODUCTION

THE PRESENT CHAPTER analyses Nepal's current post-conflict constitution-making endeavours in light of the increasing politicisation of socio-cultural identity along ethno-linguistic, regional, gender, religious and caste-based lines. Nepal's ongoing peace process began in April 2006 to resolve a decade-long armed internal conflict between the Communist Party of Nepal (Maoist) and the Nepal government (1996–2006). Significantly, constitutional change has been integral to the peace process, but has remained – to a certain extent – subordinate to critical political issues, eg arms management, the position of the Shah monarchy in the political system until May 2008, the unification of the two armies, and the role of the United Nations Mission in Nepal (UNMIN) in the peace process negotiations. The resolution of the armed conflict has been inextricably intertwined with constitutional change in the country since 2001 when the Maoists' demands for the abrogation of the embattled 1990 Constitution and the elections of a Constituent Assembly (CA) became non-negotiable. The rationale behind demands for extensive constitutional reform was the goal of achieving a greater degree of social inclusion through a radical programme of state restructuring to accommodate Nepal's high degree of socio-cultural diversity and ultimately address the country's endemic socio-economic imbalances.[1]

[1] The 2001 Census identified 92 languages spoken as mother tongues in Nepal, with only 48.61% of the total population naming Nepali as its mother tongue – although Nepali is constitutionally the country's official language. In terms of caste/ethnicity the Census recorded 102 groups, of which only six constitute more than 5% of the total population (Nepal Central Bureau of Statistics 2002). The two largest groups, the Chetri (15.8%) and Hill Brahmins (12.74%), together constitute the Parbatiya group, ie the dominant Hindu high castes of the Pahari (hilly) region of the country, to which the royal family and the majority of the country's elites belong. 10 religions are identified as practised on Nepal's territory. Hinduism has the largest following, with 81% of the total population. The Census has, however, been contested by many as a governmental attempt at downsizing the non-Parbatiya and non-Hindu population (UNDP/CASU, 2008a: iii). The Asian

The analysis concentrates on the relationship between constitutional rights and the changing definition of the Nepali nation in the 1990 Constitution, the 2007 Interim Constitution, and the ongoing discussions within the CA elected in April 2008. It is argued that the 1990 Constitution's combination of 'constitutional nationalism' – based on the privileged position of the Shah monarchy, Hinduism and the Nepali language – with a traditional set of individual rights centred on a negative form of equality anchored in the principle of non-discrimination produced specific patterns of legal exclusion in Nepal.[2] These exclusionary patterns made the document an increasingly embattled one and contributed to its progressive delegitimation. Therefore, Nepal's post-conflict constitution-making endeavours strive towards the creation of more inclusive state institutions by toning down the rhetoric of 'traditional' Nepali constitutional nationalism – especially since the abolition of the Shah monarchy in the CA's first meeting on 28 May 2008 – and, conversely, by expanding the fundamental rights contained in the Constitution to include provision for group-based rights and forms of devolution to empower marginalised groups at the local level like the proposed model of ethnic federalism.

Notably, the relationship between the 'symbolic' constitutional provisions defining Nepal's national identity and fundamental rights needs to be investigated in light of the extensive powers that the Nepali judiciary – especially the Supreme Court – has acquired since 1990 in order to evaluate the implementation of Nepal's constitutional language. In this respect, the chapter's core argument is that the translation of socio-cultural identities – whether at the national or sub-national level – into legally defined categories raises the question of legally sanctioned exclusion and discrimination as possible derogations from the principle of equality. Thus, the chapter's central question is to what extent Nepal's ongoing 'constitutional re-design' towards an institutionalised politics of recognition through legal reform can effectively tackle the country's historical imbalances and inequalities.

II. METHODOLOGICAL AND THEORETICAL FRAMEWORK

This chapter analyses three different phases of post-conflict constitutional transformation in Nepal since April 2006: the 18 May 2006 Proclamation of the reinstated House of Representatives, the drafting and promulgation of the Interim Constitution on 15 January 2007, and the work of the various CA Committees to prepare a new Constitution (originally within two years) – the

Development Bank calculated that Nepal in 2007 had a Gini coefficient of 0.473, the highest in Asia (Lal, 2007), and a literacy rate of only 57.9%. Additionally, according to a World Bank estimate, Nepal has the lowest GDP per capita (US$ 427) amongst South Asian countries (see http://data.worldbank.org/indicator/NY.GDP.PCAP.CD).

[2] M Malagodi, *Constitutional Nationalism and Legal Exclusion in Nepal (1990–2007)* (SOAS, University of London, PhD Thesis, 2009).

seventh in the country's history. The CA was unable to complete its work within the established time frame and its deadline has now been extended for the fourth time to 29 May 2012.

At the time of writing, Nepal faces a serious political impasse due to the difficulty of completing the drafting of the new Constitution, even after the election of the new Prime Minister on 28 August 2011. Dr Baburam Bhattarai, the Vice-Chairman of the United Communist Party of Nepal (Maoist), was voted in with the support of a number of Terai-based parties in the first round of elections following the resignation of his predecessor, Mr Jhalanath Khanal on 14 August 2011. The Constitution-drafting process is delayed by the profound differences amongst the 32 political parties represented in the Assembly (25 at the time of elections in 2008) over the nature of federalism, the form of government, positive discrimination, group rights, the electoral system and the position of the judiciary to be adopted in the new document. By January 2010, the CA Constitutional Committee and the Thematic Committees submitted their draft reports, which, however, remained silent on the most contentious issues.[3] To resolve the drafting stalemate in October 2010 a seven-member taskforce led by Maoist Chairman Pushpa Kamal Dahal was created to iron out the difference amongst the stakeholders and enable the CA to meet its deadline.

The uneven distribution of seats and the fragmentation of Nepal's political forces in the CA, however, still leave plenty of room for shrewd political manoeuvring.[4] The initial two-year term of the CA has already been extended four times by amending Article 64 of the Interim Constitution: on 28 May 2010, 29 May 2011, 29 August 2011 and 29 November 2011. Nepal's Supreme Court has adjudicated twice on the legality of extending the CA term: on 25 May 2011, limiting the lawful extension of the CA to a further six-month period, and then on 28 August 2011, confirming the legality of the previous extension. Nepal's new Prime Minister has pledged the completion of a full draft by the extended 29 May 2012 deadline, but should the CA be unable to do so, the question as to whether it will be constitutional to further extend the Assembly's term or it will be necessary to dissolve the CA remains a disquieting one.

Constitutional reform in Nepal has acquired a central place in the discourse about socio-political change in the country since 1990. One of the objectives behind the analysis here is to understand why negotiations over social inclusion,

[3] For the Nepali text and English translation of the various Constituent Assembly Committees' reports see www.ccd.org.np/new/index.php.

[4] Nepal's new Prime Minister was elected with 340 votes by the 601-member CA; however, a two-thirds majority vote in the Assembly will be needed to promulgate the new Constitution, requiring at least 401 votes. It will be difficult to achieve this qualified majority vote with the CA's second and third biggest parties, the Nepali Congress and UML, as the opposition. At the time of CA elections in 2008, of the 25 political parties represented in the Assembly the biggest three controlled about 75% of the seats: the Maoists 38%, Congress 19% and UML 18%. The fourth biggest party, the Madhesi People's Rights Forum, held 9% of the seats. Only five parties after the biggest four controlled respectively more than 1% of the seats, while the representation of each of the remaining 16 parties was below 1%. Over the last three years, the composition of the CA has been further fragmented: at the time of writing 32 political parties are represented in Nepal's Assembly.

socio-economic justice, democracy and even the resolution of the Maoist insurgency have been conducted in legal-institutional terms. One of the significant aspects of the Nepali case study is the primacy that has been given to institutional reform as a tool for conflict resolution, anchored in the belief that significant and durable *socio-political* change can be achieved primarily by *legal* means. Therefore, on a normative level, it is crucial to understand the central role of law in these debates which are otherwise of an essentially political nature. The progressive reconfiguration of law primarily as *right* has produced a shift in the relationship between law and politics that has been recently described as 'the triumph of law over politics'. As Martin Loughlin has argued, it is now a matter of ascertaining 'whether this conception of law as right provides an adequate representation of contemporary arrangements, one which is able to make a decisive impression on the current structure of government'.[5]

As a result, this chapter aims to asses to what extent the redefinition and expansion of constitutional rights in Nepal's ongoing process of constitutional change can provide a basis for the unity of the Nepali people and supplant exclusionary forms of constitutional nationalism. However, Nepali nationalism has proven over the years to be particularly resilient to change, even after the democratic transition of 1990. I maintain that this is due to the legacy of the country's historical processes of state formation and nation-building anchored in the institution of Hindu kingship since the creation of modern Nepal by King Prithvi Narayan Shah in the late eighteenth century.[6] Significantly, Nepal was never colonised and the dynastic lineage of the Shah Kings has remained uninterrupted for centuries. Therefore, the core empirical question underlying the present analysis is whether Nepal's current CA process will be capable of being a 'critical juncture', as understood in Historical Institutionalist literature, and act as catalyst to ignite enduring institutional change in Nepal. Historical Institutionalism embraces the view that institutional change is particularly difficult to achieve; institutions are a product of history, but at the same time, once in place, contribute to shaping historical developments. As a result, Historical Institutionalism adopts the concept of path-dependence according to which '[politics] involves some elements of chance (agency, choice), but once a path is taken, then it can become "locked in," as all the relevant actors adjust their strategies to accommodate the prevailing pattern'.[7] This is the case because the cost of reversing the initial institutional choice is particularly high. A specific path is adopted at a certain historical moment regarded as a critical juncture:

> There are brief moments in which opportunities for major institutional reforms appear, followed by long stretches of institutional stability. Junctures are 'critical' because they place institutional arrangements on paths or trajectories, which are then

[5] M Loughlin, *Sword and Scales* (Oxford, Hart Publishing, 2000) 229.

[6] M Malagodi, 'Forging the Nepali Nation through Law: A Reflection on the Use of Western Legal Tools in a Himalayan Kingdom' (2008) 8 *Studies in Ethnicity and Nationalism* 433.

[7] K Thelen 'Historical Institutionalism in Comparative Politics' (1999) 2 *Annual Review of Political Science* 385.

> very difficult to alter. [. . .] Critical junctures are often attributed to big exogenous shocks. In this literature, major events such as war or economic crisis constitute a catalyst for enduring institutional changes.[8]

Therefore, the ultimate question at the heart of the present inquiry is whether the CA process will be able to bring significant change in the relationship between the constitutional definition of 'Nepali-ness' and the constitutional rights and alter the balance in favour of a more meaningful notion of equality to which Nepalis are entitled by virtue of being citizens of the Nepali state.

III. MAOIST CONFLICT AND IDENTITY POLITICS IN NEPAL (1996–2006)

The drafting of Nepal's new Constitution by the CA is part of the ongoing peace process which began in April 2006 to bring a decade of internal armed conflict to an end. The conflict and the peace process need to be analysed within the broader context of Nepal's post-Cold War 1990 transition to constitutional democracy following 30 years of Panchayat monarchical autocracy (1960–90). Following the promulgation of the 1990 Constitution, leftist groups, dalits, women and ethno-linguistic, regional and religious minorities criticised the document because they felt it disregarded Nepal's socio-cultural diversity in favour of a homogenising vision of the Nepali nation anchored in the 'traditional' markers of Nepali nationalism: the Shah monarchy, Hinduism and the Nepali language. In fact, it has been argued that the 1990 Constitution represented 'the source of exclusion' for many of Nepal's marginalised socio-cultural groups.[9] The political change of 1990 progressively brought the grievances of many historically marginalised groups to the forefront of Nepal's public debate, especially groups defined in ethno-linguistic terms:

> In the changed context after the restoration of democracy in 1990, those historically excluded groups began to assert their identities and rights. The demands of the ethnic groups pertain to three major themes: an assertion of ethnic identities shorn of the caste-labels that the state slapped on ethnic groups, the sharing of national resources, and a greater representation of the diverse groups in the political structure. The 1990 Constitution recognized Nepal as a multiethnic, multicultural and multilingual nation, but it did not include provisions that would translate that call to promote diversity into inclusive processes. Nevertheless, the democratic atmosphere that the restoration of democracy in 1990 created proved conducive for ethnic activism and uprising.[10]

[8] P Pierson, *Politics in Time* (Princeton, Princeton University Press, 2004) 134–35.

[9] M Lawoti, *Towards a Democratic Nepal Inclusive Political Institutions for a Multicultural Society* (New Delhi, Sage Publications, 2005) 115–16.

[10] K Hacchethu et al, *Nepal in Transition: A Study on the State of Democracy (Kathmandu, IDEA*, 2008) 73–74.

The long-brewed resentment of many social groups came into the public eye with the end of the Panchayat regime, resulting in the formation of social movements demanding socio-economic advancement, political and cultural recognition.

Additionally, in February 1996 the faction of the radical United Left Front, not recognised by the Electoral Commission to contest the 1994 mid-term elections, soon renamed itself as the Communist Party of Nepal (Maoist) and launched a 'people's war' against Kathmandu's central government. Significantly, the insurgency began only six years after Nepal's return to democracy in 1990. The Maoists submitted a list of 40 demands to the central government before launching their armed attack on police posts in the western districts. The list included demands for renegotiating a number of agreements with India, for ending Nepal's 'feudal' monarchical political system and reforming the economy, for declaring Nepal a secular state, for granting equal rights to women, ethno-linguistic minorities and dalits, and, significantly, for the drafting of a new Constitution by the people's elected representatives.[11] The argument underlying the demands was that the adoption of the institutional forms of parliamentary democracy and constitutional monarchy through the promulgation of the 1990 Constitution had not led to substantive changes in Nepal's economic, social and political spheres.

The decade of Nepal's conflict between 1996 and 2006 claimed over 13,000 lives; hundreds of people disappeared and became victims of rape, torture, displacement and gross human rights violations.[12] The insurgency had its stronghold in the mid-western districts of Rukum and Rolpa where Nepal's far-left was historically deep-rooted. In fact, following the Nepali Congress's victory in the 1991 general elections, these districts saw intense clashes between Congress and Leftist activists which culminated in the violent police clampdown in Operation Romeo in 1995. While the government was slow in responding to the challenges posed by the insurgency, by 2001 the Maoists exercised almost complete control over the mid-western districts.[13] The 'royal massacre' in June 2001 resulted in the accession to the throne of unpopular King Gyanendra,[14] while the escalation of violence in the Maoist attacks in the following months led to a ceasefire and negotiations between the two sides. The peace talks collapsed over

[11] M Hutt (ed), *Himalayan People's War* (London, Hurst, 2004) 285–87.

[12] International Crisis Group, *Nepal: Peace and Justice* (International Crisis Group Asia Report N 184, 14 January 2010) i.

[13] M Hutt, 'Introduction: Monarchy, Democracy and Maoism in Nepal' in M Hutt (ed), *Himalayan People's War* (London, Hurst, 2004) 6.

[14] On 1 June 2001 King Birendra, Queen Aiswarya and seven other members of the Royal Family were shot dead inside Kathmandu's Royal Palace of Narayanhiti allegedly by Crown Prince Dipendra who then attempted to commit suicide and died two days later. The country was ridden by shock, uncertainty and fear as the vast majority of Nepal's population did not accept the official explanation for the killings. See Manjushree Thapa *Forget Kathmandu* (Delhi, Penguin Viking, 2005) 7–47. Moreover, the succession to the throne of Gyanendra, late Birendra's second brother, was looked at with suspicion. Rumours spread about the involvement in the royal massacre of the new King and his son Paras. The accusation was made explicit by the Maoist ideologue Baburam Bhattarai's letter published on 6 June 2001 in the daily *Kantipur*. Gyanendra was accused of being India's pawn, while late Birendra was described as a 'patriotic King'.

the government's refusal to entertain the Maoist demand for the election of a Constituent Assembly. At that point it was clear that institutional reforms through constitutional change had become a top priority in the Maoists' political agenda. On 25 November 2001 the insurgents broke the ceasefire and launched coordinated attacks on a number of police posts; the government responded by declaring a state of emergency, deploying the army alongside police on the battlefield, and declaring the Maoists a 'terrorist group'.[15]

Nepal's political crisis deepened with the dissolution of the House of Representatives called by Prime Minister SB Deuba in May 2002 over his inability to secure the sufficient parliamentary majority to further extend the state of emergency. Until April 2006 Nepal was ruled by way of governmental decree without the legislature in place. This opened the way for a more direct intervention of King Gyanendra in politics. The new King assumed absolute powers twice: Nepal experienced two bouts of monarchical autocracy in 2002–03 and 2005–06, which sidelined the mainstream political parties. Then a second bout of emergency rule was declared by King Gyanendra when he took over for the second time on 1 February 2005. The struggle had become a tripartite one between the Shah monarchy, the Maoists and the parliamentary political parties. A radical shift in the political balance came in November 2005 when the Maoists and the ousted parliamentary parties (Nepali Congress, UML, RPP, Nepali Congress Democratic, NWPP etc) signed the Twelve-Point Agreement to strike up an alliance and launch a pro-democracy movement against the autocratic monarchy. Nationalism was evoked to oppose the monarchy:

> People, representatives of people and political parties are the real bulwark of nationalism. We are committed to protecting our independence, national unity and sovereignty, and safeguarding geographical integrity. [. . .] We appeal to all patriotic Nepalis to be wary of the Mandale[16] brand of nationalism preached by the monarch and his sycophants to protect their rule and interest.

Importantly, the parliamentary political parties gave in to the long term Maoist demand for the election of a Constituent Assembly. The two sides also agreed on the implementation of 'absolute democracy' through a 'forward-looking restructuring of the state' to address the issue of inclusion of the various groups defined in terms of gender, class, caste, language, region, ethnicity and region.[17]

[15] The declaration of the emergency under art 115(8) of the 1990 Constitution entailed the suspension of many Articles of Fundamental Rights of the 1990 Constitution such as sub-cl (a) freedom of speech and expression; (b) freedom of peaceful assembly without arms; and (d) freedom of movement of cl (2) of art 12; cl (1) press and publication pre-censorship of art 13; art 15 preventive detention; art 16 right to information; art 17 right to property; art 22 right to privacy; and art 23 right to constitutional remedies, apart from *habeas corpus*.

[16] The term Mandale originally meant the members of the Nepal Rashtrabadi Swatantra Bidyarthi Mandal, the pro-Panchayat official student organisation disbanded in 1979, but during the 1980s the term came to be used of any conservative or reactionary member of the political system. See John Whelpton et al, *People Politics and Ideology* (Kathmandu, Mandala Book Point, 1999) 99.

[17] See www.unmin.org.np/downloads/keydocs/12-point%20understanding-22%20Nov%202005 pdf .

It is crucial at this point to briefly analyse the root causes of the Maoist insurgency and thereby elucidate the multidimensional nature of Nepal's conflict, a conflict which never had the kind of clear-cut divide, for instance, of the Sri Lankan scenario. The roots of the conflict also illuminate the complex issues behind the ongoing peace process. Deepak Thapa has identified the appeal of the Maoist ideology in their focus on social and economic structural inequalities inherent in the Nepali system: pervasive poverty, low levels of developments (notwithstanding the presence of many development agencies in the country), acute disparities within society, low levels of social mobility due to resilient caste and class structures, the historical marginalisation of many social groups on the basis of gender, ethno-linguistic, regional, religious, caste affiliation, and the sharp urban/rural divide. As a result, the Maoists were able to capitalise on the discontent towards the Nepali state which was widely perceived as an extractive, exclusionary and clientelar institution.[18] Moreover, the Maoist leadership includes many Parbatiya high-caste Hindus and so the Maoist Party cannot be in any way defined as an 'ethnic' one. In this context, the Maoist demand for secularism seems instrumental to challenge the underlying basis for the putative legitimacy of the Shah monarchy and, at the same time, opening the political space for an equal recognition of Nepal's many marginalised socio-economic groups.

In short, the Maoist insurgency was not an 'ethnic conflict' although it certainly included an 'ethnic dimension'. The Maoist agenda encompassed demands for recognition of Nepal's marginalised groups, but many of these groups have remained well organised outside the Maoist Party. In April 1990 the *Nepāl Janajāti Mahāsangh* (Nepal Federation of Nationalities) was founded to preserve the cultures and defend the interests of the country's many ethnolinguistic minorities. Nepal's Janajati define themselves both in positive terms, as the indigenous people of Nepal, and in negative terms, adopting an explicitly anti-Hindu definition masking, however, a far more heterogeneous social reality.[19] The umbrella organisation was renamed as *Nepāl Ādivāsī Janajāti Mahāsangh* (Nepal Federation of Indigenous Nationalities, NEFIN). In 2002 Parliament passed the National Foundation for the Development of Indigenous Nationalities (NFDIN) Act recognising 59 groups as Janajati on the basis of their distinct mother tongue, traditional rights, cultural identity, social structure and written/unwritten history.[20]

In terms of regional groups, the Madheshi issue in the southern plains of the Terai has been largely ignored by Nepal's government and has come to the forefront of the political debate only since January 2007 with the mass protests against governmental discrimination in the Terai. The main grievances through-

[18] D Thapa with B Sijapati, *A Kingdom under Siege: Nepal's Maoist Insurgency, 1996 to 2004* (London, Zed, 2004) 51–82.

[19] W Fisher, 'Nationalism and the Janajati' (1993) 6 *Himal* 11.

[20] Section 2 and Schedule, *Ādivāsī Janajāti Utthān Rāṣṭriya Pratiṣṭhān Ain, 2058*, National Foundation for the Development of Indigenous Nationalities Act 2002.

out the 1990s regarded the issue of citizenship with estimates of about 3.5 million people without citizenship certificates.[21] The beginning of the so-called *Madheshī Āndolan* (Madheshi movement) engendered a long string of demonstrations, strikes, *bandh* (shut-downs) and high rates of casualties – including violent clashes with Maoist cadres.[22] As illustrated by a 2010 report by International Crisis Group, Nepal's post-April 2006 transitional politics has been particularly turbulent; 'the peace process has not delivered a linear progression from conflict to stability. Instead it has prompted new conflicts and reinforced more cyclical patterns of political violence'.[23] The situation is complex and multilayered as identity politics plays an ever greater role in both inter-party and intra-party politics. It is in light of these considerations that Nepal's post-conflict constitutional developments ought to be analysed.

IV. CONSTITUTIONAL NATIONALISM AND FUNDAMENTAL RIGHTS

The present section analyses the relationship between constitutional provisions defining the Nepali nation and fundamental rights in the 1990 Constitution, the 2007 Interim Constitution and the Reports submitted by the CA Constitutional Committee on 4 January 2010,[24] the Committee for Fundamental Rights and Directive Principles on 9 November 2009[25] and the Committee on the Protection of the Rights of Minorities and Marginalised Communities on 21 April 2009.[26]

In April 2006, the pro-democracy alliance launched a People's Movement against the monarchy and, on 24 April, succeeded in having the House of Representatives reinstated; this was the beginning of the peace process. On 30 April, the recently reinstated House of Representatives unanimously endorsed a proposal to hold elections for a CA with a mandate to draft a new Constitution. On 18 May, the House issued a Proclamation declaring Nepal a secular state, curtailing the powers of the King, concentrating legislative powers in the hand of the Lower House, and reforming provisions regarding citizenship.[27] The Proclamation was not an amendment of the Constitution in the technical procedural sense, but it significantly altered the spirit and letter of the document. The 1990 Constitution was effectively in legal limbo. The courts were not implementing the Proclamation as it was not part of the constitutional text, but at the same time its validity was challenged by at least three writ petitions filed in the

[21] International Crisis Group, *Nepal's Troubled Tarai Region* (International Crisis Group Asia Report N 136, 9 July 2007) 4–5.

[22] Kiran Nepal, 'Gore in Gaur' *Nepali Times* 341, 23–29 March 2007. See www.nepalitimes.com.np/issue/341/Headline/13351.

[23] International Crisis Group, *Nepal's Political Rites of Passage* (International Crisis Group Asia Report N 194, 29 September 2010) 2.

[24] See www.ccd.org.np/new/indexphp?cipid=12.

[25] See www.ccd.org.np/new/indexphp?cipid=22

[26] See www.ccd.org.np/new/indexphp?cipid=21.

[27] See www.unmin.org.np/downloads/keydocs/2006-05-18-Proclaimation_of_HOR.pdf .

Supreme Court.[28] The Court was the only state body which could invalidate an Act of Parliament; but the Court sidestepped the issue and kept the petitions pending until the abrogation of the 1990 Constitution by the legislature. On 11 June, Nepal's Parliament stripped the King of his veto power, further eroding the powers and position of the monarchy in Nepal's political system.

On 16 June 2006, Maoist leader Prachanda and Prime Minister Koirala agreed that the Maoists should be brought into an interim government and signed the Eight-Point Agreement. They also created a six-member team to draft the Interim Constitution: the Interim Constitution Drafting Commission (ICDC). Following protests from women and the minorities, on 15 July, the ICDC was extended to 15 members, including four women. The drafting of the Interim Constitution by the ICDC was effectively carried out from 6 July to 25 August 2006, when the Chairman submitted the draft to the heads of the government and Maoist negotiating teams.[29] The draft was heavily based on the structure and principles of the 1990 Constitution; it was, however, incomplete due to the lack of agreement on the issues of the constitutional status of the monarchy, the modality of the Interim Legislature, the process and modalities of the CA, and who would be the institutional actor empowered to promulgate the Interim Constitution. The negotiations over the finalisation of the document were delayed owing to the political difficulties in reaching a compromise over the issue of the decommissioning of weapons. Then, on 21 November, the government and the Maoists finally signed the Comprehensive Peace Agreement, which paved the way for a process of institutional reform to 'build a new Nepal'.[30]

In December 2006, the text of Interim Constitution was finalised by Home Minister Kishna Prasad Sitaula and Maoist ideologue Baburam Bhattarai; significant changes were made to the ICDC draft.[31] The Interim Constitution remained silent on the issue of the monarchy, declared Nepal a secular state, retained ample similarities with the 1990 Constitution, created a unicameral Interim Legislature, preserved the wide powers of the Nepali judiciary, and ultimately paved the way for the elections of the CA. On 15 January 2007, the 1990 Constitution was abrogated and the new Interim Constitution was promulgated. The Maoist delegates subsequently joined the Interim Legislature and the Cabinet, respectively in January and April of 2007.

[28] Kanak Bikram Thapa, Personal Communication, Kathmandu, Nepal Law Campus, 21 February 2007.

[29] *The Kathmandu Post*, 26 August 2006, 1.

[30] See www.unmin.org.np/downloads/keydocs/2006-11-29-peace_accord-MOFA.pdf.

[31] *The Kathmandu Post*, 16 December 2006, 1. The Prime Minister was entitled to use all the powers of the head of state; a fresh oath of office became mandatory for judges; reservations of seats in the Constituent Assembly were confined to the proportional quota; the provisions for education, health-care and employment were moved out of the Fundamental Rights and into the Directive Principles; no changes were made to the national symbols (the cow as Nepal's national animal was retained); and the six-member security council was empowered to mobilise the national army.

Following a period of uncertainty in which the CA elections were postponed twice – in June and November 2007 – finally the interim government succeeded in holding peaceful elections on 10 April 2008 which resulted in the Maoists gaining most seats out of the 601 amongst the 25 parties.[32] Significantly, part of the CA seats were allocated on the basis of proportional representation; 33 per cent of the allocated seats were to women, additionally the following proportionality was adopted: 13 per cent dalits, 37.8 per cent marginalised groups, 4 per cent backward regions, 31.2 per cent Madheshi and 30.2 per cent Other Groups. In its first meeting on 28 May 2008, the Constituent Assembly voted in favour of declaring Nepal a Federal Democratic Republic, to abolish the monarchy and create the office of President of the Republic.[33] As a result, the Nepali Congress's Madhesi politician, Ram Baran Yadav, was sworn in as Nepal's first President on 23 July 2008. Shortly after, on 18 August 2008, Maoist leader Pushpa Kamal Dahal (aka 'Prachanda') was sworn in as Nepal's new Prime Minister. On 25 May 2009 he was replaced by Madhav Nepal following Dahal's unsuccessful attempt to sack the Chief of Army Staff. In the midst of the country's political instability, the CA strived to proceed with the task of constitution-drafting; in December 2008 14 Thematic Committees were created and began their work.[34]

A. Constitutionalism and National Identity in Post-1990 Nepal

The present section investigates the link between Nepal's post-1990 constitutional arrangements and the identity of the Nepali nation. The argument put forward is that patterns of constitutional nationalism have been progressively diluted in parallel with the shrinking role of the Shah King in Nepal's constitutional edifice. The tension between the unity and diversity of the Nepali nation plays out in different phases of Nepal's recent constitutional transformations. As Hanna Lerner highlights,

> constitutions are not merely expected to establish the institutional structure of government and regulate the balance of power. Constitutions also play a foundational role by expressing the common identity and norms of the nation. Constitutions serve as the state's charter of identity.[35]

Therefore, the analysis here concentrates on the articulation of the notion of 'We, the People' in Nepal's post-1990 constitutional developments, with specific emphasis on the post conflict transformations.

[32] For Constituent Assembly's electoral system and results, see www.election.gov.np/reports/CAResults/reportBody.php.

[33] Interim Constitution of Nepal (Fourth Amendment) Act 2008.

[34] See www.ccd.org.np/new/resources/CA_Rules_ENG.pdf.

[35] H Lerner, 'Constitution-Writing in Deeply Divided Societies: The Incrementalist Approach' (2010) 16 *Nations and Nationalism* 68, 69.

The expression 'constitutional nationalism' has been adopted to describe the institutionalisation of the Nepali nation in the 1990 Constitution in ethno-cultural terms and, to a certain extent, also in the current 2007 Interim Constitution. In this specific context, the expression describes the process of enshrining in the constitutional text the narratives which have historically come to define the Nepali nation over the years: namely Hinduism, the Shah monarchy and the Nepali language. The concept of constitutional nationalism is defined by Robert Hayden as 'a constitutional and legal structure that privileges the members of one ethnically defined nation over other residents in a particular state'.[36] In this regard, it is particularly useful in analysing Nepal's highly divided polity. Constitutional nationalism also reflects the hegemony of a particular social group – the groups whose history and culture inform the institutionalised legal definition of the nation (eg, high caste *Pahari* Hindu males) over other groups subsumed into the monolithic constitutional definition of the nation. As a result, the hegemony of one group conversely translates into patterns of legal exclusion of other groups.[37]

Nepal's 1990 Constitution was drafted with a view to establishing a stable constitutional monarchy and parliamentary democracy after three decades of monarchic autocracy. It was expected to inaugurate, sanction and set in motion *the* political and institutional change that democratic forces in Nepal have always envisaged, but somehow many of the desired changes from the previous Panchayat regime did not take place. The 1990 Constitution has been blamed for institutionalising, legitimising and engendering patterns of exclusion and discrimination by virtue of the ethno-cultural Panchayat-style version of the Nepali nation enshrined in the new document. The state was accused of discriminating against and excluding many groups in Nepali society on the basis of religion, caste, gender, language and ethnicity and, conversely, of allowing for the privileged treatment and enduring hegemony of the country's Hindu upper caste elites from the Pahari (hill) region, ie the Parbatiya group. In this regard, the 1990 Constitution became so embattled, specifically because it was expected to give substance to democratic reforms and guarantee the protection and enforcement of fundamental rights – *in primis* the right to equality. These claims were at the heart of demands for radical institutional change in the country made by the Maoists and other social and ethnic activists.

[36] R Hayden, 'Constitutional Nationalism in the Formerly Yugoslav Republics' (1992) 51 *Slavic Review* 654, 655.

[37] D Gellner, 'Caste, Ethnicity and Inequality in Nepal' (2007) 42 *Economic and Political Weekly* 20, 1825.

1990 Constitution	2007 Interim Constitution	CA Committee Report
Preamble	**Preamble**	**Preamble**
Whereas, We are convinced that the source of sovereign authority of the independent and sovereign Nepal is inherent in the people, and, therefore, We have, from time to time, made known our desire to conduct the government of the country in consonance with the popular will; [. . .] I, King Birendra Bir Bikram Shah Deva, by virtue of the State authority as exercised by Us, do hereby promulgate and enforce this Constitution of the Kingdom of Nepal on the recommendation and advice, and with the consent of the Council of Ministers.	WE, THE PEOPLE OF NEPAL, IN EXERCISE OF THE SOVEREIGN POWERS AND STATE AUTHORITY INHERENT IN US; [. . .] NOW THEREFORE, in order to institutionalize the achievements of the revolution and movements till this date, hereby promulgate this INTERIM CONSTITUTION OF NEPAL, 2063 (2007), prepared through a political consensus and to be in force until a new Constitution is framed by the Constituent Assembly	WE, THE PEOPLE OF NEPAL, IN EXERCISE OF THE SOVEREIGN POWERS INHERENT IN US; Maintaining the independence, sovereignty, territorial integrity and national unity, liberty and dignity of Nepal, [. . .] NOW THEREFORE, in order to fulfil the desire for sustainable peace, prosperity and development through a system of federal democratic republic rule while ending all kinds of the remains of feudalism, hereby promulgate this CONSTITUTION, framed through the Constituent Assembly.

The comparison between the Preambles of the three constitutional moments reveals the watershed represented by the 2007 Interim Constitution in asserting the primacy of the Nepali People. While the 1990 Constitution was promulgated by the King, even if state sovereignty was recognised as vested in the Nepali people, since 2007 we find the familiar start 'We, the People' reminiscent of the American Constitution, in line with the spirit of the May 2006 Proclamation of the House of Representatives after the success of the pro-democracy movement. In this regard, the Maoist contribution to the drafting of the 2007 document is illustrated by the direct reference to the 'revolution'. (See table over).

A comparison of the constitutional definitions of the nation also illustrates the shift in the representation of the Nepali nation. In the 1990 Constitution Article 2 stresses the unity of the nation *notwithstanding* the many socio-cultural differences of the Nepali population. This provision needs to be read together with Article 27(2) which defines His Majesty as 'the symbol of the Nepali nationality and the unity of the Nepali People'. Significantly, under Article 27(1) His Majesty means 'His Majesty the King for the time being

1990 Constitution	2007 Interim Constitution	CA Committee Report
Article 2 – The Nation Having common aspirations and united by a bond of allegiance to national independence and integrity of Nepal, the Nepalese people irrespective of religion, race, caste or tribe, collectively constitute the nation.	**Article 3 – The Nation** Having multi-ethnic, multi-lingual, multi-religious, multi-cultural characteristics with common aspirations, and being committed to and united by a bond of allegiance to national independence, integrity, national interest and prosperity of Nepal, all the Nepali people collectively constitute the nation.	**Article 3 – The Nation:** Having multi-ethnic, multi-lingual, multireligious, multi-cultural characteristics with common aspirations, and being committed to and united by a bond of allegiance to national independence, integrity, national interest and prosperity of Nepal, all Nepali people collectively constitute the nation.

reigning, being a descendant of the Great Prithvi Narayan Shah and an adherent of Aryan culture and Hindu religion'. In contrast, since 2007 the nation itself is defined as diverse and, for the first time in Nepali constitutional history, as 'multi-religious'; the unity of the nation thus derives from the allegiance to national independence and integrity.

1990 Constitution	2007 Interim Constitution	CA Committee Report
Article 4 – The Kingdom (1) Nepal is a multiethnic, multilingual, democratic, independent, indivisible, sovereign, Hindu and Constitutional Monarchical Kingdom.	**Article 4 – The State of Nepal** (1) Nepal is an independent, indivisible, sovereign, secular, inclusive and *federal democratic republican* State.* * Inserted by Interim Constitution of Nepal (Fourth Amendment) Act, 2008.	**Article 4 – State of Nepal:** (1) Nepal is an independent, indivisible, sovereign, secular, inclusive, socialism oriented, republic and multinational State which shall be called Nepal in brief. (2) The State of Nepal shall comprise the federal units as set out in Schedule 1.

Article 4(1) of the 1990 Constitution was one of the most embattled provisions of the entire document and famously made Nepal constitutionally the world's only Hindu Kingdom, although without declaring Hinduism as the state religion. The 2006 House of Representatives Proclamation had already declared Nepal to be a secular state, but it was the 2007 Interim Constitution that constitutionalised secularism. Significantly, the Nepali term adopted for 'state' in 1990 was *adhirājya*, which refers specifically to the notion of a Kingdom with an explicit association to the institution of the monarchy. Significantly, the Interim Constitution employs the expression *Nepāl rājya* and drops the term *adhirājya* entirely. The term *rājya* has more neutral connotations and it is in fact used to refer to the state as the institutional apparatus and legal entity without much emphasis on its historically salient cultural features. The Interim Constitution was silent on the issue of the monarchy until its Fourth Amendment on the first meeting of the Constituent Assembly which proclaimed Nepal a Federal Democratic Republic. The Article is almost identical in the Constitutional Committee Report and further emphasises that a federal structure is to be adopted. The provision defining the Nepali state is where the most radical constitutional change took place.

1990 Constitution	2007 Interim Constitution	CA Committee Report*
Article 6 – Language of the Nation (1) The Nepali language in the Devanagari script is the language of the nation of Nepal. The Nepali language shall be the official language. (2) All the languages spoken as the mother tongue in the various parts of Nepal are the national languages of Nepal.	**Article 5 – Language of the Nation** (1) All the languages spoken as mother tongues in Nepal are the national languages of Nepal. (2) The Nepali language in the Devanagari script shall be the language of official business. (3) Notwithstanding whatever is written in clause (2), the use of one's mother tongue in a local body or office shall not be barred. The State shall translate the language used for such purposes into the language of official business for the record.	**Article 5 – Language of the Nation** (1) The Nepali language in the Devanagari script shall be the language of official business of Nepal and a *lingua franca* between the provincial states. (2) All the languages spoken as mother tongues in different parts of Nepal are the languages of the nation and the State shall provide equal treatment to all mother tongues. (3) The Provincial or State Executive shall choose one or more languages spoken by a majority of people in the State as an official language of the Province or State. (4) English shall serve as an international contact language. (5) Deaf citizens shall have the right to use and communicate in the Nepali sign language. (6) Persons with no eye-sight shall have the right to use the Braille script. (7) There shall be a Commission on the Languages of the Nation to identify, study, research, standardize, protect and promote all languages spoken within Nepal. (8) The formation, functions, rights, duties and procedures of the Commission formed as per Sub-Article (7) shall be as prescribed by law.

Article 6 of the 1990 Constitution institutionalises the difference between Nepali and the other languages of the country. Nepali is placed on a higher level, being the sole *rāṣṭrabhāṣā* (language of the nation), while all the other languages are defined as *rāṣṭriya bhāṣā* (national language). The use of different expressions in the Nepali text is significant and ought not to be overlooked. Moreover, Article 6 makes Nepali also the official language of Nepal. From a practical point of view, however, Nepali has been the de facto *lingua franca* of the Western Pahari region since the fourteenth century AD and it is understood by the majority of the country's population, even if in the 2001 Census only 48.61 per cent of the population named Nepali as their mother tongue.

The Interim Constitution now defines all the languages spoken as mother tongues in Nepal as languages of the nation (*rāṣṭrabhāṣā*), but Nepali in the Devanagari script remains the country's only official language, hence granting the legal basis for the same kind of preferential treatment of the Nepali language under the 1990 Constitution. However, due to a controversial Supreme Court decision in 1999 which banned the use of languages other than Nepali in local government offices whose decision date was referred to by language ethnic activists as Nepal's 'Linguistic Black Day', subsection (3) was inserted to prevent similar occurrences in the future.[38] Importantly, the Article pertaining to language was not drafted by the Constitutional Committee which had purview of the Preliminary Part, but by the Committee on the Protection of the Rights of Minorities and Marginalised Communities. The language issue has become so central to debates over identity in Nepal that it was dealt with separately. Moreover, special provisions have been made with regard to the use of official languages other than Nepali in the government of the various federal units. (See table opposite).

The 1990 Constitution maintained Nepal's old national anthem, *Shrīmān Gambhīr*, in Article 7(1). The lyrics had been composed by poet Chakrapani Chalise in 1924 during the reign of the Rana Prime Minister Chandra Shamsher (1901–29) and the tune was known as Nepal's royal salute (*shrī pāncko salāmī*) praising the virtues of the King. The Interim Constitution left room for the government to choose Nepal's anthem after the old one had been scrapped by the 18 May 2006 House of Representatives Proclamation. In August 2007 a new national anthem was selected, *Sayau Thungā Phūlkā* (Made of Hundreds of Flowers); the tune celebrates Nepal's socio-cultural diversity and makes no mention of the monarchy.[39] With regard to the national symbols adopted in subsection (2) under the 1990 and 2007 Constitution, the criticism was that especially the colour (crimson) and the animal (cow) reflected Hindu symbolism, notably this subsection does not feature in the Committee Draft.

[38] *Adv Lal Bahadur Thapa and Others v Kathmandu Metropolitan City and Others*, Writ N 2931 of the year 2056/1999, unpublished Supreme Court decision.

[39] M Hutt, 'Singing the New Nepal' *Nations and Nationalism* (forthcoming).

1990 Constitution	**2007 Interim Constitution**	**CA Committee Report**
Article 7 – National Anthem, etc. (1) The national anthem of Nepal shall be as provided in Schedule 2. (2) The Rhododendron Arboreum shall be the national flower, Crimson Colour shall be the national colour, the Cow shall be the national animal and the Lophophorus shall be the national bird of Nepal. (3) The coat-of-arms of Nepal shall be as set forth in Schedule 3. The coat-of-arms may be enlarged or reduced as required, and such colour shall be used therein as specified by His Majesty's Government.	**Article 7 – National Anthem, etc.** (1) The national anthem and the coat-of-arms of Nepal shall be as determined by the Government of Nepal. (2) The Rhododendron Arboreum is the national flower, Crimson is the national colour, the Cow is the national animal and the Lophophorus is the national bird of Nepal.	**Article 7 – National Anthem and Coat-of-Arms** (1) The national anthem of Nepal shall be as set out in Schedule 3. (2) The coat-of-arms of Nepal shall be as set out in Schedule 4. *(The issue whether the provinces shall have their separate coats-of-arms or not shall be finalized after receiving the report of the Committee of State Restructuring and Distribution of State Power.)*

Yash Ghai notes: 'a state does not need a religion; and in the same way doesn't need a national animal/plant etc., and suggested that having, as in Nepal, the cow as the national animal was unnecessarily divisive'.[40] Moreover, the preservation of this Hindu national symbolism was particularly problematic in the context of the Interim Constitution and after the restoration of democracy. Maoist ideologue Baburam Bhattarai and current Prime Minister, during my interview with him, responded that it was the outcome of the negotiations behind the finalisation of the document: 'We took the King and we gave the cow'.[41] Other political commentators, instead, argued that the Maoists relented on the issue of the cow because they were aware that the majority of the Nepali public would have not supported the decision.

To conclude, Nepal's post-conflict constitutional transformations led to a greater degree of recognition of the diverse socio-cultural nature of the Nepali nation, while reinforcing the unity and integrity of the state (notwithstanding the decision to adopt a federal structure). The CA Committee Reports represent quite a departure from the model of constitutional nationalism enshrined in the 1990 Constitution, while the Interim Constitution currently in force is still an intermediate step between the two. However, only when the CA promulgates the new Constitution, will it be possible to assess to what extent Nepal has moved away from an ethno-cultural constitutional definition of the nation.

[40] UNDP/CASU, *Constitution-Making in Nepal* (Kathmandu, UNDP, 2007) 18.
[41] Interview with Baburam Bhattarai, Kathmandu, 16 August 2010.

B. Fundamental Rights in Post-1990 Nepal

The present section analyses the post-conflict constitutional changes which took place in the formulation of fundamental rights with particular reference to the right to equality. It is immediately evident that there has been a significant increase in the number of fundamental rights included under the various constitutional documents: the 1990 Constitution listed 13, the 2007 Interim Constitution 21 and the CA Committee Draft 31. There has also been an expansion in the kind of rights recognised under the CA Draft; the set of fairly traditional civil and political individual rights under the 1990 Constitution has been expanded to a more detailed protection of particular groups under the Interim document and to socio-economic rights under the CA Draft. Significantly, the first Article listed in the Committee Draft concerns the Right to a Dignified Life, in line with the Maoist demands for radical socio-economic change in the country. In my view, the Interim Constitution retains an individual rights approach similar to the 1990 Constitution, while the CA Draft significantly tilts the balance in favour of group rights.

1990 Constitution	2007 Constitution	CA Committee Report
11. Right to Equality	12. Right to Freedom	Right to a Dignified Life (Live with Dignity)
12. Right to Freedom	13. Right to Equality	Right to Liberty (Freedom)
13. Press & Publication Right	14. Right against Untouchability & Racial Discrimination	Right to Equality
14. Right Regarding Criminal Justice	15. Rights Regarding Publication, Broadcasting & Press	Right of Mass Communication
15. Right against Preventive Detention	16. Rights Regarding Environment & Health	Right to Justice
16. Right to Information	17. Education & Cultural Rights	Right of the Victims of the Crime
17. Right to Property	18. Rights Regarding Employment & Social Security	Right against Torture
18. Cultural & Educational Right	19. Right to Property	Rights against Preventive Detention
19. Right to Religion	20. Rights of Women	Right against Untouchability and Discrimination

1990 Constitution	2007 Constitution	CA Committee Report
20. Right against Exploitation	21. Right to Social Justice	Right to Property
21. Right against Exile	22. Rights of Children	Right to Religious Freedom
22. Right to Privacy	23. Right to Religion	Right to Information
23. Right to Constitutional Remedy	24. Rights Regarding Justice	Right to Secrecy (Privacy)
–	25. Right against Preventive Detention	Right against Exploitation
–	26. Right against Torture	Right to Environment
–	27. Right to Information	Right to Education
–	28. Right to Privacy	Right to Language and Culture
–	29. Right against Exploitation	Right to Employment
–	30. Right Regarding Labour	Right to Labour
–	31. Right against Exile	Right to Health
–	32. Right to Constitutional Remedy	Right to Food
–	–	Right to Accommodation (Housing)
–	–	Rights of Women
–	–	Rights of Children
–	–	Rights of Dalit Community
–	–	Right to Family
–	–	Right to Social Justice
	–	Right to Social Security
–	–	Consumers' Rights
–	–	Right against Exile
–	–	Right to Implementation of Fundamental Rights and Constitutional Treatment

The present analysis concentrates on the right to equality, its corollary provisions, and the right to religion in order to assess the relationship of fundamental constitutional rights with the notion of 'We, the People'.

1990 Constitution	2007 Constitution	CA Committee Report
Article 11 – Right to Equality (1) All citizens shall be equal before the law. No person shall be denied the equal protection of the laws. (2) No discrimination shall be made against any citizen in the application of general laws on grounds of religion, race, sex, caste, tribe or ideological conviction or any of these. (3) The state shall not discriminate citizens amongst citizens on grounds of religion, race, sex, caste, tribe or ideological conviction or any of these: Provided that special provisions may be made by law for the protection and advancement of the interests of women, children, the aged or those who are physically or mentally incapacitated or those who belong to a class which is economically, socially or educationally backward. (4) No person shall, on the basis of caste, be discriminated against as untouchable, be denied access to any public place, or be deprived of the use of public utilities. Any contravention of this provision shall be punishable by law. [. . .]	**Article 13 – Right to Equality** (1) All citizens shall be equal before the law. No person shall be denied the equal protection of the laws. (2) There shall be no discrimination against any citizen in the application of general laws on grounds of religion, race, gender, caste, tribe, origin, language or ideological conviction or any of these. (3) The State shall not discriminate among citizens on grounds of religion, race, caste, tribe, gender, origin, language or ideological conviction or any of these. Provided that nothing shall be deemed to prevent the making of special provisions by law for the protection, empowerment or advancement of women, Dalits, indigenous ethnic tribes [*Adivasi Janajati*], Madhesi or farmers, labourers or those who belong to a class which is economically, socially or culturally backward, or children, the aged, disabled or those who are physically or mentally incapacitated. [. . .]	**Right to Equality:** (1) All citizens shall be equal before the law. No person shall be denied the equal protection of the laws. (2) The State shall not discriminate against any citizen in the application of general laws on grounds of religion, colour, caste, tribe, gender, sexual orientation, biological condition, disability, health condition, marital condition, pregnancy, economic condition, origin, language or region, ideological conviction or other similar grounds. Provided that, nothing shall be deemed to prevent the making of special provisions by law for the protection, empowerment or advancement of women, *dalits*, indigenous ethnic tribes (*adivasis janjatis*), Madhesis or farmers, workers, oppressed region, Muslims, backward class, minority, marginalized and endangered communities or destitute people, youths, children, senior citizens, gender or sexual minorities, disabled or those who are physically or mentally incapacitated and helpless people, who are economically, socially or culturally backward. [. . .]

The 1990 Constitution favoured a negative view of equality based on the principle of non-discrimination. In fact, the document presented a formulation of the Article defining the right to equality in which cultural, linguistic, ethnic and religious affiliation did not provide any basis to claim a positive legal right. Such features, instead, were treated as possible causes for negative discrimination. Sub-clause (3) allowed for future enactments of special legislation for the advancement of the unprivileged segments of Nepali society; however forms of future positive discrimination, as defined by the legislator, were not based on membership in a group defined in ethno-linguistic or religious terms. Additionally, the 1990 Constitution maintained Nepal's tradition of legal uniformity, with no personal laws system like in India, and attempted to further centralise state power in order to consolidate state sovereignty to a greater extent. The Interim Constitution takes an additional step towards the recognition of group rights based on socio-cultural criteria such as ethno-linguistic, caste and regional identity. The CA Committee report advances the Interim Constitution and explicitly lists an even wider number of groups entitled to special protection as defined by the legislator. Additional Articles further qualifying equality are added to the 2007 Constitution (Cultural and Educational Rights, against Untouchability, for Women, Children, and Social Justice) and in the CA Draft (Language and Culture, Untouchability, Women, Children, Dalits, Family and Social Justice). Socio-economic rights figure even more prominently in the work of the CA Committee, with rights relating to education, employment, labour, health, food, accommodation, social security and social justice.

1990 Constitution	2007 Constitution	CA Committee Report
Article 19 – Right to Religion	**Article 23 – Right to Religion**	**Right to Religious Freedom**
(1) Every person shall have the freedom to profess and practise his own religion as handed down to him from ancient times having due regard to traditional practices; provided that no person shall be entitled to convert another person from one religion to another. [. . .]	(1) Every person shall have the right to profess, practise and preserve his or her own religion as handed down to him or her from ancient times paying due regard to social and cultural traditions. Provided that no person shall be entitled to convert another person from one religion to another and no person shall act or behave in a manner which may infringe upon the religion of others. [. . .]	(1) Every person shall have the freedom to profess, practice and preserve his or her own religion in accordance with his or her faith, or to refrain from any religion. Provided that no person shall be entitled to act contrary to public health, decent behaviour and morality, to indulge in activities of jeopardizing public peace or to convert a person from one religion to another, and no person shall act or behave in a manner which may infringe upon religion of others. [. . .]

The right to religion has, since the 1959 Constitution, gone virtually unchanged: the 1990 and 2007 constitutional reforms use the same formulation as the 1962 Panchayat Constitution. In this respect, the right to religion represents another element of continuity with Nepal's past. That being said, the formulation of the right to religion has changed dramatically in the CA Report, to the point of extending constitutional protection to non-believers. The ban on religious proselytism, however, was preserved also in the CA Draft and hints at the recurring theme of preserving Nepal's status quo. Religious conversion in Nepal has always been a thorny issue, historically being interpreted as a more or less direct attack on the country's independence – Nepal's sovereignty was thought to be best protected through the preservation of the country's Hindu identity.

V. CONSTITUTIONAL CONTROVERSIES AND THE NEPALI JUDICIARY

The changes in the relationship between the constitutional definition of the nation and fundamental rights in Nepal's post-conflict constitutional developments cannot be satisfactorily assessed without taking into account the role of the judiciary as arbiter and enforcer of that legal balance. The promulgation of the 1990 Constitution marked an extraordinary transformation of the Nepali judiciary, especially with regard to the extensive powers granted to the Supreme Court following the Indian model.

The current Interim Constitution preserves the framework of the 1990 Constitution with respect to the judiciary. The Supreme Court under Article 107(3) of the Interim Constitution has appellate and original jurisdiction. Article 107(1) grants to the Court the power of judicial review of the constitutionality of legislation and the power to void such legislation on grounds of unconstitutionality, hence departing from the traditional Westminster principle of parliamentary sovereignty. Under Article 107(2) the Supreme Court is empowered to exercise its extraordinary jurisdiction in Public Interest Litigation (PIL) cases. As developed in India, PIL has become a new kind of constitutional litigation *tout court*; abandoning a strict adversarial system, the Court can proceed *suo motu* or entertain the petition of any individual acting out of public concern. Significantly, Article 32 on the Right to Constitutional Remedy directly links the protection and enforcement of fundamental rights to judicial intervention. In this regard, the Supreme Court has also been empowered to issue directive orders and prerogative writs. Under Article 107(4), the Supreme Court is not bound by its previous decisions and it is permitted to review its own judgments and final orders. The position and powers of the Nepali judiciary have been embattled in the discussion within the Constituent Assembly, especially with regard to the power of judicial review of legislation. The Report of the CA Committee on the Judicial System submitted in September 2009 envisions the creation of a Special Judicial Committee of the Federal Legislature, which is elected by the federal legislature amongst its members under Article 29(1)(c) and empowered to judicially review legislation under Article 29(2)(a) and appoint and discipline judges under Article 29(2)(c)–(d). The adoption of these provisions would seriously undermine the independence of the judiciary, its powers, functions and, ultimately, its credibility.

At this time we can reach a tentative evaluation of the kind of balance that Nepal's Supreme Court has struck between socio-cultural diversity, the constitutional definition of the nation, and fundamental rights (including the right to equality). Elsewhere I have argued that the analysis of the Supreme Court-level case law in which Nepal's apex court has interpreted the Articles defining the Nepali nation in the 1990 Constitution reveals that the aforementioned Articles had *substantive* exclusionary outcomes rather than just a merely *symbolic* value as is claimed by the Constitution-makers. Their interpretation and implementation primarily by Nepal's Supreme Court and legislature has directly engendered and sanctioned already existing patterns of legal exclusion. Legal challenges to these exclusionary patterns have been primarily focused on gender issues. Indeed, the majority of post-1990 legal reform has concerned this area.[42] These efforts resulted in the Eleventh Amendment of the Muluki Ain (Country Code), the Gender Equality Act 2006 and the 33 per cent reservation of seats in the Constituent Assembly. Under the 1990 Constitution, the legal treatment of linguistic,[43] religious and caste issues,[44] instead, has taken a back seat and was not the subject of any challenge in the Nepali Supreme Court, with the notable exception of the issue of untouchability.[45]

The 2006 return to democracy and the promulgation of the Interim Constitution in 2007 opened the way to a fresh bout of constitutional litigation pertaining to Nepal's socio-cultural diversity and the traditional symbols of Nepali nationalism. The basis of this litigation was the principle of equality. These cases have concerned, inter alia, the case regarding the rights of the Kumari (Virgin child goddess),[46] a constitutional challenge to the criminalisation of cow slaughter,[47] a review of the Vice-President's decision to take his oath of office in Hindi and not in Nepali, and a well-known case on the rights of

[42] See *Mira Gurung v Department of Immigration*, NKP, 2051/1993, Vol 35, N 1, p 68; *Mira Dhungana v Ministry of Law and Justice*, NKP, 2052/1995, Vol 37, N 6, p 462; *Dr Canda Bajracharya v Secretariat of Parliament*, NKP, 2053/1996, Vol 38, N 7, p 537; *Adv Sapana Pradhan-Malla for FWLD v Ministry of Law and Justice*, NKP, 2053/1996, Vol 38, N 2, p 105; *Tara Devi Poudel v Cabinet Secretariat*, NKP, 2058/2001, Vol 43, N 7/8, p 375.

[43] See *Dr Cudanath Bhattarai v Public Service Commission*, NKP, 2054/1997, Vol 39, N 7, p 360, *Adv Lal Bahadur Thapa and Others v Kathmandu Metropolitan City and Others*, Writ N 2931 of the year 2056/1999, unpublished Supreme Court decision. See Narendra Prasad Pathak and Narendra Prakash Khanal (eds), 2001/2058 BS *Samvaidhānik Vivādmā Sarvocca Ādālatkā Phaisala* (Supreme Court Judgements on Constitutional Issues), Vol 1 (Kathmandu, Shakuntala Khanal) 523–29.

[44] See *HMG/N v Charles Mendez and Others*, NKP, 2046/1989, Vol 31, N 6, p 648; *HMG/N v Prem Bahadur Karki*, NKP, 2059/2002, Vol 44, N 9/10, p 697.

[45] See *Man Bahadur Vishvakarma v Ministry of Law and Justice*, NKP, 2049/1993, Vol 34, N 12, p 1010.

[46] *Adv Pundevi Maharjan v HMG Nepal*, NKP, 2065/2008, Vol 50, N 6, p 751.

[47] *Om Prakash Aryal v HMG Nepal*, NKP, 2065/2008, Vol 50, N 9, p 1063.

sexual minorities.[48] The kind of constitutional litigation under the Interim Constitution is very reminiscent of that which took place under the previous Constitution, both in terms of modalities and outcomes: the Supreme Court found itself in the position to navigate the difficult line between national unity and socio-cultural diversity, with an eye on politically sensitive issues. As a result, the 'national' custom of the Kumari was not considered violative of the little girls' rights, the legal validity of the ban on cow slaughter was upheld, the Vice-President was ordered to retake his oath in Nepali but allowed to take his oath in his mother tongue (Maithili) first, and sexual minorities were granted legal recognition in a ground-breaking judgment. Post-conflict litigation also took the shape of transitional justice with many victims of the armed conflict seeking legal redress for their injuries (sadly, however, as the joint report *Still Waiting for Justice* by Human Rights Watch and Advocacy Forum illustrates, impunity in Nepal remains the norm).[49]

VI. CONCLUSION

The Drafts prepared by the various CA Committees seek to significantly tone down the Panchayat-style kind of Nepali nationalism and alter the balance between individual and groups rights in favour of the latter, while at the same time limiting the powers of the judiciary in favour of a model of parliamentary sovereignty. In this regard, Yash Ghai has argued that the 1990 Constitution featured 'a fairly comprehensive set of traditional human rights', i.e. individual fundamental rights, and that 'these freedoms have brought little benefits to most groups'. According to Ghai, socio-economic and cultural rights were unenforceable under the 1990 Constitution and that this factor hindered any form of affirmative action for the excluded groups.[50] I agree with this argument to a limited extent: the 1990 Constitution provided the judges with sufficient 'legal leverage' to take more progressive decisions had they implemented the principle of non-discrimination and made use of the full extent of their judicial review powers. Even in the two cases on linguistic rights where the Constitution clearly grants privileged status to the Nepali language under Article 6, the Supreme Court could have used the constitutional definition of the Kingdom as multilingual in Article 4(1) to strike a more equitable balance between linguistic nationalism and the rights of the linguistic minorities. Similarly, in the many cases on gender justice the Court could have adopted a more activist approach and struck down the provisions of the Muluki Ain which are violative of the right to equality but are a legal manifestation of certain social practices and customs. I agree entirely with Ghai's argument on the point of redistributive justice through

[48] *Sunil Babu Pant v HGM Nepal*, NKP, 2065/2008, Vol 50, N 4, p 485.
[49] See www.hrw.org/en/reports/2009/10/15/still-waiting-justice.
[50] UNDP/CASU, *Human Rights, Diversity and Social Justice* (Kathmandu, UNDP, 2008) xi–xii.

socio-economic rights, especially in a country whose Gini coefficient of 0.473 has been calculated as the highest in Asia.[51]

On the issue of special group rights in Nepal, as Loughlin reminds us, 'the rights discourse remains intrinsically a form of political discourse [. . .] Rights are local, historically-rooted claims, not fixed universals'. The judicial interpretation of the constitutional text – as much as the drafting of the Constitution itself – is both a culturally specific legal and a political exercise:

> That the recognition and status accorded to particular rights is a political matter is also highlighted by the fact that today many of the most intractable political issues concern the question of how disputes between conflicting rights claims are to be resolved.[52]

As a result, the respect and preservation of culture have come to play a critical role in discourses about rights, for instance in the Janajati demands. At the same time law is asked to fulfil a modernising function by eradicating cultural practices such as untouchability. Nepal's conflict exposed structural inequalities within Nepali society and promised to redress historical wrongs and exclusionary patterns. I remain unconvinced that the best strategy for Nepal to resolve social imbalances is to turn to a legal categorisation of socio-cultural diversity.

To conclude, the tension between national integration and cultural recognition in Nepal's 1990 Constitution played out in favour of the first element. My argument is that this was the case because the adoption in 1990 of the model of constitutional nationalism reinforced patterns of legal exclusion, not because the Fundamental Rights enshrined in the 1990 Constitution were defective or insufficient. A similar analysis can be applied so far to the constitutional experience under the 2007 Interim document in which we witness a positive opening towards Nepal's socio-cultural diversity. Hopefully, the Constituent Assembly will be able to negotiate a viable post-conflict institutional settlement capable of respecting the aspirations of both groups and individual Nepalis without jeopardising political stability.

[51] CK Lal, 'Polls or Bust Elections Will Address Economic Inequity' *Nepali Times* 362, 17–23, August 2007.

[52] Loughlin, *Sword and Scales* (n 5) 203.

Part IV

Pluralism

9

The Charter of Rights and Freedoms and Canadian Unity

DANIEL WEINSTOCK

I. INTRODUCTION

CONSTITUTIONS ARE NOTORIOUSLY Janus-faced. On the one hand, they are unavoidably possessed of dry, technical aspects that spell out such things as divisions of power, amending formulas, and the like. They provide a blueprint for how a polity is to function, and a blueprint is not the sort of thing that makes the heart of the average citizen swell. As exciting as constitutions may be to constitutional scholars and to legal historians, it is hard to see when they are viewed in this manner how they can serve as anchors for the kind of identification that Jürgen Habermas famously supposed they might when he popularised the phrase 'constitutional patriotism'.[1]

But constitutions possess another, more aspirational dimension. They tell a story about who we, the people, are. By placing certain aspects of our political lives beyond the reach of ordinary politics, they speak to what we take the more permanent aspects of our national identity to be and what values we want to affirm as foundational to our collective life. They do this in a number of different ways. They sometimes contain lofty language, often placed in Preambles, that indicate to the reader that the dry and technical words through which constitutional articles are expressed should not be allowed to hide from view the fact that these articles somehow constitute higher law.[2]

But the Janus-faced nature of constitutions also consists in the fact that the narratives and ideals that constitute a constitution's more aspirational dimension are implicit in the dry and technical language of the constitutional provisions concerning the nuts and bolts of such things as the division of powers and

[1] See J Habermas, 'The European Nation State. Its Achievements and Its Limitations: On the Past and Future of Sovereignty and Citizenship' (1996) 9 *Ratio Juris* 125.

[2] Influential analyses of constitutions as self-binding mechanisms are contained in S Holmes, 'Precommitment and the Paradox of Democracy' in J Elster and R Slagstad (eds), *Constitutionalism and Democracy* (Cambridge, Cambridge University Press, 1988); and J Elster, *Ulysses Unbound* (Cambridge, Cambridge University Press, 2000).

the amending formula. Reflecting upon Canada's amending formula, which requires (for most amendments) the assent of seven provinces containing at least 50 per cent of the total population of the country, reveals a whole theory of what the country is.[3]

Constitutionalised bills of rights also present us with this dual nature, but they do so in a way that is, as it were, the mirror image of other parts of constitutions. Whereas one has to look beyond the technical language of such things as amending formulas in order to detect the ideals and national narratives that are implicit within them, the ideals implicit in bills of rights jump off the page. In liberal democracies (and even in some countries that could not plausibly be taken to function as liberal democracies) they contain commitments to inspirational ideals such as individual freedom, equality and the democratic rights of all citizens. The Janus-faced nature of charters of rights arises from the fact that these lofty ideals have to be operationalised by courts through adjudicative formulas. What does equality (to take but one example) mean, exactly, and how can that meaning be brought to bear on particular cases? Equality is a hotly contested concept (as are all of the other notions standardly contained in a bill of rights – forests have been felled in the attempt to articulate with precision a workable and plausible conception of freedom of expression![4]) and the job of the courts that are charged with enforcing the constitution is to disambiguate the concepts and to incorporate the resulting understandings into some kind of test or formula that can be used over time in a predictable and non-arbitrary manner. Needless to say, that specification will be contestable, and it will doubtless be contested by members of the polity who read the concepts in question in a manner different from the one adopted by the court.

The Janus-faced nature of constitutions, and of bills of rights in particular, poses a challenge for those who would purport to use constitutions to foster national unity in divided societies.[5] One risk is that the unifying, inspirational language contained most notably in bills of rights is undercut by the particular ways in which the ideals that make up this language are operationalised over time by the constitutional court charged with the interpretation of the constitution and its application to particular cases. The devil is in the details, as the saying goes, and the details of rights-based jurisprudence might very well end up alienating segments of the population that otherwise identify with the lofty, abstract, but ultimately indeterminate terms in which the bill of rights is framed.

[3] See, eg, PC Oliver, *The Constitution of Independence* (Oxford, Oxford University Press, 2005) especially 316–23; and S Tierney, *Constitutional Law and National Pluralism* (Oxford, Oxford University Press, 2004) especially ch 5.

[4] Notable contributors to the debate over freedom of expression include F Schauer, *Free Speech: A Philosophical Enquiry* (Cambridge, Cambridge University Press, 1982); and more recently, L Alexander, *Is there a Right of Freedom of Expression?* (Cambridge, Cambridge University Press, 2005).

[5] *cf* S Choudhry, 'Bills of Rights as Instruments of Nation Building in Multinational States: The Canadian *Charter* and Quebec Nationalism' in JB Kelly and CP Manfredi (eds), *Contested Constitutionalism: Reflections on the Canadian Charter of Rights and Freedoms* (Vancouver, UBC Press, 2009) 233–50.

So potentially unity-eroding conflicts can arise between the language of the bill of rights and the way in which it is ultimately implemented.

Conflicts can also arise among the ideals embedded in the constitution, whether explicitly or implicitly. Again, the ideals latent in the abstract language of the bill of rights may very well inspire identification across national fault lines. But these fault lines can be exacerbated if, for example, a national narrative is either explicitly or implicitly incorporated in the constitution. So conflicts can arise *between* the ideals and narratives that a constitution is composed of.

Moreover, these two problems can interact: indeed the national narrative that is dominant in a constitution can have an impact on the specific manner in which the abstract terms contained in bills of rights are applied by courts to specific cases.

So, for at least these two reasons, constitutions and bills of rights can fail to contribute to national unity. What is more, they can positively detract from national unity by holding up the promise of principle-based unification in the abstract language of rights charters, only to betray that promise in the eyes of some in the nuts and bolts of constitutional adjudication.

In this chapter I want to analyse the manner in which these dynamics have played out in the Canadian case. I want to suggest that although the principal line of division threatening Canadian unity seems at the time of writing to be as dormant as it has been in recent memory, the potential is there for the application of the Canadian Charter of Rights and Freedoms to give rise to a major unity crisis. I will proceed as follows. First, I will show that, although the Charter refers to values with which Quebeckers identify just as much (if not more) as other Canadians, these values are embedded within the Canadian Charter alongside a national narrative that is profoundly foreign to the self-understanding of Quebeckers. I will then show that the dominance of the rival, English-Canadian national narrative in the Charter has had practical effects on the manner in which the Supreme Court of Canada has interpreted section 1 of the Charter, a constitutional provision that on the face of it might have been thought to provide Quebec with latitude with which to enact legislation essential to Quebec's distinct status within Canada even in cases when this legislation impinges upon constitutionally protected rights. These effects have served to further distance Quebec from the 1982 constitutional pact. I will also suggest that the other provision of the Charter that might have been thought to facilitate the protection of Quebec's distinct culture even in the absence of the recognition of the nationalist narrative, the 'notwithstanding' or override provision contained in section 33, also fails to make up for the Charter's adverse effects on Quebec's place in Canada. After offering a brief reminder of the failed attempt at amending the Charter so as to accommodate the nationalist narrative, I will end by providing reasons to believe that while the failure to find a way to integrate Quebec to the Canadian constitutional order has not threatened national unity in the past 20 years or so, present political dynamics may very well bring matters to a head in the very near future. These dynamics have to do with the increasing rift that exists between Quebec and the rest of Canada as to the proper way to handle cultural and religious diversity.

II. COMPETING NATIONAL NARRATIVES

Two national narratives coexist within the Canadian political imaginary.[6] According to one – which I will hereafter refer to as the nationalist narrative – Canada results from the historical compact between two founding peoples: a French-speaking nation (a majority of whose members descend from the colonists who made up New France between the sixteenth and seventeenth centuries) who have over time been joined by waves of immigrants and by a substantial anglophone minority, and an English-speaking nation resulting from the conquest of New France by the British and by the cession of New France in 1763. On this view, Confederation was premised on the idea of the equality of the two founding peoples, and on a commitment by the more powerful and more numerous English-speaking nation to allow French-Canadians substantial self-determination within Confederation with which to protect and develop their distinct culture.

According to the nationalist narrative, the province of Quebec therefore has a distinct status within Canada as the home of a distinctive nation. Though French-speaking Canadians are spread out throughout Canada, it is only in Quebec that they constitute a majority, and it is thus only through the democratic political institutions of Quebec that it can exercise meaningful self-determination. Though the English-Canadian nation is spread out over nine provinces, the ideal of provincial equality makes no sense from the point of view of the nationalist narrative because it would end up denying the constitutive relationship upon which Canada was founded, namely the relationship between two equal founding people.[7]

According to a second narrative, which I will refer to as the linguistic narrative, Canada is a single nation, whose constitutive cultural duality is, firstly, linguistic, and secondly, not territorially concentrated. English and French coexist from coast to coast, and the constitutive commitment growing out of Canada's founding compact is not to the preservation of a territorially based minority nation, but rather toward English and French language groups, and in particular to English and French linguistic minorities, wherever they happen to find themselves on the Canadian territory. According to the linguistic narrative, there is no reason to detract from the federalist default of provincial equality.[8]

[6] *cf* W Kymlicka, *Finding our Way: Rethinking Ethnocultural Relations in Canada* (Oxford, Oxford University Press, 1998) especially ch 10. I have written at greater length about the importance of the moral psychology of federal constitutionalism and about the 'myths' that underpin it in 'The Moral Psychology of Federalism' in J Gaudreault-Desbiens and F Gélinas (eds), *The States and Moods of Federalism* (Montreal, Éditions Yvon Blais, 2005).

[7] A good contemporary formulation of this vision of Canada is contained in G Laforest, *Trudeau and the End of a Canadian Dream* (Montreal and Kingston, McGill-Queens Press, 1995).

[8] The *locus classicus* of this vision is found in the early writings of Pierre-Elliott Trudeau, *Le fédéralisme et la sociétécanadienne –française* (Montreal, Les Éditions HMH, 1967).

The 1982 Constitution, and in particular its Charter of Rights and Freedoms, largely incorporates the linguistic narrative. Quebec's distinct status within the federation, so central to the nationalist narrative, is nowhere present in the final constitutional document. The Constitution does not endow Quebec with the kind of constitutional veto power that one would expect were the constitutionally operative understanding of the country to be one in which two nations were seeking to achieve meaningful national self-determination within the context of a federal entity. What is more, the Charter of Rights and Freedoms devotes a great deal of attention and detail, in its sections 16 to 23, to the rights of English and French linguistic minorities throughout the country to be served and educated by public institutions in their language. The Charter thus evinces a commitment to minority language groups rather than to the Quebec minority nation that the exponents of the nationalist narrative would have emphasised.

Which of these two narratives is correct? Many commentators in Quebec have held that the linguistic narrative represents a rewriting of history, a betrayal of an original agreement perpetrated by an almost pathological anti-nationalist political leader, Pierre-Elliott Trudeau. But questions of historical accuracy are beside the point when it comes to the kinds of national narratives that are contained, either explicitly or implicitly, in constitutional texts. What matters is whether or not the people who fall under the Constitution's jurisdiction recognise themselves within this narrative or not. Constitutionally embedded national narratives are as much about who 'we the people' aspire to be as it is about who we are or who we were. Obviously, the historical and aspirational, future-directed aspects of identity are not empirically completely divorced from one another. People will not consent to an aspirational narrative if they perceive it as requiring that they turn their back on a historical narrative to which they ascribe positive valence.

Quebeckers are as drawn as other Canadians to the values of the Charter (at least in their abstract formulations), but they have rejected the national narrative that is contained within it. The sovereigntist *Parti Québécois* that was in power at the time of patriation refused to sign it, but significantly, the unacceptability of the Charter in its present form is at the centre of an all-party consensus. What has distinguished political parties in Quebec since 1982 has not had to do with whether the Constitution is acceptable or not, but with what political conclusions to draw from its unacceptability.

III. SECTION 1 AND THE 'NOTWITHSTANDING' CLAUSE

The 1982 Charter does contain some provisions that allow provincial legislatures to assert their legislative will even when legislation is found to impinge upon constitutionally protected rights. In principle, therefore, it might have been possible for the legislature of Quebec to exercise meaningful self-determination to the satisfaction of both politicians and the electorate within the post-1982 Canadian constitutional order even in the absence of an explicit constitutional incorporation of the nationalist narrative that is largely dominant in Quebec.

Section 1 of the Charter asserts that the rights enumerated in the Charter are not without limit, but rather that they are 'subject only to such reasonable limits prescribed by law as can be demonstrably justified in a free and democratic society'. Moreover, section 33 of the Charter allows legislatures to enact legislation even when the legislature believes that it would be in violation of a constitutionally protected right as understood by the Supreme Court and even in the face of an adverse Supreme Court judgment.

The two provisions function quite differently. In *R v Oakes*, the Supreme Court devised a test in the years immediately following the adoption of the 1982 Constitution which expressed the vague language of section 1 into a test.[9] According to what has come to be known as the '*Oakes* Test', legislation that is found to infringe upon a constitutionally protected right can nonetheless be 'saved' if it can be shown to meet a multi-pronged justificatory burden. First, it must be shown to serve 'an objective related to concerns which are pressing and substantial in a free and democratic society'.[10] Legislation impinging upon rights cannot be upheld if it is judged to be trivial, or if it is in clear opposition to the values of a free and democratic society.

Second, it must satisfy a series of proportionality requirements. The measure that infringes upon a constitutionally protected right must be shown to be rationally connected to the legislative purpose. Moreover, it must involve the most parsimonious limitation of a right that is compatible with the attainment of this purpose. Finally, the harms occasioned by the rights limitation must not be out of proportion with the goods realised by the legislative measure in question. According to the judges that formulated the test, the standard of proof that is implied in the various tests is the civil test of 'preponderance of evidence', rather than the more exacting criminal standard requiring that proof be 'beyond a reasonable doubt'.[11] This latter standard is deemed in the context of section 1 analysis to be incompatible with concepts such as 'reasonableness', 'justifiability' and 'free and democratic' society, presumably because it would set up an onus that legislators could never meet, given the uncertainties that are inevitable in the area of public policy. The Justices however recognise that the civil standard is inherently vague, and that the specific manner in which it is understood should be 'dependent upon the subject-matter'.[12]

Three features of this multi-pronged test are important to note for present purposes. The first, quite obviously, is that it is the Court rather than legislatures that are to determine whether legislation can be saved or not according to an analysis based on section 1. Observers and participants who feared at the

[9] [1986] 1 SCR 103.
[10] ibid para 69.
[11] ibid para 67.
[12] ibid.

time of patriation that the Charter and the corresponding practice of judicial review would detract from the distinctively democratic nature of the Canadian political process would hardly be placated by a constitutional provision that gives unelected judges the ultimate say in the determination of whether or not democratically enacted legislation can be justified. Those who feared that the Charter would detract from *federalism* by taking away from the decision-making powers of provincial politicians and vesting these powers in the hands of judges appointed by the federal government would also find much cause for dissatisfaction in a constitutional clause of this kind.

The second point to be highlighted is that although the *Oakes* Test goes some way toward disambiguating the terms contained in section 1, it does not completely do away with the need for interpretation of inherently controversial terms. It requires that the judges work on the basis of a substantive theory about the requirements of a 'free and democratic society'. It also requires that they fill in the detail of the view about the appropriateness of standards of proof to different circumstances that had only been sketched in *Oakes*. Both of these tasks are inherently evaluative. Neither one can be entirely disposed of simply by adverting to black-letter law, though, quite obviously, their interpretations are to a significant degree constrained by the law. The irreducibly evaluative dimension of legal interpretation corresponds to an area over which reasonable people might disagree. I return to this point below.[13]

The fact that section 1 tilts decision-making power in favour of the Court explains why provincial premiers insisted on adding another disposition to the Charter in order to chart another path for legislatures seeking to enact legislation that might limit rights. Section 33 contains what has come to be known as the 'notwithstanding clause' that allows legislatures to enact legislation 'notwithstanding' the fact that it might fail to conform to the fundamental freedoms and rights guaranteed by the Charter.

In opposition to section 1, the procedure laid out in section 33 vests the power to enact legislation that limits rights in the hands of legislators. What's more, the standard that has to be met for such legislation to be justified is procedural rather than substantive. Though legislators may very well be possessed of a substantive theory lying at the basis of the legislation that they propose, section 33 merely requires of legislatures that the appeal to the 'notwithstanding' clause pass a legislative vote for every five-year period that the legislation is in force. The hurdle that thus has to be cleared by every use of section 33 is that legislators be convinced of its justification. Beyond that, legislators who make use of section 33 must take into account the will of the electorate who may choose to

[13] I have written more extensively about the *Oakes* Test in my 'Philosophical Reflections on the Oakes Test' in LB Tremblay and G Webber (eds), *The Limitation of Charter Rights: Critical Essays on R. v. Oakes* (Montreal, Éditions Thémis, 2009). For other analyses of the Court's interpretation of s 1, see J Hiebert, *Limiting Rights: The Dilemma of Judicial Review* (Montreal and Kingston, McGill-Queens Press, 1996); and S Choudhry, 'So What is the Real Legacy of Oakes? Two Decades of Proportionality Analysis Under the Canadian Charter's Section 1' (2006) 34 *Supreme Court Law Review* 501.

reward or to punish politicians for the uses that they make of the power that is granted them through the notwithstanding clause.

IV. RECONCILING QUEBEC THROUGH SECTIONS 1 AND 33?

Having briefly laid out the mechanisms through which legislatures are able to offset the loss of decision-making power that the Charter and the accompanying practice of judicial review arguably involve,[14] I want in this section to reflect on the following question: To the extent that the disaffection of Quebeckers and their provincial representatives towards the 1982 Constitution stems from the impact that the absence of the nationalist narrative might have on the range of decisions over which Quebec's National Assembly is sovereign, might the use of sections 1 and 33 have served as a functional equivalent to the incorporation of that narrative in the Constitution?

A first point to make in reflecting upon that question is that its antecedent is dubious. In other words, though it is clear that the national narrative that is incorporated in a constitutional document has an impact on the manner in which courts will interpret even the most narrowly technical clauses of the Constitution in particular cases (a point to which I will return in what follows), it is also a mistake to assume that the only thing about such narratives that matters to citizens is their functional correlates and implications. Symbolic recognition matters to people, and in some circumstances it matters quite justifiably. It would fall well beyond the confines of this chapter to rehearse the philosophical literature that has emerged in recent years around the concept of recognition.[15] Though I have expressed scepticism elsewhere about the ambitious claims that have been made in recent years on behalf of the concept of recognition as a necessary ingredient of all healthy social and political relations,[16] I do think that recognition is important in order to address the distrust that lingers in relationships that have previously been marked by inequality and oppression. Recognition might very well be a necessary ingredient in the transition from relationships premised on inequality to ones grounded in equality and mutual respect.

If this is the case, it could be that the absence of a national narrative that is clearly important to the people of Quebec constitutes a reason for them to with-

[14] James Kelly argues that the impact of the Charter and of judicial review on provincial autonomy has been exaggerated by those who have criticised the Charter on federalist grounds. By his reckoning, the Court had only nullified provincial legislation in 25 cases between 1984 and 2003, and 17 of these 25 cases gave rise to 'legislative sequels' on the part of provincial legislatures. See JB Kelly, *Governing the Charter: Legislative and Judicial Activism and Framers' Intent* (Vancouver, University of British Columbia Press, 2005) especially ch 6.

[15] See especially C Taylor, *Multiculturalism and the Politics of Recognition* (Princeton, Princeton University Press, 1992); and A Honneth, *The Struggle for Recognition: The Moral Grammar of Social Conflicts* (Cambridge, Polity Press, 1995).

[16] D Weinstock, 'Trois concepts de reconnaissance' in J Payet and A Battegay (eds), *La reconnaissance à l'épreuve* (*Villeneuve-d'Ascq*, Presses Universitaires de Septentrion, 2008).

hold their assent from the Constitution, even absent any identifiable impact of this lacuna on the scope of the decision-making power of Quebec's National Assembly.

But (and I come here to a second way of looking at the question with which I began this section) it is far from clear that the absence of the nationalist narrative from the Constitution and the Charter has not had an impact on the degree to which Quebeckers have been able to make use of their National Assembly in order to achieve meaningful self-determination.

Let us begin by looking at the manner in which the Supreme Court of Canada has dealt with Quebec's language Charter, Bill 101. The legislation is arguably most central to the National Assembly's ability to use its powers to protect Quebec's language and culture from the encroachment of the continentally much more powerful anglophone language and culture. In *Quebec Assn. of Protestant School Boards v Quebec (Attorney General)*, the Supreme Court struck down provisions of the language Charter on the grounds that they offended against the educational rights of linguistic minorities guaranteed by section 23 of the Charter. The Court refused to engage in a section 1 analysis because it considered the violation of section 23 to be 'so blatant' as to preclude the impugned provisions from being considered a 'reasonable limit' on rights in the context of a 'free and democratic' society.[17] This decision clearly is a direct consequence of the dominance of the linguistic narrative in the Charter: Canada's cultural duality is understood in terms of the protection of linguistic minorities rather than in the recognition of the prerogatives of the representatives of a minority nation within the federation.

In *Ford v Quebec*, moreover, the Supreme Court struck down articles of the language charter that had to do with the language of commercial signs.[18] In order to maintain the francophone nature of Quebec's 'linguistic face' (*visage linguistique*), the language charter prohibited all languages but French from commercial signs. This provision of the law was successfully challenged through the Quebec court system by shopkeepers in predominantly anglophone neighbourhoods. The Attorney General of Quebec appealed the matter to the Supreme Court, which rejected the appeal. The Court's reasoning followed the steps laid down in the *Oakes* Test. Having determined that the provisions of the language law concerning signage violated citizens' rights to freedom of expression, protected under section 2b of the Charter, the Court proceeded to a section 1 analysis. The Court recognised the importance of the legislative purpose of the language law, and also noted that the limitation on rights involved in the prohibition on all languages but French in public commercial signage was rationally connected to the purpose of securing the French language from encroachment by English.

[17] *A.G. (Que.) v Quebec Protestant School Boards* [1984] 2 SCR 66.
[18] [1988] 2 SCR 712.

But the legislation was struck down because in the view of the Justices the government of Quebec had not demonstrated that the legislative end of protecting the French language could not be achieved by less intrusive means, such as the requirement that French be present on all commercial signs, or that it be predominant on such signs:

> [W]hereas requiring the predominant display of the French language, even its marked predominance, would be proportional to the goal of promoting and maintaining a French '*visage linguistique*' in Quebec and thus justified under the Quebec *Charter* and the Canadian *Charter*, requiring the exclusive use of French has not be so justified.[19]

This decision reflects the absence of the nationalist narrative in a more subtle way than had been the case in *Quebec Assn of Protestant School Boards*. Key to the decision of the Court in *Ford* is its determination that Quebec had not met its justificatory burden under the second prong of the proportionality test incorporated in the *Oakes* Test. The Court held that it had not shown that the same legislative intent could not have been realised through a lesser infringement of expressive rights guaranteed under section 2 of the Charter. In so doing, it imposed a much stricter burden of proof on Quebec's National Assembly than it would impose on other cases where freedom of expression would be at stake. For example, the Supreme Court in *R v Butler* upheld the criminal prohibition of certain forms of violent and dehumanising pornography in the absence of any empirical evidence to the effect that such pornography causes harm.[20] In this context, it held the legislature that had enacted the relevant statute to the much lower standard of a 'reasoned apprehension of harm'. The Court traces the use of this standard back to another case involving freedom of commercial expression. In *Irwin Toy*, the Court held that a section analysis of legislation restricting advertising directed at children could be justified even in the absence of strong empirical evidence proving the harmful consequences of such advertising. It also ascribed the kind of expression that is involved in pornography to a lower standard of constitutional protection: 'In my view, the kind of expression which is sought to be advanced does not stand on an equal footing with other kinds of expression which directly engage the 'core' of the freedom of expression values'.[21]

Taken together, these three decisions – all of which involved legislation restricting free expression – raise two questions: First, why does the court invoke a more stringent standard of proof in the case of Quebec's language law than it does in the cases of laws restricting pornography and advertising aimed at children? Second, and related, why does the court ascribe the kind of importance to commercial speech in *Ford* that it seems to deny it in *Irwin Toy*? Commercial speech seems to be treated more like pornography where it is aimed at children,

[19] *Ford v Quebec (Attorney General)* [1988] 2 SCR 712, 773.
[20] [1992] 1 SCR 452.
[21] *Irwin Toy Ltd v Quebec (Attorney General)* [1989] 1 SCR 927.

and seems to lie more at the core of the right in *Ford,* where commercial signage is at stake.

The decision to impose a more stringent burden of proof on Quebec in its restriction of commercial signs, and the decision to accord great importance to the expressive interests involved in being able to put up commercial signs in the language of one's choice (provided that French is clearly predominant) are both reasonable, but they are also reasonably debatable. As mentioned above, the substantive theory that the Court has to deploy in order to generate determinate results on the basis of section 1 analysis are not dictated by black-letter law. The nature of the exercise that is required of them by section 1 analysis unavoidably involves the judges in substantive theories (about the nature of liberal democracy, about the kind of polity that Canada is) that are only partially constrained by positive law. They must, in other words, engage in the kind of interpretive exercise that according to Ronald Dworkin is part and parcel of judicial reasoning.[22]

Now, had the Charter included language that incorporated something of the nationalist narrative within it, then that might have introduced more of a constraint for the Court to defer to the National Assembly in its determination of what level of limitation of the right of freedom of expression is required in order to secure the objective of protecting the French language. After all, while it reasonable to think that the mere presence of French on all commercial signs will suffice to secure the legislative end in question, it is also reasonable to think that the *exclusive* presence of French is required, or at the very least that it is required in order to protect it more securely or with a higher degree of probability than would be the case under a linguistic regime in which other languages are permitted on commercial signage. Indeed, it is difficult to know what would count as incontrovertible or even plausible empirical proof here. As in many other cases of public policy, in evaluating the impact of different linguistic regimes on the long-term goal of protecting a vulnerable language, the reasonable apprehensions of policy-makers acting in good faith might in fact be all we have to go on.

Moreover, the Court might also have been constrained to weigh the expressive value of *commercial* signage differently relative to the value of preserving the French language had the Constitution included language according to which Quebec is to be thought of as a distinct nation whose legitimate claims to self-determination need to be accommodated within the context of a federal constitution.

In short, the presence or absence of a national narrative in the Constitution makes a difference to the way in which the Supreme Court is likely to apply the various tests that it has devised in order to give legal expression to the vague terms included in the Charter's various articles. Other decisions that it has taken in matters related to freedom of expression suggest that the conceptions of freedom of expression and the ways of understanding the burden of proof that

[22] See generally R Dworkin, *Law's Empire* (London, Fontana Press, 1986).

must be met by legislatures in section 1 analyses suggest that could have 'saved' more of Quebec's language laws than it did in *Ford* and in *Quebec Assn. of Protestant School Boards.* The presence of the nationalist narrative in the Constitution would have at the very least provided legal constraints inclining the Court in that direction.

Given the foregoing, absent language giving the nationalist narrative weight within the constitution, section 1 cannot serve as a functional equivalent to the incorporation of a nationalist narrative.

What then of section 33? On the face of it, it would seem better suited than section 1 to such use, since it places the decision-making authority squarely in the hands of legislators, subject only to the sanction of voters and, more generally, of public opinion.

The Quebec government of Robert Bourassa made use of the notwithstanding clause in order to shelter Quebec's language law from the effects of the Supreme Court judgment in *Ford*.[23] This touched off a firestorm both inside Quebec and in the rest of Canada that contributed to the failure of what has come to be known as the 'Meech Lake Accord'. The Accord was an attempt by the federal government to bring Quebec into the constitutional fold, most notably through the incorporation within the constitutional document of an interpretive clause that would have recognised Quebec as a 'distinct society' within Canada. English Canadians viewed the recourse to the notwithstanding clause as something of a betrayal, proof that Quebeckers could not be trusted.

Historical ironies abound here. The incorporation of the kind of interpretive clause contained in the Meech Lake Accord would presumably have had a decisive impact on the Court's degree of deference to Quebec's National Assembly on linguistic matters. Had the clause been in place at the time of the legal challenges to Quebec's language law, it might very well (as will be argued below) have led the Court to 'save' the legislation in spite of its prima facie incompatibility with the right to freedom of expression. This raises the question: Why was English Canada prepared to grant Quebec a constitutional amendment that would have allowed it to enforce the entirety of its language law, but unwilling to countenance the province's use of the notwithstanding clause to achieve precisely the same end? And why be so opposed to the use of a perfectly valid constitutional clause, one that was insisted upon by anglophone Premiers from the West as a condition of their signing up to the 1982 constitutional pact?

There are several plausible answers to the second of these questions. First, the negotiations over the Meech Lake Accord were tense and often acrimonious, and probably did much to deplete the fund of trust upon which relations between Quebec and the rest of Canada rested. The Accord, which I will devote the next section to considering, represented the maximal constitutional conces-

[23] This episode is recounted by Bourassa himself in his *Gouverner le Québec* (Montreal, Éditions Fides, 1995) 181–87.

sion that English Canadians felt they could make in order to recognise Quebec's specificity, but it was seen by many in Quebec as the absolute minimum that Quebeckers could accept in order to join the new Canadian constitutional order. The attempt to articulate this very tenuous area of overlap led to a situation in which any display of apparent unreasonableness on the part of Quebeckers would be magnified many times over in the perceptions of English Canadians.

A second explanation has to do with the emergence in English Canada of what has come to be known as 'Charter Patriotism'. According to some analyses, the attempt by Pierre Elliott Trudeau to replace the – in his view necessarily divisive – historical roots of Canadian identity by a more forward-looking and inclusive identity based on the principles of the Charter has to a large degree succeeded in English Canada. Whatever vestigial trace there may have been before the patriation of the Constitution and the promulgation of the Charter of an Anglo-Celtic ethnic element to the identity of English Canadians was quickly swept away by an idea of Canada as bringing diverse people together under the protection afforded by the Charter. Now, this may have had more to do with demographic facts on the ground as with the putatively greater amenability of English Canada to a kind of constitutional patriotism – lower birth rates in English Canada and the correspondingly greater proportional impact that immigration has had most notably in Canada's most populous English-speaking provinces, Ontario and British Columbia, have meant that there simply no longer is an Anglo-Celtic majority in English Canada to which the idea of an historically oriented, ethnic identity could have even prima facie appeal. Be that as it may, the identity vacuum left behind by English Canada's rapidly changing demographic profile was easily filled by the inspirational language of the Charter.[24]

If this is the case, then attitudes toward section 33 may have changed dramatically in English Canada between the 1970s when the Constitution was being debated, and the early 1990s, when the Quebec government invoked it in the context of the language law. Whereas English Canadians might have originally been amenable to the positive interpretation given to it by provincial politicians such as Allan Blakeney and Stirling Lyon, basically as a bulwark against the potentially undemocratic centralism that the Charter and an unfettered practice of judicial review would have represented, they were by the early 1990s more inclined to see it as an attack upon Charter values themselves.[25]

The evolution of the Charter as an anchor for English-Canadian identity was probably impossible to predict when negotiations over the patriation of the

[24] *cf* P Russell, 'The *Charter* and Canadian Democracy' in JB Kelly and Christopher P Manfredi (eds), *Contested Constitutionalism* (Vancouver, University of British Columbia Press, 2009) especially 300–02.

[25] For a more detailed attempt at understanding the strange fate that s 33 has had in Canadian public opinion, see J Hiebert, 'Compromise and the Notwithstanding Clause: Why the Dominant Narrative Distorts our Understanding' in JB Kelly and Christopher P Manfredi (eds), *Contested Constitutionalism* (Vancouver, University of British Columbia Press, 2009) 107–25.

Constitution began. Thus, it was impossible to predict just how much of a constraint on the use of the 'notwithstanding' clause public opinion and the threat of electoral sanction would be. But as Andrew Petter puts it, 'the political pressures against overriding the Charter makes it extraordinarily difficult for governments to make use of section 33. Thus, governments will be loath to invoke section 33 to protect all but the most vital aspects of their legislative program'.[26]

So, though section 33 would seem on the face of it better suited than section 1 as an *ersatz* for constitutional recognition of the nationalist narrative in virtue of the fact that it ultimately makes the Quebec National Assembly the ultimate judge of whether legislation that limits rights does so in a manner that can be justified as reasonable in a free and democratic society, the fact is that it is no longer considered by Canadians to be part of normal politics. Its use by Quebec in order to protect its language law had enormous costs in terms of finding constitutional common ground with the rest of Canada, even though this putative common ground would have included an interpretive clause that would have 'saved' that very same language law on the basis of section 1 analysis. This irony can only be saved from outright contradiction if we suppose that Canadians actually see a substantive difference between the justification of rights limitations resulting from section 1 analysis carried out by judges, and the same limitations resulting from political decisions on the part of elected politicians. Even though sections 1 and 33 are both integral parts of the Charter, Canadians may have reached a point where they view the former process as still somehow 'internal' to the logic of the Charter, and the latter as foreign to it. Simply put, Canadians seem to trust judges more than they do politicians with the task of limiting their rights in order to achieve legislative purposes.

Whatever the explanation and rationale for the strange fate that section 33 has undergone in Canadian public opinion, it simply can no longer be viewed (if it ever could) as a tool whereby Quebec's National Assembly could assert its right to determine for itself what the proper balance between individual rights and collective legislative goals was to be. The potential political costs are simply too high.

V. THE MEECH LAKE ACCORD

The Meech Lake Accord resulted from the attempt by Canadian Prime Minister Brian Mulroney, whose Progressive Conservative Party was elected to power after the Trudeau era ended in 1984, to bring Quebec back into the constitutional fold. It was an ingenious attempt to satisfy Quebec's constitutional demands without violating the principle of provincial equality that was so important to Canadians in other provinces. It achieved this squaring of the

[26] A Petter, *The Politics of the Charter: The Illusive Promise of Constitutional Rights* (Toronto, University of Toronto Press, 2010) 60.

circle for example by granting *all* provinces a range of powers that Quebec would have made disproportionate use of, such as increased power of immigrant selection and integration, and an expansion of the program whereby provinces receive compensation from the federal government when they opt out of federal programs that fall under provincial jurisdiction.

Key to the accord was a new section that would have been added to an amended Charter immediately following section 1. It would therefore have been placed within the Charter in such a way as to signal that its role within the Charter was analogous to that of section 1, in that it would have also provided the Supreme Court with grounds to limit rights by reference to a fundamental characteristic of Canadian society. The new section would have recognised Quebec as a 'distinct society' within Canada, and it would have affirmed 'the role of the legislature and Government of Quebec to preserve and promote the distinct identity of Quebec'.[27] In order not to violate the principle of the equality of the provinces or to displace the linguistic narrative that holds pride of place within English Canada, the same section includes a reference to the presence of English and French linguistic minorities throughout the territory of Canada as a fundamental feature of the country, and to the role of the all levels of government in preserving that feature. Thus, the Meech Lake Accord did not so much replace the Trudeau vision of Canadian binationalism with the Quebec nationalist vision so much as it juxtaposed them.

It is perhaps idle to speculate on how the Court would have rendered the language of the interpretive clause operational. But a number of points seem at least at least plausible on the basis of the manner in which it operationalised section 1.

First, as was the case with section 1, the interpretive clause on Quebec's status within the federation contained some important but vague concepts that required disambiguation by the Court. Chief among these is the idea of Quebec as a 'distinct society', along with the accompanying idea of a distinct Quebec identity. But the idea of the Quebec government's responsibility to 'protect and promote' Quebec's distinctiveness is equally open to interpretation, and opens some of the evidentiary issues that had already been raised by section 1. By what standard is the Court to determine whether an item of legislation, and the limitation of individual rights that it involves, is necessary to the protection and/or the promotion of Quebec's distinct society and identity? The interpretive task is made even more daunting by the fact that the 'distinct society' clause of the proposed constitutional amendment coexists with a clause according to which the federal and provincial governments also have the responsibility to protect Canada's linguistic minorities, including, presumably, the anglophone minority of Quebec.

[27] The Meech Lake Accord, www.solon.org/Constitutions/Canada/English/Proposals/Meech Lake.html.

As in the case of section 1, the Court would require a case in which the proposed new section 2 was invoked in order to elaborate a test, analogous to the *Oakes Test*, making the abstract language of the amendment useful in judicial decision-making. As in the case of the *Oakes Test*, therefore, it would have had to elaborate, over time, a working substantive theory of what Quebec's constitutionally relevant 'distinctiveness' resides in. One of the principal issues that the Court would have had to determine would have been just how narrowly culturalist a reading to give to the idea of Quebec as a distinct society. Would it have restricted the applicability of the 'distinct society' clause solely to issues of language and culture narrowly understood, or would it have countenanced the possibility that the kind of cultural justification for the limitation of rights envisaged by the proposed section 2 might have encompassed broader issues of value?

There are intimations of the manner in which the Court would have handled the challenge of coming up with a test to reflect the abstract language of the 'distinct society' clause proposed by the Meech Lake Accord in decisions taken by the Court subsequent to the rejection of the Accord in 1990. I will mention two. First, in *Reference re Secession of Quebec*, the Court affirms that 'the principle of federalism facilitates the pursuit of collective goals by cultural and linguistic minorities which form the majority within a particular province' and recognises the special historical role played by the concern that French Canadians be able to constitute a majority in a province in order to pursue collective goals.[28] It does however in the very next section remind readers of just how important federalism was to Nova Scotia and New Brunswick in joining Confederation, given 'their will *to protect their individual cultures* and their autonomy over local matters'.[29] The inclusion in this context of Nova Scotia, a province with an overwhelmingly Anglophone majority, strongly suggests that, in the Court's view, the kinds of matters that the federalist principle applies to have to do with culture broadly understood, including presumably a province's ethical culture, which might sometimes place it at odds with other provinces.

In a bitterly divided reference on Canada's *Assisted Human Reproduction Act*, moreover, four Justices rendered a judgment that would have invalidated the Act on the basis of an argument according to which the proper delineation between health law and criminal law ought to be determined by deference to the principle of federalism.[30] In their view, there is no fact of the matter as to whether technologies and practices of assisted procreation ought to be governed by the criminal law, a federal jurisdiction, or by health policy, a provincial sphere. In their view, the Attorney General of Canada's contention that new reproductive technologies ought to be included under the purview of the criminal law does violence not to some independent construal that we might have about the kinds of actions that the use of these technologies involves. Rather, a

[28] *Reference re Secession of Quebec* [1998] 2 SCR 217, 59.

[29] *Reference re Secession of Quebec* [1998] 2 SCR, 59–60 (emphasis added).

[30] *Reference re Assisted Human Reproduction Act*, 2010 SCC 61, [2010] 3 SCR 457.

view of the criminal law that in the Canadian context encompasses them 'is incompatible with the federal nature of Canada; it not only upsets the constitutional balance of powers in the field of health, but also undermines the very definition of federalism'.[31]

There is thus evidence to suggest that the Court would not have been averse to employing the proposed section 2 of the Charter as a manner of enhancing and expanding the power of provinces to legislate freely, especially in matters that are deemed to be central to these provinces' distinctive cultures. But in the absence of an explicit constitutional provision, there is certainly no guarantee that the logic that I have gingerly suggested might be present in some Supreme Court decisions would be pursued or that it would play out in a manner that corresponds with the sense that Quebeckers have of the kind of legislation that is necessary for the preservation and promotion of their distinctive culture.

VI. THE DEBATE OVER RELIGIOUS ACCOMMODATION AND THE FUTURE OF THE CANADIAN CONSTITUTIONAL ORDER

In 2006, the Supreme Court of Canada handed down a decision in the case of *Multani v Commission Scolaire Marguerite Bourgeoys*.[32] The case involved a young Sikh boy who was sent home from a Montreal school because he was wearing a *kirpan*, a religious object that resembles a dagger. The school board and the parents agreed to an accommodation that would see the boy wear his *kirpan* under his garments in a sheath that made the object difficult to access. But the governing body of the school rejected the accommodation, claiming that school rules prohibited weapons of any kind being introduced into school grounds.

The Supreme Court of Canada, having decided that the case fell under the purview of the Charter of Rights and Freedoms, determined that the decision of the school commissioners did not survive section 1 analysis. The restriction on the right of the Sikh boy was justified by reference to the importance of ensuring the security of all children in the school. The Supreme Court Justices accepted that security represented a pressing objective that the school commissioners were perfectly justified in pursuing, and they recognised that the banning of *kirpans* was clearly rationally connected to this goal. However, they determined that banning *kirpans* failed the test of minimal impairment, since the available evidence suggested that if they were to be hidden from view and sheathed in the manner proposed by the original accommodation, they would pose no serious threat to the security of the other children in the school.[33]

The decision was perfectly in keeping with other decisions that the Court has rendered on matters of religious freedom. The Court has tended to be quite

[31] ibid 256.

[32] *Multani v Commission scolaire Marguerite-Bourgeoys*, 2006 SCC 6, [2006] 1 SCR 256.

[33] ibid.

expansive in its defence of religious liberty. Not only does it not recognise any a priori internal limit on the concept, preferring to balance it against other values and rights on the basis of section 1 analysis, but it has also tended to apply and to interpret constitutional guarantees to religious freedom in the light of section 27 of the Charter, according to which 'this Charter shall be interpreted in a manner consistent with the preservation and enhancement of the multicultural heritage of Canadians'. The very first case decided by the Court on matters of religious freedom made plain that the protection of the religious freedom of minority religious groups mattered not only from the point of view of the individual believer whose religious rights can be threatened by legislation, but from the point of view of Canadian society as a whole, one of the defining values of which is a commitment to multiculturalism.[34]

The *Multani* decision was hardly noticed in the rest of Canada, but it led to a major political crisis in Quebec. Media commentators and politicians hostile to the extent of religious and cultural accommodation that the Charter seemed to impose on Quebeckers mounted a vigorous campaign against what they perceived to be the excesses of the Canadian multicultural model that the Supreme Court was making itself the vehicle of.[35] When the governing Liberal Party started to feel like it might pay a political price for what many Quebeckers felt to be its quietism in the face of a multiculturalist ideology deeply alien to Quebec's political culture, it named a Commission, chaired by two eminent academics, the philosopher Charles Taylor, and the historian and sociologist Gérard Bouchard, to inquire into whether the practice of cultural accommodation in Quebec had indeed gone too far.

The *Report* that the Commission produced did little to quell public dissatisfaction.[36] The Commissioners felt that the practices of accommodation that obtained in Quebec fell well within justifiable liberal democratic principles, and devoted a good part of their Report to the task of attempting to identify the causes of the deep dissatisfaction that was felt by many Quebeckers with the kind of accommodation of which *Multani* was taken to be emblematic.

Criticisms of the philosophy of accommodation that seemed to underlie the *Multani* decision can be seen as falling under a number of rubrics. Some critics feel that when interpreted as the Court seems to have done as responsive to the value of muticulturalism, accommodation risks becoming a ghettoising practice incompatible with policies designed to achieve a robust sense of shared citizenship.[37] Others put forward the feminist concern that accommodation might end

[34] *R v Big M Drug Mart Ltd* [1985] 1 SCR 295, 11

[35] The decision and the ensuing controversy generated a huge academic response. See in particular M Jezéquel (ed), *La justice à l'épreuve de la diversitéculturelle* (Montreal, Éditions YvonBlais, 2007); and J Gaudreault-Desbiens (ed), *Le droit, la religion et le 'raisonnable' – le fait religieux entre monismeétatique et pluralisme juridique* (Montreal, Éditions Thémis, 2009).

[36] The final report of the Commission is entitled *Building the Future: A Time for Reconciliation*, and can be found at www.accommodements.qc.ca/.

[37] In Canada, the most influential expression of this concern came from N Bissondath, *Selling Illusions: The Cult of Multiculturalism in Canada*, 2nd edn (Toronto, Penguin Books, 2002).

up countenancing unacceptably patriarchal practices via the pretext of respect for cultural diversity.[38] Others still feared that religious accommodation would represent a major setback for Quebec, which had spent the last decades attempting to rid itself of the impact in all spheres of life of the Catholic Church. It would also be incompatible with the robust affirmation of the religious neutrality of the state, which might be threatened were decisions like *Multani* to require of state institutions that they accommodate the religious demands either of users of public institutions or of those who work within them.[39]

In an attempt to placate growing popular discontent with what are seen as excessively generous policies of cultural and religious accommodation, the Liberal Party recently introduced legislation that would have prohibited, at least in a number of public institutional contexts, the wearing of the full-face Muslin veils – the *niqab* and the *burqa* – which are widely perceived as the most unacceptable emblems of a multicultural policy run amuck. It is unclear that this proposed legislation would survive Charter scrutiny. But it is quite certain that legislation imposing a complete ban on all religious accommodation in public institutions proposed by the opposition *Parti Québécois* (which the Party is almost certain to enact once it is returned to power) would be struck down.

The *Parti Québécois* has threatened to invoke section 33 of the Charter were this to happen while it was in power. Given the perception that is now dominant in the rest of Canada concerning the 'notwithstanding' clause, to wit, that it is contrary to the values of the Charter which so many Canadians now view as fundamental to the Canadian identity, the use by Quebec of the clause in order to immunise its laws on *laïcité* from Charter scrutiny risks disturbing the cold peace that has characterised the relationship between Quebec and the rest of Canada since the 1995 referendum on Quebec sovereignty was narrowly defeated. A sovereigntist political Party like the *Parti Québécois* intent on awakening Quebec's nationalist sentiment long enough to produce winning referendum conditions might find that the opening up of a clear rift between Quebec and the rest of Canada on the issue of cultural and religious accommodation and on the use of section 33 makes political sense.

Decisions on a whole spate of cases to do with religious freedom, which, as I have indicated above, have been very generous towards claimants of religious accommodation. Thus, given the absence in the Charter of any language that might have provided the Court with reasons to defer on such matters to the obviously quite different vision that is dominant in Quebec as to the proper way of balancing religious freedom against considerations of gender equality, secularism and minority integration, the Court would have no choice but to uphold challenges that are sure to be mounted against a law on *laïcité* that banned

[38] See Y Geadah, *Accommodement sraisonnables: Droit à la difference et non difference des droits* (Montreal, VLB, 2007).

[39] These latter two concerns were clearly expressed in a manifesto published by leading Quebec intellectuals partly as a reaction to the report of the Bouchard/Taylor Commission. See 'Pour un Québec laïque et pluraliste',www.quebeclaique.org/.

religious accommodation outright in the public sphere. True, the *Court* has in a pair of recent decisions shown that its openness to accommodation is not without bounds, and that it is at times willing to limit religious freedom for the sake of gender equality (as in the Jewish divorce case *Bruker v Marcovitz*),[40] and for the sake of security (as in the case of *Alberta v Hutterian Brethren of Wilson Colony*.[41] But the wholesale ban of any religious accommodation within public institutions envisaged by the *Parti Québécois*, an idea which enjoys wide public support in the province, is well beyond what the Court would be prepared to countenance under the present constitutional order. The Charter mandates that Justices interpret fundamental rights in a manner that takes into account the multicultural heritage of Canada.[42] The Charter does not contain what might have been at least potentially countervailing language that would have required that they also interpret the Charter in a manner that recognises the role of the National Assembly of Quebec in promoting Quebec's distinct culture and identity. Consequently, the Court may have no choice but to hand down decisions invalidating large sections of an eventual law on *laïcité*. This may well provoke a unity crisis in the same way that its striking down of large sections of the language charter of the province had touched off a unity crisis in the early 1990s that culminated in the 1995 referendum (which came within a few thousand votes of providing the provincial government with a mandate to negotiate secession from Canada).

VII. CONCLUSION

I have argued that, far from contributing to Canadian unity, the 1982 Constitution and its entrenched Charter of Rights and Freedoms have at various points exacerbated tensions between Quebec and the rest of Canada and risk doing so again in the near future around the issue of religious and cultural accommodation.

Throughout this chapter, I have emphasised costs that the present constitutional order exacts upon Canadian unity. I have steered clear of saying anything about the *justice* of the rival narratives that contend with one another within the Canadian polity. Nor have I said anything about the justice of the positions that have been defended by Quebec legislators with respect to issues of language and religious accommodation, and which seem to offend against the Supreme Court of Canada's way of interpreting the Charter.

I have in other writings opposed certain aspects both of Quebec's language laws and of its stance on religious accommodation on grounds of justice.[43] It

[40] *Bruker v Marcovitz* [2007] 3 SCR 607, 2007 SCC 54.

[41] *Alberta v Hutterian Brethren of Wilson Colony*, 2009 SCC 37, [2009] 2 SCR 567.

[42] See s 27.

[43] D Weinstock, 'The Antinomy of Language Rights' in W Kymlicka and A Patten (eds), *Language Rights and Political Theory* (Oxford, Oxford University Press, 2000); D Weinstock, 'Laïcité ouverte ou laïcité stricte' in N Baillargeon (ed), *Le Québec en quête de laïcité* (Montreal, Écosociété, 2011).

might therefore seem odd that I emphasise problems that the Supreme Court's opposition to these policies pose for Canadian unity and stability. If Quebec's positions on these issues are unjust, should they not be opposed on Charter grounds, even if the unity and stability of the country were adversely affected?

I can only respond to these questions briefly here. The first point that I want to make is that though I consider that Quebec's policies on language and religious accommodation are not optimal from the point of view of liberal justice, they nonetheless belong to a family of views that are reasonable. They represent a plausible way of attempting to achieve balance among a number of rival normative considerations that I would balance in a somewhat different way.

The second point, following from this, is that I think it would be normatively preferable – as well as being more conducive to the stability of the Canadian federation – for Quebeckers to decide through democratic deliberation which among a number of reasonable ways of balancing these normative considerations should be enshrined in laws, rather than having one of these reasonable dispensations imposed upon them by the Court. The presence of a constitutional clause providing the judges on the Court with reasons to defer to the legislature of Quebec on such matters as long as it remains within the bounds of the reasonable still strikes me as the best way in which to reconcile Quebec to the Canadian constitutional order. Our recent political history provides me with little hope that language striking this balance will be agreed to any time soon.

10

Education, Crucifixes and Headscarves: The Appropriation of Meanings and the Content of Rights in Divided Societies

RUTH RUBIO-MARÍN AND LEONARDO ÁLVAREZ-ÁLVAREZ

I. INTRODUCTION

ON 24 SEPTEMBER 1995, around 25,000 people demonstrated in Munich against the decision by the German Federal Constitutional Court to ban the cross from public classrooms. Almost a decade later, 17 January 2004 was declared the international protest day against the French headscarf ban and public demonstrations were held in dozens of locations, from Washington to Cairo; Amman to Khartoum; Montreal to Beirut. On 2 February 2008 more than 100,000 people demonstrated in Ankara against a bill which would lift the prohibition to wear the headscarf at Turkish universities, and 28 June 2010 saw around 5,000 people taking to the streets in Kosovo to protest against a government decision to ban pupils from wearing Muslim headscarves in public schools. In November 2009, after the European Court of Human Rights issued its first decision condemning Italy's unwillingness to remove the crucifix from public classrooms,[1] the mayors of several Italian towns in different Italian provinces and regions including Ancona, Bolzano, Monza, Sicily, Padova, Venice, Treviso and Taranto took action to protest. These included verbal or written orders not to remove the crucifixes from public schools, sometimes under threat of a financial fine, as well as an initiative to sign a petition to formally protest against the Strasbourg Court decision, with a reward of free crucifixes for all those willing to join. These actions were justified in the name of preserving Italian tradition and Christianity, but their proponents also appealed to the civic dimension of the crucifix as a symbol of peace

[1] *Lautsi v Italy*, no 30814/2006, ECHR 47 (2009) (*Lautsi I*).

and love and to the Christian origins of Italian constitutional values, including freedom, mutual respect, solidarity and non-discrimination.[2] Eventually, the Grand Chamber of the European Court of Human Rights came to support the reasoning of the Italian government,[3] finding that the decision as to whether to allow the display of religious symbols at school falls within the margin of appreciation of Member States, and that the crucifix can indeed be interpreted not only as a religious symbol but also as the expression of a historical tradition and of the values that inspire western democracies and civilisation.

These controversies must be placed in their proper context. Religious diversity in increasingly multicultural European societies is prompting legal scholars to think about the role of the law in setting the conditions for and limits to the expression of religious pluralism, especially in public settings. The controversies are particularly strong in the educational domain, a domain which is naturally expected to play a crucial role in the integration of migrants. Given the highly topical discussions around immigrants' integration strategies in countries such as France, Germany, the United Kingdom and also in the Nordic countries which represent the core of Europe's social democratic tradition, we anticipate that the religious symbols dispute is unlikely to subside any time soon. The virulence of the public reactions just described is telling in this respect.

The European Court of Human Rights, like several constitutional courts, has already had the opportunity to address interesting questions around religious meanings such as whether students should be allowed to attend school or university wearing religious garments, or whether it is acceptable that they be educated under the influence of certain religious symbols including crucifixes hanging from the walls or Islamic headscarves worn by their teachers or peers.[4] Likewise, European courts have had to decide whether students can be exempted from exposure to religious symbols and representations and from participation in symbolic ceremonies such as military parades.[5] The right to conscientious objection, asserted now in the educational context, has replicated the old American debate about homeschooling in Europe.

[2] For a more detailed description of the different initiatives see http://antiuaar.wordpress.com/2010/06/21/grazie-alluaar-migliaia-di-crocifissi-in-piu-nelle-scuole-e-nei-comuni-italiani/.

[3] *Lautsi v Italy* [GC], no 30814/06 of 18 March 2011 (*Lautsi II*).

[4] See respectively the decisions from the ECtHR, *Leyla Sahin v Turkey,* (GC n 44774/98, ECHR 2005-XI) on the use of the headscarf in public universities); *Lautsi I* and *Lautsi II* and *Dahlab v Switzerland,* n 42393/1998, ECHR 2001-V on the use of headscarf by a public school teacher.

[5] See ECHR, *Efstratiuou v Greece* – n 24095/1994, ECHR 1996-VI (on the mandatory participation of students in a military parade on a national holiday which the Court considered not to be in violation of the rights of parents, members of Jehovah's Witnesses, to choose the moral and philosophical (in this case pacifist) education of their children under art 2 of the Additional Protocol to the ECHR, resting its case on the pacifist meaning of the national holiday) and *Hassan Eylem Zengin v Turkey* n 1448/2004 ECHR 2007-XI (where the Court considered contrary to the parents' rights and to the due respect of pluralism and objectivity the teaching of the Sunni version of Islam to their Alevite children, including their exposure to text books enshrining religious symbols and ceremonies that were foreign to their faith).

In spite of the important contribution of some of these European courts it is our claim that the proper doctrinal approach is still wanting and that the conditions and limits for the spread of religious pluralism within the educational context have not been identified clearly. Often, we suggest, such educational controversies have been framed both in the scholarly doctrine and case law in terms of the conflicting fundamental rights of the parties involved (students, parents and teachers). In part, this is because the relevant legal norms – including European human rights or fundamental rights charters as well as the constitutions of many European countries – often limit themselves to spelling out the set of rights and rights holders that can be identified in the educational domain.[6]

Nevertheless, on closer analysis, one realises that a theory of fundamental rights is not, by itself, able to provide the answers to many of the issues that are being raised. Indeed, the standard categories provided by such a theory do not give a conclusive answer to many of the specific questions that need to be resolved in addressing the set of claims raised, such as the content and limits of each of the fundamental rights involved; the coordination of the educational powers attributed by different legal orders to the state and to private parties; the relationship between education as transmission of knowledge and education as transmission of values; or the limits of educational neutrality or indoctrination.

The proposition that we would like to advance in this chapter is that these answers can only be consistently provided by a proper *theory of education* articulated around a systematic response to the questions of *in what*, *how* and *who* has to educate. Until now, we claim, courts and scholarly doctrine in Europe have mostly failed to address such school controversies from the premises of a theory of education. To the extent that they have, we will show that the theory of education that has been most commonly relied upon – a theory which we could identify as a classical liberal theory – has clear shortcomings, especially for our increasingly diverse societies. In such societies these questions, we argue, must be addressed from a democratic liberal theory of education. Such a theory views the educational experience as a context for preparing citizens to act with the necessary degree of civility and tolerance required for peaceful coexistence in the context of pluralism.[7] The aim of this contribution is to

[6] Such sets of rights include the rights of parents to choose for their children an education which reflects their philosophical and religious convictions; the right of the minor to be educated and the right of private parties to establish private educational centres (see, eg, art 2 of the First Protocol to European Convention of Human Rights; art 14 of the Fundamental Rights Charter of the European Union; arts 33 and 34 of the Italian Constitution and arts 6.2 and 6.3 and 7 of the German Basic Law).

[7] To be sure, the very roots of liberal thought are connected to the affirmation of religious pluralism and the creation of the conditions for religious tolerance. However, the focus of *classical* liberal doctrines on a notion of individual autonomy to be defended primarily against state interference almost inevitably leads the discussion of the display of religious symbols in schools to what we see as a rather sterile terrain of competing claims of positive or negative individual rights and freedoms and to the affirmation of the elusive goal of state neutrality. Instead, we claim, a liberal *democratic* theory primarily focuses on the generation of the conditions and civic virtues necessary to sustain democratic institutions and to guarantee the peaceful coexistence and exercise of fundamental rights in ever-increasing diversity. It better accounts for the central authority of states in the

explore how such a theory could help to interpret the complex set of rights and powers that come together in the educational setting and provide a principled answer to the question of the display of religious symbols there.

II. THE DISPLAY OF RELIGIOUS SYMBOLS IN EDUCATIONAL SETTINGS AND THE NEED FOR A THEORY OF EDUCATION

A. The School as a Domain of Confluence of Competing Fundamental Rights

Any legal approach to education has to take as its starting point the fact that the school is a space in which several fundamental rights collide. Indeed, it appears that the display of religious symbols in public schools presents a degree of complexity which can hardly be reproduced elsewhere; it entails the confluence of one fundamental right (religious freedom) which has both a positive and a negative dimension, which is attributed at the same time to a plurality of subjects who participate in the educational domain (students, parents and teachers), a domain which is generally organised by the state but where parents are also commonly given authority and which is ultimately oriented to guarantee another fundamental right, the right to education (a right which is at the same time also a legal duty).[8]

In principle, the combination of these elements can generate up to four types of conflicts. First of all, religious freedom has both a positive and a negative side; it can mean the right to profess a certain religion and exercise religious practices but also the right not to do either. Thus, the display of religious symbols by students can be interpreted as the expression of their religious freedom, but it may also come into conflict with the religious freedom of all those other students who do not want to be exposed to them. This is, for instance, the problem generated when the wearing of the Islamic headscarf by students who thereby express their religious convictions is seen as conflicting with the freedom of religion of those who do not want to be exposed to and educated under their symbolic effect.[9] An even clearer case would present itself if some students wanting to be taught under a crucifix were not allowed to on the grounds that this would amount to an encroachment of the religious freedom of other students. Secondly, we can identify a conflict of a similar nature when teachers,

educational domain and recognises the impossibility and the undesirability of a value-free or strictly speaking neutral public education, especially in deeply diverse societies. In these societies, liberalism's historical concern with the accommodation of mostly inter-Christian pluralism is insufficient to respond to contemporary religious pluralism, more plural in nature.

[8] Indeed most international and European norms establish the mandatory nature of primary and secondary education.

[9] See, eg, the ECtHR decision *Leyla Sahin v Turkey*, on the prohibition of the headscarf in Turkish universities presented as a clash between positive and negative sides of the freedom of religion of university students and upholding such prohibition for the sake of preserving the rights of others and the public interest in ensuring 'religious peace' and 'public order' (art 9 ECHR).

and not just students, are the ones asserting their right to wear religious symbols. In that case, given the aura of authority that teachers arguably possess, the problem presents itself in an aggravated manner.[10] Thirdly, all of the possible conflicts we have mentioned so far would also invariably generate at the same time a conflict between the religious freedom of teachers and/or students on the one hand, and the right (and duty) to education with respect to students on the other. Finally, the display of religious symbols in public schools may also be seen as either a fulfilment of or an encroachment on the rights of parents to ensure that the education and teaching of their children is in conformity with their own religions and philosophical convictions.[11] Moreover, identifying the possible set of rights involved is essential but not sufficient in order to solve the conflicts generated by the display of religious symbols at school. It is just as important to understand the source of educational authority, an authority which many European constitutional orders recognise primarily, if not exclusively, in favour of the state.[12] It is the state that is primarily in charge of organising the educational system and of doing so in a way that duly respects the rights of those involved, including those of religious minorities.

B. The Insufficiency of the Fundamental Rights Doctrine; the Need for a Theory of Education

The categories and the interpretive criteria provided by the doctrine of fundamental rights are not sufficient to provide a solution to the definition of the scope and limits of each of the rights and powers that come together in the educational setting. Doctrinal debates and case law have paid insufficient attention to this and have instead continued to think of education almost exclusively in terms of the relation and tension between different fundamental rights. In particular, both scholars and courts have exhibited a certain circularity, first defining in the abstract the object and content of the rights involved and then trying to come up with proper criteria of interpretation to resolve the tensions between them. Instead, we claim, the better approach would be to deduce the purpose of education from a theory of education and then to define the object, content and limits of the rights involved in light of that theory. The limited regulatory framework established in both international instruments as well as

[10] This was for instance the case of *Dahlab v Switzerland* where the ECtHR had to decide whether a public school teacher ought to be allowed to wear a headscarf. In fact the conflict here is three-dimensional. At stake is the positive religious freedom of the teacher as well as the positive religious freedom of the students willing to be taught by somebody endorsing such religious symbolism. In tension is the negative religious freedom of those students that were opposed to it, either because they belong to a different religious faith or to none at all, something which is of course also covered by the religious freedom clause (art 9 ECHR).

[11] See, for instance, art 2 of the First Additional Protocol to the ECHR. Indeed, this was the claim the court addressed in *Lautsi I*, where a parent alleged that the imposition on their children of the obligation to study under the crucifix violated her children's and also her own rights.

[12] See, eg, art 2 of the First Additional Protocol to the ECHR.

national constitutions of European countries regarding the concept and purpose of education is partly to blame for the problem we are describing.[13]

The possibility of arriving at almost diametrically opposite positions in the conflict around the display of religious symbols at school reveals the most serious limitations of an approach derived from a doctrine of fundamental rights. First of all, it is impossible to come up with a principled criterion for determining the fundamental rights which have to be taken as an argumentative starting point.[14] Likewise, a theory of fundamental rights does not provide us with a principled way to determine the scope of the state and parental authority in the educational domain. Consider the following examples.

First, under the fundamental rights theory, the controversies around the use of religious symbols at school have sometimes been framed as being primarily about the freedom of religion. Thus, the fact that the setting of the controversy happens to be a school classroom or an educational setting is taken to be of secondary importance at best. The solution advanced then is one that looks at how to reconcile colliding claims to religious freedom (taking into account the positive–negative strands and the rights of all parties concerned), attaching little if any significance to the right to education itself.[15] This is why the kinds of limitations placed on the expression of religious freedom under this approach could in principle be extended to any other domain.[16] An example of this approach can be seen in the case *Leyla Sahin v Turkey* where the European Court of Human Rights upheld the prohibition of wearing the headscarf in Turkish public universities and the subsequent limitation of the religious

[13] Indeed most international covenants limit themselves to typifying the set of rights and sometimes powers which come together in the school setting but say virtually nothing about how those rights and faculties must be consistently interpreted. As a result, the 'educational relationship' ends up being primarily understood as a competition of rights. See, eg, art 2 of the First Protocol to the ECHR and, more recently, art 14 of the European Charter of Fundamental Rights of the European Union.

[14] Linked to this, we can also deplore the fact that in trying to render rights pulling in different directions compatible with each other, the technique put into place has been that of the *balancing of rights* which in the end has entailed attaching a higher value to some fundamental rights to the detriment of others without there being a principled way of establishing a priori the proper hierarchy of rights. On the technique of the balancing of rights see R Alexy, *A Theory of Constitutional Rights* (Oxford, Oxford University Press 2004) 54ff.

[15] This was the approach taken by the French *Conseil d'Etat* in its traditional doctrine on the headscarf, prohibiting the use of religious symbols when they are ostensible or imply an act of pressure, provocation or proselytising (Resolution of 29 November 1989). Religious peace is thus considered the operative criterion expressing the limits that the negative religious freedom of some places to that of the positive freedom of others.

[16] Indeed, the ECtHR has called on the principle of 'religious peace' to decide other controversies around religious freedom outside the school. See, eg, *Otto Perminger Institut* v *Austria* (n 13470/87 (ECtHR 1994-XXVI) where the ECtHR declared that the limitation of freedom of expression (art 10 ECHR) entailed by the censoring of the movie 'Das Liebeskonzil', which denigrated the feelings of Catholics, was proportional to the goal of ensuring religious peace in the South-Tyrol, an Austrian province inhabited by a Roman Catholic majority. This example also shows that, when the argument of religious peace is taken as the main concern, in the end the religious feelings of the majority end up prevailing. This of course does not per se follow from the collision of rights pulling in different directions.

freedom it entailed on the grounds that the prohibition served the purpose of achieving religious peace in the Turkish state.[17] The problem with this approach is that it offers little room for principled solutions. On the one hand, the positive and negative strands of freedom of religion can be seen as reciprocally cancelling each other out resulting in the possibility of religious majorities and minorities asserting opposing claims. On the other, this framing of the question does not allow any meaningful discussion of the specific problem of religious indoctrination which is arguably relevant when the display of religious symbols takes place in the public educational settings in non-confessional states.

A different take consists of approaching the issue of the display of religious symbols in schools primarily from the perspective of the right to education. Starting from such premises, as the German Federal Constitutional Court has done in its crucifix[18] and veil decisions,[19] the school is not just one of the settings in which the controversy around the religious freedom of different individuals can take place but rather the very reason for the limitation of such freedoms in a non-confessional state bound to respect the principle of religious neutrality. The question then becomes what type of limitation on the right to education can be accepted in the name of respecting religious tolerance as a constitutionally enshrined right and value.

Taking the right to education as a point of departure can be useful, among other things, to give due visibility to the problem of educational indoctrination. In spite of this, the classic categories of theories of fundamental rights (delimitation of object, content and limits of rights) are not enough to explain what kinds of limits can be set on religious freedom and its symbolic expressions for the purpose of avoiding undue indoctrination. Instead, to decide whether or not such indoctrination is taking place, one must first decide what are the contents and values that can be the object of teaching and hence, what kinds of symbolic displays may put such education at risk. This is precisely one of the central questions that a theory of education tries to address, but this is not a question that naturally flows from the right to education per se.

The controversy around the homeschooling doctrine, American in origin, and now widely diffused in Europe, provides yet another illustration of the inadequacy of the fundamental rights approach with respect to this type of question. According to that doctrine, a child's right to education entails an education in accordance with her family's values, and so the right can only or mainly be effectively guaranteed where parents constitute the chief legitimate educational authority. Thus, according to this view, the state or the school's authority to decide on the display of religious symbols under which students are to be educated is problematic. In Europe this doctrine is difficult to reconcile with a legal framework which reflects the view that the primordial educational function pertains to the state and that acquiring an education is also a citizen's

[17] 44774/98 [2005] ECHR 819 (10 November 2005).
[18] See BVerfGE 93, 1 of 16 May 1996.
[19] See BVerfGE 108, 292 of 24 September 2003.

duty (and not just a right). However, the relevant point for us is that, in and of itself, the theory of fundamental rights is (once again) unable to provide interpretive criteria for norms which, on the one hand, recognise the rights of parents to choose the philosophical and religious education of their children and, on the other, recognise the educational authority of the state (see, for instance, Article 2 of the First Additional Protocol to the ECHR). In the end, the answer to this question can only be provided by a theory of education which first determines the 'in what' of education and then derives from that starting point the 'how and by whom'.[20]

III. EDUCATIONAL LIBERALISM AND THE DEFINITION OF THE CONTENT OF FUNDAMENTAL RIGHTS IN THE SCHOOL SETTING

Liberal theories of education, rooted in the classical liberal doctrines of political thought, and following the postulates of Aristotelian and Platonic thought,[21] have the merit of offering a systematic analysis of the rights and powers involved in the educational relationship. Categories that are by now consolidated in the legal literature and case law – such as the proper function of education, the prohibition of indoctrination, or the principle of neutrality at school – all flow from such liberal premises. Although there are indeed several theories of liberalism, what characterises what we are here calling *liberal* theories of education is that they start from the premise that the transmission of certain liberal principles or values is the primary object of education, deducing from them the *how* and *who* of education.

Liberal educational theories have thus far flourished in the domains of pedagogy, sociology and, more recently, in the domain of political theory.[22] But they have not been adopted to the same extent by legal scholars and actors when trying to articulate rights and powers in the educational domain. The legacy of such theories can, however, still be detected in several *topoi* or argumentative perspectives which are recurrent in the European debate over the use of religious symbols. Interestingly, their impact owes more to the ever-increasing number of social demands of parents – who have come closest to articulating a legal liberal theory of education – than to the success of such educational theories in providing for a systematic interpretation of fundamental rights. It is not our task here to analyse in any meaningful depth the classical doctrines of educational liberalism but rather to assess how much the European debate on religious symbols is indebted to them and to show that educational liberalism is not able to offer

[20] These are the elements of a theory of education. Gutmann refers to the purpose, distribution and authorities of education. See A Gutmann, *Democratic Education* (Princeton, Princeton University Press, 1987) 22.

[21] See Aristotle, *Politica*, V, 107(a), Plato *Nomoi* XII, 961(a).

[22] See, by way of example, among the classics, JS Mill, *On Liberty*, 2nd edn (John W Parker & Son, London, 1859) 188–90 and, among the contemporary, B Ackerman, *Social Justice in the Liberal State* (New Haven, Yale University Press, 1980) 141–43.

a consistent interpretation of the rights and powers foreseen under the various legal systems in increasingly pluralistic societies.

A. The '*in what*' of Liberal Education: Individual Autonomy and the Position of Religious Symbols in Schools

What all the liberal doctrines of education have in common is that they conceive of education as being fundamentally in the service of the freedom of students; this the *in what* of education.[23] The primary function of liberal education is thus perceived as that of enabling individual autonomy by allowing the young person to freely develop and pursue his or her vision of the good life.[24] Several legal instruments seem to reflect this understanding of education when linking the educational process to the development of one's personality. Thus, Article 26.2 of the Universal Declaration of Human Rights recognises that 'education shall be directed to the full development of the human personality'. Similarly, Article 13.1 of the International Covenant on Social, Economic and Cultural Rights provides that: 'The education shall be directed to the full development of the human personality and the sense of its dignity, and shall strengthen the respect for human rights and fundamental freedoms'.[25] In contrast, most European constitutions do not mention the primary purpose of education in general, or the pursuit of individual autonomy in particular, but rather, as mentioned above, only recognise the set of rights and powers that come together in the educational setting.

The most obvious legal consequence that derives from this conception of the right to education for the interpretation of other fundamental rights which may be asserted in the classroom (such as the freedom of religion of teachers) is that the latter may be limited for the purpose of ensuring the freedom of students who are obviously the primary beneficiaries of the educational process.[26] Similarly, the display of religious symbols at school may also be restricted as undue *educational indoctrination* contrary to the required educational *neutrality* of the state. In Europe, the principle of non-indoctrination has been fully embraced by both the legal doctrine and the case law.[27]

[23] See Mill, *On Liberty* (n 22) 115.

[24] See E Callan, *Creating Citizens: Political Education and Liberal Democracy* (Oxford, Oxford University Press, 1997) 10 ff.

[25] Notice that also among the scholarly doctrine one finds a clear emphasis on individual freedom among those discussing the right to education. See, in general, S Detrick, *A Commentary on the United Nations Convention on the Rights of the Child* (The Hague, Kluwer Law International, 1999) 93. Within the European Union, see G Gori, *Towards an EU Right to Education* (The Netherlands, Kluwer Law, 2001) 320 ff.

[26] As recognised by art 3 of the Convention of the Rights of the Child.

[27] As a landmark case discussing the neutrality/non-indoctrination principle see the ECtHR case *Kjeldsen, Busk Madsen and Pedersen v Denmark* (*Series A* n 23, 1 EHRR 711) of 7 December 1973 in which the ECtHR decided that teaching sexual education in public schools did not amount to undue indoctrination as long as the subject was taught in an 'objective, critical and pluralistic manner'.

The problem with this understanding of education is that the guarantee of neutrality is much easier to promise than to actually deliver. First of all, as some authors have rightly pointed out, an education geared towards enhancing individual freedom is not strictly speaking *neutral* in terms of values; it enshrines the idea of individual autonomy as a fundamental value asserting it against those whose moral, religious or philosophical convictions lead them to think otherwise, including those who think that there is more to a good life and good society than freedom (such as the virtues of honesty, industriousness and kindness).[28] Indeed, citizens of a religiously and ethnically diverse society disagree on the relative values of freedom and virtue.

Maybe the solution lies in drawing a distinction between the transmission of objective knowledge and the transmission of values and limiting the realm of authority of the state to the former while leaving the latter to the parents. This would at least allow parents (and not the state) to be primarily responsible for shaping their children's autonomy according to their own system of moral and religious beliefs.[29] However, this too is an elusive goal; ultimately there is no educational system which can limit itself to the transmission of value-free knowledge and development of skills. As has been pointed out, what facts are taught, who and how they are taught, and basic things such as who is allowed into the classroom, the sitting arrangement of students, rules of conduct or dress code, and the order and type of courses taught, all reflect a value system whether or not this is explicitly recognised.[30]

Given the impossibility of a purely value-free education for the sake of preserving individual autonomy, we increasingly observe the following phenomenon: rhetorically, the principle of neutrality and non-indoctrination is paid lip-service to; substantively, the values that are tacitly and often unconsciously endorsed through the state school system are those that simply reflect the cultural, political and religious values that are dominant in a society at any given point in time. In this way, the promise of furthering individual autonomy is implicitly reduced to enabling choice among competing visions of the good life but only within the range of options legitimised by the majority culture. In this scenario education comes to play a different function from that which is explicitly recognised, becoming a tool for preserving the homogeneity of the majority and its values. Doctrinally, the shape this process takes is that, when the process of the balancing of conflicting rights takes place, more weight is automatically granted to those rights and public interests that are instrumental to the assertion of majority values.

That the preservation of dominant political, cultural and/or religious values has come to play a role in the European debate on the display of religious

[28] Gutmann, *Democratic Education* (n 20) 92.

[29] More on this below.

[30] See W Kymlicka, *Politics in the Vernacular: Nationalism, Multiculturalism and Citizenship* (New York, Oxford University Press, 2001) 291. On the notion of hidden curriculum see PW Jackson, *Life in Classrooms* (Columbia, Teachers College Press, 1990) 34–35.

symbols can hardly be denied. In its most extreme and communitarian version – the one that would be more difficult to reconcile with any pretence of liberal neutrality – it has come to endorse the obligation to display the religious symbols of the majority unabashedly. Think of Austria, for example, where the law indeed *requires* that in those public schools with a majority of Christian students a crucifix shall be displayed.[31]

More often, the process whereby majoritarian beliefs are imposed (and consequently the realm of applicability of fundamental rights which serve to assert minority beliefs is restricted) is more subtle and comes dressed in robes that are more agreeable to liberal thinking. One example which comes to mind is the prohibition of girls and women from wearing religious headscarves in school on the grounds that the practice reflects a model of society that enshrines female subordination, a recurrent argument in the European headscarf debate.[32] This argument was endorsed by the European Court of Human Rights in *Dahlab v Switzerland*. The Court justified the prohibition imposed on a Muslim teacher from wearing the Islamic headscarf to class on the grounds that, inter alia, because doing so meant endorsing a Koranic precept sanctioning inequality between the sexes.[33] No reference is made in these decisions to the fact that, according to liberal orthodoxy, freedom of thought or of expression do not allow for content-based limitations, not even for the purpose of defending constitutionally enshrined values other than those strictly necessary for the protection of the rights of others. It is also problematic that the majority is allowed to assume the role of defining 'the' concrete meaning of a symbol which the minority uses, even though, as we know to be the case with the use of the headscarf, there may be competing interpretations of its proper meaning even within the minority community. Thus seen, the question of the display of religious symbols becomes one of what those symbols 'symbolise' or 'mean' for the majority,[34]

[31] See, in this respect, the very recent decision by the Austrian Constitutional Court (VfGH G287/09) of 9 March 2011, affirming that the display of the crucifix in nurseries does not infringe against art 2.1 of the First Additional Protocol to the ECHR which, in Austria, has constitutional ranking.

[32] On the different positions around the wearing of the headscarf at school see, among many others, AK Wing and MN Smith, 'Critical Race Feminism Lifts the Veil?: Muslim Omen, France and the Headscarf Ban' (2005–06) 39 *Davis Law Review* 743, 767–70 and B Wynter, *Hijab & the Republic: Uncovering the French Scarf Debate* (Syracuse, Syracuse University Press, 2008) 21ff.

[33] The argument was also endorsed by the Commission in *Karaduman v Turkey* (Commission decision of 3 May 1993 (no 16278/90)) upholding the decision of Turkish authorities to deny the expedition of a university diploma to two students whose pictures were taken while wearing headscarves. Similar arguments have been endorsed by the French *Conseil d'Etat* (see the decision from 27 July 2008). Also, the famous Stasi Report of the presidential committee to examine how the principle of *laicité* should be applied in the French Republic (11 December 2003) affirms that the wearing of the headscarf violates the principles and values that the school has to teach, mainly that of equality between men and women.

[34] Interestingly, notice that the argument is never made that the crucifix should not be displayed because it is a symbol of a religious faith, the Christian faith, which arguably and like all other major religions endorses the inferior social position of women. See S Moller Okin, 'Is Multiculturalism Bad for Women?' in Joshua Cohen, Matthew Howard and Martha Nussbaum (eds), *Is Multiculturalism Bad for Women?* (New Jersey, Princeton University Press, 1999) 12–16.

a majority which then considers the interpretive content of the symbol sufficient to limit precisely those fundamental freedoms whose primary purpose is to allow for ideological, cultural and religious pluralism and hence, for minority dissent.[35] The end result then is inevitably educational assimilationism disguised as liberal education.[36]

This hermeneutic privilege of the majority is also exercised when the argument put forward to defend the display of religious symbols of the majority (typically, the Christian crucifix) is that it does not represent religion but only western secular values. This position has been defended by many Italian courts as well as by the Italian government in front of the ECtHR, first unsuccessfully in *Lautsi I* and then successfully in *Lautsi II* before the Grand Chamber.[37] Similar arguments were also made years ago in Germany in reaction to the controversial decision of the Federal Constitutional Court asking for the removal of the crucifix from public schools in Bavaria. The crucifix, the argument went, does not instantiate religion as such, but merely symbolises values that are common to the European cultural tradition.[38]

The process of engineered blending of the concepts of culture, tradition and religion can maybe accommodate different degrees of religious sensitivities among members of a culturally dominant group. To that extent, it is not surprising that the display in public places of certain religious symbols may raise relatively little concern when applied to societies so long as they remain relatively homogenous from a cultural or religious point of view. Practicing members of different faiths sharing a common religious tradition (such as Christianity) and non-practicing members sharing strong cultural ties and common religious traditions may indeed not be as offended by the display of certain religious symbols, such as the crucifix; they may even show an openness to interpreting them as symbols which have come to be associated with shared secular

[35] The argument is then different and would not necessarily lead to the same conclusions to one that would look at the practice of allowing or prohibiting girls from wearing the headscarf in view of the impact that such a prohibition may have on their possibility to meaningfully enjoy the right to education.

[36] See W Gaston, 'Civic Education in the Liberal State' in NL Rosenblum (ed), *Liberalism and the Moral Life* (Cambridge MA, Harvard University Press, 1989) 89.

[37] See by way of example the decision of the Aquila Court from 23 October 2003. To follow the fascinating doctrinal debate on the crucifix in Italian public schools see the work of R Bin and others (eds), *La laicità crocifissa. Il nodo costituzionale dei simboli religiosi nei luoghi pubblici* (Turin, Giapichelli, 2004).

[38] See BVerfE 93.1. One can find this line of argumentation in the dissenting opinion of Justices Seidl, Soellner and Haas. The academic literature has extensively criticised the decision of the Constitutional Court on three grounds including 1) that the crucifix must be considered part of the western cultural heritage and that Muslim students must respect the values of the state and society in which they live; 2) that the crucifix must be interpreted as representing religious values that are shared by all religions, including the Muslim religion and 3) that the crucifix must be interpreted as endorsing secular values including peace and solidarity between different societies. On the different positions in this debate see, by way of sample, W Gut, *Kreuz und Kruzifix in öffentliche Raumen* (Zurich, NzV, 1996) 16–20 and A Hollerbach, 'Der Staat ist kein Neutrum' in Hans Mayer (ed), *Das Kreuz im Widerspruch: Der Kruzifix- Beschluss des Bundesverfassungsgerichts in der Kontroverse* (Freiburg/Breisgau, Herder, 1996) 26–30.

values of a common culture. However, much more controversy can be expected when the symbols are displayed in front of believers from different religious traditions or people professing strong anti-religious sentiments; such people are much more likely to experience the crucifix as a religious symbol that is foreign to them and alienating. Whereas if silently worn by peer students, the crucifix might be seen as expressing religious pluralism – an expression of religious tolerance – when displayed in the classroom by the school it is much more likely to be perceived as an official endorsement of the Christian faith.[39]

B. The 'how and who' in Liberal Education: The Principle of Neutrality, Educational Authority, and Religious Symbols in School

As we have seen, according to liberal doctrines the right to education aspires to protect individual autonomy and can only be adequately realised when the principle of neutrality in education is affirmed and indoctrination is prohibited. According to the most radical liberal conception of neutrality, this requires the denial of all forms of deliberate transmission of values through the school. Neither parents nor the state are to educate. Rather, education comes to be understood as entailing the exposure of minors to competing forces and interests as they are otherwise displayed in society at large.[40] This position, however, has been increasingly abandoned and criticised as unrealistic. It is definitely not the one enshrined in most legal orders which make some form of schooling until a certain age mandatory.

Nowadays many more authors defend the view that the true addressee of the principle of neutrality and non-indoctrination is the state because the largest threat of undue moral indoctrination comes from public schools. What the authors seem to endorse, in one form or another, is the possibility and need to draw a distinction between education, as the transmission of values, and teaching, as the transmission of knowledge. What they seem to suggest is that the latter is the only legitimate task for the state to engage in.[41] In other words, what this means is that the *who* in many liberal theories of education is ultimately the parents and the family, as was openly acknowledged by Locke.[42] This is how, in what we could describe as an almost patrimonial understanding of parenthood, parents come to be recognised as having exclusive authority to decide on the

[39] On the tradition and history of the crucifix and its different connotations for the Christian and Jewish communities see, eg, S Luzzatto, *Il crocifisso di Stato* (Turin, Einaudi, 2011) 17–29.

[40] A classic defence of this position can be found in AO Hirshmann, *The passions and the interests. Political Arguments for Capitalism Before Its Triumph* (Princeton, Princeton University Press 1977) 14–15. Similarly, in his theory of education Rousseau attributed a natural educational role to nature and objects. See J Rousseau, *Emile* in J Rousseau, *Oeuvres Complètes. Tome II* (Paris, Gallimard 1861) 447–48.

[41] Initially, the ECtHR also endorsed the distinction between these two concepts. See, eg, ECtHR *Campbell and Cosans v United Kingdom* (*Series A* n 48, 4 EHRR 293).

[42] See J Locke, *Two Treatises on Government* (London, R Butler et al, 1821) para 68; and Mill, *On Liberty* (n 22) 189.

moral and religious education of their children thereby shaping the process of their personality formation and their autonomy. Such premises are for instance the ones underlying the American movement of homeschooling asserting parents' rights to educate their children at home instead of under the educational system organised by the state.

Clearly, this is not the only possible interpretation of what a liberal commitment to the notion of individual autonomy means for the question of educational authority. Amy Gutmann, for instance, has identified the above-mentioned position as one which reflects the liberal tradition of the 'State of families' and offered it in contrast to the one she describes as the liberal tradition of the 'State of individuals' which, she claims, is the one that focuses on a notion of individual autonomy that can be asserted against parents as well.[43] The two competing positions are elegantly contrasted in the landmark US Supreme Court decision of *Wisconsin v Yoder* which represents a paradigm of the assertion of maximum parental authority. Decided in 1972, that case concerned the request of Amish parents that their children, ages 14 and 15, be exempted from attending the mandatory public school (which in the State of Wisconsin continues until the age of 16) to allow them to receive education within the Amish community in conformity with their value system. The Court granted the parents' claims, finding that the State had failed to show that there was a compelling state interest in educating the children those two extra years, an interest sufficient to justify the restriction of the freedom of religion of the parents for whom the extra time spent in the public school system could seriously threaten their children's moral upbringing and the chances that in the future they would decide to stay in the Amish community.[44] Although the decision represents the liberal vision that gives pre-eminence to the role of parents in the transmission of moral and religious values, it has also been criticised by those liberals who, placing an emphasis on individual autonomy, think that children should receive a broad education to enable them to choose their life path even if this goes against parental expectations. This view was in fact the one articulated by Justice Douglas in his dissent.[45]

Coming back to the European continent, a similar question of interpretation arose in a very controversial decision of the Germany Federal Administrative

[43] See Gutmann, *Democratic Education* (n 20) 28. In her work Gutmann criticises, as we also do here, the shortcomings of both and openly endorses the need for a democratic liberal theory of education in which parents and the state both share educational authority and are entitled to inculcate values on to the children, the question then becoming, for the state, one of what values and within what limits.

[44] See 406 U.S. 205.

[45] Notice, in any event, that the case beautifully portrays the elusive nature of the promise of neutrality which in the end cannot be satisfied by any of the alternatives. Either the children are expected to attend the two extra years and this diminishes the chances that they will thereafter remain within the Amish community leading an Amish lifestyle, or they are exempted to do so and end up with limited options to access other life projects that the majority culture renders available. Neither option is therefore strictly neutral and both are value-laden, as they both have an impact on what the students are to perceive as valuable life options.

Court concerning the possibility of exempting a girl from attending gym classes.[46] The girl's parents asked for an exemption for the girl on religious freedom grounds because of their opposition to their daughter wearing gym clothes that exposed her body in front of her male peers, a claim which the school authorities had disregarded. Reversing the decision, the Federal Administrative Court granted the exemption, indirectly recognising the higher educational authority of the parents.

This notion of the educational authority of parents over the religious and moral education of their children underlies the different forms of parental objections expressed in several European states against the inclusion of certain subjects in the public curriculum, subjects which are considered to touch upon moral issues such as citizenship education, sexual education, religion and/or ethics.[47] However, most of the scholars and courts which have dealt with the question of the display of religious symbols at school have not conclusively accepted the theory that attributes the task of educating values to parents and families on the one hand, and to the state the task of teaching knowledge on the other, not the least because it would go against the grain of most legal systems which do recognise that the state has a central (and not just a marginal) educational authority. But this central authority, we claim, is more difficult to sustain on principled grounds if our only or main concern is with ensuring individual autonomy. A liberal democratic theory of education which explicitly articulates the foundations (and also the limits) of such public powers is much more promising, especially if one shares the belief in both the impossibility and the undesirability of a value-free or strictly neutral public education.

IV. EDUCATIONAL DEMOCRACY AND THE DEFINITION OF THE CONTENT OF FUNDAMENTAL RIGHTS IN THE SCHOOL DOMAIN

We have seen that the main elements of classic liberal theories of education flow directly from traditional philosophical premises of liberal doctrines. The same is not true with respect to democratic theory which has flourished since the twentieth century. This is partly due to the fact that, with some significant exceptions,[48] democratic theorists have not traditionally thought that the defence of the state and its constitution would fundamentally depend on

[46] See BVerwGE 32, 98 of 25 August 1993.

[47] Demands of this sort have occasionally been supported by the literal wording of some legal provisions, including art 6.2 of the German Basic Law (1949), which explicitly refers to the 'natural' right of parents over the education of their children; art 42.1 of the Irish Constitution (1937), which refers to family as the 'primary and natural educator of the child', or art 17.1 of the *Staatsgrundgesetz* (1867) in Austria, which openly recognises the right of parents to educate their children in the home. With time however, these provisions have less and less frequently been interpreted as sanctioning parents as the exclusive educational authority.

[48] One of these exceptions is Hans Kelsen, a democratic theorist who explicitly defended the view that one of the requirements for democracy is the inculcation of democratic values through education: *Vom Wesen und Wert der Demokratie* (Aalen, Scientia, 1994) 18.

education. This is why, for the most part, we still lack well-articulated theories of democratic education based on securing the conditions for pluralism. Instead, we have well developed theories of the defence of the democratic State grounded on the need to protect the state against those expressions and forces actively fighting against it, including for instance political parties.[49]

For the most part, political scientists and philosophers only began to articulate a democratic theory of education at the end of the twentieth and beginning of the twenty-first centuries. These efforts were triggered by several factors, including the felt need to resuscitate basic civic virtues such as public spiritedness and social responsibility in what some see as politically apathetic and selfish capitalist societies, but also the interest in tightening the bonds of citizenship in increasingly diverse and multicultural societies. As the fiction of a homogenous ethno-cultural social substratum presupposed in the traditional nation state construct becomes increasingly illusory, there is a felt need to find instruments which can ensure a minimum level of social cohesion in European societies.[50] Thus democratic theory has come to the conclusion that it is only by inculcating principles that allow for the respect of social diversity and pluralism in the school system that European societies can remain cohesive. The recent Recommendation (2002) 12 of the Council of Ministers of the state members of the EU, on education for democratic citizenship endorses precisely this vision.[51]

This being said, we are still far from identifying the contours of a legal doctrine of education which, seeking to ensure the health of our democratic societies, allows us to systematically interpret the complex set of rights that come together in the school setting, even though some of what could be its essential features appear sporadically in the European literature and jurisprudence. In the following pages we outline the principles upon which such a liberal democratic theory of education should be built[52] and explain how these principles could help us in identifying and setting proper limits to the relevant fundamen-

[49] On militant democracy see the seminal work of K Loewenstein, 'Militant Democracy and Fundamental Rights' (1937) 3 *The American Political Science Review* 417ff. This democratic theory of the defence of the Constitution came as a response to the threats, during the inter-war period, from political parties proposing the destruction of democracy. On the different models of militant democracy see K Stern, *Das Staatsrecht der Bundesrepublik Deutschland* (München, CH Beck, 1977) 148ff.

[50] Europe is of course not reducing its search for social cohesiveness to the educational domain. Instead it is experimenting with other means including integration contracts for foreigners of the kind that have been applied so far with little success in different countries including the Netherlands, Austria, France and the UK.

[51] Point 1 of the Recommendation affirms that one of the educational objectives of the Member States consits on: *'defending the values and principles of freedom, pluralism, human rights and the rule of law, which are the foundations of democracy.'* On the recent discussions around the role of education for citizenship in different European states see JA Banks (ed), *Diversity and Citizenship Education: Global Perspectives* (San Francisco, John Wiley & Sons Inc, 2004).

[52] In doing this we are largely indebted to the theories developed by Amy Gutmann within American political theory. See Gutmann, *Democratic Education* (n 20) developed on the premises originally explored by John Dewey in the field of pedagogy, *Democracy and Education. An Introduction to the Philosophy of Education* (Los Angeles, Indo-European Publishing 2010) 59ff.

tal rights, thereby providing a coherent answer to the question of the display of religious symbols in the classroom.

A. The '*what*' of Liberal Democratic Education: Pluralism and Religious Symbols in School

Not unlike educational liberalism, a *liberal democratic* theory of education maintains that one of the primary functions of education is to enable students to develop autonomously. The democratic emphasis however shifts the framework of the educational experience from the exercise of individual rights (the right to education or to religious or ideological freedom) to the generation of the conditions, including the promotion of civic virtues, that enable the preservation and proper functioning of democratic institutions as well as the egalitarian and responsible exercise of rights.[53] In multicultural conditions the emphasis must be put on the active promotion of tolerance and mutual respect to prepare students to navigate the complex reality of social and religious pluralism in which they live.[54] The importance of mutual respect and tolerance for difference in facilitating peaceful coexistence and citizenship in pluralistic societies is such that they ought to be pedagogically inculcated.[55] The explicit recognition of these values defies the pretence of pure axiomatic neutrality.[56] In other words, education in democratic societies must prepare persons to be citizens and, as such, to take part in collective decision-making and contribute to shared enterprises in the societies they inhabit. This requires the development of certain dispositions and skills, including those that can enable them to evaluate the performance of public officials and to engage in public discourse and responsible voting. They also need the dispositions and skills to sustain the necessary level of civility with peer citizens of different cultures, ethnicities and religions.[57]

This conception of democratic education, applied to the question of defining the confines of the relevant fundamental rights, means that the fundamental right to education is infringed when pluralism is not duly affirmed in schools.[58] With respect to the display of religious symbols, this means that, in principle,

[53] On the need to educate citizens in what he calls *civic liberalism*, relying on education to transform citizens and further the civic virtues that the defence of a liberal order requires see also S Macedo, *Diversity and Distrust: Civic Education in a Multicultural Democracy* (Harvard, Harvard University Press 2003) 8, 11 and 175.

[54] See, in this regard, art 26.2 of the Universal Declaration of Human Rights and art 13.1 of the ICESCR. See also art 5(c) of the UN Convention against discrimination in education, of 14 December 1960.

[55] See Gutmann, *Democratic Education* (n 20) 31.

[56] In the end, as Gutmann puts it, the goal of axiomatic neutrality is elusive for 'any political understanding of education depends on some conception of a good society and every conception of a good society rests on some conceptions of a good life'. See A Gutmann, 'Unity and Diversity in Democratic Multicultural Education: Creative and Destructive Tensions' in JA Banks (ed), *Diversity and Citizenship Education* (2004) 82.

[57] Kymlicka, *Politics in the Vernacular* (n 30) 299.

[58] Defending this view see ECtHR *Kjeldsen, Busk Madsen and Pedersen v Denmark*.

the wearing of veils and crucifixes by students and teachers must be allowed, not only as generic expressions of the exercise of religious freedoms, but also because this display actually enhances the democratic function of education by representing the religious pluralism of the larger society. The underlying premise is that the transmission of democratic dispositions, such as tolerance or respect for diversity, cannot simply be a question of educational curriculum (for instance, through a mandatory course on citizenship education) but, as many have observed, depends as much (if not more) on the hidden curriculum which is linked to the educational experience. The experience of sharing a classroom with students who express their different religious faiths through their dress code and other practices is therefore an experience of democratic education.

The democratic theory of education explicitly rejects assimilationism and instead seeks to integrate cultural and religious pluralism[59] following pedagogic doctrines which see school as a social microcosm.[60] This is why the democratic function of education is diminished when the representation of symbols in the classroom, instead of reflecting the value of pluralism, affirms one particular religious truth over others; instead of engendering a notion of citizenship built around respect for diversity, it implies the superior political value of some religious symbols and identities (those which get official recognition) over others (those which do not). For a democratic theory of education, the undue indoctrination does not consist in the transmission of values by the state[61] – as an improper limitation of individual autonomy or the freedom of parents to pass on their value system to their children – but rather in the transmission of religious truths which clash with competing claims of truth. The promise of non-indoctrination in this democratic theory is thus fulfilled by setting the expression of religious meanings in its proper context, which means by allowing the display of religious symbols as expressions of pluralism and not as expressions of religious truth.[62]

In Europe such notions have rightly inspired the prohibition of the display of the crucifix in public schools. In its 2009 *Lautsi I* decision the ECtHR was asked to determine whether the refusal of Italian public authorities to remove the crucifix from the public school to which Ms Lautsi sent her children entailed a violation of the Convention. The European Court determined first that, con-

[59] See Callan, *Creating Citizens* (n 24) 13.

[60] See L Kohlberg, *Essays on Moral Development. The Psychology of Moral Development* (San Francisco, Harper and Row 1984) 498–500.

[61] Indeed, a democratic theory of education sees the task of moral education as shared between parents and family, who may be essential in teaching children what it means to be committed to a concrete way of life, and the state, which has the task of teaching responsibilities and rights within a larger and more diverse community. See Gutmann (n 20) 54. On this, more below.

[62] The fact that religious symbols embody a set of transcendental truths which cannot be reconciled with those of competing religions is what makes the possibility of relying on religious nationalism to ensure a common shared identity to ensure the well functioning of democratic institutions particularly implausible. Other forms of cultural nationalism, such as, for instance, those based on the sharing of a common language or a common sense of history may in this respect be more promising.

trary to what the Italian government claimed, the crucifix was unequivocally to be considered a religious sign, something which could not be denied by simply attaching a symbolic or a secular meaning to it.[63] The Court held that the crucifix, just like the Islamic veil, ought to be considered a *strong* religious symbol capable of religiously indoctrinating students.[64] Thus, the ECtHR in *Lautsi I* considered that the permanent display of the crucifix, and the inability of students to protect themselves from its symbolic effect, created the danger of religious indoctrination. This is in line with the interpretation that the meaning of improper indoctrination for a democratic theory of education in a multicultural society is not so much connected to the arguably proselytising effect of a religious symbol when it is officially sanctioned, and hence, with its capacity to unduly alter the religious convictions of non-religious citizens or citizens with a different religion. Rather, the danger lies in the potential that the official sanctioning of a certain religious symbol may fracture the citizenry by separating those whose system of belief deserves public recognition from the others, attaching higher status to the former.

This doctrine has been rejected by the ECtHR in its Grand Chamber decision (*Lautsi II*) of March 2011 in which the Court considered that the display of the crucifix in a public school does not necessarily have to be considered unduly indoctrinating. In particular, the Court argued first, that although the crucifix

[63] This is the same doctrine that the Court had established in its decision *Buscarini and others v San Marino* [GC] 24645/94. In this case, elected deputies of the San Marino Parliament refused to swear their oath of loyalty on the Bible, as the protocol established in the electoral legislation required, on the grounds that this infringed against their religious freedom under art 9 ECHR. The European Court granted their petition, and stated that the symbolic nature of the ceremony did not redeem the act or the Bible from its natural religious connotation.

[64] See *Dahlab v Switzerland* where the Court takes as relevant, in order to characterise the Islamic headscarf worn by the teacher as a powerful external symbol with indoctrinating potential, the fact that the meaning of the symbol is undeniably religious as well as the fact that the students subjected to it are young and therefore in the midst of the process of personality formation. But see, in contrast, the German decision by the Federal Constitutional Court, *Ludin* (BVerfG (108, 282) of 24 September 2003) in which the Court established that, contrary to what happens with the crucifix, the Islamic headscarf does not have an unequivocal religious connotation, given the fact that other social meanings may be attached to it. Notice in any event that in *Ludin* there is an interesting evolution in the definition of what amounts to a religiously indoctrinating symbol when compared with the doctrine advanced by the *Crucifix* decision of the same German Court (see BVerfGE 93, 1 of 16 May 1995). In the *Crucifix* decision the German Court had considered that one of the essential elements to decide that the crucifix unduly indoctrinates students is that it expresses the core of Christian beliefs. This seemed to suggest that other Christian religious symbols, less central to the 'core Christian beliefs' would not necessarily be indoctrinating. We think that this way of reasoning sanctions the hermeneutic privilege of the majority. The question, we claim, of deciding what amounts to undue indoctrination, must rest on the likely perception of the meaning of a certain symbol by non-believers, at least to the extent that such perception is not unreasonable. Hence, whether or not the symbol is the expression of a core belief according to some purportedly objective theological standards is less relevant and probably something not for a court to decide. What is crucial is whether non religious students or students belonging to a different religion are exposed to a symbol which they can 'reasonably' experience as having religious meaning and that this symbol is officially endorsed because it hangs on the walls. Of course, 'reasonable' is a vague notion, and what is essential is that the cultural bias of the majority does not get naturally infiltrated in the interpretation.

has primarily a religious meaning, nothing prevents the public authorities from attaching other historical or cultural meanings to it. Secondly, the Court considered that the crucifix constitutes only a passive as opposed to an active symbol, unlike the mandatory teaching of religious doctrines or participation in religious activities. Finally, the Court took into account the fact that the Italian authorities also allow for the display of other religious symbols and dresses, such as the Islamic headscarf. By taking all of this into account the European Court felt that it was able to reconcile the public display of the crucifix with democratic pluralism.

This reasoning is, in our view, highly questionable. The affirmation that the crucifix can be deprived of its religious meaning and rather linked to shared historical and cultural traditions is probably just as offensive to many Christian believers as it is implausible to non-believers. Similarly, the fact that the wearing of other religious symbols in the classroom, such as the Islamic headscarf, is allowed cannot counteract the fact that the display on the school walls of the crucifix represents an official endorsement of the symbol whereas the individual wearing of religious garments remains the affirmation of individual autonomy and hence, constitutes an expression of religious tolerance. Finally, the idea that the crucifix constitutes at best a passive symbol and therefore has lesser indoctrinating potential simply reinforces the hermeneutic privilege of the majority. To say the least, it seems hard to reconcile the Court's second decision with its 2001 decision in *Dahlab v Switzerland*. In that case, the ECtHR upheld the prohibition of a Muslim teacher from wearing a *foulard* in the classroom by the canton of Geneva in Switzerland on the grounds that the *foulard* had to be unequivocally reputed as a *powerful external* religious symbol able to disrupt the 'religious peace' needed in a democratic society.

But why is the *foulard* 'powerful' and the crucifix 'passive'?; why does the *foulard* threaten religious peace and the crucifix does not? While we certainly empathise with the need to ensure the orderly delivery of public services (including education), to call on 'peace' as the public interest that justifies the restrictions of fundamental rights[65] is to fail to recognise the need to further a set of dispositions and civic virtues that citizens must develop to ensure peaceful coexistence in religiously pluralistic societies, including tolerance and mutual respect. Otherwise, we are buying peace at the price of privilege, or, to put it differently, striving for a kind of peace which consists primarily in reassuring the cultural and religious majority that its position of power is not being threatened. This is peace as power, not peace as justice.[66]

[65] Notice that this criterion was also endorsed by the ECtHR in its decision *Leyla Sahin v Turkey* justifying the prohibition of the headscarf in public universities and has been sanctioned also in the legislation of several states. See, eg, in Germany, the Länder of Baden-Württemberg, Bavaria, Berlin, Bremen, Hesse, Lower Saxony, North Rhein Westfalia and Saarland. France and Switzerland have also justified their statutory prohibition of the display of religious symbols in the educational setting for the sake of preserving peace in schools.

[66] From the perspective of a democratic theory of education the better approach is exemplified in the decision on the Muslim headscarf by the German Federal Constitutional Court (BVerfGE 102,

B. The '*how* and *who*' of Liberal Democratic Education; Educational Authority and Religious Symbols

When education is placed in the service of creating the conditions for democratic pluralism certain consequences follow with respect to *how* and *who* has the responsibility to educate: all the elements combined should allow for the proper definition of the boundaries and limits of the fundamental rights at stake. Thus far, the European debate on school and religion has failed to provide a satisfactory answer as to who is to be considered the primary source of educational authority and how such authority must be exercised. This has had some bearing on the debate about religious symbols and dress code at school. There has not been a consistent approach to the question of whether or not students could be exempted from attending certain classes or school activities because of a conflict with their parents' system of belief or religious dress code.[67] Whether or not the homeschooling doctrine can be considered compatible with a democratic theory of education is also a recurring source of controversy.[68]

288 (2003)) which upheld a public school teacher's right to wear the headscarf on the basis of the principle of pluralism. The Court reasoned that the veil could be assigned different meanings, beyond the religious one, and that, in any event, students of other faiths could not claim to have their negative religious freedom violated especially given the fact that the teacher taught only one subject per week so that, under those circumstances, the symbol could barely be interpreted as indoctrinating. In this case, contrary to what it had held in the *Crucifix* decision the Court did not think it was relevant to decide whether the Islamic headscarf expressed or not the core of Islamic religious convictions. Rather, it focused on whether students could reasonably detract themselves from its religious symbolic effect. This, we claim, depends on whether the conditions are given so that the symbol displayed may be interpreted as an expression of existing pluralism rather than of officially sanctioned religious truth. In making this kind of determination courts will have to take a contextual approach and decide whether this is the case on the basis of concrete circumstances, including whether one or all teachers or students display the same, none, or many different religious symbols, and, more importantly, whether it is the teachers, the students or the school per se which displays the symbol at stake. This is why, in principle, we can agree with both the German Court and the ECtHR that the legislator must enjoy a certain discretion in drawing the right balance between the competing considerations. Such balancing however must be subject to judicial review.

[67] See, eg, ECtHR in *Hassan Eylem Zengin v Turkey* (n 5) and the decision of the German Federal Administrative Tribunal allowing the exemption of a girl from gym classes (n 46).

[68] In the European context, two German cases, exemplify the kinds of questions that the homeschooling doctrine is currently raising. The first decision, *Leuffen v Germany*, deals with the claims of a mother who wanted to educate her child at home in the understanding that God had given her the responsibility and authority to do so, as well as because of her concern with the academic and moral degradation of the public school system. In view of her unwillingness to enrol him at school, the social services of Düsseldorf had assigned a tutor to the child, and eventually imposed custodial limitations on the mother. Affirming the state decision, the European Commission confirmed that the primary responsibility for the education of citizens pertains to the state (see n 19844/92, Decision of the Commission of 9 July 1992). The second case decided by the ECtHR is *Konrad and others v Germany*. Christian parents wanted to educate their children at home following the *Philadelphia School* programme, alleging that the public education offered by the authorities of the *Land* of Baden-Württemberg infringed against their religious beliefs because of sexual education and its reference to fairy tales and fiction and mythical characters. The ECtHR denied the parents' claims arguing that the mandatory nature of education has as its primary goal the due socialisation of minors (n 35504/03, ECHR 2006-XIII).

The core of the debate has to do with whether or not, in a democracy, parents ought to be considered as the only/mainly ones responsible for the education of their children and what consequence this has for preparing students for pluralism. The debate has become highly sophisticated because in reality most parental claims in Europe have not simply denied the relevance of pluralism but rather used the very concept of pluralism to back their argument for educational authority. Thus, instead of denying the state any role in the education of values as opposed to the transmission of knowledge, many recent demands assert a division of tasks and educational authority suggesting that moral and religious upbringing pertains to the parents, leaving the rest, including the teaching of civic values, to the state. This type of claim is often based on parents' recognised right to choose the religious and moral education of their children, a right which some legal instruments explicitly endorse.[69] According to them, the democratic function of education in the service of pluralism would thus be achieved by confronting students with a plural reality: the perspective offered by the state in the schools and the perspective offered by parents at home.[70] The idea then is to reinterpret the liberal doctrine of *homeschooling* by limiting its reach to the strictly religious and moral domains. This is also the proposed re-interpretation of legal clauses like that in the Austrian *Staatsgrundgesetz* which recognise the right of parents to educate their children at home.[71]

According to this position, the function of democratic education would be denied were the state to assume powers over religious or moral education or to unilaterally decide on the kind of religious symbols that the students must be exposed to while at school. This was the position successfully defended by some Norwegian parents before the ECtHR in the case of *Folgero v Norway*.[72] As members of the Norwegian Humanist Association, the plaintiffs of the case claimed that the inclusion in the public curriculum of the mandatory subject of 'Christianity, religion and philosophy' infringed their rights to ensure that the education of their children was in conformity with their own religious and philosophical convictions, a right recognised under Article 2.1 of the First Additional Protocol to the ECHR. The parents objected, *inter alia*, to the fact that their children were expected to take part in religious-symbolic ceremonies such as prayers and religious singing.[73]

This proposed delimitation of the fundamental rights of parents and of the educational powers of the state fails to live up to the promise of democratic

[69] See, eg, art 26.3 UDHR and art 2 of the First Additional Protocol to the ECHR.

[70] The notion of the creation of 'parallel societies' has been coined in the European educational discourse to refer to this schizophrenic vision of society whereby the state forms one society and families a different one. Criticising the vision of the parallel societies, see BVerfGE 1 BvR 436/2003.

[71] See art 17.1 of the *Staatsgrundgesetz* (1867).

[72] (2008) 46 EHRR 47.

[73] Similar arguments were put forward by Danish parents in the case of *Kjeldsen, Busk Madsen y Pedersen v Denmark*, (*Series A* n 23, 1 EHRR 711) of 7 December 1973 where the violation of the same provision was grounded on the inclusion of the subject of sexual education in the curriculum. In their view, sexual education is strictly tied to religious convictions, and hence falls under their educational authority.

education in the service of pluralism. While in the exercise of their religious freedom, individuals can legitimately reject religious, moral and philosophical beliefs that are contrary to their own, they must accept that democratic education in diverse societies needs to prepare students to accept pluralism – including religious pluralism – and the respect of equal fundamental rights of all citizens. This is what the Christian fundamentalist parents in the landmark US case of *Mozert v Hawkins Board of Education*[74] failed to realise. They had objected to their children taking part in reading classes on the grounds that, amongst other things, they were being taught about the options that women have to develop outside of the home, something which they saw in tension with their religious beliefs. Although the religious claims of parents can of course be considered an expression of democratic pluralism, as the Court rightly understood, they cannot be considered sufficient to provide the *pluralistic* education that the democratic theory of education requires.

A democratic theory of education seeks to make citizens aware not only of their own rights but also of those of their citizen peers. This is precisely one of the primary goals of citizenship education. Parents must be able to live with the fact that in the educational domain their children may be exposed to religious symbols and moral conceptions that do not necessarily match their own. The mandatory nature of primary and secondary school, widely recognised in international norms, is only justified when it satisfies a clear democratic function by preparing students to be active members of a democracy. In our multicultural societies this requires not only the ability to read and write to the extent necessary to participate in a political debate and exercise critical judgment over their representatives' performance, but also the cultivation of the civic virtues of tolerance and mutual respect that peaceful coexistence in diverse societies requires. This trend of thought seems to have inspired the European Court in *Kjeldsen, Busk Madsen y Pedersen v Denmark*, when deciding that the inclusion of sexual education in the academic curriculum contrary to the plaintiffs' religious and moral convictions could not be seen as an infringement against the parents' right to ensure that education and teaching be provided in conformity with their own religions and philosophical convictions (in respect of Article 2.1 of the First Additional Protocol of the ECHR). In denying such a claim, the Court appealed to the need for students to be confronted with diverse views on sexuality.

In other words, under a democratic theory of education we cannot a priori grant parents or children the right to be protected from the display of certain religious symbols that contradict their religious convictions, as long as such displays are done in such a way that clearly expresses religious pluralism instead of officially endorsed religious truths. What parents can in principle expect when exercising the right to determine the religious and moral education of their children is that the state, as an educational authority, exhibits or allows the exhibition of those other symbols that express their own religious convictions.

[74] 827 F.2d 1058 (1987).

Precisely this type of consideration is what allowed the ECtHR to agree with the parents in the above mentioned case of *Folgero v Norway*. The problem, the way the Court saw it, was not with the fact of having a mandatory subject on 'Christianity, religion and philosophy' in which Christianity was taught, but with the fact that such teaching was not done in a critical and pluralistic manner giving due recognition to the existence of other religious faiths. In other words, in this context, the rights of parents must be interpreted as a guarantee in the service of pluralism.[75]

V. CONCLUSION

In Europe, as in many other parts of the world, popular, academic and legal disputes around the display of crucifixes and headscarves in educational settings are unlikely to subside any time soon. The discussion, we claim, has thus far been rather unhelpful because scholars, courts and the parties involved have tended to frame the problem in terms of conflicting fundamental rights. Instead, as we have argued, the proper approach is one that frames the debate from the perspective of a theory of education. In highly pluralistic democratic societies where education is mandatory and the state is granted an important role as a source of educational authority, the most plausible theory of education is one that conceives of the educational experience as intended to prepare citizens to act with the necessary degree of civility and tolerance for difference that peaceful coexistence in diverse societies requires. Confronting pluralism by insisting instead on strict educational value neutrality, as some do, and condemning the transmission of values in the educational context by the state as undue indoctrination, hides the fact that no educational experience can limit itself to the transmission of value-free knowledge. When neutrality, non-indoctrination and religious peace are asserted as objectives to be achieved or limits to be respected, more often than not what we find are dominant groups tacitly and or even unconsciously promoting their own cultural, political and religious values. This, we claim, is educational assimilationism disguised as liberal education.

With respect to the display of religious symbols, we have argued that, in principle, the wearing of veils and crucifixes by students and teachers must be allowed, not only as generic expressions of the exercise of religious freedoms, but also because this display actually enhances the democratic function of education by mirroring the religious pluralism of society. The transmission of democratic dispositions, such as tolerance or respect for diversity, cannot simply be a question of educational curriculum but also depends upon the

[75] See *Hassan Eylem Zengin v Turkey*, for a successful challenge of the Turkish educational system by Alevite parents claiming an exemption for their children on the grounds that parents, and not the state, were the primary authority in terms of the religious education of their children, something they claimed was not respected by the compulsory Sunni-oriented religious teaching offered by the Turkish state.

hidden curriculum of the educational experience. It is crucial that the conditions are provided for the symbol displayed to be interpreted as an expression of existing pluralism rather than of officially sanctioned religious truth. In making this kind of determination a contextual approach must be taken and bias prevented. A judgment which, by definition, sees the Muslim headscarf as a 'powerful' symbol threatening religious peace and the crucifix as a 'passive' one which does not is one that seems more concerned with reassuring the nation that its dominant and traditional cultural and religious identify features will not be threatened, than with reassuring minorities about their equal citizenship stature and inculcating in both majorities and minorities the necessary civic virtues for peaceful and respectful coexistence with one another. The latter, we argue, should be the primary purpose of a democratic liberal theory of education in pluralistic societies.

11

Forcing Consensus: Challenges for Rights-based Constitutionalism in Chile

AMAYA ALVEZ MARIN*

I. INTRODUCTION

FROM THE PERSPECTIVE of liberal constitutionalism, the central figure is the judge; the core of law is human rights; and the overarching context is that of a pluralistic society.[1] Chile, like most currently existing constitutional orders, falls short of this ideal. The reasons for this (as always) are contested, but this contribution aims to expose how one particular feature of the Chilean context, the divisive legacy of authoritarianism, has hindered the development of rights-based constitutionalism. On the one hand, this inquiry reveals yet another iteration of the perennial tension between the democratic ideal (that gives priority to the public autonomy of citizens) and the existence of rights under a constitutional text (that allows institutions, like courts, to enforce them even against majority-rule).[2] On the other hand, Chile is a special example of an attempt to force a consensus about constitutional rights in lieu of opening the space for the expression of the very deep ideological cleavages that continue to divide the polity. Thus, although Chile is not divided by strong ethnic, religious or nationalist antagonisms, it is in fact a very 'divided society' when it comes to the question of constitutional rights. Nevertheless, I will argue that

* I would like to express enormous gratitude to Alex Schwartz for thoughtful comments and amicable support throughout this project. I would also like to thank for valuable comments on previous versions of the manuscript Bruce Ryder, Joel Colon-Rios, Kim Stanton, Amar Bathia and Dave Christie. All remaining errors are my sole responsibility. Please address correspondence to Amaya Alvez Marin, School of Law, Faculty of Social and Legal Sciences, University of Concepción, Concepción, 4030000, Chile; e-mail: aalvez@udec.cl.

[1] D Kennedy, 'Three Globalizations of Law and Legal Thought: 1950–2000' in D Trubek and A Santos (eds), *The New Law and Economic Development. A critical appraisal* (New York, Cambridge University Press, 2006) 66.

[2] J Colón-Ríos, 'The end of the Constitutionalism – Democracy debate' (2010) 28 *Windsor Review of Legal and Social Issues* 25, 32.

the courts can play a constructive role in helping the polity to work through these divisions, provided that adjudication is properly guided by the right methodology.

In Part I, I analyse the negotiated transition from a military dictatorship to a democracy in the early 1990s. As I will explain, the transition discouraged debate and contestation among actors, imposing a forced constitutional consensus and isolating judicial decisions from political debate; this was the ostensive price of achieving political stability. Part II appraises the Constitutional Court's definition and defence of fundamental rights during the era of democratic transition and the hindrances for achieving an understanding of the appropriate role of judges in a constitutional democracy. Finally, in Part III, I discuss the diverse range of human rights adjudication methodologies, focusing upon the recent migration of proportionality analysis as an interpretative technique to solve collisions between constitutional rights. In the Chilean context, I argue that the use of a three-pronged proportionality test may help to promote a dialogue of democratic responsibility among the branches of government. This will require the courts to turn away from a legal culture characterised by judicial restraint and embrace its role as a legitimate interpreter of the 1980 Constitution, a role that is unavoidably political in nature.

II. THE CONSTITUTION-BUILDING PROCESS IN CHILE: A 'DEMOCRACY OF AGREEMENTS'

Chile's transition to a democratic regime in the early 1990s had paradoxical effects on constitutional politics. The catalogue of justiciable human rights was extremely restricted between September 1973 and March 1990 because of the legal state of emergency under which Chile was governed. The concept of law as detached from politics was entrenched in Chile and it had been exploited by the authoritarian regime to legitimate its repressive legal framework. The government's actions were, nevertheless, criticised through the language of human rights by victims of abuse, political actors, and within the general population.[3] Following the restoration of democratic rule, the catalogue of rights and freedoms used to seek justice and redress were derived from the 1980 Constitution, which ironically was originally constructed by the Military Junta.[4]

[3] There is evidence that during the military dictatorship 3195 murders or disappearances by state organs occurred and 28459 arrests where individuals or groups were subjected to torture due to political motives, as documented in the First Annual Report on the Human Rights Situation in Chile (December, 2010) National Human Rights Institute, 153, www.indh.cl. Those considered 'enemies of the regime' were also forced into exile that resulted in the disregard of their right to live or enter into Chile. Decree Law 81 (6 November 1973) established that the right to live in Chile depended upon administrative decisions with decree law 604 (10 August 1974) authorising the government to deny access to Chilean territory to Chilean citizens considered a 'danger to national security'.

[4] Although the Constitution was originally ratified by 67% of voters in a plebiscite, authors like Renato Cristi argue that it was a vote without legal effect because all advertisements concerning the plebiscite focused upon the image of Augusto Pinochet as a political leader, with the text or its

A. Constitutional Amendments and the 'Elite Bargaining' Model

The failure of the authoritarian regime to protect human rights might have provided a legitimate reason for the new political elite who came to power in the 1990s to withdraw support for the established constitutional order. According to Bernhard Schlink, this could have been a way to come to terms with the [authoritarian] past, based in the idea that 'law's specific contributions are the forms and procedures it provides'.[5] However, the elite decided to maintain the 1980 Constitution. Nevertheless, given the illegitimate origins of the Constitution, some kind of democratic transformation was required in order to secure legitimacy. The solution was to abolish the 'authoritarian enclaves', regarded as an unwanted legacy of the military dictatorship. This transformation was to occur through a series of constitutional amendments, with 28 amendments having been made to date since 1989.[6] Political representatives, using majority-rule as a decision-making method, focused upon institutional amendments that sought to provide civilian oversight of the armed forces.[7] The primary intention of such a focus was to ensure that human rights abuses could not be precipitated by the armed forces in the same manner as had occurred under the autocratic regime.

This transitional model, dubbed a 'democracy of agreements', was essentially a pact among political elites. The process involved those centre and left-wing parties who were members of the 'Concertación de Partidos por la Democracia' (as the former opposition to the authoritarian regime) and the right-wing parties that supported the military regime (and would constitute the political opposition after 1990). Joseph Colomer labelled the centre and left-wing coalition as 'openists', as their goal in the late 1980s was to encourage the softening of the authoritarian regime through moderate reforms.[8] However,

implications barely discussed and the consequences of its rejection unknown; R Cristi, 'The Metaphysics of Constituent Power, Carl Schmitt and Genesis of Chile's 1980 Constitution' (1999) 21 *Cardozo Law Review* 1749, 1774–75.

[5] B Schlink, *Guilt about the Past* (Toronto, University of Queensland Press, 2009) 66.

[6] A first constitutional amendment was passed in a referendum in July 1989 (still under the Pinochet regime) that sought to remove some of the most objectionable 'authoritarian features' of the original text. The process of negotiating the referendum was ground-breaking because all major political forces sat around the same table for the first time since the democratic breakdown in 1973. The referendum was carried out in July 1989 with 85% of voters in favour of the amendments and 8.2% against. The remaining 27 amendments were approved by the National Congress with the participation of the executive as co-legislator.

[7] Among the most relevant amendments was the required agreement of the National Congress to declare states of emergency and the elimination of designated members of the Senate so that all members of the National Congress are democratically elected representatives; Law 20.050 amended s 49 of the 1980 Constitution, Official Gazette, 26 August 2005. In addition, the institutional dependency of the armed forces was placed upon the Minister of Defence, the executive could request the forced retirement of any commander-in-chief with prior notification to the Senate and the Chamber of Deputies, and the 'National Security Council' was transformed into an advisory executive institution with a majority of civilian members.

[8] JM Colomer, 'Transitions by Agreement: Modeling the Spanish Way' (1991) 85 *American Political Science Review* 1283, 1296.

faced with the danger of violent confrontation or civil war, the opposition preferred to join the 'continuists' of the authoritarian regime represented by right-wing parties.[9] Thus, the preferred option was a strategy of 'particular agreements' that sought to achieve a consensus between the political antagonists. Furthermore, because the parties were still working within the parameters set by the 1980 Constitution, in practical terms the democratic government required a political accord with the opposition, represented by 'continuists', to secure the necessary constitutional amendments.

Jorge Contesse notes that aversion to political dissent was seen as a positive quality in a country fractured by disagreements. However, in his opinion, this forced constitutional consensus damaged a real understanding of what a democratic regime entails.[10] In the same vein, Manuel Antonio Garretón criticised this 'consensual path' because it did not strengthen the democratic model, forced the government to act tactically, and did not allow for a coherent strategy to be adopted on crucial themes like human rights.[11] This is exactly one of the problems underlined by the literature on political cleavages in divided societies (although not in ethnically divided societies); where divisions are seen as temporary, moderation and consensus are valued at the expense of addressing or even acknowledging the underlying cleavage itself.[12]

In short, the transitional process was mostly undertaken behind closed doors in an 'elite bargaining' model without providing real possibilities for citizens to become protagonists of constitutional transformation.[13] Interestingly enough, the 1980 Constitution, at least in its formal text, contains a particular mechanism in which the direct participation of the citizenry could potentially be required in order to accept or reject a constitutional amendment. If a proposal is approved by the majority of the plenary congress but objected to by the President, the President can consult the citizens through a plebiscite where congress continues to demand the proposed amendments. If the citizens approve the proposed text, it will be incorporated as a constitutional amendment to the Constitution.[14] Since the restoration of democracy in Chile, however, these provisions have never been used.

The catalogue of rights and freedoms creates a more ambitious relationship between democracy and the rule of law. However, the debate so far has been very restricted. While a number of laws and amendments have sought to create

[9] ibid 1285.

[10] J Contesse, 'Las Instituciones Funcionan: Sobre la Ausencia de Diálogo Constitucional en Chile' (2008) *Chilean Yearbook of Legal and Social Philosophy* 335, 347.

[11] MA Garretón, 'La redemocratización política en Chile: transición, inauguración y evolución' (1991) 42 *Revista Estudios Publicos* 101, 127.

[12] S Choudhry, 'After the Rights Revolution: Bills of Rights in the Post-Conflict State' (2010) 6 *Annual Review of Law and Social Science* 301, 309–10.

[13] See S Mainwaring and T Scully (eds), *Building Democratic Institutions: Party Systems in Latin America* (Stanford, Stanford University Press, 1995).

[14] 1980 Constitution, c 15: Amendment to the Constitution, ss 127–29.

and enforce the existing catalogue,[15] fundamental provisions like the right to life, the physical and psychological integrity of the individual, and the equality clause, have remained unchanged since they were drafted under military rule. The right to personal freedom and individual security is one of the sections that has been more thoroughly changed in order to incorporate limits to the state 'police power', with the goal of avoiding the abuses that occurred under the authoritarian regime.[16] In addition, law 20.050 of 2005 created a new right of access to public information and, more recently, another constitutional amendment forced political representatives to declare economic interests and patrimony. Both amendments aim to further the principle of probity and make political representatives accountable to the citizenry.[17]

Because of this approach Chile successfully achieved a measure of political stability in the 1990s. Esteban Montes and Tomas Vial emphasise that the most outstanding characteristic of the Constitution-building process in Chile is that it demonstrates how 'an authoritarian constitution, both in its origin and content, may allow for a transition to a stable democracy'.[18] However, this conclusion is dubious. The use of constitutional amendments, as the path chosen to legitimise the content of the Constitution, achieved some important democratic objectives (mainly in civilian oversight over military institutions). However, the model of a 'democracy of agreements' limited popular participation, failed to initiate debate about the democratic role of courts, avoided a closer examination of justiciable rights, and excluded the possibility of competing interpretations or new approaches to certain rights. This limited democratic openness also failed to encourage an open debate as to whether the military dictatorship could be considered a rule-of-law regime, which would have required a re-foundation of the legal order in place and the areas where the discretion of the political authorities had previously been uninhibited by law or judicial review, particularly in regard to the mass violation of human rights. A related consequence was that elements of continuity with the previous authoritarian regime have remained in place, ensuring that the processes of liberalisation and democratisation have been rather slow. Political dissent was often dismissed for being contrary to the 'consensual spirit of the moment' and popular participation in transforming the 1980 Constitution as a political forum for new political norms was initially denied. At the same time, the system fostered a low level of political involvement by citizens and the political accountability of the ruling elites was limited to elections. In sum, the approach that was taken meant a lack of

[15] The pursuit of a neo-liberal economic framework meant that property rights received an enhanced protection while a special framework called 'economic public order' was created.

[16] Three constitutional amendments addressed this area. law 19.055 Official Gazette, 1 April 1991; law 19.519 Official Gazette 16 September 1997; and law 20.050, Official Gazette 26 August 2005.

[17] Constitutional amendment law 20.414, Official Gazette, 1 January 2010.

[18] E Montes and T Vial, 'The Constitution building process in Chile. the authoritarian roots of a stable democracy' (2005) in *The Role of Constitution-building processes in Democratization* (International IDEA) available at www.iidea.int/conflict/cbp/.

debate about the imposed legal order of the 1980 Constitution. The populist uprising with massive street marches and strikes to demand government reforms held during 2011 made the Chilean political class recognise with hindsight the consequences of forced constitutional consensus as a transitional strategy.[19]

A more inclusive public debate in the political public sphere and participatory mechanisms with regards to future amendments to the Constitution is needed. To paraphrase Habermas, we might say that 'the catalogue of human rights in Chile has been paternalistically foisted on sovereign citizens'.[20] If the protection of rights and freedoms ought also to reflect the basic ideas, principles and values of a polity, consultation about constitutional change needs to be much broader. For example, women, indigenous peoples and sexual minorities have traditionally been excluded from constitutional politics in Chile and their inclusion is necessary to ensure attentiveness to the views of all sectors of Chilean society. As Jennifer Nedelsky argues, if we also endorse the idea that rights are 'a particular institutional and rhetorical means of expressing, contesting and implementing the values of a certain polity',[21] the case for a broader discussion about the values that Chile upholds as a polity is even greater.

III. BARRIERS FOR THE CONSTITUTIONAL COURT IN ITS ROLE IN A DEMOCRACY

In addition to the role of the democratically elected and accountable branches of government in creating and enforcing legal norms, the meaning of the catalogue of rights and freedoms needs to be elaborated and enforced by the judiciary; rights are not self-defining or self-enforcing. After World War II, it came to be understood that even democratically elected governments can commit abuses through the disproportionate limitation on rights of minorities and individuals. Therefore, judicial review, as a control of the constitutionality of laws, became one of the key features of the 'modern constitutional state'.[22] The debate about the democratic legitimacy of judicial review is better positioned if it is focused on the capacity of judges to articulate decisions and make political choices that promote contemporary political values like democracy, equality or autonomy.

[19] See S Borzutzky and GB Weeks, The *Bachelet Government. Conflict and consensus in Post-Pinochet Chile* (Gainesville FL, The University Press of Florida, 2010).

[20] J Habermas, 'On the Internal relation between the Rule of Law and Democracy' in R Bellamy (ed), *Constitutionalism and Democracy* (Burlington VT, Ashgate Dartmouth Publishing Company, 2006) 272.

[21] J Nedelsky, 'Reconceiving Rights and Constitutionalism' (2008) 7 *Journal of Human Rights* 139, 145.

[22] For the concept of 'modern constitutional state' see L Weinrib, 'Canada's Constitutional Revolution: From Legislative to Constitutional State' (1999) 33 *Israel Law Review* 13. On the global trend towards greater judicial responsibility for the definition and enforcement of constitutional rights, see N Tate and T Vallinder (eds), *The Global Expansion of Judicial Power* (New York, New York University Press, 1995); R Hirschl, *Towards Juristocracy: The Origins and Consequences of the New Constitutionalism* (Cambridge MA, Harvard University Press, 2004).

Such an approach blurs the distinction between the work of judges and legislators in a democratic society. Since a democratic system must be capable of reflecting the aspirations of the citizens, legislators and judges need to understand that current political values upheld in the Constitution are essentially contested and in need of revision. Courts can be seen as democratic institutions with 'a vital and complementary role to play in the continuous process of discussion and reflection about what democracy means and demands'.[23]

A major obstacle in overcoming the legacy of oppressive regimes is the judiciary's deferential attitude.[24] Chile was not an exception to this rule. During the period of military dictatorship, opponents claimed that the judiciary regularly applied and interpreted the law in a manner that was biased in favour of the authoritarian regime. However, as in many other transitional democracies, the Constitutional Court was made the primary institution in charge of the interpretation, defence and implementation of constitutional rights in Chile. Although the 'democracy of agreements' model meant that the debate about basic political norms was restricted to the National Congress, the criticism of the judiciary has obscured the role that the Constitutional Court could potentially have in the implementation of rights protection. There were at least two obstacles here: firstly, the misguided effort made by the Chilean Constitutional Court to establish institutional continuity; and secondly, democratic objections to the use of an originalist method of constitutional interpretation.

A. The Constitutional Court's Institutional [Dis-]Continuity

The Constitutional Court was originally incorporated into the pre-1973 Chilean political structure by way of a constitutional amendment in 1970.[25] The creation of a court distinct from the regular judiciary was intended to assist with the institutional and political crisis that had developed between the Supreme Court, the executive and the National Congress. The Constitutional Court's main role was to conduct constitutional reviews of law and international treaties that were awaiting the legislature's approval, called 'a priori' review. In its first epoch (1970–73), the Constitutional Court decided only 16 cases.[26] At this time, the Court gave standing only to political representatives. The Court is generally considered to have been a failure, given that it could not help to prevent the collapse of Chilean democracy in 1973.

After seizing the constituent, legislative and executive functions by force in a coup d'état in September 1973, the military junta dissolved the Constitutional

[23] A Hutchinson, 'The Rule of Law Revisited: Democracy and Courts' in D Dyzenhaus (ed), *The Rule of Law: The Limits of Legal Order* (Oxford, Hart Publishing, 1999) 196, 218.

[24] T Ginsburg and T Moustafa (eds), *Rule by Law: The Politics of Courts in Authoritarian Regimes* (Cambridge, Cambridge University Press, 2008).

[25] Amendment of the 1925 Constitution, law 17.284, Official Gazette, 23 January 1970.

[26] See E Silva, *El Tribunal Constitucional de Chile (1971–1973)* (Caracas, Editorial Jurídica Venezolana, 1977).

Court in November 1973.[27] The reason given was that due to the dissolution of the National Congress, the mediating function of the Court was obsolete. This gave free rein to authoritarian rule.

The constitutional text approved in 1980 under the authoritarian regime re-established the Constitutional Court as an independent institution outside of the regular judiciary. It was one of the few institutions that came into being in March 1981 and its main competence was the 'a priori' constitutional review of law during the drafting process before the National Congress.

There are concrete differences between the Constitutional Court created in 1970 and the version reincarnated in 1980.The first was intended to assist with the institutional crisis that had developed between the branches of government. The second was part of the 'transitional period' from the dictatorship to democratisation and, it was intended to shield the framework constructed by the drafters of the 1980 Constitution. The appointment process of the seven members of the Constitutional Court in 1980 saw three members designated from the Supreme Court, one lawyer appointed by the executive which at that time was exercised by Pinochet, two lawyers elected by the National Security Council with a military majority, and one lawyer elected by the Senate replaced during the transitional period by the military Junta. So judges were either part of the deferential regular judiciary or designated by military authorities. Lisa Hilbink argues that the Chilean case in the 1980s fits some aspects of Ran Hirschl's rational–strategic theory of judicial empowerment which attributes the rise of judicial review to an alignment of the interests of political and legal elites.[28] In the Chilean case, where the military government tried to create a new constitutional order based on a neo-liberal model, judicial empowerment helped to shield the legal framework from opposing political forces. Moreover, Hilbink even compared the highly hierarchical and centralised structure of Chile's judiciary with the military organisation underlining common characteristics such as an internal culture of discipline, fear of innovation and a risk-averse attitude.[29] However, Hilbink proposes an alternative to Hirschl's account, underlining how the Constitutional Court was:

> a creature of Chile's long tradition of conducting government affairs in legalist terms, making judicial empowerment a logical move in the regime's bid for legitimacy; and second, that the leaders of the authoritarian regime viewed adjudication as an 'apolitical' function and judges (hence) as natural allies in the effort to create and protect their new and improved type of democracy.[30]

[27] Decree Law 119, Official Gazette, 10 November 1973.

[28] See R Hirschl, *Towards Juristocracy* (n 22).

[29] L Hilbink, *Judges beyond Politics in Democracy and Dictatorship: Lessons from Chile* (Cambridge, Cambridge University Press, 2007) 161.

[30] L Hilbink, 'The Constituted Nature of Constituents' Interests: Historical and Ideational Factors in Judicial Empowerment' (2009) 62 *Political Research Quarterly* 781, 791.

Nevertheless, the Court played a puzzling transitional role in the 1980s; in some decisions it paved the path for the return to a democratic regime,[31] while in other cases it simply decided to act as guardian of the institutional design of the military regime.[32]

The institutional history shows the misguided effort made so far by the Constitutional Court to establish institutional continuity between the Constitutional Court established in 1970 under the 1925 Constitution and the court created in 1980 under the authoritarian regime. The creation of the Constitutional Court in 1970 aimed to fulfil a political role, the idea of preventing political conflicts among the branches of government and, in 1980, the legal ideal presented the Constitutional Court as a 'technical' institution in charge of protecting the institutional framework created by the regime. The desire to prove institutional continuity meant that the Constitutional Court of Chile officially celebrated 40 years of existence in 2011. The historical–institutional elements show how problematic is it to view the Chilean Constitutional Court as a monolithic institution that has functioned uninterruptedly since 1970 (and that just happened to be closed between 1973 and 1981). It is also problematic not to mark a clear division between the role of the court under the authoritarian regime (1981–90) and the role of the Constitutional Court under a democratic regime (1990–to date). As I will explain, a clear division would facilitate rights protection.

B. A Democratic Objection to Originalist Constitutional Interpretation

The second hindrance to a rights-based constitutionalism is a consequence of the illegitimate origin of the 1980 Constitution. The first step of the 1980 Constitution drafting process saw a commission of jurists work between September 1973 and August 1978. These sessions were the only stage of the drafting process that was made public during the authoritarian regime.[33] This Commission was predominantly composed of constitutional and political science university professors, and was commonly referred to as the 'Ortúzar Commission' (named after its President). Initially recognised as a 'constituent commission', the Commission later renamed itself as the 'Comision de Estudio de la Nueva Constitución' having realised that the constituent power was in the hands of the military Junta. However, legal scholars, practitioner lawyers and judges all refer to the Commission as the 'constituent power' to offer constitutional interpretations of the text. In fact, one of the members of this junta-appointed commission, Raúl

[31] Decision No 33 where the Court delivered a crucial judgment in 1985 concerning the National Electoral Tribunal and, decision No 43 where the Court considered the scope of protection for freedom of expression and the regulation of political parties.

[32] In decision No 21 in 1985 and decision No 46 in 1987 the Court endorsed the model of 'restricted democracy' established in s 8 of the original text of the 1980 Constitution.

[33] Library of the National Congress: www.bcn.cl/lc/cpolitica/constitucion_politica/Actas_comision_ortuzar/.

Bertelsen Repetto, was created a judge of the Constitutional Court for the period 2006–2015 and recently elected as President of the Court.[34]

Interpretative methodology in the constitutional realm is generally more demanding than regular statutory interpretation. The question about the link between the political order and the interpretation of fundamental rights is not commonly considered by legal doctrine in Chile. The consideration that is always taken into account to interpret the 1980 Constitution is the original will of those who drafted the text. This is problematic because the interpretation of the Constitution needs to evolve to take into account the democracy Chile has enjoyed since 1990. By interpreting the rights and freedoms contained in the Constitution, judges are supposed to declare a 'collective choice' about the meaning of a legal right.[35] An approach is needed that takes into consideration the new threshold imposed by a democratic regime. This would shed new light on events that took place when the 1980 Constitution was in place under the authoritarian regime. It has become a common practice for the Court to mistakenly disregard the influence of the political system in place when deciding cases in a democratic era using judgments rendered under Pinochet's authoritarian regime.[36] A related interpretative challenge is the application of the catalogue of rights and freedoms to events that occurred before the 1980 Constitution was enacted. This situation needs to be (and has not yet been) carefully considered by the Constitutional Court. So far the approach that has been adopted by the regular judiciary has been to admit the application of the right if the violation of the guarantee is ongoing.[37]

C. The 1990s: the Constitutional Court and the Democratic Threshold

The return to democracy in 1990 meant renewed challenges for the Court in the implementation of the 1980 Constitution and the rights and freedoms enshrined in the text. Due to limitations imposed upon the participation of citizens by the 'democracy of agreements' model, the judicial forum and the mechanism of judicial review was, throughout the 1990s, a significant medium for debate concerning individual rights and public freedoms and also for contesting 'official' interpretations of constitutional provisions. Indeed, as Jorge Contesse points

[34] Official judges' biographies are online: www.tribunalconstitucional.cl/index.php/integraciones/index .

[35] J Nedelsky, 'Reconceiving Rights and Constitutionalism' (n 21) 144.

[36] Decision No 541 issued by the Constitutional Court on 26 December 2006 relied extensively on the commission of experts that drafted the 1980 Constitution to interpret the individual property rights guarantee established in s 19(24); a second example is decision No 976 decided by the Constitutional Court on 26 June 2008, that used as an informal precedent decision No 98 decided by the Constitutional Court on 15 February 1990, a few days before Pinochet left power and therefore known as part of the 'mooring regulation'.

[37] The Supreme Court debated in the 1990s the 'legal status' of political prisoners that were abducted during the military dictatorship, establishing that abduction was an ongoing crime in order to avoid the prescription of the criminal and civil liability and to avoid being enclosed by the 1978 amnesty law.

out, some Latin American scholars and activists even urged the courts to emulate the 'Warren Court era'[38] in the United States in crucial areas like racial discrimination, freedom of speech, privacy and reproductive rights, amongst others.[39] Non-governmental organisations believed that progressive agendas could be better furthered by 'activist' courts.[40]

Huneeus, Couso and Sieder argue that there has been a recent process of 'judicialization of politics' in Latin America characterised by:

> firstly, claims for social justice and redistribution are stated in rights terms and linked to a legal instrument and the struggle over authoritarian legacies have been definitively judicialized; secondly, [the] toolkit of legal language has expanded through constitutions and international treaties hand in hand with a process of democratization; and finally, an acceleration in the use of legal language, instruments and institutions in politics.[41]

Nevertheless, the general Latin American picture seems to be at odds with the concrete Chilean example. During the first 15 years of transitional democracy, the Court has been highly deferential to the legislature, showing restraint in its role as 'guardians' of the institutional framework inherited from the authoritarian regime, preferring a very formal or mechanical application of the 1980 Constitution. Javier Couso observes how the Constitutional Court in the first period of democratic transition suffered from 'political insignificance' with 'relative obscurity in the eye of the public', which was fostered through its 'diminished status by its very jurisprudence'.[42]

A major restructuring of the system of constitutional adjudication occurred in 2005 through law 20.050.[43] This constitutional amendment, considered by a majority of scholars and politicians to be the major milestone of the transition to a democratic system in Chile, gave the Constitutional Court a central role. The changes addressed the main criticisms of the Court, including the appointment, tenure and role of the judges. The intent was to equip the system to better serve democracy. Concrete reforms included changes to the appointment process of the 10 judges. The democratically elected and accountable branches of government appoint the majority of judges, with the executive designating three judges and the National Congress designating four judges. The Supreme Court designates three judges that cannot be members of the regular judiciary. The

[38] See LA Powe, *The Warren Court and American Politics* (Cambridge MA, Harvard University Press, 2000).

[39] J Contesse, 'Las Instituciones Funcionan: Sobre la Ausencia de Diálogo Constitucional en Chile', 351.

[40] One example of the outstanding work done by Centro de Estudios Legales y Sociales (CELS); Litigio Estratégico y Derechos Humanos: La Lucha por el Derecho (Buenos Aires, Siglo Veintiuno Editores, 2008).

[41] A Huneeus, J Couso and R Sieder (eds), *Cultures of legality: Judicialization and Political Activism in Latin America* (New York, Cambridge University Press, 2010) 9–11.

[42] J Couso, 'The Judicialization of Chilean Politics: The Rights Revolution That Never Was' in R Sieder, L Schjolden and A Angell (eds), *The Judicialization of Politics in Latin America* (New York, Palgrave MacMillan, 2005) 105, 115.

[43] Law 20.050, Official Gazette, 26 August 2005.

consequence is that these three candidates must be drawn from outside the judiciary and, therefore, will provide a broader legal expertise.[44] Tenure was also limited to nine years and, for the first time ever, the role of a constitutional judge was considered to be a full-time judicial activity (thereby addressing the critique of being only part-time judges). For the first time, judges of the regular courts and the ordinary citizens could access the Constitutional Court when they required a decision about the constitutionality of statutory law. Moreover, a further procedural change that greatly helped in the democratisation of the Court was the introduction of signed opinions, including concurrences and dissents, and the disclosure of judicial votes.[45] Abstention is no longer a possibility and judges must give reasons to support their decisions. The Court's new role as the principal interpreter of fundamental law awakened the interest of constitutional scholars in the Court's performance.[46]

The consequence of opening the Constitutional Court to individual citizens has been to create a real 'judicial forum' where political decisions of the authorities can be examined or questioned with respect to their constitutionality. Cases also helped to show how law is applied and understood as an everyday experience. It also transformed the ability of minority groups or non-governmental institutions to access the Court in order to advance progressive agendas. The latter meant a huge increase in the number of cases presented before the Constitutional Court.[47]

IV. RIGHTS ADJUDICATION METHODOLOGIES AND CONCEPTIONS OF RIGHTS

A missing debate amongst the Chilean legal community is the question of the appropriate methodology for deciding human rights cases. The aim here is to explore the link between a doctrinal conception of constitutional rights and

[44] Among the current judges, 9 out of 10 hold academic appointments at universities. Only Marcelo Venegas is not listed as an academic. Two of the judges have PhDs in law, Gonzalo García and Raúl Bertelsen. Most of the judges have publications in the area of public law, mainly constitutional law and administrative law. One member was a diplomat, Francisco Fernández. Four were politicians either as part of the executive cabinet (Gonzalo García and IvánAróstica) or as Deputy and Senator in the 1990s (José Antonio Viera-Gallo and HernánVodanovic) and two were civil servants, one under the military regime (Marcelo Venegas) and one after the return to a democracy in 1990 (Carlos Carmona). The above information is drawn from the official judges' biographies published at the constitutional court website: www.tribunalconstitucional.cl/index.php/integraciones/index.

[45] Section 39, Law 17.997 Organic Constitutional Law of the Constitutional Court, Official Gazette, 10 August 2010.

[46] L Ríos, 'El Nuevo Tribunal Constitucional' in F Zuñiga (ed), *Reforma Constitucional* (Santiago, LexisNexis, 2005) 627; and G Gómez, 'La Reforma Constitucional a la Jurisdicción Constitucional: El Nuevo Tribunal Constitucional Chileno' in the same volume, 651.

[47] From an average number of 20 cases per year since 1990 the Constitutional Court received 236 cases in 2006, 320 in 2007, 270 in 2008 and 289 cases in 2009. Since 2005 the Constitutional Court has published an annual report of activities: www.tribunalconstitucional.cl/index.php/documentos/memorias_cuentas.

methodologies of rights adjudication. The work of Jorge Contesse on judicial accountability sheds some light on the hindrances affecting rights-based constitutionalism and, in particular, fundamental rights adjudication in Chile.[48] Similarly, Allan Hutchinson's concept of 'persuasive judgments' helps us to conceptualise how judicial performance can be evaluated. As Hutchinson explains, 'a judgment will gain acceptance or rejection because the judge is able to persuade others that it is a reasonable interpretation and that it has earned its legitimacy through the persuasive force of its supporting arguments'.[49] There are various methods for the adjudication of constitutional rights. Some methods reject the very idea of balancing (like the concept of absolute rights), while others adopt a different way of resolving collisions between constitutional rights (like subsumption). My aim in what follows is not to argue for or against particular decisions of the Chilean Constitutional Court, but to explore how different methods of rights adjudication can further or foreclose a constitutional dialogue with other branches of government.

A. The Traditional Deductive Formal Structure of Adjudication

The method chosen to solve disagreements about rights in Chile was a rule-based system of adjudication. Robert Alexy presents this system as an approach that considers rules as definitive commands that 'contain fixed points in the field of the factually and legally possible'.[50] The latter is based on the idea that legal validity does not accept degrees, therefore, a legal rule is either fulfilled or not. Judges confronted with such a system must use the traditional canons of interpretation – the grammatical, historical or systematic elements contained in the Civil Code – to solve questions connected with the application of constitutional rights. The objective is to provide greater certainty in the outcome and in terms of legal predictability; it is desirable that the Constitution and the norms contained in it are considered to be rules. However, the complexity of constitutional rights, as particular forms of legal norms, does not allow them to be considered solely as rules (an argument that will be developed further in this chapter). The normative solution created to overcome collisions of rules is that of categorisation. A conflict between rules can only be solved through a formal exception, implying that one of the rules will not be applied or will be declared invalid. Categorisation imposes a hierarchy upon rights with one rule regarded as superior to the exclusion of another.

Rights adjudication in Chile was conducted in this categorical fashion, where a constitutional right connects semantic rules with a particular case and the legal judgment follows in a logical way. According to this deductive formal

[48] J Contesse, 'Responsabilidad por la interpretación constitucional' (2005) 11 *Revista de Derecho y Humanidades* 281, 289.

[49] A Hutchinson, 'The Rule of Law Revisited: Democracy and Courts' (n 23) 214.

[50] R Alexy, *A Theory of Constitutional Rights* (Oxford, Oxford University Press, 2002) 33.

structure of adjudication, often called 'subsumption', constitutional rights are rules with an empirical trigger and a determinate response, a design which is said to foster certainty and uniformity.[51] Subsumption can also be constructed as a formula. As John Merryman described it: 'the whole process of judicial decision is made to lift into the formal syllogism of scholastic logic. The major premise is in the statute, the facts of the case furnish the minor premise, and the conclusion inevitably follows'.[52]

The problem is that in Chile the use of a rule-based system of adjudication in constitutional rights claims, due to its formalistic structure combined with a conception of judges as mechanical law-appliers, encouraged a detachment of the judiciary from the social-political process, marginalised judges from social change, and promoted minimal judicial discretion with a failure to account for the decisions that were adopted. Under this method legal certainty and uniformity may be achieved, but at the expense of openness to competing interpretations or new approaches to rights.

B. Absolute Constitutional Rights – a Conservative 'Move'

Another methodological option is to portray constitutional rights as absolute, with no legal limits. As a result, constitutional rights would protect a domain equal to their scope. This means that neither a public interest, nor the individual rights of others, can limit the scope of the protected right or diminish its protected domain. In Chile, the right to life has been presented as absolute in several cases denying the option of a collision. In 2008, the Chilean Constitutional Court was asked to decide upon the constitutionality of a Ministry of Health policy relating to the regulation of fertility through the use of the emergency contraceptive pill (also known as the 'day-after pill' policy).[53] This decision exposed how judicial methodology hindered the debate about rights and the relevance of judges to admit its essentially contested nature. In a paradoxical move, the Court in a 277-page judgment showed awareness of the importance of considering extrinsic medical evidence as well as the relevance of considering the societal interest in the case. Furthermore, the Court allowed three public audiences that permitted argumentation from institutions and individual claimants as well as from the Deputies that initiated the writ of inapplicability. The migration of judicial mechanisms such as the legal figure of an amicus curiae[54] was accepted by the Court. Most contributions sought to offer

[51] P Schlag, 'Rules and Standards' (1985–86) 33 *UCLA Law Review* 379, 382–83.

[52] JH Merryman and R Pérez-Perdomo, *The Civil Law Tradition: An Introduction to the Legal Systems of Europe and Latin America*, 3rd edn, (Stanford, Stanford University Press, 2007) 36.

[53] Decision No 740, issued on 18 April 2008.

[54] Amicus curiae means 'friend of the court', and it is applied to someone that has no right to appear in a suit but who wants to bring attention to a matter of public interest, to prevent injustices or to represent a point of law that may have been overlooked. In Chile there are no specific rules and regulations as to when an amicus curiae may be used in the court's proceedings.

evidence that the encroachment of the right to life through an emergency contraception and the abortive effect of the 'day-after pill' were highly contested in the medical arena and that the debate should consider as well the reproductive rights of women. Contradicting the argumentative openness previously showed, the Court decided to consider the right to life as absolute and offering protection to unborn children from the initial moment of conception by considering them persons entitled to protection and rights.

In a concurrent opinion judge Marcelo Venegas, although supporting the judgment, argued openly about the alternative option of accepting the idea of abortion as one of the mechanisms for contraception. The judge made an appeal to the legislature in order to initiate a dialogue about the societal views about contraception and abortion in Chile.[55] Moreover, through a dissenting opinion, Judge Hernan Vodanovic argued against the declaration of unconstitutionality based on the existence of a conflict between the right to life and the reproductive rights of the women involved. Judge Vodanovic also pointed out the absence of a proportionality analysis in this case.[56] In another dissenting opinion, Judges Jorge Correa and Francisco Fernandez placed an emphasis upon the medical extrinsic evidence provided in order to prove that the emergency contraception did not have abortive effects and, therefore, it was not unconstitutional as a public policy.[57]

This judgment constitutes the most contested judicial decision in the Court's history.[58] Here, of course, neither interpretation of the collision nor balancing was necessary. The concept of absolute rights in Chile has been mostly related to conservative perspectives on rights, in a situation where the objective is to avoid the necessity of balancing the 'protected' right against another right or interest. The view furthered in this chapter is that this conception of rights, as absolute, overlooks the political function that is now integral to the concept of human rights.

C. The Migration of Proportionality Analysis: Opportunities and Limits

The dominant rights adjudication doctrine in the western world, after the consolidation of the new template of so-called 'new constitutionalism', is proportionality analysis.[59] Proportionality, as a balancing mechanism, is seen as the threshold that limits a constitutional right and is justified in terms of the relationship between the means used and the aims pursued. Proportionality as a

[55] Decision No 740, issued on 18 April 2008 concurrent opinion Judge Marcelo Venegas, 160–68

[56] Decision No 740, issued on 18 April 2008 dissenting opinion Judge Hernan Vodanovic, 193–201.

[57] Decision No 740, issued on 18 April 2008 dissenting opinion Judges Jorge Correa and Francisco Fernandez, 201–75.

[58] C Bucciferro, 'President Michelle Bacheler and the Chilean Media: A complicated affair' (2009) 2 *Journal of Global Communication* 289, 302.

[59] See especially M Cabonell (ed), *Neoconstitutionalismo(s)* (Madrid, Editorial Trotta, 2005).

formula is a three-pronged test that determines whether: a measure interfering with a right is constitutionally legitimate; that measure is suitable to achieve its objective; it is the least restrictive means to achieve that purpose; and the burden imposed on the right is proportional compared with the benefits it aims to secure.[60] The aim is to make a case for a more serious and sophisticated embrace of proportionality analysis on the part of the Chilean judges, which would have salutary effects on Chile's constitutional democracy.

The Chilean Constitutional Court partially incorporated the principle of proportionality as a criterion to resolve conflicts between competing constitutional rights and freedoms in 2006.[61] The proportionality methodology has only been partially adopted by the Chilean Constitutional Court in the last five years, but, as Humberto Nogueira underlines, in most cases the Court only uses the first steps of a proportionality framework requiring a legitimate purpose for the statute and the requirement of a relationship between the means and the aims. Rarely has the Court referred to the possibility of analysing the existence of the least restrictive means that would achieve the same aim; it has not even structured a concrete case where the limitation of a constitutional methodology uses the proportionality 'stricto senso' step.[62]

A first area where proportionality analysis might address the problems in Chile's post-authoritarian constitutionalism is by recognising the complexity of constitutional rights, as particular forms of legal norms, under the structure of principles and rules. For this aim, Robert Alexy's theory of constitutional rights and proportionality, which he arrived at through an analysis of German Federal Constitutional Court case law, is especially relevant. In 2009–10, a group of scholars close to Alexy published similar books regarding proportionality analysis in numerous Latin American countries.[63] Eduardo Aldunate, a constitutional scholar, argues that Alexy's reception in Chile has been superficial and uncritical because Alexy's critics (among them Jürgen Habermas) have not been translated accordingly.[64] In Alexy's account, principles are norms that 'require that something be realised to the greatest extent possible given the legal and factual possibilities' and where principles can be fulfilled to different degrees.[65] Given that

[60] A Barak, 'Proportionality and Principled Balancing' (2010) 4 *Law & Ethics of Human Rights* 1, 12.

[61] Decision No 541, issued on 26 December 2006 used proportionality analysis for the first time.

[62] H Nogueira, 'El Principio de Proporcionalidad y su aplicación en Sudamérica por la Jurisdicción Constitucional, con especial mención al Tribunal Constitucional Chileno' in Miguel Carbonell (ed), *El Principio de Proporcionalidad en la Interpretación Jurídica* (Santiago, UNAM & CECOCH, 2010) 353, 403.

[63] On Chile, see M Carbonell (ed), *El Principio de Proporcionalidad en la interpretación jurídica* (Santiago, UNAM & CECOCH, 2010); on Peru, see M Carbonell and P Grández, (eds), *El Principio de Proporcionalidad en el Derecho Contemporáneo* (Lima, Palestra Editores, 2010); on Argentina see L Clérico, *El Examen de Proporcionalidad en el Derecho Constitucional* (Buenos Aires, Eudeba, 2009); on Mexico, see M Carbonell (ed), *El Principio de Proporcionalidad y protección de los derechos fundamentals* (Ciudad de México, Comisión Nacional de los Derechos Humanos, 2008).

[64] E Aldunate, 'A conceptual and critical approach towards neo-constitutionalism' (2010) 23 *Revista de Derecho Universidad Austral de Chile* 79, 85.

[65] R Alexy, *A Theory of Constitutional Rights*, 47.

there has been a 'forced consensus' about constitutional rights in Chile imposed by the ruling elites and given that there could be potentially strong disagreement about the content and scope of protection among the rights population, how should constitutional judges proceed? In Alexy's framework, constitutional rights – like freedom of expression, the right to health-care or even the right to life – will be considered as principles at first sight but, following the consideration of the legal and factual circumstances and the competing principles, a principle will be transformed into a rule valid in that particular case through proportionality analysis. When a constitutional court transforms a principle into a rule, it is a judicial attempt to declare what the constitution stipulates in that particular setting. However, the ideal of the principle will remain alive behind the particular rule.[66] The Chilean case resonates well with this proposal. Judges could try to reconcile disagreements about rights with judgments that offer an immediate answer to a concrete case where a principle is transformed into a rule with very little in the way of 'theory' or of fully theorised rights.[67]

A second area where proportionality analysis might address the problems in Chile's post-authoritarian constitutionalism is by requiring substantive grounds to limit a constitutional right. Rights are presented throughout this chapter as ideals that ought to be realised to the greatest extent possible. This concept rejects the scheme that rights are absolute, and sees protected rights and freedoms as subject to limitations. Courts will have the task of interpreting the constitutional right granted but also the limitation applicable. Constitutional rights are formulated in a way that allows disagreement within the scope of protection. In a democratic regime the state organs need to accomplish certain substantive requirements in order to legitimately encroach upon a fundamental right.[68] A 'limitation of rights' generally establishes a two-stage sequence. First, the right-holder carries the onus of establishing the content of the right and its scope based on the constitution, the facts and their application to the right, and the infringement. The right-holder needs to establish that a constitutional right has been limited. In the second stage, the state carries the onus of justifying the limitation of a particular right.[69] Again the situation in Chile is such that the onus carried by the right-holder and the onus carried by the state has not been clearly defined. While the 1980 Constitution opted for specific limitation clauses,[70] there

[66] R Alexy, 'The Construction of Constitutional Rights' (2010) 4 *Law & Ethics of Human Rights* 20, 23.

[67] See CR Sunstein, 'Incompletely Theorized Agreements' (1994–95) 108 *Harvard Law Review* 1733.

[68] M Kumm, 'Political Liberalism and the Structure of Rights: On the Place and Limits of the Proportionality Requirement' in S Paulsen and G Pavlakos (eds), *Law, Rights, Discourse: themes of the work of Robert Alexy* (Oxford, Hart Publishing, 2007).

[69] L Weinrib, 'Canada's Constitutional Revolution: From Legislative to Constitutional State' (n 22) 30.

[70] eg, s 19(6) guarantees the freedom of conscience and religion but establishes a limitation clause that curtails the activities of 'cults that are opposed to morality, appropriate customs and public order'; and private property (s 19(24)) is limited by its social function established by law that includes 'the requirements of the Nation's general interests, the national security, public use and health, and the conservation of the environmental patrimony'.

is no clear general limitation clause against which the collision of fundamental rights can be evaluated. It is still unclear as to whether the interpretative work of the Constitutional Court or a constitutional amendment by the legislature could establish a general limitation clause in Chile. One option that would not require a constitutional amendment would be to interpret section 4 of the 1980 Constitution that declares 'Chile is a democratic republic' as the justificatory criteria against which limitations on rights must be confronted, helping to underline how the action of public authorities must be highly respectful of rights and that limitations are the exception. It might also foster a conversation as to what being a democratic political regime entails.

A third area where proportionality analysis might address the problems in Chile's post-authoritarian constitutionalism is by providing an updated interpretation of the political norms contained in the 1980 Constitution. It would be a major advance even to acknowledge that the values and principles have evolved since 1980 and that a consensus might be difficult or impossible to obtain in certain domains. The role of courts can be evaluated from a democratic point of view by their capacity to adequately grasp the evolving debate about political norms and not by their capacity to be objective and impartial. One concrete example is decision No 976 issued in 2007 by the Chilean Constitutional Court where for the very first time the Constitutional Court declared that social, economic and cultural rights can have normative force against the intent of the framers of the 1980 Constitution who traditionally considered social, economic and cultural rights to be simply 'political aspirations'. The recognition of social rights as positive rights that require the exercise of precise actions to be adequately guaranteed by the state triggered a new understanding of the constitutional right to health-care in Chile.[71] However the Court's performance lacks coherence and so it has not been able to respond to the critical reaction from the legal community.

A fourth area where proportionality analysis might address the problems in Chile's post-authoritarian constitutionalism is by restoring a dialogue of democratic responsibility among the branches of government. A proportionality analysis framework determines the proper purpose of the legislative act as a first step. Furthermore, one of the appealing features of proportionality analysis is the ability to follow the judges' decision-making process and be able to evaluate judicial performance. Unfortunately, so far the Chilean Constitutional Court has been hesitant to challenge the culture of judicial restraint. For example, in the very first case in 2006 where proportionality was articulated, the Court declared 'that although the constitutional justice is forbidden to qualify

[71] Decisions No 976 and No 1218 decided as unconstitutional limitation of the equality clause (s 19(2)) and the right to health-care (s 19(9)); and decisions No 1273 and No 1287 added to the two constitutional provisions already cited an unconstitutional limitation to the right to social security (s 19(18)). These cases triggered an action of unconstitutionality, decision No 1710, issued on 6 August 2010 by the Chilean Constitutional Court, a case initiated unilaterally by the court where part of the existing legislation on private health-care contracts was struck down.

the merit of the legislative decision, it is still possible to examine the constitutionality of the statutory norm and . . . the requirement of a legitimate aim'.[72] If the Court decides to discuss the legislative reason for the limitation upon a constitutional right it will need to abandon the notion that constitutional judges cannot offer opinions with regards to legislative outcomes. By considering proportionality analysis as a potential limitation upon the discretionary power of political representatives, judges have the potential to engage in a dialogue concerning the evolving state of constitutional rights and offer a more structured, open and transparent judgment. The focus on a case-by-case analysis aims to foster the currently non-existent public conversation between the legislature and the Constitutional Court about the concept, structure and normative force of fundamental rights, the way in which two or more rights compete and collide, and the ability to address particular disagreements about rights.

V. CONCLUSION

The Chilean model of constitution-building process has mostly been achieved at the expense of an open democratic debate. The argument advanced here suggests that a closer look at what is normally considered a successful transition to democracy requires that we challenge the lack of debate about how rights are defined and defended. In Chile, the challenge has been to achieve rights protection and democracy in a context of legal continuity with an authoritarian regime. So far the Chilean Constitutional Court has suffered from inconsistencies in its self-proclaimed institutional continuity, bias in the use of an originalist method of constitutional interpretation, and a lack of coherence in the methodology for human rights adjudication.

The use of techniques like proportionality analysis promoting a clear general limitation clause as the democratic parameter against which the collision of fundamental rights will be evaluated, would require a departure from historical sources under the authoritarian regime and concentration upon the constitutional amendments approved by the National Congress since 1990. This approach will also need to depart from the traditional canons of interpretation to make better sense of the legal context and political circumstances under which a case is decided. The purpose of the constitutional guarantee could also be illuminated by international human rights treaties ratified by Chile and the previous jurisprudence of the Constitutional Court under democratic rule. Proportionality provides a structured path for the use of rational judicial power rather than an excuse for withdrawing it. In this sense, proportionality, as an interpretative technique, can be used as a mechanism for the legitimation of an otherwise contested Constitution.

[72] Decision No 541, issued on 26 December 2006, para 15.

The approach favoured in this chapter is the view that legislators and judges are partners in a democratic society and the evaluation of Chilean democracy needs to include both. Since a democratic system must be capable of reflecting the aspirations of its citizens, legislators and judges need to understand that norms included in the 1980 Constitution are in need of revision. It is only recently that scholars have begun to look at the decline of consensus in Chile, 20 years after the return to a democratic regime. This work has attempted to show how the Constitutional Court could take a more systematic approach to breaking with the past.

Index

www.ingramcontent.com/pod-product-compliance
Ingram Content Group UK Ltd.
Pitfield, Milton Keynes, MK11 3LW, UK
UKHW020248290926
15470UKWH00002B/800

9 781849 461009